QuietTime

one-year daily
devotional with
commentary

QuietTime

one year daily devotional with commentary

Word of Life Local Church Ministries
A division of Word of Life Fellowship, Inc.
Joe Jordan – Executive Director
Don Lough - Director
Jack Wyrtzen & Harry Bollback - Founders
Mike Calhoun – VP of Local Church Ministries

USA
P.O. Box 600
Schroon Lake, NY 12870
talk@wol.org
1-888-932-5827

Canada
RR#8/Owen Sound
ON, Canada N4K 5W4
LCM@wol.ca
1-800-461-3503 or
(519) 376-3516

Web Address: www.wol.org

Publisher's Acknowledgements
Writers and Contributors:

Dr. Tom Davis	1 & 2 Thessalonians, 2 Peter, Acts, Jude Proverbs, Ruth
Dr. Paul Enns	Colossians
Gary Ingersoll	Galatians
Don Kelso	Ezra, Haggai, Leviticus, Nehemiah, Numbers, Psalms
Dr. Chuck Scheide	1 Timothy, 1,2,3, John
Dr. Charles Wagner	Mark

Editor: Dr. Tom Davis
Curriculum Manager: Don Reichard
Cover and page design: Chris Boire

ISBN - 978-1-931235-81-5
Printed in the United States of America

Helpful Hints For a Daily Quiet Time

The purpose of this Quiet Time is to meet the needs of spiritual growth in the life of the Christian in such a way that they learn the art of conducting their own personal investigation into the Bible. Consider the following helpful hints:

1. Give priority in choosing your quiet time. This will vary with each individual in accordance with his own circumstances. The time you choose must:
   - have top priority over everything else
   - be the quietest time possible.
   - be a convenient time of the day or night.
   - be consistently observed each day.

2. Give attention to the procedure suggested for you to follow. Include the following items.
   - Read God's Word.
   - Mark your Bible as you read. Here are some suggestions that might be helpful:

     a. After you read the passage put an exclamation mark next to the verses you completely understand.
     b. Put a question mark next to verses you do not understand.
     c. Put an arrow pointing upward next to encouraging verses.
     d. Put an arrow pointing downward next to verses which weigh us down in our spiritual race.
     e. Put a star next to verses containing important truths or major points.
   - Meditate on what you have read (In one sentence, write the main thought). Here are some suggestions as guidelines for meditating on God's Word:

     a. Look at the selected passage from God's point of view.
     b. Though we encourage quiet time in the morning, some people arrange to have their quiet time at the end of their day. God emphasizes that we need to go to sleep meditating on His Word. "My soul shall be satisfied and my mouth shall praise thee with joyful lips: when I remember thee upon my bed, and meditating on thee in the night watches" (Psalm 63:5,6).

c. Deuteronomy 6:7 lists routine things you do each day during which you should concentrate on the portion of Scripture for that day:
   — when you sit in your house (meals and relaxation)
   — when you walk in the way (to and from school or work)
   — when you lie down (before going to sleep at night)
   — when you rise up (getting ready for the day)

- Apply some truth to your life. (Use first person pronouns I, me, my, mine). If you have difficulty in finding an application for your life, think of yourself as a Bible SPECTator and ask yourself the following questions.

  S – is there any sin for me to forsake?
  P – is there any promise for me to claim?
  E – is there any example for me to follow?
  C – is there any command for me to obey?
  T – is there anything to be thankful for today?

- Pray for specific things (Use the prayer sheets found in the Personal Prayer Diary section).

3. Be sure to fill out your quiet time sheets. This will really help you remember the things the Lord brings to your mind.

4. Purpose to share with someone else each day something you gained from your quiet time. This can be a real blessing for them as well as for you.

My Personal Prayer Journal

daily prayer list

date | REQUEST	date | ANSWER

daily prayer list

date | REQUEST	date | ANSWER

daily prayer list

date | REQUEST	date | ANSWER

daily prayer list

date | REQUEST	date | ANSWER

sunday

Family

date | REQUEST	date | ANSWER

Christian Friends

date | REQUEST	date | ANSWER

Unsaved Friends

date | REQUEST	date | ANSWER

Missionaries

date | REQUEST	date | ANSWER

monday

Family

date | REQUEST	date | ANSWER

Christian Friends

date | REQUEST	date | ANSWER

Unsaved Friends

date | REQUEST	date | ANSWER

Missionaries

date | REQUEST	date | ANSWER

tuesday

Family

date	REQUEST	date	ANSWER

Christian Friends

date	REQUEST	date	ANSWER

Unsaved Friends

date | REQUEST	date | ANSWER

Missionaries

date | REQUEST	date | ANSWER

wednesday

Family

date | REQUEST	date | ANSWER

Christian Friends

date | REQUEST	date | ANSWER

Unsaved Friends

date | REQUEST	date | ANSWER

Missionaries

date | REQUEST	date | ANSWER

thursday

Family

date | REQUEST	date | ANSWER

Christian Friends

date | REQUEST	date | ANSWER

Unsaved Friends

date | REQUEST	date | ANSWER

Missionaries

date | REQUEST	date | ANSWER

Family

date	REQUEST	date	ANSWER

Christian Friends

date	REQUEST	date	ANSWER

Unsaved Friends

date | REQUEST	date | ANSWER

Missionaries

date | REQUEST	date | ANSWER

saturday

Family

date | REQUEST	date | ANSWER

Christian Friends

date | REQUEST	date | ANSWER

Unsaved Friends

date | REQUEST	date | ANSWER

Missionaries

date | REQUEST	date | ANSWER

daily praise list

date | I AM PRAISING GOD FOR...

date | I AM PRAISING GOD FOR...

daily praise list

date | I AM PRAISING GOD FOR...

daily praise list

date | I AM PRAISING GOD FOR...

Something for everyone

Some people just can't get enough! That is why we have several dimensions in the Word of Life Quiet Time. Along with the daily reading, content and application questions for each day, two reading programs are given to help you understand the Bible better. Choose one or both.

Reading Through the New Testament Four Times In One Year

Turn the page and discover a schedule that takes you through the New Testament four times in one year. This is a great method to help you see the correlation of the Gospels and other New Testament books.

Reading Through the Whole Bible In One Year

Turn another page and find a program of several pages that will guide you through a chronological reading of the entire Bible. Follow this schedule and you will move from Genesis through Revelation in one year.

The Choice is Up to You

Whether you have a short quiet time, a quiet time with more scripture reading or one with a mini-Bible study each day, we trust your time with God will draw you closer to Him in every area of your life.

Read through the new testament

Weeks 1-13

- ❑ Matthew 1-3
- ❑ Matthew 4-6
- ❑ Matthew 7-9
- ❑ Matt. 10-12
- ❑ Matt. 13-15
- ❑ Matt. 16-18
- ❑ Matt. 19-21
- ❑ Matt. 22-24
- ❑ Matt. 25-26
- ❑ Matt. 27-28
- ❑ Mark 1-3
- ❑ Mark 4-5
- ❑ Mark 6-8
- ❑ Mark 9-11
- ❑ Mark 12-14
- ❑ Mark 15-16
- ❑ Luke 1-2
- ❑ Luke 3-5
- ❑ Luke 6-7
- ❑ Luke 8-9
- ❑ Luke 10-11
- ❑ Luke 12-14
- ❑ Luke 15-17
- ❑ Luke 18-20
- ❑ Luke 21-22
- ❑ Luke 23-24
- ❑ John 1-3
- ❑ John 4-5
- ❑ John 6-7
- ❑ John 8-10
- ❑ John 11-12
- ❑ John 13-15
- ❑ John 16-18
- ❑ John 19-21
- ❑ Acts 1-3
- ❑ Acts 4-6
- ❑ Acts 7-8
- ❑ Acts 9-11
- ❑ Acts 12-15
- ❑ Acts 16-18
- ❑ Acts 19-21
- ❑ Acts 22-24
- ❑ Acts 25-26
- ❑ Acts 27-28
- ❑ Romans 1-3
- ❑ Romans 4-6
- ❑ Romans 7-9
- ❑ Rom. 10-12
- ❑ Rom. 13-16
- ❑ 1 Cor. 1-4
- ❑ 1 Cor. 5-9
- ❑ 1 Cor. 10-12
- ❑ 1 Cor. 13-16
- ❑ 2 Cor. 1-4
- ❑ 2 Cor. 5-8
- ❑ 2 Cor. 9-13
- ❑ Galatians 1-3
- ❑ Galatians 4-6
- ❑ Ephesians 1-3
- ❑ Ephesians 4-6
- ❑ Philippians 1-4
- ❑ Colossians 1-4
- ❑ 1 Thes. 1-3
- ❑ 1 Thes. 4-5
- ❑ 2 Thes. 1-3
- ❑ 1 Timothy 1-3
- ❑ 1 Timothy 4-6
- ❑ 2 Timothy 1-4
- ❑ Titus 1-3
- ❑ Philemon
- ❑ Hebrews 1
- ❑ Hebrews 2-4
- ❑ Hebrews 5-7
- ❑ Hebrews 8-10
- ❑ Hebrews 11-13
- ❑ James 1-3
- ❑ James 4-5
- ❑ 1 Peter 1-3
- ❑ 1 Peter 4-5
- ❑ 2 Peter 1-3
- ❑ 1 John 1-3
- ❑ 1 John 4-5
- ❑ 2 Jn, 3 Jn, Jude
- ❑ Rev. 1-3
- ❑ Rev. 4-6
- ❑ Rev. 7-9
- ❑ Rev. 10-12
- ❑ Rev. 13-15
- ❑ Rev. 16-18
- ❑ Rev. 19-22

Weeks 14-26

- ❑ Matthew 1-3
- ❑ Matthew 4-6
- ❑ Matthew 7-9
- ❑ Matt. 10-12
- ❑ Matt. 13-15
- ❑ Matt. 16-18
- ❑ Matt. 19-21
- ❑ Matt. 22-24
- ❑ Matt. 25-26
- ❑ Matt. 27-28
- ❑ Mark 1-3
- ❑ Mark 4-5
- ❑ Mark 6-8
- ❑ Mark 9-11
- ❑ Mark 12-14
- ❑ Mark 15-16
- ❑ Luke 1-2
- ❑ Luke 3-5
- ❑ Luke 6-7
- ❑ Luke 8-9
- ❑ Luke 10-11
- ❑ Luke 12-14
- ❑ Luke 15-17
- ❑ Luke 18-20
- ❑ Luke 21-22
- ❑ Luke 23-24
- ❑ John 1-3
- ❑ John 4-5
- ❑ John 6-7
- ❑ John 8-10
- ❑ John 11-12
- ❑ John 13-15
- ❑ John 16-18
- ❑ John 19-21
- ❑ Acts 1-3
- ❑ Acts 4-6
- ❑ Acts 7-8
- ❑ Acts 9-11
- ❑ Acts 12-15
- ❑ Acts 16-18
- ❑ Acts 19-21
- ❑ Acts 22-24
- ❑ Acts 25-26
- ❑ Acts 27-28
- ❑ Romans 1-3
- ❑ Romans 4-6
- ❑ Romans 7-9
- ❑ Rom. 10-12
- ❑ Rom. 13-16
- ❑ 1 Cor. 1-4
- ❑ 1 Cor. 5-9
- ❑ 1 Cor. 10-12
- ❑ 1 Cor. 13-16
- ❑ 2 Cor. 1-4
- ❑ 2 Cor. 5-8
- ❑ 2 Cor. 9-13
- ❑ Galatians 1-3
- ❑ Galatians 4-6
- ❑ Ephesians 1-3
- ❑ Ephesians 4-6
- ❑ Philippians 1-4
- ❑ Colossians 1-4
- ❑ 1 Thes. 1-3
- ❑ 1 Thes. 4-5
- ❑ 2 Thes. 1-3
- ❑ 1 Timothy 1-3
- ❑ 1 Timothy 4-6
- ❑ 2 Timothy 1-4
- ❑ Titus 1-3
- ❑ Philemon
- ❑ Hebrews 1
- ❑ Hebrews 2-4
- ❑ Hebrews 5-7
- ❑ Hebrews 8-10
- ❑ Hebrews 11-13
- ❑ James 1-3
- ❑ James 4-5
- ❑ 1 Peter 1-3
- ❑ 1 Peter 4-5
- ❑ 2 Peter 1-3
- ❑ 1 John 1-3
- ❑ 1 John 4-5
- ❑ 2 Jn, 3 Jn, Jude
- ❑ Rev. 1-3
- ❑ Rev. 4-6
- ❑ Rev. 7-9
- ❑ Rev. 10-12
- ❑ Rev. 13-15
- ❑ Rev. 16-18
- ❑ Rev. 19-22

four times in one year

Read through the new testament

Weeks 27-39

- ❑ Matthew 1-3
- ❑ Matthew 4-6
- ❑ Matthew 7-9
- ❑ Matt. 10-12
- ❑ Matt. 13-15
- ❑ Matt. 16-18
- ❑ Matt. 19-21
- ❑ Matt. 22-24
- ❑ Matt. 25-26
- ❑ Matt. 27-28
- ❑ Mark 1-3
- ❑ Mark 4-5
- ❑ Mark 6-8
- ❑ Mark 9-11
- ❑ Mark 12-14
- ❑ Mark 15-16
- ❑ Luke 1-2
- ❑ Luke 3-5
- ❑ Luke 6-7
- ❑ Luke 8-9
- ❑ Luke 10-11
- ❑ Luke 12-14
- ❑ Luke 15-17
- ❑ Luke 18-20
- ❑ Luke 21-22
- ❑ Luke 23-24
- ❑ John 1-3
- ❑ John 4-5
- ❑ John 6-7
- ❑ John 8-10
- ❑ John 11-12
- ❑ John 13-15
- ❑ John 16-18
- ❑ John 19-21
- ❑ Acts 1-3
- ❑ Acts 4-6
- ❑ Acts 7-8
- ❑ Acts 9-11
- ❑ Acts 12-15
- ❑ Acts 16-18
- ❑ Acts 19-21
- ❑ Acts 22-24
- ❑ Acts 25-26
- ❑ Acts 27-28
- ❑ Romans 1-3
- ❑ Romans 4-6
- ❑ Romans 7-9
- ❑ Romans 10-12
- ❑ Romans 13-16
- ❑ 1 Cor. 1-4
- ❑ 1 Cor. 5-9
- ❑ 1 Cor. 10-12
- ❑ 1 Cor. 13-16
- ❑ 2 Cor. 1-4
- ❑ 2 Cor. 5-8
- ❑ 2 Cor. 9-13
- ❑ Galatians 1-3
- ❑ Galatians 4-6
- ❑ Ephesians 1-3
- ❑ Ephesians 4-6
- ❑ Philippians 1-4
- ❑ Colossians 1-4
- ❑ 1 Thes. 1-3
- ❑ 1 Thes. 4-5
- ❑ 2 Thes. 1-3
- ❑ 1 Timothy 1-3
- ❑ 1 Timothy 4-6
- ❑ 2 Timothy 1-4
- ❑ Titus 1-3
- ❑ Philemon
- ❑ Hebrews 1
- ❑ Hebrews 2-4
- ❑ Hebrews 5-7
- ❑ Hebrews 8-10
- ❑ Hebrews 11-13
- ❑ James 1-3
- ❑ James 4-5
- ❑ 1 Peter 1-3
- ❑ 1 Peter 4-5
- ❑ 2 Peter 1-3
- ❑ 1 John 1-3
- ❑ 1 John 4-5
- ❑ 2 Jn, 3 Jn, Jude
- ❑ Revelation 1-3
- ❑ Revelation 4-6
- ❑ Revelation 7-9
- ❑ Rev. 10-12
- ❑ Rev. 13-15
- ❑ Rev. 16-18
- ❑ Rev. 19-22

Weeks 40-52

- ❑ Matthew 1-3
- ❑ Matthew 4-6
- ❑ Matthew 7-9
- ❑ Matt. 10-12
- ❑ Matt. 13-15
- ❑ Matt. 16-18
- ❑ Matt. 19-21
- ❑ Matt. 22-24
- ❑ Matt. 25-26
- ❑ Matt. 27-28
- ❑ Mark 1-3
- ❑ Mark 4-5
- ❑ Mark 6-8
- ❑ Mark 9-11
- ❑ Mark 12-14
- ❑ Mark 15-16
- ❑ Luke 1-2
- ❑ Luke 3-5
- ❑ Luke 6-7
- ❑ Luke 8-9
- ❑ Luke 10-11
- ❑ Luke 12-14
- ❑ Luke 15-17
- ❑ Luke 18-20
- ❑ Luke 21-22
- ❑ Luke 23-24
- ❑ John 1-3
- ❑ John 4-5
- ❑ John 6-7
- ❑ John 8-10
- ❑ John 11-12
- ❑ John 13-15
- ❑ John 16-18
- ❑ John 19-21
- ❑ Acts 1-3
- ❑ Acts 4-6
- ❑ Acts 7-8
- ❑ Acts 9-11
- ❑ Acts 12-15
- ❑ Acts 16-18
- ❑ Acts 19-21
- ❑ Acts 22-24
- ❑ Acts 25-26
- ❑ Acts 27-28
- ❑ Romans 1-3
- ❑ Romans 4-6
- ❑ Romans 7-9
- ❑ Romans 10-12
- ❑ Romans 13-16
- ❑ 1 Cor. 1-4
- ❑ 1 Cor. 5-9
- ❑ 1 Cor. 10-12
- ❑ 1 Cor. 13-16
- ❑ 2 Cor. 1-4
- ❑ 2 Cor. 5-8
- ❑ 2 Cor. 9-13
- ❑ Galatians 1-3
- ❑ Galatians 4-6
- ❑ Ephesians 1-3
- ❑ Ephesians 4-6
- ❑ Philippians 1-4
- ❑ Colossians 1-4
- ❑ 1 Thes. 1-3
- ❑ 1 Thes. 4-5
- ❑ 2 Thes. 1-3
- ❑ 1 Timothy 1-3
- ❑ 1 Timothy 4-6
- ❑ 2 Timothy 1-4
- ❑ Titus 1-3
- ❑ Philemon
- ❑ Hebrews 1
- ❑ Hebrews 2-4
- ❑ Hebrews 5-7
- ❑ Hebrews 8-10
- ❑ Hebrews 11-13
- ❑ James 1-3
- ❑ James 4-5
- ❑ 1 Peter 1-3
- ❑ 1 Peter 4-5
- ❑ 2 Peter 1-3
- ❑ 1 John 1-3
- ❑ 1 John 4-5
- ❑ 2 Jn, 3 Jn, Jude
- ❑ Revelation 1-3
- ❑ Revelation 4-6
- ❑ Revelation 7-9
- ❑ Rev. 10-12
- ❑ Rev. 13-15
- ❑ Rev. 16-18
- ❑ Rev. 19-22

four times in one year

Bible reading schedule

Read through the Bible in one year! As you complete each daily reading, simply place a check in the appropriate box.

- ❑ 1 Genesis 1-3
- ❑ 2 Genesis 4:1-6:8
- ❑ 3 Genesis 6:9-9:29
- ❑ 4 Genesis 10-11
- ❑ 5 Genesis 12-14
- ❑ 6 Genesis 15-17
- ❑ 7 Genesis 18-19
- ❑ 8 Genesis 20-22
- ❑ 9 Genesis 23-24
- ❑ 10 Genesis 25-26
- ❑ 11 Genesis 27-28
- ❑ 12 Genesis 29-30
- ❑ 13 Genesis 31-32
- ❑ 14 Genesis 33-35
- ❑ 15 Genesis 36-37
- ❑ 16 Genesis 38-40
- ❑ 17 Genesis 41-42
- ❑ 18 Genesis 43-45
- ❑ 19 Genesis 46-47
- ❑ 20 Genesis 48-50
- ❑ 21 Job 1-3
- ❑ 22 Job 4-7
- ❑ 23 Job 8-11
- ❑ 24 Job 12-15
- ❑ 25 Job 16-19
- ❑ 26 Job 20-22
- ❑ 27 Job 23-28
- ❑ 28 Job 29-31
- ❑ 29 Job 32-34
- ❑ 30 Job 35-37
- ❑ 31 Job 38-42
- ❑ 32 Exodus 1-4
- ❑ 33 Exodus 5-8
- ❑ 34 Exodus 9-11
- ❑ 35 Exodus 12-13
- ❑ 36 Exodus 14-15
- ❑ 37 Exodus 16-18
- ❑ 38 Exodus 19-21
- ❑ 39 Exodus 22-24
- ❑ 40 Exodus 25-27
- ❑ 41 Exodus 28-29
- ❑ 42 Exodus 30-31
- ❑ 43 Exodus 32-34
- ❑ 44 Exodus 35-36
- ❑ 45 Exodus 37-38
- ❑ 46 Exodus 39-40
- ❑ 47 Leviticus 1:1-5:13
- ❑ 48 Leviticus 5:14-7:38
- ❑ 49 Leviticus 8-10
- ❑ 50 Leviticus 11-12
- ❑ 51 Leviticus 13-14
- ❑ 52 Leviticus 15-17
- ❑ 53 Leviticus 18-20
- ❑ 54 Leviticus 21-23
- ❑ 55 Leviticus 24-25
- ❑ 56 Leviticus 26-27
- ❑ 57 Numbers 1-2
- ❑ 58 Numbers 3-4
- ❑ 59 Numbers 5-6
- ❑ 60 Numbers 7
- ❑ 61 Numbers 8-10
- ❑ 62 Numbers 11-13
- ❑ 63 Numbers 14-15
- ❑ 64 Numbers 16-18
- ❑ 65 Numbers 19-21
- ❑ 66 Numbers 22-24
- ❑ 67 Numbers 25-26
- ❑ 68 Numbers 27-29
- ❑ 69 Numbers 30-31
- ❑ 70 Numbers 32-33
- ❑ 71 Numbers 34-36
- ❑ 72 Deuteronomy 1-2
- ❑ 73 Deuteronomy 3-4
- ❑ 74 Deuteronomy 5-7
- ❑ 75 Deuteronomy 8-10
- ❑ 76 Deuteronomy 11-13
- ❑ 77 Deuteronomy 14-17
- ❑ 78 Deuteronomy 18-21
- ❑ 79 Deuteronomy 22-25
- ❑ 80 Deuteronomy 26-28
- ❑ 81 Deuteronomy 29:1-31:29
- ❑ 82 Deuteronomy 31:30-34:12
- ❑ 83 Joshua 1-4
- ❑ 84 Joshua 5-8
- ❑ 85 Joshua 9-11
- ❑ 86 Joshua 12-14
- ❑ 87 Joshua 15-17
- ❑ 88 Joshua 18-19
- ❑ 89 Joshua 20-22
- ❑ 90 Joshua 23 - Judges 1
- ❑ 91 Judges 2-5
- ❑ 92 Judges 6-8
- ❑ 93 Judges 9
- ❑ 94 Judges 10-12
- ❑ 95 Judges 13-16
- ❑ 96 Judges 17-19
- ❑ 97 Judges 20-21
- ❑ 98 Ruth
- ❑ 99 1 Samuel 1-3
- ❑ 100 1 Samuel 4-7
- ❑ 101 1 Samuel 8-10
- ❑ 102 1 Samuel 11-13
- ❑ 103 1 Samuel 14-15
- ❑ 104 1 Samuel 16-17

Bible reading schedule

Day 105-199

- ❑ 105 1 Samuel 18-19; Psalm 59
- ❑ 106 1 Samuel 20-21; Psalm 56; 34
- ❑ 107 1 Samuel 22-23; 1 Chronicles 12:8-18; Psalm 52; 54; 63; 142
- ❑ 108 1 Samuel 24; Psalm 57; 1 Samuel 25
- ❑ 109 1 Sam. 26-29; 1 Chronicles 12:1-7, 19-22
- ❑ 110 1 Samuel 30-31; 1 Chronicles 10; 2 Sam. 1
- ❑ 111 2 Samuel 2-4
- ❑ 112 2 Samuel 5:1-6:11; 1 Chronicles 11:1-9; 2:23-40; 13:1-14:17
- ❑ 113 2 Samuel 22; Psalm 18
- ❑ 114 1 Chron. 15-16; 2 Sam. 6:12-23; Psalm 96
- ❑ 115 Psalm 105; 2 Sam. 7; 1 Chronicles 17
- ❑ 116 2 Sam. 8-10; 1 Chronicles 18-19; Psalm 60
- ❑ 117 2 Sam. 11-12; 1 Chron. 20:1-3; Psalm 51
- ❑ 118 2 Samuel 13-14
- ❑ 119 2 Samuel 15-17
- ❑ 120 Psalm 3; 2 Samuel 18-19
- ❑ 121 2 Samuel 20-21; 23:8-23; 1 Chronicles 20:4-8; 11:10-25
- ❑ 122 2 Samuel 23:24-24:25;
- ❑ 123 1 Chronicles 11:26-47; 21:1-30, 1 Chronicles 22-24
- ❑ 124 Psalm 30; 1 Chronicles 25-26
- ❑ 125 1 Chronicles 27-29
- ❑ 126 Psalms 5-7; 10; 11; 13; 17
- ❑ 127 Psalms 23; 26; 28; 31; 35
- ❑ 128 Psalms 41; 43; 46; 55; 61; 62; 64
- ❑ 129 Psalms 69-71; 77
- ❑ 130 Psalms 83; 86; 88; 91; 95
- ❑ 131 Psalms 108-9; 120-21; 140; 143-44
- ❑ 132 Psalms 1; 14-15; 36-37; 39
- ❑ 133 Psalms 40; 49-50; 73
- ❑ 134 Psalms 76; 82; 84; 90; 92; 112; 115
- ❑ 135 Psalms 8-9; 16; 19; 21; 24; 29
- ❑ 136 Psalms 33; 65-68
- ❑ 137 Psalms 75; 93-94; 97-100
- ❑ 138 Psalms 103-4; 113-14; 117
- ❑ 139 Psalm 119:1-88
- ❑ 140 Psalm 119:89-176
- ❑ 141 Psalms 122; 124; 133-36
- ❑ 142 Psalms 138-39; 145; 148; 150
- ❑ 143 Psalms 4; 12; 20; 25; 32; 38
- ❑ 144 Psalms 42; 53; 58; 81; 101; 111; 130-31;141;146
- ❑ 145 Psalms 2; 22; 27
- ❑ 146 Psalms 45; 47-48; 87; 110
- ❑ 147 1 Kings 1:1-2:12; 2 Samuel 23:1-7
- ❑ 148 1 Kings 2:13-3:28; 2 Chron. 1:1-13
- ❑ 149 1 Kings 5-6; 2 Chronicles 2-3
- ❑ 150 1 Kings 7; 2 Chronicles 4
- ❑ 151 1 Kings 8; 2 Chronicles 5:1-7:10
- ❑ 152 1 Kings 9:1-10:13; 2 Chron. 7:11-9:12
- ❑ 153 1 Kings 4; 10:14-29; 2 Chronicles 1:14-17; 9:13-28; Psalm 72
- ❑ 154 Proverbs 1-3
- ❑ 155 Proverbs 4-6
- ❑ 156 Proverbs 7-9
- ❑ 157 Proverbs 10-12
- ❑ 158 Proverbs 13-15
- ❑ 159 Proverbs 16-18
- ❑ 160 Proverbs 19-21
- ❑ 161 Proverbs 22-24
- ❑ 162 Proverbs 25-27
- ❑ 163 Proverbs 28-29
- ❑ 164 Proverbs 30-31; Psalm 127
- ❑ 165 Song of Solomon
- ❑ 166 1 Kings 11:1-40; Ecclesiastes 1-2
- ❑ 167 Ecclesiastes 3-7
- ❑ 168 Ecclesiastes 8-12; 1 Kings 11:41-43; 2 Chronicles 9:29-31
- ❑ 169 1 Kings 12; 2 Chronicles 10:1-11:17
- ❑ 170 1 Kings 13-14; 2 Chron. 11:18-12:16
- ❑ 171 1 Kings 15:1-24; 2 Chronicles 13-16
- ❑ 172 1 Kings 15:25-16:34; 2 Chronicles 17; 1 Kings 17
- ❑ 173 1 Kings 18-19
- ❑ 174 1 Kings 20-21
- ❑ 175 1 Kings 22:1-40; 2 Chronicles 18
- ❑ 176 1 Kings 22:41-53; 2 Kings 1; 2 Chronicles 19:1-21:3
- ❑ 177 2 Kings 2-4
- ❑ 178 2 Kings 5-7
- ❑ 179 2 Kings 8-9; 2 Chronicles 21:4-22:9
- ❑ 180 2 Kings 10-11; 2 Chron. 22:10-23:21
- ❑ 181 Joel
- ❑ 182 2 Kings 12-13; 2 Chronicles 24
- ❑ 183 2 Kings 14; 2 Chronicles 25; Jonah
- ❑ 184 Hosea 1-7
- ❑ 185 Hosea 8-14
- ❑ 186 2 Kings 15:1-7; 2 Chron. 26; Amos 1-4
- ❑ 187 Amos 5-9; 2 Kings 15:8-18
- ❑ 188 Isaiah 1-4
- ❑ 189 2 Kings 15:19-38; 2 Chronicles 27; Isaiah 5-6
- ❑ 190 Micah
- ❑ 191 2 Kings 16; 2 Chron. 28; Isaiah 7-8
- ❑ 192 Isaiah 9-12
- ❑ 193 Isaiah 13-16
- ❑ 194 Isaiah 17-22
- ❑ 195 Isaiah 23-27
- ❑ 196 Isaiah 28-30
- ❑ 197 Isaiah 31-35
- ❑ 198 2 Kings 18:1-8; 2 Chronicles 29-31
- ❑ 199 2 Kings 17; 18:9-37; 2 Chronicles 32:1-19; Isaiah 36

Bible reading schedule

Day 200-288

- ❑ 200 2 Kings 19; 2 Chron. 32:20-23; Isaiah 37
- ❑ 201 2 Kings 20; 2 Chron. 32:24-33; Isaiah 38-39
- ❑ 202 2 Kings 21:1-18; 2 Chronicles 33:1-20; Isaiah 40
- ❑ 203 Isaiah 41-43
- ❑ 204 Isaiah 44-47
- ❑ 205 Isaiah 48-51
- ❑ 206 Isaiah 52-57
- ❑ 207 Isaiah 58-62
- ❑ 208 Isaiah 63-66
- ❑ 209 2 Kings 21:19-26; 2 Chronicles 33:21-34:7; Zephaniah
- ❑ 210 Jeremiah 1-3
- ❑ 211 Jeremiah 4-6
- ❑ 212 Jeremiah 7-9
- ❑ 213 Jeremiah 10-13
- ❑ 214 Jeremiah 14-16
- ❑ 215 Jeremiah 17-20
- ❑ 216 2 Kings 22:1-23:28; 2 Chron. 34:8-35:19
- ❑ 217 Nahum; 2 Kings 23:29-37;
- ❑ 2 Chron. 35:20-36:5; Jeremiah 22:10-17
- ❑ 218 Jeremiah 26; Habakkuk
- ❑ 219 Jeremiah 46-47; 2 Kings 24:1-4, 7; 2 Chronicles 36:6-7; Jeremiah 25, 35
- ❑ 220 Jeremiah 36, 45, 48
- ❑ 221 Jeremiah 49:1-33; Daniel 1-2
- ❑ 222 Jeremiah 22:18-30; 2 Kings 24:5-20; 2 Chron. 36:8-12; Jeremiah 37:1-2; 52:1-3; 24; 29
- ❑ 223 Jeremiah 27-28, 23
- ❑ 224 Jeremiah 50-51
- ❑ 225 Jer. 49:34-39; 34:1-22; Ezekiel 1-3
- ❑ 226 Ezekiel 4-7
- ❑ 227 Ezekiel 8-11
- ❑ 228 Ezekiel 12-14
- ❑ 229 Ezekiel 15-17
- ❑ 230 Ezekiel 18-20
- ❑ 231 Ezekiel 21-23
- ❑ 232 2 Kings 25:1; 2 Chronicles 36:13-16; Jer. 39:1; 52:4; Ezekiel 24; Jer. 21:1-22:9; 32:1-44
- ❑ 233 Jeremiah 30-31, 33
- ❑ 234 Ezekiel 25; 29:1-16; 30; 31
- ❑ 235 Ezekiel 26-28
- ❑ 236 Jeremiah 37:3-39:10; 52:5-30; 2 Kings 25:2-21; 2 Chronicles 36:17-21
- ❑ 237 2 Kings 25:22; Jeremiah 39:11-40:6; Lamentations 1-3
- ❑ 238 Lamentations 4-5; Obadiah
- ❑ 239 Jer. 40:7-44:30; 2 Kings 25:23-26
- ❑ 240 Ezekiel 33:21-36:38
- ❑ 241 Ezekiel 37-39
- ❑ 242 Ezekiel 32:1-33:20; Daniel 3
- ❑ 243 Ezekiel 40-42
- ❑ 244 Ezekiel 43-45
- ❑ 245 Ezekiel 46-48
- ❑ 246 Ezekiel 29:17-21; Daniel 4; Jeremiah 52:31-34; 2 Kings 25:27-30; Psalm 44
- ❑ 247 Psalms 74; 79-80; 89
- ❑ 248 Psalms 85; 102; 106; 123; 137
- ❑ 249 Daniel 7-8; 5
- ❑ 250 Daniel 9; 6
- ❑ 251 2 Chronicles 36:22-23; Ezra 1:1-4:5
- ❑ 252 Daniel 10-12
- ❑ 253 Ezra 4:6-6:13; Haggai
- ❑ 254 Zechariah 1-6
- ❑ 255 Zech. 7-8; Ezra 6:14-22; Psalm 78
- ❑ 256 Psalms 107; 116; 118
- ❑ 257 Psalms 125-26; 128-29; 132; 147; 149
- ❑ 258 Zechariah 9-14
- ❑ 259 Esther 1-4
- ❑ 260 Esther 5-10
- ❑ 261 Ezra 7-8
- ❑ 262 Ezra 9-10
- ❑ 263 Nehemiah 1-5
- ❑ 264 Nehemiah 6-7
- ❑ 265 Nehemiah 8-10
- ❑ 266 Nehemiah 11-13
- ❑ 267 Malachi
- ❑ 268 1 Chronicles 1-2
- ❑ 269 1 Chronicles 3-5
- ❑ 270 1 Chronicles 6
- ❑ 271 1 Chronicles 7:1-8:27
- ❑ 272 1 Chronicles 8:28-9:44
- ❑ 273 John 1:1-18; Mark 1:1; Luke 1:1-4; 3:23-38; Matthew 1:1-17
- ❑ 274 Luke 1:5-80
- ❑ 275 Matthew 1:18-2:23; Luke 2
- ❑ 276 Matthew 3:1-4:11; Mark 1:2-13; Luke 3:1-23; 4:1-13; John 1:19-34
- ❑ 277 John 1:35-3:36
- ❑ 278 John 4; Matthew 4:12-17; Mark 1:14-15; Luke 4:14-30
- ❑ 279 Mark 1:16-45; Matthew 4:18-25; 8:2-4, 14-17; Luke 4:31-5:16
- ❑ 280 Matthew 9:1-17; Mark 2:1-22; Luke 5:17-39
- ❑ 281 John 5; Matthew 12:1-21; Mark 2:23-3:12; Luke 6:1-11
- ❑ 282 Matt. 5; Mark 3:13-19; Luke 6:12-36
- ❑ 283 Matthew 6-7; Luke 6:37-49
- ❑ 284 Luke 7; Matthew 8:1, 5-13; 11:2-30
- ❑ 285 Matt. 12:22-50; Mark 3:20-35; Luke 8:1-21
- ❑ 286 Mark 4:1-34; Matthew 13:1-53
- ❑ 287 Mark 4:35-5:43; Matthew 8:18, 23-34; 9:18-34; Luke 8:22-56
- ❑ 288 Mark 6:1-30; Matthew 13:54-58; 9:35-11:1; 14:1-12; Luke 9:1-10

Bible reading schedule

Day 289-365

- ❑ 289 Matthew 14:13-36; Mark 6:31-56; Luke 9:11-17; John 6:1-21
- ❑ 290 John 6:22-7:1; Matthew 15:1-20; Mark 7:1-23
- ❑ 291 Matthew 15:21-16:20; Mark 7:24-8:30; Luke 9:18-21
- ❑ 292 Matthew 16:21-17:27; Mark 8:31-9:32; Luke 9:22-45
- ❑ 293 Matthew 18; 8:19-22; Mark 9:33-50; Luke 9:46-62; John 7:2-10
- ❑ 294 John 7:11-8:59
- ❑ 295 Luke 10:1-11:36
- ❑ 296 Luke 11:37-13:21
- ❑ 297 John 9-10
- ❑ 298 Luke 13:22-15:32
- ❑ 299 Luke 16:1-17:10; John 11:1-54
- ❑ 300 Luke 17:11-18:17; Matthew 19:1-15; Mark 10:1-16
- ❑ 301 Matthew 19:16-20:28; Mark 10:17-45; Luke 18:18-34
- ❑ 302 Matthew 20:29-34; 26:6-13; Mark 10:46-52; 14:3-9; Luke 18:35-19:28; John 11:55-12:11
- ❑ 303 Matthew 21:1-22; Mark 11:1-26; Luke 19:29-48; John 12:12-50
- ❑ 304 Matthew 21:23-22:14; Mark 11:27-12:12; Luke 20:1-19
- ❑ 305 Matthew 22:15-46; Mark 12:13-37; Luke 20:20-44
- ❑ 306 Matthew 23; Mark 12:38-44; Luke 20:45-21:4
- ❑ 307 Matthew 24:1-31; Mark 13:1-27; Luke 21:5-27
- ❑ 308 Matthew 24:32-26:5, 14-16; Mark 13:28-14:2, 10-11; Luke 21:28-22:6
- ❑ 309 Matthew 26:17-29; Mark 14:12-25; Luke 22:7-38; John 13
- ❑ 310 John 14-16
- ❑ 311 John 17:1-18:1; Matthew 26:30-46; Mark 14:26-42; Luke 22:39-46
- ❑ 312 Matthew 26:47-75; Mark 14:43-72; Luke 22:47-65; John 18:2-27
- ❑ 313 Matthew 27:1-26; Mark 15:1-15; Luke 22:66-23:25; John 18:28-19:16
- ❑ 314 Matthew 27:27-56; Mark 15:16-41; Luke 23:26-49; John 19:17-30
- ❑ 315 Matthew 27:57-28:8; Mark 15:42-16:8; Luke 23:50-24:12; John 19:31-20:10
- ❑ 316 Matthew 28:9-20; Mark 16:9-20; Luke 24:13-53; John 20:11-21:25
- ❑ 317 Acts 1-2
- ❑ 318 Acts 3-5
- ❑ 319 Acts 6:1-8:1
- ❑ 320 Acts 8:2-9:43
- ❑ 321 Acts 10-11
- ❑ 322 Acts 12-13
- ❑ 323 Acts 14-15
- ❑ 324 Galatians 1-3
- ❑ 325 Galatians 4-6
- ❑ 326 James
- ❑ 327 Acts 16:1-18:11
- ❑ 328 1 Thessalonians
- ❑ 329 2 Thessalonians; Acts 18:12-19:22
- ❑ 330 1 Corinthians 1-4
- ❑ 331 1 Corinthians 5-8
- ❑ 332 1 Corinthians 9-11
- ❑ 333 1 Corinthians 12-14
- ❑ 334 1 Corinthians 15-16
- ❑ 335 Acts 19:23-20:1; 2 Corinthians 1-4
- ❑ 336 2 Corinthians 5-9
- ❑ 337 2 Corinthians 10-13
- ❑ 338 Romans 1-3
- ❑ 339 Romans 4-6
- ❑ 340 Romans 7-8
- ❑ 341 Romans 9-11
- ❑ 342 Romans 12-15
- ❑ 343 Romans 16; Acts 20:2-21:16
- ❑ 344 Acts 21:17-23:35
- ❑ 345 Acts 24-26
- ❑ 346 Acts 27-28
- ❑ 347 Ephesians 1-3
- ❑ 348 Ephesians 4-6
- ❑ 349 Colossians
- ❑ 350 Philippians
- ❑ 351 Philemon; 1 Timothy 1-3
- ❑ 352 1 Timothy 4-6; Titus
- ❑ 353 2 Timothy
- ❑ 354 1 Peter
- ❑ 355 Jude; 2 Peter
- ❑ 356 Hebrews 1:1-5:10
- ❑ 357 Hebrews 5:11-9:28
- ❑ 358 Hebrews 10-11
- ❑ 359 Hebrews 12-13; 2 John; 3 John
- ❑ 360 1 John
- ❑ 361 Revelation 1-3
- ❑ 362 Revelation 4-9
- ❑ 363 Revelation 10-14
- ❑ 364 Revelation 15-18
- ❑ 365 Revelation 19-22

Our English word "Psalms" is derived from a Greek word denoting, *poems sung to the accompaniment of string instruments.* The English translation of the Hebrew title is *Book of Praises.* The Book of the Psalms is actually an artistic arrangement of five collections of psalms – each collection ending with a *doxology* Psalm (a Psalm of Praise). The superscriptions in the Hebrew text ascribe authorship of seventy-three Psalms to David and twenty-seven to various other writers. Fifty Psalms are anonymous. However, New Testament references and textual content indicate that some of the fifty are authored by David. Truly, David is "raised up on high, the anointed of the God of Jacob" not only to be king, but also as "the sweet psalmist of Israel" (2 Samuel 23:1).

The Psalms contain praise, petition, prophecy and perspective on the past history of God's people. A number of them are songs about the creation, glorifying the Creator. Others extol the veracity and the power of God's Word. The prophetic Psalms are especially intriguing. Sixteen of these are designated *Messianic* because, in whole or in part, they foretell events concerning either the first or the second coming of the Messiah which in Greek is *the Christ.* The words of the risen Christ Himself in Luke 24:27 and 24:44 should alert us to search for our Lord in many of the Psalms.
Several Scriptures let us know that the human authors of the Psalms, as well as other Old Testament books, are aware that they are writing under the power and in the wisdom of a Divine Author. See 2 Samuel 23:2, Psalm 102:18-19 and 1 Peter 1:10-12.

If you'll find time to meditate on the words of the Psalms, here are some promises for you. You will be fruitful and prosperous in all that you do (1:2-3). You will sleep well (4:4, 8). Your soul will be satisfied (63:5-6). You will be glad in the Lord (104:34). You will not sin against your God (119:11) but will have respect unto His ways (119:15). You will be wiser than your enemies and understand more than your teachers and your elders (119:97-100).

Please note that each year in the Word of Life Quiet Time, we cover a different portion of the Psalms, which means that this year we break into the Psalms at Psalm 51 and will study through to Psalm 76. Be patient, in six years you will work your way through all 150 Psalms!

Psalm 51:1-19

What is the writer saying?

David is talking to God and asking him to cleanse his heart.

How can I apply this to my life?

Take my sinnful thoughts from my mind + heart. Help me stop my thoughts

pray *Japan – Continued success of youth ministries working among the 3,000,000 university students.*

King David wrote four Penitential Psalms (meaning *to express, with a sorrowful heart, regret for sin.* It includes *a willingness to atone for the transgression*). David is confronted by the prophet Nathan concerning David's sin with Bathsheba (2 Samuel 12:7-9). He pens these Psalms in this sequence: Psalm 38, 6, 51, and 32. Read in that order, we see David's spiritual recovery from overwhelming remorse (38:1-11) to overflowing joy in assurance of restoration (32:11).

"Transgressions" (v. 1) is overstepping the boundaries of conduct – such as the breaking of the Ten Commandments. "Iniquity" (v. 2) is evil coming from an evil heart (Mark 7:21-23). "Sin" (v. 2) is coming short of God's required righteousness. In confessing these *three aspects of wrongdoing*, David makes a threefold plea – blot out, wash and cleanse.

David has been taught by the Spirit that all sin is ultimately against God (2 Samuel 12:13). Thus, in the historical perspective, Uriah is killed by David's wicked actions but, in the eternal perspective, the harm to Uriah is made right by God as a part of God extending forgiveness and restoration to David. In Glory, there will be no barrier to the restored fellowship between Uriah and David.

But who will compensate for the injury our sins do to the tender heart of the eternal God of Heaven? God the Father has only to look to the *compensation* paid by the death of His Son, Jesus Christ on the Cross!

The steps back from sin to communion with God are: (a) *confession* (vv.1-6), (b) *cleansing by the blood* (vv.7-10), (c) *joy and empowering by the Spirit* (vv.11-12), (d) *service* (v. 13) and (e) *worship* (vv. 14-17).

Perhaps sin has robbed you of your joy in your salvation. Use this Psalm as the guide it is intended to be. Like David, you too can return to a walk with God with a "clean heart," a renewed "right spirit" and a restored "joy" (vv. 10-12)!

1 Monday

QT

Psalm 52:1-9

What is the writer saying?

We choose either the wide road to evil or the narrow rode to good. We have to make make our choices good.

How can I apply this to my life?

Not judge others, live for God, teach others that don't believe and help lead them down the path of good

pray *Brazil – For godly, seminary – trained men, willing to serve among the 139 unreached tribal groups.*

The superscription to Psalm 52 gives its historical setting (1 Samuel 22:9-23). At the command of a vengeful King Saul, Doeg, the powerful and wealthy Edomite, Saul's chief-herdsman, slays eighty-five priests and their families. The high priest, Ahimelech, has unwittingly supplied bread to David (1 Samuel 21:2-6) and his men as they flee from Saul's army.

Part 1: David to his Enemy: (vv.1-5) David begins by lashing out at the treacherous Doeg. While it is true that Doeg only reports to Saul the facts of David's meeting with Ahimelech, David also sees Doeg's heart, which is the source of Doeg's malicious intent. Doeg's purpose is to deliver David to Saul so that David might be destroyed. In verse 5, David makes a fourfold pronouncement of Doeg's doom at the hand of God.

Part 2: The Righteous shall see the Abundance of God's Riches: (vv. 6-7) Verse 6 assures the reader that the righteous will have the last "laugh," even though the wicked seem to prevail. A righteous person's ultimate well-being depends upon making "God his strength" (v. 7)!

Part 3: The True Picture of David's Situation: (vv. 8-9) David now turns from his problems to praise God as he reflects on his true spiritual situation; David is "like a green olive tree in the house of God" (v. 8). This is an ancient Hebrew saying which pictures the believer's fellowship with God (Psalm 1:3; Luke 23:31; Revelation 22:2). A specially-selected olive tree would be brought into the main enclosure of a landowner's household. Here it could receive daily protection, care, and watering, thus allowing it to be green, fruitful and lovely to behold (Jeremiah 11:16). Notice the contrast with the judgment upon Doeg; he would be like a tree that is plucked out and dragged from the land of the living (v. 5)!

Even if your words are true, you must ask, what is the true purpose of my speaking? Do you speak the truth with intent to bring hurt?

QT Tuesday 1

Psalm 53:1-6

What is the writer saying?

Talking about people that don't believe in God and heaven

How can I apply this to my life?

When I come across people who don't so my knowledge and explain why I know there is a God

pray *Australia – Effective outreach to youth as Sunday school attendance has seen a dramatic decline.*

It is interesting to note that Psalm 53 appears to be a later revision of Psalm 14. Both end with the same prayer asking the Messiah to set up His kingdom on earth (Daniel 2:44). Psalm 53:5 replaces 14:5-6. Psalm 53:1-4 is substantially the same as Psalm 14:1-4, except that 53 revises the text to use only *Elohim* (translated God) as its designation for God; whereas 14 also utilizes *Jehovah* (translated LORD; used to emphasize a personal relation to God). *Elohim* is used to declare that God is the "true God" or the "Supreme One in Heaven." Thus it is likely that the psalmist makes the revision of names after God demonstrates His greatness in a major victory over a strong enemy (and also the enemy's god!) in a battle fought after Psalm 14 is written. Note that by these name changes, Psalm 53 is giving that same thought a different emphasis on God's care for His people (v. 6).

"Fool" in verse 1 does not indicate mental deficiency, but indicates a disregard for God and therefore, *devoid of wisdom*. Romans 3:10-12 quotes from verses 1-3 to begin a series of quotes that describe the depravity of the unregenerate human heart. The fool of verse 1 has the same *heart problem* as does Pharaoh (Exodus 9:34-35), who disregards God (Exodus 5:1-2). Ananias (Acts 5:4) and Simon the Sorcerer (Acts 8:21) are afflicted with the same ailment. The Hebrew word, "fool," is a word that pictures a disease that corrupts (v. 1) by rotting away the morals of a person so that he is now in a ruined state.

Be aware! God's people today can still contract the disease of "the fool." The cure to this corrupting condition is to remember that the opposite of "there is no God" (v. 1) is the Truth. The cure which heals rotten morals is to "seek God" (v. 2) several times each day as you face those moral issues. So then, what moral issues threaten you today? In preparation, spend a few minutes now to "seek God" for direction.

1 Wednesday

Psalm 54:1- 7

What is the writer saying?

How can I apply this to my life?

pray *Pray for God to show your church leaders creative ways to minister to, and meet the needs of your community.*

Many psalms have opening inscriptions. Some contain odd sounding Hebrew words, like "Maschil" in today's Psalm. This ancient word derives from the idea of *insight* and thus means, *a poem of contemplation.*

The historical events which occasion Psalm 54 are recorded in 1 Samuel 23:19-29. David's hiding location is betrayed to King Saul, who then sends his army to destroy David and his men. Verses 1-3 express an urgent plea to God for protection. David bases his petition upon the premise that his pursuers have no regard for God. In contrast, he declares his reliance upon the Lord's deliverance and vindication.

The "Selah" at the end of verse 3 is a musical term that indicates a pause, which in this Psalm tells us that verses 1-3 are the prayer of David, with verses 4-6 being David's later praise to God for answering.

David begins his later praise by declaring that God helped David (v. 4) by rewarding "evil" upon the ungodly actions of Saul (v. 5). 1 Samuel 23:27-29 says that just as Saul's men are closing in on David's band, a messenger arrives to warn Saul that the Philistines have invaded Israel, forcing Saul to leave to deal with this new problem.

In verse 6, David announces that he will offer a sacrifice of verbal praise unto God (Psalm 50:13-15; 69:30-31, see also Hebrews 13:15).

In verse 7, David explains that the foundation of his faith in God for deliverance is recalling the faithfulness of the Lord to deliver in the past. Obviously, verse 7 is David's realization that God had worked out the timing of the Philistine invasion as an answer to David's prayer!

Do you ever find yourself in dire circumstances with your faith wavering? Start by recalling the times in your past when you have experienced help from the Lord. Then contemplate the truth that today He desires to continue to be your faithful deliverer! Take some time to tell God that you are going to again rely upon Him to bring the needed help!

Psalm 55:1-14

What is the writer saying?

How can I apply this to my life?

pray *Kenya – Over half of Kenya's population is under 15. Pray for God to call out a generation devoted to Him.*

The Prophet Nathan has declared (2 Samuel 12) that as a result of David's sin with Bathsheba, there is to be rebellion in David's kingdom. Psalm 55 portrays the anguish suffered by David when he learns the rebellion has come about by his own son, Absalom, and by betrayal of close friends. This Psalm is likely uttered during David's flight from Absalom, who has taken over the kingdom. The Psalm is divided into three parts:

(1) A Prayer of Distress, as David complains to God, (vv. 1-8)

(2) A Proclamation of Indignation against his betrayers, (vv. 9-15)

(3) A Prayer of Confidence in God's work to sustain David . [see tomorrow's passage and commentary].

Notice the progression in David's thoughts:

(1) In the first section, we see David *thinking of himself,*

(2) In the second, we see David *thinking of his foes,*

(3) In the third, we see David *thinking about God*!

In 2 Samuel 15:31 and 16:23, we are told that David learns that his counselor, Ahithophel, is also a conspirator. We deduce that he is in view from verses 12-14 of our Psalm. Here, David's bitter disappointment is expressed for this trusted friend who, through "wickedness" (v. 15), has become an enemy who brings strife (v. 9) and oppression (v. 3) to Israel.

Notice David's condition: a heart sore from pounding in his chest (v. 4), with fears so great that he is trembling (v. 5)! And what does David do? He takes all to God in prayer, asking God to "give ear" (v. 1)! Even though it takes several verses for David to get through his worrying and complaining, David does go to his only true source of help, God Himself!

Follow David's pattern when facing impossible situations: take your worries and complaints to God Himself. Take time to *bend His ear*!

Psalm 55:15-23

What is the writer saying?

How can I apply this to my life?

pray *Peru – For a softening of hearts among the 700,000 unusually resistant, university students.*

This is a difficult passage of Scripture. It is called an *Imprecatory* Psalm. In it, David calls upon God to bring judgment upon wicked men who were also David's enemies. The rest of the story of David's life shows that he knows well that vengeance belongs to God (Deuteronomy 32:35, i.e., God Himself will deal with wicked men.). Verses like 55:15 are building upon earlier pronouncement of judgment by God. For instance, 2 Samuel 23:3b says, "He that ruleth over men must be just, ruling in the fear of God." Thus, the reason David could ask God to "bring them down into the pit of destruction" (v. 23) is because "they fear not God" (v. 19).

It is important to understand David's complete prayer life, so as to give balance to this harsh prayer. Note that David prays in the morning as he is fleeing from Absalom. Read Psalm 3, where his prayer carries him from troubled (vv. 3:1-2), to trusting (vv. 3:3-4), to tranquil (vv. 3:5-6), and finally to triumphant (vv. 3:7-8). His evening prayer is Psalm 4 and his prayer for guidance throughout the day is Psalm 5. We gain insight into the result of all that praying from our Psalm. In spite of a situation that causes David to tremble with fear (v. 5), David is able to find "peace from the battle *that was* against me" (v. 18).

An important principle is given here; David demonstrates the right road to triumph over evil antagonists. He calls upon the Lord evening, morning, and at noon. He casts his burdens upon the Lord and trusts Him for deliverance and vindication. We too can find "peace" in the midst of the hard situations of life when we follow David's pattern of prayer.

Yes, it takes David a while in his prayer to work through all of his fears and complaints. But notice that he comes to the place where he can say, "As for me, I will call upon God; and the LORD shall save me" (v. 16). What troubles are you facing that require you to work through in prayer your fears, hurts, and anger so that you too can come to a place where you have spiritual peace knowing you trust in God to be your Help?

Psalm 56:1-13

What is the writer saying?

How can I apply this to my life?

pray *Taiwan – For an end to the misconception that Christianity is for intellectuals and the wealthy.*

The superscriptions of Psalms 34 and 56 and the story in 1 Samuel 21 explain David's dire distress when he writes this Psalm. Fleeing from King Saul, he seeks refuge in Gath, a main city of the Philistines, the main adversaries of Saul. Achish, the king of Gath (Abimelech is his title), has received David, but the servants of Achish recognize David as the slayer of thousands of Philistines. He escapes captivity by successfully feigning insanity before King Achish who drives him away.

Failing to save himself by his own devices, David, in this Psalm, finally comes to the place where he completely trusts in the Most High God to protect him from any harm of men. He makes his faith concrete by praising God for His "word" (vv. 4, 10).

Although pursued by some and forsaken by others, David perceives that God's eye of protection is upon him (vv. 8-9). His faith is sustained by repeatedly announcing his trust in God and by praising God with tongue and pen. To better see the insights that lead to David's trust in God, let us make questions out of David's statements in this Psalm:

1. In God I put my trust, what can "flesh" do to make me fear? (v. 4)
2. In God I put my trust, can anything make me afraid? (v. 11)
3. If I walk before God, what can cause my feet to fall? (v. 13)

The Psalm concludes with David looking back to instances in his past when God preserved him from death (v. 13). This gives him the confidence to believe that he would "walk before God in the light of the living" until God's purposes for him on earth are finished.

Consider a difficult circumstance of your own, how can you follow this pattern of David's? (1) Renounce any confidence in yourself. (2) Trust in the promises of God's Word. (3) Believe that He has a purpose for your life. (4) Keep praising Him for His Word and His provision.

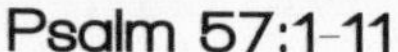

Psalm 57:1-11

What is the writer saying?

How can I apply this to my life?

pray *Romania – Outreach to thousands of street children and orphans who possess Europe's highest HIV rates.*

The superscription tells us that this Psalm is written from a cave. Scripture records two instances of David taking refuge in a cave while fleeing from Saul, 1 Samuel 22 and 24. Psalm 57 is probably written during the first, following his escape from Gath (1 Sam. 22:1).

We also note that Psalm 57 has the same structure as 56, consisting of two stanzas, each followed by a refrain (see 56:4, 11 and 57:5, 11). Since Psalm 56 includes a vow (a promise to God) that David would "render praises" unto God (56:12, to "render" = *to repay an obligation*), it is likely that Psalm 57 is David's *payment* that fulfills the vow of Psalm 56. Also note the victorious tone of Psalm 57, since David has seen that God *completes* or *accomplishes* in His people all that he undertakes (v. 2).

Now notice again the two refrains (a poetic device that *stops action* so one will consider the repeating phrase; vv. 5, 11). David points out that God is "exalted" through His care of David during his troubles.

"In the shadow of Thy wings" (v. 1) is also a favorite image for David (see 17:8; 61:4; 63:7). It pictures him as a helpless chick nestling under the mother's wing due to a danger. There he finds complete rest without fear of the predator that would "swallow me up" (56:1, 2; 57:3).

Many who live wicked lives receive little retribution for their wicked deeds on this side of the grave. But some "fall into the pit" they have dug for their prey (Psalm 7:15, Prov. 26:27; 28:10). Like Haman who died on the gallows he had prepared for Mordecai (Esther 7:10), they are "taken in the devices that they have imagined" (Psalm 10:2). God does this so men might fear before Him.

Have you trusted God to take care of your needs during your times of troubles? Then would you now take a minute to "render praises" to God for accomplishing all He has intended to do in your life?

Psalm 58:1-11

What is the writer saying?

How can I apply this to my life?

pray *Ask the Lord to make you aware of one person that you can encourage today.*

David begins with an outcry against the governmental authorities (likely Saul's advisors) and especially against judges (vv. 1-2). On earth they sit as God's agents (Romans 13:1), who are thus obligated to rule in righteousness (v. 1). Yet they rule in wickedness, since they are wicked (v. 2). They refuse to listen to God on whose behalf they are appointed (Daniel 4:17). Dr. Graham Scroggie offers this outline:

(a) vv. 1-5, The Sin of Injustice by the *speakers* of justice!

(b) vv. 6-9, The Sentence against the Serpents; let them be swept away!

(c) vv. 10-11, The Satisfaction of the Righteous; God will judge rightly!

David begins with a question to the Judges, *Are you really righteous if you do not speak when you should have spoken for righteousness?* (v. 1). Later he calls them "deaf" (v. 4) since they are completely indifferent to the voice of God who is pictured as their *Charmer*. Snake "charmers" or *handlers* are common in the ancient east. As a Charmer, God is illustrated as directing and controlling His agents in government. David continues to use colorful language in the Psalm as he beseeches God to destroy these *snakes*, who could not be tamed since they would not listen to their Charmer and would continue their evil ways. Thus David requests for God to "break out the great teeth" (v. 6).

The Psalm closes with a reminder that God is the final judge of all that transpires on earth. One day the righteous will rejoice and the wicked will meet their doom. While today "a man shall say" God does not seem to judge the wicked, in that future day every "man shall say" ... *I see it now, God does reward the righteous and does judge the wicked!*

Watching the news, we too might be fooled into believing that, while crime pays, right-living is never rewarded. How can you display a *David-like* confidence towards God in your world? How can you speak up for what is right?

Psalm 59:1-17

What is the writer saying?

How can I apply this to my life?

pray *Angola – For committed translators to bring the scriptures to the 20 language groups that have none.*

King Saul is determined to kill David because God, through Samuel, has made it clear that David would be king. Saul's plan is to require David to slay one hundred Philistines to receive his daughter, Michal, for a bride. Saul is confident that David would be killed (1 Samuel 18:25). David slays two hundred and claims his bride. Saul now fears David since he "knew that the Lord was with David" (18:28-29).

Furious, Saul tries to thrust David through with a javelin. David escapes to his house. Saul sends soldiers to surround it so they might kill him in the morning (1 Samuel 19:9-11). According to the superscription, this is the situation that leads to David writing Psalm 59.

In verses 1-5, David recognizes his predicament and calls upon his God to deliver, defend and save. He declares his innocence and reminds God of His future plan to use David to reach the nations. Verses 6 and 7 are David's poetic description of Saul's soldiers. David declares his confidence that God will *defend* him against his adversaries (vv. 8-10).

Also notice that David, in the Psalm's two refrains (vv. 9, 17, a device that *stops action* to allow the reader to consider), wants us to look at the phrase, "God is my defense!" Finally, let's note that the Psalm, several times, focuses upon this *defending* character of God:

(1) "O my God," thus a personal claim to God as his Defender (v. 1).

(2) "O Lord God of hosts," thus God has a heavenly army (v. 5).

(3) "O Lord our shield," thus God stops all arrows of the wicked (v. 11).

(4) "O my strength," thus confidence that "in the morning" (vv. 16-17), when the enemy attacks, they will fail in their challenge of God's strength.

At times do you feel like you have a figurative *army of evil* seeking to destroy you at their first opportunity? If not, those days will surely come! So then, adopt David's *plan of defense!*

QT Wednesday 2

Psalm 60:1-12

What is the writer saying?

How can I apply this to my life?

pray *Papua New Guinea – Effectiveness of literacy ministries that enable nationals to study God's Word.*

King David is up in the far northeast in Aram, (Syria) during his first Syrian campaign. Apparently, there is an attack resulting in a severe defeat by Israel. Then the Edomites launch an invasion in the far south of Israel (near the Dead Sea, called the *Sea of Salt*). Joab is dispatched with a part of the army of Israel to meet this invasion. In the battle that follows, twelve thousand Edomites are killed.

While summaries of David's final victories over Syria and Edom are given in 2 Samuel 8:10-16 and 1 Chronicles 18:3-15, these come after "hard things" (v. 3) that are dealt with in this Psalm. Here, Israel feels as though God has "cast us off" (used to describe the throwing away of a broken pot).

This Psalm has three, four-verse stanzas that can be divided as follows:

(1) *Tragic Events* cause Israel "to tremble" and to seek God again, vv. 1-4.

(2) A reminder that *God Promises Victory* throughout the region, vv. 5-8.

(3) A *Prayer of Confidence* in God that He would bring victory, vv. 9-12.

Notice how God answers David's prayer (vv. 6-8). God reminds David that blessings from Him are based upon "holiness." God, by means of "holiness" (v. 6), has already delivered to them the six areas of the land mentioned in verses 6-7. Now God declares, with three "I will" statements (vv. 6, 8), that He is granting David victory over three surrounding enemy nations.

In verses 9-12 David proclaims his dependence upon God and God alone, and thereby appropriates God's might for the coming battles.

There is a two-sided principle for us in this Psalm: Victory in life comes by means of a walk in God's own holiness. Defeats in life are often God-directed so that we might see our own sin. Take time, as David did, to express a desire to walk in God's holiness.

2 Thursday

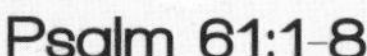

Psalm 61:1-8

What is the writer saying?

How can I apply this to my life?

pray *Kenya – For the 500 Kenyans working as missionaries within sub-cultures and other countries.*

We safely assume that 2 Samuel 17:24-29 is the historical setting for Psalm 61. David is in flight, having been banished from Jerusalem and the Tabernacle, because his son, Absalom, has taken over the kingdom of Israel. David has escaped to the "end of the earth" (v. 2), which means *far ends of the land,* and is again in need of God's help. While David is in Mahanaim, a rocky region to the far northeast of Jerusalem, this phrase emphasizes the emotional cry of one who is feeling *far from God!*

First, notice David's situation, "my heart is overwhelmed" (v. 2) which pictures a man *covering his face in sorrow* from overpowering distress.

Now notice his request for God to, once again, "lead me to the rock that is higher than I" (v. 2). David's need is for someone with a capability higher than his own. David observes that God has previously been David's "shelter" and "strong tower." Additionally, David longs to continue as a guest in God's *tent* (a request for spiritual fellowship with God). He also states that he trusts in the "covert of thy wings," (as a young bird finds refuge under its mother's wings).

Notice the contrast between the tenses of verses 5 and 6. Verse 5 *looks back,* "hast heard …," while verse 6 *looks forward* to God's future dealings with David, "Thou wilt …"!

Because God is merciful and truthful, David can be confident that God will fulfill all that He promised David in the Davidic covenant (2 Samuel 7:16). Therefore, David will "sing praise unto thy name forever."

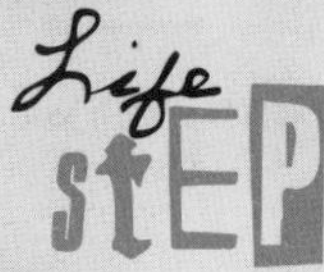

Feeling overwhelmed by the flood of life's problems? Then let this be your Quiet Time: where you fellowship as a permanent guest *in God's Tent* … where you allow God to be your *Rock fortress* that is "higher" (a sure protection!) than your problems … where you find refuge under "thy wings"!

Psalm 62:1-12

What is the writer saying?

How can I apply this to my life?

pray *North Korea – For the abandoned children on the streets to find a place of refuge.*

In the Hebrew text, verses 1, 2, 4, 5, 6 and 9 begin with the word, *Akh* which is translated into English as "truly," "only," and "surely." The word is the equivalent of "verily" in the Gospels. It affirms a truth, regardless of circumstances! The truth to be announced here is *confidence in God.*

First, note that David continues to build on a Hebrew metaphor for God, He is our "rock" (v. 2). Moses first proclaims this metaphor just prior to his death as he sought to encourage Israel to continue their confidence in God (Deuteronomy 32:4,15,18, 31).

Notice that vv. 5-6 repeats vv. 1-2 except v. 2 ends with a declaration that David will "not be greatly moved." But after reflecting for a time, v. 6 gives the greater declaration that David will *not be moved at all!*

Finally, notice the other vivid descriptors of God which David claims as his many shields for his own defense:

- God is my "salvation" (vv. 1, 2, 6), that is, *God brings deliverance.*
- God is my "defense" (vv. 2, 6), that is, *my high safe place; fortress.*
  - Thus, David will not be "moved," which is to say his enemies will not cause him to *shake with fear.*
  - Notice the contrast presented: His enemies, who trust in money and fame, will be like crumbling walls and tottering fences.
- God is my "glory" (v. 7). Thus, nothing can defame David since his *fame* is not to be found within his own person or accomplishments.
- God is my "strength" (v. 7). Thus, God was his strongest support.
- God is my "refuge" (v. 7). Thus, God is a safe sanctuary.

Note the change from God is "my refuge" (v. 7) to God is "a refuge for us" (v. 8)!

Use these many shields of defense which God offers you. How can you wait upon God to be your *Rock* during your hard "times" (v. 8)?

Psalm 63:1-11

What is the writer saying?

How can I apply this to my life?

pray *Austria – Pray for this nominal Christian society where only a small minority has heard the gospel.*

This most beautiful Psalm has been set in the Book of Psalms to form a climax to a trio of Psalms (61, 62, and 63). The probable historical setting of this psalm is when David is being relentlessly pursued by his son, Absalom, (2 Samuel 15-17). The recurring phrase, "my soul" (1, 5, and 8) mark the three divisions of the Psalm, as David reflects upon his faith in the power and glory of God.

In verses 1-7, David shows us the pathway to joy in the midst of the direst of circumstances (Hebrews 12:2). He begins by acknowledging that *The* God is *his* God. He tells his God that he seeks, thirsts, and longs for Him. He praises and blesses his God with lips and uplifted hands. When he awakes during the night, he presently appropriates the total future satisfaction that will be his in God's presence. His faith becomes sufficient as he meditates on how God has sheltered him in the past.

David is upheld because of his dedication to follow God's leading and by trusting God for future vindication. Let us meditate again upon the psalm, as we observe David acknowledging, seeking, thirsting, longing, seeing, praising, blessing, meditating and rejoicing. The psalm shows us the right perspective concerning the past, present and future. As we live in the present, we constantly keep in mind how God has dealt with us in the past. All the while, we rejoice in that which He has promised for our future. We are upheld in the present "in hope of eternal life, which God, that cannot lie, promised before the world began" (Titus 1:2).

David has the perfect cure for insomnia. He doesn't need sleeping pills (v. 6). He trusts God to turn meditation into restful sleep when He foresees that sleep is needed for tomorrow's tasks (Psalm 3:5; 4:4).

Psalm 64:1-10

What is the writer saying?

How can I apply this to my life?

pray *Pray for the elderly in your church and those who are shut-ins.*

The theme is *The Hurtful Tongue.* Its history is not known, but it fits into two periods of David's life: (1) when Doeg speaks to King Saul, intending to harm young David (1 Samuel 22); or (2) when Ahithophel joins Absalom's rebellion and gives counsel to him (2 Sam. 15:31).

The Psalm has a simple structure of two parts:

1. 64:1-6, David's Complaint of wicked men who "shoot" at him!

Note that they "fear not" (v. 4) when they do evil.

2. 64:7-10, David's Consolation, God will suddenly shoot them!

Note that "all men shall fear" when they see God's "doing" (v. 9).

The "wicked" (v. 2) denotes the character of his enemies; literally it means *those who break things into pieces,* thus implying evil people who desire to injure other people. This is the opposite of God's character, for He always desires to help people – rebuilding their lives!

Verses 3-6 describe actions of the wicked. Their "tongue" (v. 3) is a sharpened sword that cuts others. Their "words" are arrows shooting from ambush (v. 4, "secret"), so that these "arrows" can hit the "perfect" (those *blameless ones* in whom God works to complete a righteous character). The wicked act as though no one is watching their evil deeds.

Note the transition, "But God" (v. 7) – the wicked have forgotten that it is a "work of God" (v. 9) that defends the righteous! God knows the intent of their wicked hearts; therefore His timing is perfect so that their arrows of evil words fall on them (v. 8). This "work of God" will cause all men to "wisely consider" their actions for they will "fear" (v. 9) God. The righteous will then be "glad" that they trusted (*to take refuge*) in the Lord.

Is that tongue of yours also a sharpened, cutting sword and drawn bow that shoots poisoned arrows? Ask the LORD to help you to "wisely consider" your words before you speak!

3 Monday

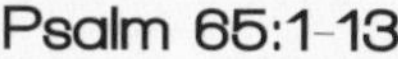

Psalm 65:1-13

What is the writer saying?

How can I apply this to my life?

pray *Paraguay – For God to call laborers to the more than 400 interior villages that remain unreached.*

Psalm 65 is a restating of verses from other Psalms, arranged here for use at the beginning of worship at the "Feasts of the Lord" (Leviticus 23). There is a three-part progression of thought as the congregation worships:

1. The Congregation, with Praises Waiting, Approaches God: Verses 1-4 express the anticipation of the festive proceedings.

2. The Congregation Celebrates the Mighty Deeds of God:
Verses 5-8 present to God the honor due Him as their Sustainer.

3. The Congregation Thanks God for the Rich Harvest:
Verses 9-13 sing to God for His benevolent and gracious provision.

Notice how the Psalm develops its praise: First the congregation declares that God is their "salvation" and "confidence" (v. 5). Then it gives examples of God's "power" over the mighty force of the world:

- vv. 6-7, God establishes the mountains (perhaps referring to Noah's great flood?) and retrains the seas (Israel at the Red Sea?)
- v. 8, God's grat deeds cause all people to notice (Red Sea?)
- vv. 9-10, God watches the land carefully so His people have grain.
- vv. 11-12a, God, each year, causes flocks and grain to flourish.
- vv. 12b-13, As an example to the congregation, even the hills, pastures and valleys rejoice every where and shout for joy!

Delving deeper, we detect prophetic implications in the Psalm. Verses 1-2 look forward to a time still future (Isaiah 66:23; Zechariah 14:16). Verse 3 anticipates that their sins will be forgiven since their animal sacrifices prefigure the work of Christ on the Cross (Hebrews 9:13-14). Verse 4 foresees the complete satisfaction we enjoy when "present with the Lord" (2 Corinthians 5:8).

A lesson for us is that we too should have *praises waiting* to proclaim about God. Tell Him why you place your "confidence" in Him!

Psalm 66:1-20

What is the writer saying?

How can I apply this to my life?

pray *Jamaica – For churches to model compassion to the poor, who receive minimal exposure to the gospel.*

This Psalm of thanksgiving is an invitation for various groups of people to come forward and praise God. It is divided into five stanzas:

1. The God of All Things: *1st Stanza,* vv. 1-4: It begins and ends with the phrase "all ye lands" and calls to people everywhere to give God the honor and praise due His name. However, fulfillment of the prophetic words of vv. 3-4 awaits the appearance of the Messiah.
2. The God of Israel: *2nd Stanza,* vv. 5-7: All Israel is exhorted to consider how God has intervened on behalf of Israel in the past. The psalmist warns them to recognize that God, in His sovereignty, overrules in the governmental affairs of nations (Daniel 2:21; 4:17).
3. Israel's God to All People: *3rd Stanza,* vv. 8-12: Next, Israel calls to all people to join in the praise of God for upholding them and preserving them; not letting their feet slip (v. 9). God is worthy of praise since He has a divine purpose in bringing trials, testings, and affliction.
4. The God of the Individual Believer: *4th Stanza,* vv. 13-15, Note the transition here from the *first-person-plural* (we, our, us) to the *first-person-singular* (I, my). David now expresses that he personally purposes to fulfill his own worship obligations to God!
5. The Individual to All Others: Join my Praises to God: *5th Stanza,* vv. 16-20: David invites "all ye that fear God" to listen to his testimonial: when David cried out to God concerning his guilt for his own sin and when he praised God, he was heard, because his heart was right before the Lord, and his "soul" was restored. He ends the Psalm by gratefully blessing God for mercifully hearing his prayer.

Are you a believer with past sins troubling your "soul" (your inner-conscience)? Then be sure to follow David's example.

Psalm 67:1-7

What is the writer saying?

How can I apply this to my life?

pray *Pray that the Lord will give you the strength to overcome temptation (Matthew 26:41).*

The psalm before us is a *missionary psalm.* It is one of several that demonstrates the nation of Israel understands that God desires for them to be a nation of priests that spreads God's saving message to the ends of the earth (v. 2). Historically, they do little to fulfill that commission. However, the promise given to Abraham, that through him all the nations will be blessed (Genesis 12:3), will not fail (Galatians 3:16).

The psalm is arranged in two parts: (1) a prayer for God's blessing and (2) the anticipated joy that results from God answering the prayer.

The psalm begins by quoting from the blessing that the priests are to say over Israel (Numbers 6:24-26). It asks for God's blessing upon Israel so that, through Israel, His "saving health" will be "known" (v. 2) to all nations. Surely Israel had seen God's way (v. 2) of mercy (v. 1), but the many nations of the world have not seen that God's ways are righteous and that He is a refuge to all that seek Him (Psalm 145:19).

Verses 3-7 are a response to the prayer of verses 1-2. It calls upon people to praise God and "sing for joy" (vv. 3-4) for He rules "righteously" (v. 4). Verses 5-6 asks these agricultural people to praise God (and not some other god), so that He will give them a bountiful harvest.

Verse 6 (based on Leviticus 26:4) expresses hope in the future as an encouragement for the present.

Verse 7 is a closing statement of expectation (it repeats the opening prayer). We can expect God's blessing upon Israel and we can expect God's ways to be known, loved, and feared by all nations.

In Matthew 28:19-20 and Acts 1:8 the Lord gave us a commission to take the *Saving Gospel Message* "unto the uttermost part of the earth." As such, how can you express, at home, at school, or at work, the joys of living in God's ways so others might know that God desires to bring to them mercy, forgiveness, and bountiful blessings?

Psalm 68:1-10

What is the writer saying?

How can I apply this to my life?

pray *Korea – Complete renewing of the mind for South Koreans saved out of Buddhism and Confucianism.*

The purpose of Psalm 68 is to extol the God of Israel as the One who brings victory over all of God's enemies and the oppressors of God's people past, present and future. In so doing the psalmist utilizes seven Hebrew names for God – *Elohim* (v. 1, God), *Jah* (v. 4, an abbreviation of Jehovah), *El Shaddai* (v. 14, Almighty), *Jehovah* (v. 16, LORD), *Jah Elohim* (v. 18, LORD-God), *Adonai* (v. 19, Lord) and *Jehovah Adonai* (v. 20, God the Lord).

In order to accomplish his purpose, the Psalmist draws upon earlier Scriptures. Verse 1 is the recorded call by Moses to Israel each time the pillar of cloud led them to resume the journey from Mt. Sinai to the Promised Land (Numbers 10:35).

The wicked (v. 2) are those who do not consider God as they conduct their lives. These will be "driven away" from God's "presence" (v. 2) as He "rideth" forward in victory (v. 4). In contrast, the righteous rejoice (v. 3) for they will remain "before" God's "presence." Thus the righteous are exhorted to be glad, rejoice, sing, praise and extol exceedingly!

Verses 5 and 6 declare that God has a very personal interest in each individual, especially those individuals that have no other protector! This powerful Victor is also a tenderhearted Father!

Verses 7 and 8 borrow from Deborah's Song (Judges 5:4-5) and are a summary of Israel's wanderings in the wilderness.

"Plentiful rain" (v. 9) is emblematic of God *raining down* gifts upon His people while in the wilderness, including water, manna and quail, as well as the "milk and honey" of the Promised Land.

Have you received God's gift of righteousness offered be means of the death of Jesus Christ? Also, are you living a life that is pleasing to the *Righteous One,* the LORD-God who scatters the wicked?

Psalm 68:11-23

What is the writer saying?

How can I apply this to my life?

pray *Italy – Maturity in believers, as more churches have resulted from bitter splits than church growth.*

Psalm 68 celebrates a great victory wrought by God on behalf of Israel. The occasion for writing may have been one of David's campaigns to enlarge the kingdom of Israel described in 2 Samuel 8.

Verses 11-13 focus on those who kept the home front while the army faced the enemy. The women celebrate in the manner instituted by Miriam (Ex. 15:20) and continued by Deborah (Judges 5:1). See also 1 Samuel 18:6. They are enriched by their share of the spoils of war.

Verses 14-16 speak of the Lord's selection of the seemingly insignificant hill of Zion as His earthly dwelling (the hill upon which Jerusalem and the Temple are built), rather than the mountains of Bashan which culminate into the majestic snow-capped Mt. Herman.

Verse 17 looks back to the host that brought the law to Moses at Sinai (Deuteronomy 33:2; Acts 7:53; Galatians 3:19). It may also look forward to the host that will accompany the Lord when He establishes His throne on Zion (Daniel 7:10; Revelation 19:14).

According to Ephesians 4:8, verse 18 prophesies the *ascension of Christ* (Acts 1:9-11, after His resurrection, Jesus "ascended" to a place of honor in Heaven!) which climaxed the victory of Jesus over Satan and death which He won on the cross (John 12:31-33; Hebrews 2:14).

Verses 19-20 declare that God should be glorified because He provides day by day, and also because He has the only answer to death.

Verses 21-23 prophesy of the ultimate defeat of the enemies of God and of the regathering of Israel at the end of the age.

As this Psalm declares that a great company of people "published" (v. 11) the wonderful deeds and words of God, so should we be *publishing* the glorious deeds and words of God! How has God *loaded benefits* daily upon your life? How can you *publish* His "salvation" to others so that they too can enjoy His blessings?

Psalm 68:24-35

What is the writer saying?

How can I apply this to my life?

pray *Dominican Republic – For believers to take a more vocal stand in a society where evil is rampant.*

Verses 24-28 tell of a victorious procession to the sanctuary David has prepared at Jerusalem for worship before Solomon's Temple (v. 29) was built. The singers are an especially appointed group of Levites. They live with their families at the place of worship. They are full-time keepers of the sanctuary provided for by special decree (1 Chronicles 9:33; 15:16; Nehemiah 11:22-23; 12:47).

Four of the twelve tribes of Israel are mentioned. The four poetically represent all the tribes of Israel who have come to give praise to God. The tribes of Benjamin and Judah are mentioned first. These occupy the far south of Israel. Zebulun and Naphtali occupy the far north.

The use of the future tense is a signal that verses 29-32 project us into the future *Millennial Reign* of Messiah. All the rulers on earth will pay homage by bringing gifts to the King at Jerusalem (Isaiah 60:6). Egypt is given as the first example here since it has always been one of the great nations of the ancient world. Ethiopia, located south of Egypt, is an example of a country from one of the farthest corners of the world that would come to praise God.

In verses 32-35, the psalm closes with a call to all the kingdoms to "sing" praises to the greatness of the God of Israel. All hearers are admonished to recognize that Israel's God is the God of the universe and all that is therein. At the time of this Psalm's writing, God was only the "God of Israel" (v. 35). The point of this prophecy is that the day is coming when God would become the God of all the Earth (v. 32), when all the nations of the earth acknowledge Him.

How has the God of all the Earth sought to make Himself the *God of all areas of your life?* David thought it important to note that all twelve tribes have submitted themselves to the worship of God. Have you made it an important point to submit all areas of your life to God?

Psalm 69:1-12

What is the writer saying?

How can I apply this to my life?

pray *El Salvador – For those taking Bible correspondence courses to gain a passion for studying the Word.*

Psalm 69 is one of the most quoted Psalms (along with Psalms 22 and 110) in the New Testament. A characteristic of Messianic Psalms is illustrated here; some verses apply only to David while others apply to both David and Christ! So then, how do we know how to apply its verses? David's distress, and resulting prayer for God's aid, is a typical pattern for all who follow (including Jesus!) when they themselves come under great distress resulting from their zeal to honor God.

The Psalm's predominant feature is the cry to God by a man under great affliction. His *soul* is described as drowning in deep, stormy waters (vv. 1-2). While David understands that his own foolishness and sins (v. 5, see 1 Samuel 21) are a source of some of his suffering, David also knows that for God's sake (v. 7) he has borne suffering, reproach and shame. Those that "reproached" God (vv. 7, 9, *to publicly insult; to bring harm upon another's reputation*) are now reproaching David!

Since David, after his foolish sin, had acted righteously (he wept, fasted, sat in sackcloth, v. 10-11; all are associated with repentance from sin), the dominant condition of the Psalm is that of a sufferer who is innocent of further alleged charges brought against him (v. 12).

Notice David's prayer also includes a request that his past foolish and sinful deeds not cause other godly people ("them that wait on thee," v. 6) to be "ashamed" (implies being *delayed* in their service to God) or be "confounded" (*to cause confusion* and *a drying up of faith in God*).

Do you face troubles and distress because of your righteous stand with things pleasing to God or because of your own foolishness and sin? If it is due to your stand with right and good things, then ask God to "save me" (v. 1) from those troubles. If it is due to foolishness and sin, you must first confess your sin and turn away from such foolish activities.

Psalm 69:13-21

What is the writer saying?

How can I apply this to my life?

pray *Canada – That Canada's churches will keep evangelism a priority.*

Verses 13-19 report David's solution to the distressful situation (v. 2-4). He is still in anguish of soul (v. 18), but his eyes have turned from his plight unto his God (v. 13). He cries to God using the names of Jehovah and Elohim (v. 13). The first name indicates David's confidence in his *personal relationship* to God, the One who *personally fellowships with* and *acts to benefit* His own. The second indicates David's confidence that God, as the *Supreme One,* is able to "deliver" (v.18) David.

David also places his faith in the unchanging character of God:

- God is all knowing (vv. 5, 19, God *sees* and skillfully *discerns* what must be done),
- God has a "multitude" of mercy (v. 13),
- God is known for His "loving-kindness" (God's *attitude of loyalty* towards His people results in His *acting as an ally*), which is then further described as "good" (meaning *bountiful* here) (v. 16).
- Similarly, God is known for His "tender mercies" (this word pictures a mother's care for her new infant!) (v. 16)

So then, David is confidently beseeching the One who sees, understands and desires to help with his problems. God will act because He will always be merciful to those who call upon Him.

To emphasize the urgency of his plea, David uses all these words: "Deliver me" (v. 14) – "Turn unto me" (v. 16) – "Draw nigh unto my soul" (v.18). – "Hide not thy face from thy servant" (v. 17). He addresses himself as a "servant" in need of help from his Master. He reasons, "How can I perform my duties as your servant until You bring deliverance?"

What should you do when you find yourself in the mire (mud pits) of despair? Follow the steps on the rescue ladder that God extends to your "soul" in drawing it out of its mire. Ask yourself, who is God and what does He desire to do for me?

Psalm 69:22-36

What is the writer saying?

How can I apply this to my life?

pray *Bahamas – For Christians to guard themselves from materialism.*

Verses 22-28 prophesy concerning Israel ("pour out thine indignation upon them," v. 24, *to be enraged by sin*) during the time of God's "great indignation" (Deuteronomy 29:28). This is the time between their rejection of the Messiahship of Jesus and the time, still future, when *the indignation* is past (Isaiah 26:20; Daniel 8:19). The Apostle Paul quotes vv. 22-23 in Romans 11:9-10, and then says that God's indignation upon Israel has resulted in God's blessings upon Christians in the Church.

In Acts 1:20, the Apostle Peter quotes from verse 25 and applies it to Judas Iscariot by changing "their" to "his." Judas, like the religious leaders of Israel, rejected Jesus as Messiah and brought disaster upon himself.

Verse 26 speaks of the Jewish treatment of the One "despised and rejected of men; a man of sorrows, and acquainted with grief: and…smitten of God" (Isaiah 53:3-4).

"Add iniquity unto their iniquity" (v. 27) – We all, like David, are "shapen in iniquity" (Psalm 51:5). By refusing to acknowledge our iniquity and receive God's provision for our sin, we add the ultimate iniquity to the "iniquity" with which we were born. Verse 27 illustrates Paul's words that Israel set "about to establish their own righteousness, have not submitted themselves unto the righteousness of God" (Romans 10:3), thereby, excluding themselves from "the book of the living" (v. 28).

Verses 29-36 look to the day when the people Israel will see themselves as "poor and sorrowful" and in need of God saving (v. 1) and delivering (v. 14) them from their own "deep mire" (vv. 2, 14). God's "indignation" will then be past and they will receive their Messiah!

God's "indignation" is upon all who continue in sin and refuse to allow God to deliver them from their sin. God also desires to bring "salvation" (v. 29) to all who admit they are "poor" in life and are "sorrowful" for their sin. What "poor and sorrowful" person do you know who needs to hear of God's salvation?

QT Wednesday 4

Psalm 70: 1-5

What is the writer saying?

How can I apply this to my life?

pray *For Christian writers to develop curriculum for churches with biblical content, clarity, and creativity.*

This psalm is an urgent petition for deliverance from pursuers and is the type of prayer David might have prayed on a number of occasions. For instance, it fits well for the experience reported in 2 Samuel 16:5-14. While fleeing from Absalom, a group of Benjamites threw stones at him while mocking and taunting. Perhaps they were angry since David replaced Saul, a Benjamite, as king of Israel.

David invokes the name of God five times in the Psalm – as *Elohim* three times and *Jehovah* twice. David calls to Elohim since it emphasizes that God is the "Supreme One" who is all powerful. David calls upon Jehovah since God is also the personal God who takes interest in the needs of His people.

David urges God to please hurry!! That is how he both begins and ends his plea. He asks for four things in regards to his pursuers: (1) Let them be ashamed, (2) Let them be confounded (humiliated), (3) Let them be turned back (twice), (4) Let them be confused (dishonored).

Then he makes a request for those who seek God and love His salvation (David is including himself in this group!) (v. 4). Let them rejoice, be glad and magnify God continually.

David closes by expressing his own complete poverty in resources (v. 5) and his entire dependence on a God who is able (*Elohim*), and a God who acts on behalf of His own people (*Jehovah*). David understands and trusts in the inexhaustible resources of God! David also wants God's greatness to be "magnified" (v. 4) as He brings deliverance to David.

What *do* you *do* when you are out of things you can *do*? David has the right answer: call upon God (who is both Elohim and Jehovah!) to use His vast resources to *do* the *doing* for you! After all, God loves to *do* such for those who "love" Him (v. 4)! So then, since you too "love" God, why not ask God, who is ready and able, to help with your need?

Psalm 71:1-13

What is the writer saying?

How can I apply this to my life?

pray *Aruba – For outreach among those who have immigrated from Latin America, the Caribbean and Asia.*

Verses 1-13 of Psalm 71 consist of a prayer, and then the remainder of the Psalm (vv. 14-24) is primarily praise. Though we are not told who authors the Psalm, it is likely David in his old age (vv. 9, 18). The word "trust" in verse 1 means *to take refuge,* and the psalmist is escaping (v. 2), so we assume the historical setting is David's flight from his son, Absalom, who had rebelled and taken over the nation (2 Samuel 15:14). In the past, God has always *delivered* David according to the request of verse 4. Therefore, he has a firm basis for hope and trust, which causes him to "praise" (v. 22) God instead of cowering in fear.

"A wonder unto many" (v. 7) – Certainly David is a source of wonder to those who curse him and throw stones in 2 Samuel 16:5-8. David, the giant-slayer and conqueror of nations, is fleeing in disgrace from his own son! They think God is punishing him and are ready to help God finish him (v. 11). Some onlookers at the crucifixion of Jesus have similar thoughts (Luke 23:35-37, 48).

Notice that David gives his readers thoughts to "wonder" about:

- This old man is still full of trust and hope in God (vv. 9, 17, 18).
- He asks God to continue to be his "rock" and "fortress" (vv. 3, 7).
- He talks of and sings praises to God "all the day" (vv. 8, 15, 24).
- He believes that God has watched over him all his life (vv. 5-6, 17).
- He was sure that God would not fail him now that he was old (vv. 9, 18).
- This old man believed God still had a work for him to do, which was to declare God's "strength" to the coming generation (v. 18).

If you are old or have an older relative, then consider carefully David's "wonder"! How has God *not failed* the elderly and what work does God *still intend* them to do for Him?

Psalm 71:14-24

What is the writer saying?

How can I apply this to my life?

pray *France – Passionate outreach to the nearly 50,000,000 people who have no contact with Christianity.*

In verses 1-13, the psalmist prays an urgent petition for deliverance from his enemies while declaring his trust and hope in the Lord God (vv. 1, 5). He also expressed a desire to praise God (vv. 6, 8).

At verse 14, he stops praying about his enemies and turns his eyes upon God's righteousness (vv. 15, 16, 19, 24), strength (vv. 16, 18) and wondrous works (vv. 17, 19). These are the qualities of God that are the foundation of the hope that he had expressed in verse 5. Firmly trusting in God's salvation (meaning here *deliverance from danger*), he praises God with his mouth "all the day" (v. 8). As a result, there is no time for worry about circumstances or enemies!

In verses 17 and 18, the psalmist reminds God that from his youth he has declared the wondrous works of God. Now in his old age, he asks for the privilege of continuing to serve God by telling present and future generations of God's delivering power.

In verse 20, David uses a figure of speech, translated "depths of the earth," that is now hard to understand. Most likely, David is expressing hope in God's deliverance from his present dire circumstance. A form of this Hebrew word is used in Genesis 1:2, "the face of the deep," to describe the vast depths of the oceans. So then, our verse likely pictures God metaphorically bringing a person back to life after rescuing him from drowning in the deepest, most forbidding *sea of perils.* Perhaps David, as an old man considering his own death, is also speaking of God literally bringing David back to life after rescuing him from the depths of the grave! Old Testament saints certainly expected to be resurrected bodily (Job 19:25-26; Psalm 17:15; Isaiah 26:19).

Since God is righteous, strong, and able to do wondrous work, how can God rescue you from the depths of your troubles? How can you tell the present generation about God's wondrous works?

4 Saturday

Psalm 72:1-11

What is the writer saying?

How can I apply this to my life?

pray *Eritrea – For Christians to be fervent for Jesus and make a significant impact on their nation and beyond.*

Psalm 72 is a song that builds upon the *Davidic Covenant* (2 Samuel 7:10-16), a collection of promises from God to David about the future of David's kingdom. These promises are partially fulfilled during the reign of Solomon, David's son, which is characterized by peace and rest (1 Chronicles 22:9). However, complete fulfillment of the Covenant awaits the setting up of the future glorious kingdom of Jesus Christ, the future *Son of David* and the promised Messiah (Daniel 2:44).

The superscription above the Psalm is likely telling us that this Psalm is *concerning* Solomon and not written *by* Solomon. We understand it to mean *concerning Solomon,* with the author, David, writing about his son and next king, Solomon (note "David," v. 20).

Verses 1-7 present the character of the kingdom. Notice the repeated use of *judgment, judge,* and *righteousness* in vv. 1-7. "Peace" then appears (v. 7) since peace *flourishes* in a climate of these three, "the work of righteousness shall be peace; and the effect of righteousness quietness and assurance forever" (Isaiah 32:17). A chief concern of the king is the protection of the poor, the needy, and those "that hath no helper" (vv. 12-14). There will be no oppressors.

Verses 8-11 present the extent of the kingdom which is "unto the ends of the earth" and to "all nations." God's original allotment to Israel is from the Red Sea to the Great Sea (Mediterranean). However, He promised to *enlarge their borders.* David extends the borders to the river (Euphrates), and Jesus when He comes as Messiah-King will extend them to the ends of the earth (Exodus 23:30, 31).

Notice God's interest in His people doing what is *just* and *right* (vv. 1-7); things like being the helper to those with "no helper" (vv. 12-14). So then, how can you be a "helper" to a "needy" person today? God will be pleased!

QT

Sunday 5

Psalm 72:12-20

What is the writer saying?

How can I apply this to my life?

pray *Pray for the peace of Jerusalem (Psalm 122:6).*

As this Psalm portrays the glorious, future kingdom of Jesus, the Messiah-King, Psalm 72 could be outlined as follows:

1. The Character of the Kingdom (vv. 1-7) – *Righteousness* and *peace*
2. The Extent of the Kingdom (vv. 8-11) – To the *ends of the earth*
3. The Prosperity of the Kingdom (vv. 12-16) – *Abundance* for all
4. The Duration of the Kingdom (vv. 17-19) – *Never ending*

The King gives special attention to the poor and needy who are often neglected in this age. All people are precious to Him (12-14).

The abundant life is expressed by God blessing this kingdom with "showers" (v. 6), grain and "fruit" (v. 16). The King will be honored by "gifts" (vv. 10, 15), by homage (vv. 9, 11) and by praise (vv. 15, 17).

The thousand-year kingdom age (millennium) will end with the destruction of both death and Satan, followed by the great white throne judgment (Revelation 20). After that thousand-year kingdom, there will be a "new heaven and a new earth" (Revelation 21:1), in which the throne of God and the Lamb (another name for Jesus Christ) will continue forever (Revelation 22:1-5). The promises to David (2 Samuel 7:13, 16) and the prophecy of Daniel (Daniel 2:44) emphatically declare the eternality of this Kingdom.

The Psalm itself ends at verse 17. The last three verses here form a doxology to the Second Book of Psalms (Psalms 42 to 72; note that the Psalms are organized into five sections or books). The doxology urges us to bless God which means *to extend worth or gratitude* to God for all the blessings He has extended to us!

Since God wants to establish the character of the future kingdom in your life now, how can your life be a testimony to all men that you are "blessed in Him" (v. 17)?

5 Monday

Psalm 73:1-14

What is the writer saying?

How can I apply this to my life?

pray *Jamaica – For quality staff and increased enrollment among Jamaica's Bible schools and seminaries.*

The Book of Psalms is traditionally divided into five sections or books. Today we start the *Third Book* (Psalms 73-89). The first eleven Psalms are ascribed to Asaph, who is King David's chief singer. He is also a "seer" of God (a prophet, 2 Chronicles 29:30).

Psalm 73 considers an old question – Why do the wicked prosper while the righteous suffer? Asaph stumbles and almost falls because of *envy* (v. 3). The same question perplexes Job, Jeremiah and Habakkuk.

"The foolish" (v. 3) denote those who arrogantly live their lives without regard to their Creator. Such appear to have lives full of life's good things. There is no evidence of God's judgment upon their evil deeds (vv. 4-5). They are full of pride and indulge themselves in every desire (vv. 6-7). They are corrupt, oppressive, and boastful (v. 8). They vaunt themselves wherever they go, defying God and man with no apparent penalty (v. 9).

Asaph observes the people of God following the ways of the wicked. These have concluded that God isn't aware of what is happening on earth (vv. 10-12). This lead Asaph to suppose: Since the ungodly increase in prosperity, is his living a clean life for God entirely "in vain" (vv. 13-14)? Asaph *almost* decides that it has been useless to live a clean life!

Providentially, Asaph does not decide to follow the ways of the "foolish" and ungodly! Go back to verse 1 to hear his conclusion, which, due to its importance, Asaph places first and noticeably out-of-order! In spite of the apparent evidence that evil men have a better life, Asaph correctly observes, "Truly God is good to Israel, even to such as are of a clean of heart."

Asaph finally remembers that he has the greatest possession; God's good care in his life (vv.1, 23). Take a minute and consider all the good stuff you *do have* from God!

Psalm 73:15-28

What is the writer saying?

How can I apply this to my life?

pray *Nigeria -- For the youth of Northern Nigeria that are enticed by the Muslims with promises of material goods to know the truth about Jesus.*

Asaph knows there is something wrong with his thinking in verses 13 and 14. What about his obligation to the generation to come (v. 15)? Someone must stay true to God for their sake. How else will they know God's way? In Psalm 78:1-7, Asaph demonstrates that he took his obligation to future generations seriously.

The "sanctuary" (v. 17) is a special place set aside so that a person may draw near to God in order to fellowship with Him; thus, often used as an alternate title for the temple at Jerusalem (Psalm 20:2; 77:13; 96:6). It is the place where God shows Asaph the foolishness of his thoughts. It is the place where Asaph finds the answer to the problem that causes his pain (v. 16). It is the place where God brings conviction to his heart and where he freely confesses (Job 42:5, 6). In the sanctuary, Asaph realizes that his God is with him, holding his hand all the while (v. 23). There Asaph gains the assurance that God would counsel and guide him during his life on earth and bring him into His very presence in the glory of heaven (v. 24). His God is his total desire here, and his portion forever (vv. 25-26).

As for those who are far from God because they shun His sanctuary, He will take care of that in His time. Those who follow after the ways of the wicked will perish with the ones who led them astray. At the end of the Psalm, we have the same man in the same circumstances, but with a new and true perspective of the role he is to play on the stage of life.

Do you have a *special place* set aside where God can quietly talk to your heart? A Quiet Time *place* is good to have! It was at his set-apart-place that God guided (v. 24) his thoughts to the truth about his worries. Ask God to give you a *spiritual sanctuary* where you can see that He is "continually" with you, holding your hand (v. 23), as He counsels (v. 24) and strengthens (v. 26) you concerning your worries.

Psalm 74:1-12

What is the writer saying?

How can I apply this to my life?

pray *Paraguay – For salvation decisions resulting from radio broadcasts to the 90,000 Germans living there.*

This Psalm of Asaph must have been compiled by his descendants known as the *sons of Asaph.* These were leaders of worship for many generations after Asaph's time (2 Chronicles 20:14; Ezra 3:10). The sad plight of the nation described in Psalm 74:3-9 resulted from the destruction of Jerusalem by the Babylonian army in 586 BC (2 Kings 25:8-12) long after Asaph served King David between 1010 to 970 BC.

Apparently, sometime after Jerusalem's destruction, the psalmist asks, "O God, why hast thou cast us off forever?" "O God, how long shall the adversary reproach?" (to publicly scorn and do harm to God's reputation, vv. 1, 10)

In Romans 11, the Apostle Paul answers these two questions. Full restoration for Israel as a nation will come. Israel's restoration comes after the three *Until's* of the New Testament are fulfilled:

- "Until the time come when ye [the nation of Israel] shall say, Blessed is he that cometh in the name of the Lord" (Luke 13:35). Israel as a whole nation must first believe Jesus is the Messiah.
- "Until the times of the Gentiles be fulfilled" (Luke 21:24). Jerusalem shall be trodden down by the Gentiles from 586 B.C. until the great *Battle of Armageddon* when Messiah will crush the world powers.
- "Until the fulness of the Gentiles be come in" (Romans 11:25). God intends to first complete His calling out (from amongst the Gentiles) of a great number of people who call upon His name (Acts 15:14).

At first, it appears that God has withdrawn His hand from acting in the affairs of the world (v. 11). Then the psalmist recognizes the truth, God has not changed; He is still the "King of old" (v. 12a). Thus He continues "working salvation in the midst of the earth" (v. 12b)!

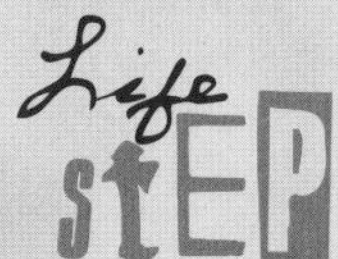

We too face times when it seems that God has *withdrawn* His hand! Maybe you need to reaffirm your old faith by declaring God is still the same "King of old"!

Psalm 74:13-23

What is the writer saying?

How can I apply this to my life?

pray *Argentina – For full-time workers to make the development of future leadership a major priority.*

In verses 13-15 the psalmist rehearses the history of how God manifested His power on behalf of Israel. The monstrous animals of verses 13 and 14 are emblematic of strong adversaries that only God's power could destroy (Isaiah 27:1; Ezekiel 29:3). Those "inhabiting the wilderness" (v. 14), speaks of the creatures of desert and sea that feast upon the slain soldiers of Egypt. Verse 15 recalls the water coming from the rock which Moses hit and the crossing of Jordan on dry ground.

Verses 16 and 17 acknowledge the work of God in Creation. The psalmist is saying to God, *I know that you have been willing in the past to rescue your people, and that you are fully capable.* In the remainder of the Psalm, the psalmist reminds God (v. 18) of the reasons why He should "arise" (v. 22) on behalf of His people:

1. It is God, Himself who has been reproached and blasphemed in the desecration of His holy habitation (v. 18b).
2. Remember that You are a merciful God. We are as helpless as a dove in a snare (v. 19a).
3. You are the Provider of the poor and needy, and they are shamefully oppressed (v. 19b).
4. Honor Your covenant with Abraham, Isaac, and Jacob (v. 20).
5. You called out a people for Your name. How can they offer praise under these circumstances (v. 21)?
6. This is Your cause, and the enemies are prevailing (v. 22)!

In Leviticus and Deuteronomy the LORD fully explained that if Israel sinned, her sin would lead to the calamity Israel is here enduring. They rejected God's warning. They would not learn by instruction, so they must learn by experience. Today, are you willing to learn by instruction or must you experience God's chastening hand? Don't forget, "The Lord shall judge his people" (Deuteronomy 32:36; Hebrews 10:30).

Psalm 75:1-10

What is the writer saying?

How can I apply this to my life?

pray *Spain – For people to be called to evangelize to the remote areas of the country.*

This Psalm is best viewed as God's answer to the two requests at the end of Psalm 74: (v. 22) "plead thine own cause," and (v. 23) "Forget not the voice of thine enemies." It can be outlined as follows:

- In verse 1, the psalmist speaks *to God* on behalf of the congregation.
- In verses 2-3, he speaks *to the congregation* on behalf of God.
- In verses 4-8, he speaks *to the oppressors* of Israel on behalf of God.
- In verse 9 he speaks *for himself.*
- Finally, in verse 10, he speaks on behalf of God *to all.*

In v. 2, God says "when I shall receive the congregation." This pictures God as a great and sovereign King who, at His *appointed time,* will act upon the requests of the congregation.

In v. 3, God says that in spite of the disorder and disruption caused by the sins of the people of the earth, He declares that He has always been in control of the ultimate course of world history.

In vv. 4-5, God speaks to the "wicked," warning them to "lift not up the horn" against God. This is an oriental saying that pictures one bull challenging another for dominance. God knows that these arrogant and foolish men were *tossing their heads* at God. Note that v. 10 says "all the horns of the wicked also will I cut off." The wicked will never be *top bull!* Rather, God remains the powerful and righteous Judge of the wicked.

The Hebrew word for lift up, used in vv. 4 and 5, is used again in v. 6 "promotion," in v. 7 "set up," and in v. 10 "be exalted." Thus, the key lesson of the Psalm is that, while wicked men search every corner of the world to find a way to *lift up themselves,* the truth is that only *God lifts up!* The Psalm concludes with the observation that God will only lift up or exalt those who live "righteous" lives (v. 10).

Have you *bowed the horn* of your will to God's righteous will (v. 10) or have you *lifted the horn* against God's righteous judgments (v. 2)?

Psalm 76:1-12

What is the writer saying?

How can I apply this to my life?

pray *No interference from civil authorities in the cities where street evangelism takes place.*

Psalm 76 is the climatic sequel to Psalm 75 where God declares that He is sovereign in the world. Psalm 75 is God's answer to the troubled psalmist of Psalm 74, *Why are You not dealing with Your enemies?*

Psalm 76 is a song of victory that arises from the destroying of 185,000 Assyrian invaders by one angel (Isaiah 36-37; 2 Kings 19:30-35). The Assyrians have besieged Jerusalem. King Hezekiah of Judah prays and God answers in a manner not seen since the great wonders from the days of Joshua, when Israel had first conquered the land.

The Psalm is divided into four *triplets* (four sets of three verses) as follows:

- vv. 1-3, God has made Himself known, by His great acts, in Judah.
- vv. 4-6, God is victorious over the stubborn nations.
- vv. 7-9, God is now feared throughout the earth.
- vv. 10-12, God will be praised by all round-about Him.

"Mountains" (v. 4) are often used figuratively to picture a kingdom (Isaiah 2:2; Daniel 2:35). The "mountains of prey" are nations, like Assyria, which prey upon other weaker countries, like Judah.

There is a lesson for us in the contrast between the proud "men of might," who will not praise God (vv. 5, 10), and the "meek" (v. 9), who submit to God's sovereignty. Even today, proud "men of might" attack us desiring to spoil (v. 5) our lives. We can be confident that God will be against those who will not allow God to be their Sovereign. Similarly, God will "save" (v. 9, *to deliver from a peril*) all those who submit to Him.

In the ancient world, a king from a small kingdom would bring "presents" (v. 11) to a king of a large kingdom to demonstrate his submission to the will of the more-powerful king. God desires "presents" such as these: willing worship of God, living a righteous life, demonstrating the fruit of the Spirit, and the doing of good works for others. Consider a "present" to bring Him today!

First Timothy is one of three books (the others: 2 Timothy and Titus) written by the Apostle Paul to two younger men, Timothy and Titus, who were serving in pastoral-like roles. Paul wants to tell them how to *behave* themselves "in the house of God, which is the Church of the living God" (1 Timothy 3:15). Due to their similar purpose and content, these three books have come to be known as the *Pastoral Epistles.*

To understand 1 Timothy, some background on all three of the books and all three of the men involved should prove to be helpful. At the time of writing, Paul is approaching the end of his life and ministry. Timothy and Titus, both a generation younger than Paul, are anticipating many years of ministry still ahead. Both of them have been greatly influenced by Paul, beginning first with their salvation. He addresses each of them as his "own son" in the faith, using the Greek word *teknon,* which literally means, "a born one," and is used to speak of "a little child." Paul also attaches "in the faith" in his address to Timothy, and "after the common faith" to Titus, leading to the conclusion that he is their spiritual father.

Timothy is born of mixed parentage, with a Greek father and a Jewish mother (Acts 16:1). Timothy's salvation apparently took place in his hometown of Lystra, in the Roman province of Galatia (modern Turkey), under Paul's ministry. He soon became one of Paul's most trusted aides, ministering with him in such places as Philippi, Thessalonica, Berea, Corinth and Ephesus. It is at Ephesus where Timothy is left on his own, becoming the *senior pastor* of the Ephesian church. It is there he receives this first of the Pastoral Epistles. The relationship between Paul and Timothy is very special and could be legitimately described as *father-son-like* in nature. Of all Paul's letters, his second epistle to Timothy, his "own son in the faith," is his most personal (apart from his unusual letter to Philemon).

Titus is a Greek believer converted from paganism and may have been the younger brother of Luke. As 2 Corinthians 2:13 points out, he is a member of Paul's ministering team. Both Titus and Timothy are ministering in exceedingly difficult places when Paul writes to them. For Timothy, it was in Ephesus, where stands the famous Temple of Diana. All sorts of violent and immoral acts take place here in the name of worship. It is a city famous for sorcery, superstition and sexual debauchery. Paul had ministered there for three years and his ministry had borne much fruit. Yet he warns that after his departure, "shall grievous wolves enter in...not sparing the flock" (Acts 20:29). It is to this work and to this condition that Timothy is called.

Titus fares no better. His assignment is to the island of Crete. The people there, by their own admission, are "liars, evil beasts, slow bellies" (lazy gluttons) (Titus 1:12).

As for Paul himself, little needs to be said. This is the great champion of the Christian faith, who at one time was a "blasphemer, and a persecutor" of those who claimed the name of Christ (1 Timothy 1:13). Then on the Damascus Road (Acts 9), he became a believer, and the change in his life became a pattern for others to follow (1 Timothy 1:16).

While these three books are written to individuals, Paul identifies himself as "an apostle of Jesus Christ." Surely neither Timothy nor Titus needs such substantiation, but what they do need is the weight of Paul's title behind them as they discharge their duties. On their own merit, they could have been challenged. So Paul gives them a hammer – the hammer of his apostleship. And in the days prior to the canonization of the Scripture, this hammer gave these young men authority they would not otherwise have had.

Three themes seem to resonate throughout all three books:

(1) Church Organization
(2) Sound Doctrine
(3) Consistent Christian Living

While all three books touch on all three themes, each book has its particular emphasis. The three themes also follow the order of placement of the three books in the Bible (though they are not written in that order).

- 1 Timothy emphasizes *Church Organization*
- 2 Timothy emphasizes *Sound Doctrine*
- Titus emphasizes *Consistent Christian Living*

Charles Erdman, in writing of these three books early in the 20th century, offers this summation of the three themes in this manner: "Church government is not an end in itself; it is of value only as it secures sound doctrine: and doctrine is of value only as it issues in life."

1 Timothy 1:1-11

What is the writer saying?

How can I apply this to my life?

pray *Venezuela – Perseverance and patience for those discipling believers from dysfunctional backgrounds.*

Paul introduces himself as an Apostle of Jesus Christ. He is writing to Timothy, his "son in the faith" (v. 1). He refers to Christ in three tenses:

- He is "Our Savior" – *the past,* looking back to redemption;
- He is "Our Lord" – *the present,* looking at present responsibility;
- He is "Our hope" – *the future,* looking to His future return.

To Timothy (*he who honors God*) he extends the salutation "Grace, mercy, and peace" (v. 2). Grace: God's assistance is extended; Mercy: God's judgment is withheld; Peace: harmony with God.

He identifies his purpose: Timothy is to rebuke false doctrine (v. 3). Paul exhorts him to *hang in there* ("abide still"), as he challenges these false teachers who teach that Christ's work on the cross was only a partial payment for sin. Works to keep the Law are also needed.

Paul introduces a basic Gospel principle: True "faith" (vv. 2, 5) results in love (v. 5, "charity"), which comes from (1) a pure heart, (2) a good conscience (see v. 19), and (3) a sincere faith. These characteristics are not found in the false teachers who are marked by "vain jangling" (*purposeless talk*) (vv. 5-6) and do not understand the purpose of the Law (v. 7), which is to show Israel its need of faith in God's grace!

"Sound doctrine" (v. 10) means *healthy teaching* or *teaching that promotes spiritual health.* The Greek word translated, "sound," gives us our English word, *hygiene.* Later Paul pictures false teaching as the opposite, a canker ("gangrene," 2 Timothy 2:17). Only sound doctrine can successfully combat the disease of false teaching!

If you have true faith in Jesus Christ as your Savior, then that should be apparent in your love for the things of God and for other people. Consider your own heart; is it "pure" before God? Similarly, do you serve others well?

1 Timothy 1:12-20

What is the writer saying?

How can I apply this to my life?

pray *South Africa – For loving outreach by those in youth ministry to a very vulnerable generation.*

Paul's tone changes here in verse 12. The emphasis is on praise and thanksgiving, an attitude prompted by his mentioning his call to the gospel ministry (see v. 11). He thanks God for: (1) Empowerment, strength to fulfill his calling; (2) Trust, God counts him faithful; (3) Calling, God puts him into the ministry (v. 12). He then reviews his past, "a blasphemer…persecutor… injurious…" Nevertheless, he received mercy, and that mercy erupts in praise. Paul next lists the three motivating forces in his life: *grace,* providing salvation; *faith,* appropriating it; and *love,* applying it (v. 14). He then offers the first of five "faithful sayings" (see 3:1; 4:9; 2 Timothy 2:11; Titus 3:8). These are likely *prophetic sayings* by early Christians prior to the completion of Scripture; they help form an early standard of faith. Here: "Christ Jesus came in to the world to save sinners" (v. 15; see Luke 19:10). Paul refers to himself as the "chief" of sinners, an indication that he never forgot God's extra grace extended to him.

His life becomes a "pattern" (v. 16) for others: turn to Christ (v. 16), experience salvation, return praise to God (v. 17) and serve Him (v. 18).

Paul then returns to the charge he has begun in verse 3. He uses military language: a "charge" (*An order that gives instructions for the coming battle*) to "war a good warfare" (v. 18). The war is to be waged on two fronts: doctrinal and moral, and to be fought using two weapons: *faith* and a *good conscience* (v. 19). Paul then mentions two men whose words were blasphemous. These are judged by excommunication, with an intended purpose ("that they may learn not to blaspheme" v. 20).

Paul's life provides a pattern for us to follow: turn to Christ, experience salvation, praise God and serve Him. As a member of the army of God, are you *warring a good spiritual warfare*? How can you praise and serve the Captain of the Army of God, the Lord Jesus?

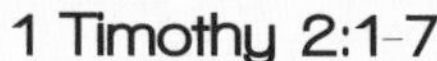

1 Timothy 2:1-7

What is the writer saying?

How can I apply this to my life?

pray *Uruguay – For the spiritual awakening of a country that is disillusioned by secularism.*

Paul now moves from "sound doctrine" to prayer. The ministry of the Word and the ministry of prayer are the main pastoral responsibilities (see Acts 6:4). The words "first of all" (v. 1) emphasize prayer's place of priority in the church. The four *Ingredients of Prayer* are: (1) "Supplications," asking for one's own spiritual needs; (2) "Prayers," suggesting expressing devotion and adoration to God; (3) "Intercessions," the coming near to God on behalf of others; and (4) "Giving of thanks," appreciation for what He has done.

In verses 2-8 we see the *Aims of Prayer*: (1) To maintain peace in society. Through prayer "for kings, and for all that are in authority," God protects His church, making possible "a quiet and peaceable life" (v. 2); (2) To please God. Prayer is good in God's sight (v. 3). If we pray only to have needs met, we have a low view of God; and (3) The salvation of the lost (vv. 4-7). Christ died for all and wants all to be saved, (see also 2 Peter 3:9).

Also we find a *Basic Rule of Prayer*: Prayer is offered *only* to God the Father through the *only* "mediator" possible, the Lord Jesus (v. 5). He is the *only* go between, between God and men (Hebrews 4:14-16). His willingness to be a "ransom" for man made salvation possible (v. 6).

Praying in the Church is to be: (1) "without wrath"– prayer is a working love in the church (v. 8); (2) "lifting up holy hands" – indicating a condition of a pure heart and cleansed life (v. 8); and (3) "without ... doubting" – doubting is the opposite of faith; faith believes that God hears (v. 8)!

How's your prayer life? Ask yourself the following: (1) What are my own spiritual needs? (2) How can I express my devotion to God? (3) How can I pray on behalf of others in need of God's help? (4) What has God already done that needs to be on my "giving of thanks" list?

QT Wednesday 6

1 Timothy 2:8-15

What is the writer saying?

How can I apply this to my life?

pray *Austria – Pray for more godly Austrian men to respond to the call to full – time Christian service.*

Paul deals with the dress (vv. 9-10), behavior (vv. 11-12) and role (vv. 13-14) of women in the church. First positively: godly women are attractive by means of their discreet, modest dress (v. 9), and by "good works," a godly woman's true adornment (v. 10). Then negatively; extreme hairstyles and attention-getting jewelry would be inconsistent with the woman professing godliness (v. 10). Immodest dress would distract others from seeing her "good works."

With verse 11, Paul speaks on the subject of the woman's behavior in the church. While Paul's ministry includes female co-workers (1 Corinthians 11:5; Philippians 4:1-3, etc.), he makes it clear that their role is one of subordination to male leadership. A woman is not "to teach, nor to usurp authority over the man" (v. 12). He supports his teaching doctrinally (Adam was created first and had precedence over Eve, 1 Corinthians 11:8-9), and observationally (Satan finds the woman easier to deceive, verse 14 with 2 Corinthians 11:3). To accept such a role of subordination demonstrates Christ-like humility, for Christ, though equal with the Father, subordinated His will to the Father's will (see John 14:7-11, 28).

Verse 15 needs to be interpreted in its context, that of the Garden of Eden. At issue is not *soul* salvation, but *societal* salvation. Adam's purpose in life was to be found in the "sweat of thy face"; his "sweat" providing for their needs (Genesis 3:19). Eve's salvation was to be found in childbirth; that is, accepting God's ordained role of subjection to her husband and bearing children. (Note: the "they" of v. 15 refers to both husband and wife.)

Paul has given us a *woman's guide to attractive living.* Everything about her draws attention to her walk in godliness! Dear lady, does your outer appearance (apparel, hair, jewelry) draw attention to an inner *well-balanced* walk that pleases God?

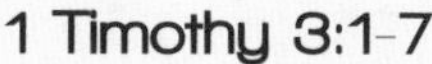

1 Timothy 3:1-7

What is the writer saying?

How can I apply this to my life?

pray *Pray that your pastor will have God's wisdom and guidance in the area of counseling.*

Verses 1-13 give the primary qualifications for church "office" (v. 1): the pastor (vv. 1-7) and the deacon (vv. 8-13). The title of pastor does not appear here. Instead we have the term, bishop. A number of New Testament passages make it clear that those two terms, plus elder, are used interchangeably. All refer to the same individual and provide a job description for his ministry: (1) As elder, he provides authority; (2) as bishop, administrative oversight; (3) as pastor, he feeds the congregation as a shepherd does his sheep (see Acts 20:17,28; 1 Peter 5:1-2.).

To be worthy of the office of the elder/pastor/bishop one must meet certain qualifications. A total of sixteen items are found here. These fall into three categories.

(1) PERSONAL QUALIFICATIONS, verses 2-3. Some thirteen are listed, beginning with being "blameless" (*irreproachable*), nothing is in his life that would discredit his witness. It continues down through "not covetous," he consistently puts Christ and his church first in his life.

(2) FAMILY QUALIFICATIONS, verses 4-5. He, not his wife, is the leader in his home. He is to be in control. After all, if he cannot rule his own house, how shall he take care of the house of God?

(3) CHURCH QUALIFICATIONS, verses 6-7. He cannot be a novice. Leadership demands experience and wisdom; serious decisions must be made. A novice could be in danger of the sin of pride. Finally, he must have a "good report" of those outside the church. The bottom line: the men who serve as pastors must be of unquestioned character.

Church leaders should take care that they measure up to their Biblical qualifications. Let us pray for them as they lead [add your pastor to your Quiet Time prayer list too], lest they fall into "the condemnation" (v. 6) and "snare" (v. 7) of the devil.

1 Timothy 3:8-16

What is the writer saying?

How can I apply this to my life?

pray *For fellow church members working in the secular world to exhibit humble, holy living that creates a thirst in others to know Christ.*

Here we have the qualifications of a deacon; many are similar to those of a pastor. Transliterated from the Greek word, *diakonos,* and often translated elsewhere as "minister" or "servant," it finds its best definition in the latter translation: servant. Collectively the term "deacons" is a reference to a class of helpers chosen to serve the church under leadership. The first deacons (Acts 6) were selected to meet the needs of church members (there had been a dispute over two groups of widows). This responsibility continues today.

As with the pastor, the emphasis of his qualifications is on character (vv. 8-10, 12). Again, there is a need for provenness (v. 10), marital fidelity and parental control (v. 12). The pastor's requirement, "apt to teach," is not repeated. The deacon who serves "well" gains the esteem of those served, allowing him to function with "great boldness" (v. 13).

In the middle of Paul's list of qualifications are four concerning the deacon's wife (v. 11). Hers are similar to his. There must be a spiritual maturity on the part of ministry wives.

Paul goes on to describe the church and its ministry. It is the household of God and "the pillar and ground of the truth" (v. 15); this is architectural language that stresses the church's responsibility of faithfully preserving, preaching and practicing the "truth" (the Word of God). Verse 15 summarizes the purpose behind Paul's writing: to give to Timothy instructions as to how to act in church.

Verse 16 is likely an early Christian hymn, beginning with "the mystery of godliness," God's hidden program to bring about godliness through Jesus Christ who has come into the world.

Do you desire to be involved in the ministry of the church? Then, what is the quality of your personal conduct?

6 Saturday

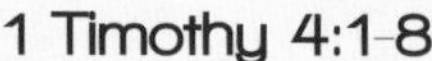

1 Timothy 4:1-8

What is the writer saying?

How can I apply this to my life?

pray *Taiwan – For godly national Bible teachers and evangelists who understand this people's unique mindset.*

Paul has previously warned the Ephesians (Acts 20:29-30) about the coming of false doctrine. Here he predicts that a falling away from the truth is imminent, in fact, already present (see 2 Thessalonians 2). Its cause: the satanic influence of demons (v.1). The marks of these teachers of false doctrines are: *first,* they are hypocritical liars, with "seared" (*without feeling*) consciences; *second,* they teach a false piety/asceticism, forbidding marriage and certain foods. This asceticism reflects pagan gnostic teaching that all matter [or *flesh*] is evil and only what is *spirit* is good. Abstinence is seen as denying the *flesh* and thus increasing one's *spirit* or holiness.

Paul's answer to the danger of verses 1-3 is found in verses 4-6, "the word of God and prayer" (v. 5). God has declared all foods clean (Genesis 1:29-31; Mark 7:14-23; 1 Corinthians 10:23-26; Acts 10). Genesis 9:3 points out that God has provided man with meat and plant life for nourishment. Through prayer, the believer thanks God and dedicates the food to His glory (1 Corinthians 10:31). The pastor who is "nourished up in the words of faith and of good doctrine," and points out these truths to his people, is judged to be "a good minister" (v. 6).

In verses 7-8 Paul instructs Timothy to "refuse profane and old wives' fables," since these always prove detrimental (a contrast with "sound doctrine," 1:10). Paul exhorts Timothy to emphasize spiritual discipline over physical discipline. This is not to ignore genuine healthy habits, but *exercising godliness is profitable eternally* (paraphrase of v. 8).

Do you have a pastor who fits the "good minister" definition of verse 6 and the "exercise" in godliness appeal of verse 7? Then would you take a minute and write him a note, telling him that you have noticed his good service and will be praying for him to continue on his path of godliness?

QT

Sunday 7

1 Timothy 4:9-16

What is the writer saying?

How can I apply this to my life?

pray *Nicaragua – Praise the Lord that the church has doubled in the last 10 years!*

Paul once again uses a "faithful saying" (v. 9, see 1:15) to drive home the truth of verse 10, the saying: "we trust in the living God, who is the Saviour of all men, specially of those that believe." The bottom line: Jesus Christ is the only Savior of people lost in sin, and His work on the cross provided an offer of salvation for all (1 John 2:2).

This prompts Paul to state that he is giving his ministry his best efforts, "we both labour and suffer reproach," and provides a backdrop for his instructions concerning Timothy's ministry. He begins: "Let no man despise thy youth" (v. 12). Likely, some older believers (Timothy is thirty to thirty five years old) are disregarding Timothy since he is not yet forty (it was believed that only someone forty or older is mature enough to be listened to). The best way to deal with fears that follow such accusations is to demonstrate such a maturity in godly living that his life would be a pattern for all others.

In verse 13 Paul emphasizes the public reading of the Word of God. It is to be read, then explained – "doctrine," a ministry of teaching; and applied – "exhortation," a ministry of encouraging. Timothy's gifting has been recognized by the church (v. 14 with 2 Timothy 1:6) and would stand him in good stead as he carries out his role – "neglect not."

Paul then challenges Timothy to "meditate" on these truths. Putting Paul's instructions into action wholeheartedly removes any opportunity for others to look down on Timothy (v. 15). Paul closes with a reminder: "Take heed unto thyself, and unto the doctrine" (v. 16). Be sure to care for your own spiritual welfare while carrying out ministry responsibilities. Proper care will result in the salvation, or *protecting*, of one's ministry.

Check through the list of qualities that Timothy needs in his life and then evaluate your own character against them. What item in particular do you need God's help to bring into your life?

7 Monday

1 Timothy 5:1-8

What is the writer saying?

How can I apply this to my life?

pray *Pray for the missionaries overseas to be encouraged in their work for the Lord.*

In chapters 5 and 6, Paul details various categories of people to whom the church must minister. Age relationships are dealt with first, and instruction given to encourage the establishment of a family mentality within the church. Older men and women are to be treated like parents; younger men and women like brothers and sisters. Added caution is to be exercised in relationships with young women: treat them "with purity" (v. 2). Impropriety in ministering to young women is never to come into question.

Verse 3 begins an extended treatment of ministry to widows. The early church cared for widows (Acts 6:1-6; James 1:27), giving them "honour" (v. 3) that would include financial assistance. To guard fund distribution, some guidelines are put in place. Four classes are mentioned: (a) Real widows, vv. 3, 5, 9-10; (b) Widows with relatives, vv. 4, 8, 16; (c) Widows living in pleasure, vv. 6-7; (d) Young widows, vv. 11-15.

A *real widow* (a "widow indeed") is truly destitute, without family, and having no means of support. These widows (vv. 5-10) are to be church supported, with the church becoming her family. For *widows with family,* the "first" responsibility for her care belongs to her family (v. 4). *Widows living in pleasure* (v. 6), having chosen a decidedly unchristian path, have placed themselves outside the church's responsibility. For *young widows* (v. 11) Paul instructs that they are to remarry. Paul instructs Timothy to pass this "charge" to the church (v. 7). When they carried out their responsibilities they would be "blameless."

Are there "real widows" in your church? How can you be that Christian son or daughter or cousin in the *church-family* who assists these widows who have God's eye of concern upon them?

1 Timothy 5:9-16

What is the writer saying?

How can I apply this to my life?

pray *Ecuador – Praise-For effective Christian radio ministry that encourages believers and spreads the Gospel.*

Paul continues detailing the qualifications necessary for a widow's inclusion on the *widow's support list.* Being without family-support is not reason enough. One's lifestyle and age (v. 9; minimum sixty years) must be considered. Paul lists ten qualifications in verses 5-10. Included would be that of an unblemished married life (v. 10) and a good testimony earned by: (a) raising of children, if so blessed; (b) hospitality, "lodged strangers"; and (c) humility, having "washed the saints' feet," a demonstration of her willingness to accept even menial tasks.

Younger widows (v. 9) are not to be included (vv. 11-16). Reason: they might pledge faithfulness to serve Christ and the church early in their widowhood, but in time turn away and be consumed by a desire to be remarried. Result: they grow "wanton" (*to feel the impulses of sexual desire*) and grow cold spiritually. They stop serving others ("they learn to be idle," v. 13) and become "tattlers also and busy-bodies" (v. 13), bringing reproach upon the name of Christ. Since they lacked the wisdom of age and experience, they tend to fall prey to their own sexual desires (v. 11).

Paul then gives instructions: Young widows should (a) remarry, (b) bear children, and (c) guide the household. In carrying out these duties she will "give none occasion [*no base of operations*] to the adversary to speak reproachfully (v. 14)," as some have already done (v. 15).

Paul then summarizes his instructions. Responsibility for the care of widows falls first as an obligation on her family. This allows the church to be free to care for the genuinely destitute (v. 16).

Widows who sow a godly lifestyle reap positive consequences. Observing their godly lifestyle, let us give them proper "honour"! How can you, like those in the early church, be actively involved in relieving the needs (v.16) of others who are genuinely in need of help?

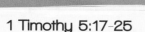

1 Timothy 5:17-25

What is the writer saying?

How can I apply this to my life?

pray *Finland – For creative, committed believers willing to invest their lives in this country's youth.*

Paul now deals with two issues relative to church leaders: (1) How they are to be paid, and (2) How to treat them when they sin. Elders who "rule well" [literally, *having taken the lead well*] are "worthy of double honour" ("honour" is also used in the matter of financial care for widows, 5:3). The qualifying word is "well," and, if that is the case, he is to receive "double pay," or at the very least, *ample* or *generous pay* would be proper. "The ox that treadeth out the corn" is not muzzled, nor should the one be who labors in the Word and doctrine (v. 18, quoting Deuteronomy 25:4; Luke 10:7). As Jesus Christ has already said, he is worthy of his reward.

When a church leader sins, how is the church to respond?:

(a) Get the facts. Accusations supported by two or three witnesses (v. 19)!

(b) Give the matter honest, non-partial appraisal (v. 21).

(c) Rebuke him publicly if proven guilty (v. 20).

Such a procedure would deter others from falling into sin (v. 20).

Verses 22, 24-25 address the issue of prematurely laying on of hands. In time, an individual's true colors emerge. Hasty actions lead to the placing of unworthy men in leadership, whether in the first or twenty first century!

In verse 23 Paul inserts a personal bit of medical advice to Timothy. Timothy has stomach problems probably from drinking polluted and unsafe water. His advice: "Drink no longer water [only], but use a little wine." Paul is offering Timothy a water purification method – the placing of a little wine in a much larger portion of water, a common procedure in that day.

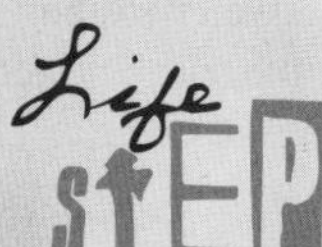

Leaders must understand that sin in a *public* leader's life merits *public* rebuke. Church members must remember that hasty action in selecting their leaders can cause great damage. Pray now for your church leaders.

1 Timothy 6:1-8

What is the writer saying?

How can I apply this to my life?

pray *Bahamas – Nearly a third of the population are bible-believing Christians. Pray that they would grow in their love for each other and the lost.*

In the Roman Empire, slaves make up about fifty percent of the population. Slaves are valued with cattle (both being agricultural commodities). Many slaves believe in Christ. Christian slaves are prone to take on a false superiority because of their new spiritual freedom in Christ, tempting them not to give their best service. Paul cautions against this, for such an attitude would cause others to blaspheme God (v. 1). Paul's desire is that a slave's actions would cause his master to see the true character and teachings of God.

Slaves with "believing masters" are tempted to take advantage of their spiritual oneness. They are to understand that such behavior would be unacceptable. They are to serve them well ("do them service") because of their faith in Christ (v. 2; See also Ephesians 6:5; Colossians 3:22).

Verses 3-5 warn about false teachers who "consent not to wholesome words," especially on matters concerning the doctrines of Christ and "godliness" (v. 3). These teachers are "proud," ignorant, have an abnormal interest in disputes (KJV, "doting"), and are argumentative (v. 4). Their behavior is disruptive and their "disputings" are "destitute of the truth" (v. 5). They are "supposing" that they gain "godliness" by their disputings about religion. The believer is not to keep their company (v. 5).

Conversely, "godliness, with contentment, is great gain" (v. 6). The point: physical possessions are temporary. Contentment and godliness are eternal possessions that go with us when we depart. All else will be left behind (vv. 6-7). Thus, having food and raiment, let us be content (v. 8).

Your boss is the "master" of your work day. God says you owe him your best service. Do your actions cause him to praise the true God of heaven or does he "blaspheme" (*speak against*) the things of God?

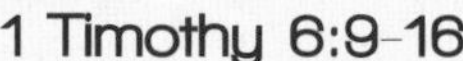

7 Friday

1 Timothy 6:9-16

What is the writer saying?

How can I apply this to my life?

pray *France – For missionaries to integrate well into French culture and to persevere amidst slow results.*

Paul moves from the positive ("godliness with contentment") to the negative (greed). In verse 9, his warning is to those whose goal in life is to become rich. Focused on gaining wealth, they are "foolish," they "fall," and then "drown" (v. 9). Paul warns them (v. 10), "The love of money is the root of all evil." Those "that will be rich" are likened to a bowman who *shoots himself* through with many arrows of sorrow!

Verses 11-16 are parenthetic. In this parenthesis, he repeats to Timothy, by way of summary, much of what he has already written. He calls him a "man of God," a mature Christian – surely a great encouragement to Timothy. Paul's "charge" to Timothy is four-fold.

(a) FLEE: pride, covetousness, false teaching (v. 10 and 11a). Sometimes the wisest thing a believer can do is run (see also 2 Timothy 2:22)!

(b) FOLLOW: righteousness, godliness, faith, love, patience, meekness. Six virtues to be evidenced in the life of a man of God (v. 11b).

(c) FIGHT "the good fight of faith," (a picture taken from the Olympics, where the contestant keeps on until attaining the prize or goal). "Fight" is a word meaning *to contend for a prize.*

(d) FOCUS on eternal life as found in Jesus Christ (1 John 5:11-13). Eternal life is both a *present possession* and *future expectation.*

Verses 15-16 are a doxology to the "King of kings and Lord of lords," a title Paul uses nowhere else. He focuses on the Lord's sovereignty and His immortality.

Paul's four-fold "charge" to Timothy is one that we can apply personally. Take a look at the little list and ask yourself, How am I doing? There are things for you to *flee* and things to *follow*. There is a *good fight* that is a part of your life of faith, and there is an *eternal focus* to maintain. What areas of your life need to change so you can stop *shooting yourself*?

1 Timothy 6:17-21

What is the writer saying?

How can I apply this to my life?

pray *Pray for those in your church who are facing health problems.*

In verses 17-19 Paul returns to the subject of *riches*. This time he addresses not those who wish to be rich (vv. 9-10), but those who are rich. He instructs them as to how to use wealth for the glory of God.

(a) BE HUMBLE ("not highminded") – recognizing that all the wealth a person has is a gift from God. Focus on the *Giver*, not the *gift*!

(b) BE TRUSTING– riches present a danger of trusting in one's own money, which can only bring uncertainty, rather than trusting in God!

(c) BE APPRECIATIVE – it has been given to be enjoyed. The danger is that money can also buy much evil. Use the money for good things.

(c) BE USEFUL – it has been given not just for enjoyment. Be sure that riches are employed to "do good." Be generous and willing to share.

(d) BE VISIONARY – or forward-looking. Invest the earthly riches in eternal treasures, "laying…a good foundation against the time to come." This is what Christ calls "treasures in heaven" (Matthew 6:20).

Paul closes the letter by challenging Timothy to remember his calling and to avoid the "profane and vain babblings" of false teachers. He is to "keep" (*to place a guard around,* see also v. 14) that which has been committed (*entrusted to his care*) to his trust (*deposited into his bank account*). Paul is using a banking term, referring to that which has been placed on deposit and which, when demanded, is to be returned in its entirety. What has been deposited with Timothy is the Gospel message, which has earlier been committed to Paul (1:11), and which Timothy would later commit in trust to others (2 Timothy 2:2).

The Gospel message came from God to Paul, and then from Paul to Timothy. He is to pass it on to others. Those others are to pass the trust on to other faithful men also (2 Timothy 2:2). And so it has continued. Now it is your turn. How are you *keeping* the Gospel message that has been *trusted* to your *account*?

In Exodus 24, the Lord called Moses to the top of Mt. Sinai to give precise details for the building of the tabernacle, a portable shrine, which permitted a holy God to dwell among a sinful people (Exodus 25:8, 22). Upon completing the construction of the tabernacle, the Lord manifested His presence in His earthly habitation (Exodus 40:34) and then spoke the words recorded by Moses in Leviticus from the tabernacle while it was still located the foot of Mt. Sinai. By comparing Exodus 40:17 with Numbers 1:1, we conclude that the entire book was given to Moses within a thirty-day period.

The phrase, "and the Lord spake unto Moses, saying," appears thirty-four times in Leviticus, including the twenty times that it begins a chapter. The phrase points out that everything contained in Leviticus was established by God's own directive. Thus, (a) all aspects of sacrifice, (b) all aspects of the work of the priests, and (c) all aspects of the service of the tabernacle are intended by God Himself to present a means of approaching God. Nothing is left to the creative imagination of Aaron and his sons. Rather, they are able to deal with the sins of the people of God because they followed God's instructions; "So Aaron and his sons did all things which the Lord commanded by the hand of Moses," Leviticus 8:36 (see also 9:6-7).

The purpose of Leviticus is to give instructions concerning how a sinful people could approach a holy God. The instructions include the procedures for presenting sacrificial offerings in order to handle the sin question until the perfect offering of the sinless Jesus Christ. Moses is also given instructions on how to live among one's neighbors and in the presence of a holy God. These instructions are necessary for the tabernacle to be used for its intended purpose. God has chosen one of the twelve Hebrew tribes to be specifically set aside for the special work of conducting the procedures pertaining to worship at the tabernacle. Thus the book is named, Leviticus, referring to the instructions *"pertaining to Levi."*

The theme of the book, "...ye shall be holy; for I am holy...," is stated first in 11:44 and repeated five more times in the book. Jesus incorporated this theme in the Sermon on the Mount (Matthew 5:48), and Peter applies it to us (1 Peter 1:15-16). There are more than forty references from Leviticus in the New Testament. While Leviticus places much stress upon ceremonial holiness, which allows common persons, animals, and objects to be used in the worship of an *uncommon* and holy God, the ceremonial practices are also intended to be the foundation for a holy life lived before God. "Speak unto the children of Israel saying..." "...ye shall therefore be holy: for I am holy" (11:2a, 45b).

Leviticus 1:1-9

What is the writer saying?

How can I apply this to my life?

pray *Pray that God will bless the ministry and outreach of your local Christian radio station.*

The first division of Leviticus is like a *Handbook of Sacrifice.* Each of the five offerings described in these first seven chapters of Leviticus points to a different aspect of the sacrificial offering of Christ; "For had ye believed Moses, ye would have believed me: for he wrote of me" (John 5:46). Chapter 1 presents the *burnt offering,* which could be a bullock (v. 5), a male sheep (v. 10), or a goat (v. 10). The bullock denotes Jesus the *obedient servant.* The sheep is the *submissive innocent one* dying for the guilty, and the goat is Christ the *sin-bearer.* The poorest people could substitute doves or pigeons (v. 14, also Luke 2:24) that represented "...he became poor, that ye through his poverty might be rich" (2 Corinthians 8:9). The point is clear; God intended that anyone could come to Him through His prescribed sacrifices.

The "male without blemish" (v. 3) depicts the sinlessness of Christ who is *the door* by which one approaches a holy God. Placing the hand of the offerer upon the head of the animal (v. 4) signifies the transfer of the sin of the guilty to the innocent one. The blood is applied to the altar (v. 5) to represent the blood of Christ shed on Calvary (Hebrews 9:22). The entire carcass is cut into pieces and consumed with fire on the altar, showing that Christ yielded up all to the Father.

The inside parts and the legs are washed before the offering is acceptable (v. 9), picturing that Jesus was completely righteous within and His walk was righteous.

The burnt offering is a "sweet savor" (*pleasing aroma,* v. 9) since the sacrifice of Christ fully satisfies the righteous demands of a holy God.

The key to enjoying the study of the Levitical sacrifices is to look for pictures of the later sacrifice of Jesus in every procedure. You may experience the same burning heart that excited the Emmaus disciples as "...he opened to us the scriptures" (Luke 24:32).

8 Monday

Leviticus 5:1-13

What is the writer saying?

How can I apply this to my life?

pray *Indonesia – For the unity and continued growth of churches in the midst of intense persecution.*

Several times in the text, the *burnt offering* (Leviticus 1), the *grain offering* (Leviticus 2), and the *peace offering* (Leviticus 3), are called "sweet savor" offerings. The three together depict Jesus Christ as the Beloved Son who, in His earthly sojourn, fulfilled all the desires of the Father "...in bringing many sons unto glory..." (Hebrews 2:10). The offerer came to the door of the tabernacle voluntarily to worship and give thanks.

Today's passage is a part of a longer section, Leviticus 4:1-6:7, that gives the details of the sin offering and the trespass offering which are designated *non-sweet savor* offerings because they present the suffering servant laden with the sins of mankind. They emphasize the demerits of the offerer (one who has "sinned" and "trespassed") rather than the merits of Christ, and they were obligatory.

A sinner is one who *misses the mark* in failure to keep God's righteous laws. A trespasser is one who *oversteps the boundaries* of established rules of conduct. The two offerings are closely related, concerning both the act and the procedures for restoration.

In 5:1-5 we see the state of the wayward one before his God: guilty. The *sin offering's* distinctive purpose is to *provide forgiveness* for unintentional (or non-defiant) sins. In verses 6-9 we see God's merciful provision for bringing him to full forgiveness. The process of restoration begins with the sinning one's own confession of guilt (v. 5).

Since Jesus became our *perfect sacrifice,* we no longer need to bring animal sacrifices when we seek God's forgiveness. Yet the process of restoration still requires confession of guilt (v. 5). "If we confess our sins, he is faithful and just to forgive us our sins, and to cleanse us from all unrighteousness" (1 John 1:9). Does your relationship with God need to be *restored* through your own *repentance* and *confession* to God?

Leviticus 17:1-14

What is the writer saying?

How can I apply this to my life?

pray *Korea – For seminary graduates to humbly commit themselves to less prominent, rural pastorates.*

The two important themes of chapter 17 are: The One Acceptable Place of Sacrifice and The Value of the Blood.

The One Acceptable Place of Sacrifice: heretofore, spiritual leaders like Noah, Job, and Abraham, selected a place, usually on an open hilltop, built an altar, and sacrificed animals to the Lord. The Lord has now manifested His presence on earth at a particular place, wherever the tabernacle is set up (Exodus 25:22; 40:34). Henceforth, only blood sacrifices offered at "the door of the tabernacle of the congregation" (vv. 3-4) would avail. Generations later, the Ark of the Covenant is placed in the temple, and the Lord manifests His presence at a permanent geographical spot (1 Kings 8:10-13). To be impressed by the imperativeness of that one place, listen in while Moses, thirty-eight years later, addresses the next generation. You may do this by reading Deuteronomy 12. Six times in that chapter (twenty times in the book), he stresses this point. All of the blood shed at that place points to the one sufficient sacrifice of Jesus Christ at that geographical location.

The Value of the Blood of the Sacrifice: Hebrews 9:22 tells us that "...without shedding of blood is no remission"; "for the life of the flesh is in the blood..." (Leviticus 17:11). There is no spiritual value in the blood of the sacrificial animal except "upon the altar" (v. 11). The value of the blood is determined by the value of the life it represents. This gives the blood of Christ its inconceivable worth. More than a century ago, Bible expositor C. H. Mackintosh observed, "The loftiest estimate which the human mind can form of the blood must fall infinitely short of its divine preciousness."

Today, places are still important to our Lord. The Lord has a place in mind, at a church, where He would have us join with other saints on the Lord's Day (Hebrews 10:25). He also has a place of service (Hebrews 10:24). What is your *place of worship* and what is your *place of service*?

8 Wednesday

Leviticus 19:9-18

What is the writer saying?

How can I apply this to my life?

pray *Australia – For young people and children to have a desire to attend Sunday school and share the Gospel.*

A major theme throughout the Bible concerns our daily conduct among those around us. This is especially true regarding our relationship with others in God's household (Galatians 6:10). We should be ever mindful of those in need (Hebrews 13:1, 16). In considering verses 11-13, here are some questions:

- Is the taking of another's possessions the only form of stealing?
- Does lying include only blatant falsehoods?
- Are the use of substitutes for divine names profaning God's name?
- How can one "defraud" (*cheat, take advantage of*) a neighbor?

And why should we obey all these things? Well, fifteen times in the chapter God gives us the *why*: "I am the Lord your God"! Obviously, the point here is that God is holy and loving and He expects all those who claim that He is their Lord will work at living out the holy life!

Jesus quotes this admonition, "Thou shalt love thy neighbor as thyself" (v. 18), on at least two occasions (Matthew 19:19; 22:39). It is also quoted and expounded upon in Galatians 5:14 and James 2:8. Further, it forms the basis for that which is called *The Golden Rule.* Jesus incorporates that rule into His *Sermon on the Mount* (Matthew 5:43). He calls this statement the second great commandment. Jesus said the first and greatest commandment is, "Thou shalt love the Lord thy God with all thy heart, and with all thy soul, and with all thy mind" (Matthew 22:37-39). It is not possible to obey these commandments from God's standard "except a man be born again" (John 3:3). Therefore, all of us must personally act upon: "Ye must be born again" (John 3:7).

To remember the point of Leviticus 19, take a *purple* color pencil [the *royal* color] and highlight all of the "I am the Lord" statements. Now consider these two questions: Which of these commandments of the Lord do you need to work on applying to your life? How can God help you?

Leviticus 20:6-10, 22-27

What is the writer saying?

How can I apply this to my life?

pray *Venezuela – Praise – for the missionary vision of this country that has sent many to the 10/40 window.*

"...Cut him off from among his people" (vv. 3, 6), "...put to death..." (vv. 2, 9, 10, 27), "...stone him with stones" (vv. 2, 27). Living in the day of God's grace, we tend to view these judgments for sin as overly harsh. However, the point for us to see is that God looks upon any involvement with the occult (such as sorcery, wizardry, necromancy, etc.) as wicked deeds being equally as sinful as sacrificing children (v. 2), cursing parents (v. 9) and committing adultery (v. 10).

Both the first and last verses of our Scripture portion deal with that matter.(see also 19:31). Notice that the one who participates in the occult suffers the same penalty as the one who practices it. That is a Bible principle (Ezekiel 14:10). See Deuteronomy 18:10-12 for a list of forbidden occult practices. To see how the New Testament classifies witchcraft and sorcery, read Galatians 5:20 and Revelation 21:8; 22:15.

Leviticus 18 and 20:10-21 recount the ways in which man is prone to pervert God's holy institution of marriage (Hebrews 13:4). A principle reason why God abhors sexual perversion is because it destroys His purposes for the family. Wrong use of sex also destroys the beautiful way in which a scriptural marriage portrays the relationship between Christ and His church (2 Corinthians 11:2; Ephesians 5:31-32). Sexual gratification is to be confined to one man joined with one woman in the bond of holy matrimony [God says, no exceptions allowed!]. Other uses of sex will surely subject the participants to God's judgment!

Yes, some stern principles in today's passage, but notice again God's foundational reason, "for I am the Lord your God" (v. 7)!

One may reason, *Since God gave me a sexual appetite, He also gives me the right to satisfy it.* That's like saying, *Since God gave me an explosive temper, I may explode whenever I please.* If you struggle with your passions, ask for God's grace to control your passions.

8 Friday

Leviticus 22:17-25

What is the writer saying?

How can I apply this to my life?

pray *For lives to be transformed as the Word of God is proclaimed around the world.*

We are looking further into two of the "sweet savor" offerings presented in the first seven chapters of Leviticus. The offerer brings these sacrifices "unto the Lord" because he wants to worship (v. 19, notice "own will"; v. 21, notice "freewill"), not because he has sinned.

The burnt offering (vv. 18-20) is consumed totally by fire on the altar of sacrifice (a large fire box placed in front of the tabernacle). Necessarily, it is "a male without blemish," because it depicts Christ giving Himself totally unto the will of the Father. The "beeves" species (v. 19, KJV uses this Old English term for *ox* or *male cow*; it is the basis for our word beef) is an example of the perfect servant. Cows give man milk, meat, clothing and shelter. Oxen, due to their great strength, bear man's burdens. The sheep portrays Christ as the innocent one, quietly submitting its life for man's needs. The goat is Christ, laden with our sins and taking them far away (Leviticus 16:21, 22).

The peace offering (vv. 21-25) looks to that work of Christ on the cross which *brought peace with God* by meeting all of His just requirements for the penalty of sin. God was propitiated (*God's righteous holiness was satisfied by Jesus as our substitute!*), and we were reconciled (*our relationship to God was restored*) that we might have fellowship with Him (1 John 1:3, 7).

After the blood of the sacrifice is applied to the altar, the fat and non-edible parts are consumed by fire, and the priest is given portions of the meat for his own food. Then the offerer is to eat the remainder with family or friends as though they were having a delightful meal with God!

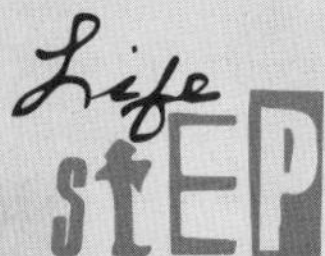

Since we no longer offer peace offerings as a part of our fellowship with God, how can we enjoy a figurative *delightful meal with God*? How about taking a minute and figuratively *lean back in your chair* and just enjoy talking to God!

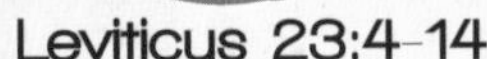

Leviticus 23:4-14

What is the writer saying?

How can I apply this to my life?

pray *Peru – Funding for more scholarships that will make Bible training accessible to the poor.*

When Moses was being instructed on Mt. Sinai, the Lord informed him of the annual feasts to be observed by Israel (Exodus 23:14-17). Thirty-eight years later, after the *first generation* died in the wilderness, he gave these instruction again to the *second generation,* telling them that the observances would be fully implemented when the Lord chose a specific place for sacrifice and worship (Deuteronomy 16:1-17)

Beginning with verse 4, Leviticus 23 sets forth the "seasons" (*appointed times*) for observing seven special Sabbaths or religious holidays, here called "holy convocations" (vv. 2, 4, 7, 8, 21), meaning *a calling of an assembly,* connected with the annual feasts. Their year begins with the new moon that follows the spring equinox (Exodus 12:2).

The set time for the killing of the Passover lamb is the fourteenth day of the first month (their religious new year begins in the Spring). The Feast of Unleavened Bread begins and ends with a special Sabbath, lasting seven days, and immediately follows the Passover meals. During the seven days, a sheaf of the new crop is waved before the Lord in thanksgiving and before any of that harvest could be eaten.

The Passover, fully explained in Exodus 12, commemorates the deliverance of Israel from Egyptian bondage for those who, by faith, applied the blood of a sacrificed lamb to the doorposts of their homes. The Feast of Unleavened Bread speaks of the holy lives God's people are to live before the Lord. The presentation of the First Fruits recognizes that all of the bounty of harvest is from the Lord.

Two lessons: (1) God wants His people to offer thanksgiving to God; (2) The multiple feasts here remind us that we are forgetful. We forget *what God has done* and *who God is*! Like a farmer who remembers to thank God for a bountiful harvest of grain, how can you praise God for the bountiful harvest of His blessings in your life?

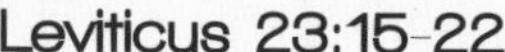

9 Sunday

Leviticus 23:15-22

What is the writer saying?

How can I apply this to my life?

pray *Venezuela – Boldness for Bible school students getting hands-on experience ministering to the lost.*

Today's passage deals with the second of the three feasts. It is called, *The Feast of the First Fruits of the Harvest* in Exodus 23 and 34. It is also called, *The Feast of Weeks* in Exodus and Deuteronomy. It is more commonly known to us as the Day of Pentecost (Greek for fifty, thus the *Feast of the Fiftieth Day*) in Acts 2:1 when the early believers are filled with the Holy Spirit as the Spirit empowers the church.

Verse 15 connects the second annual feast to the first. The second feast is to be fifty days after the first. The *Wave-Sheaf Feast* is the celebration of the first *sheaves* of grain coming from the grain fields. These are brought to the tabernacle where the priests make of them a flower which is *waved* to God as a tribute for His care that brings the new harvest. The second annual feast, the *Wave-Loaves Feast,* is similarly a tribute to God, but it comes at the end of harvest. Two *loaves of bread* are prepared and *waved* before God. These represent Israel's daily bread for the next year (normally with leaven).

The Wave Sheaf Feast is also intended by God to be a picture of *Christ in resurrection* (1 Corinthians 15:20). He is the grain of wheat that died in order to bring forth much fruit (John 12:24). The Wave Loaves Feast pictures the future *formation of the church,* when two peoples, the Jews and the Gentiles, are to be the two loaves presented as one sacrifice, a sweet savor unto the Lord. God's purpose is to break "down the middle wall of partition" between Jew and Gentile "that he might reconcile both … by the cross" (Ephesians 2:14-16).

These farmers worked hard to bring in a bountiful harvest and yet they thanked God for the harvest. They were recognizing that God did His part by providing providential care (*quiet and timely care*) of their fields. For what do you need to thank God? Yes, He has been *quietly and aptly caring* for your life too!

Leviticus 23:23-32

What is the writer saying?

How can I apply this to my life?

pray *Uruguay – Bookmobile ministry that makes Christian books accessible to believers around the country.*

While there are no feasts during the summer months, there are three special feast days in the seventh month (called Tishri, it overlaps our October/ November). On the first day of the seventh month, the trumpets sound, announcing an extra "Sabbath" at the start of this month.

The purpose of this Feast of Trumpets is for *spiritual preparation* of the approaching Feast of Atonement (notice the word, "also" at verse 27 that connects the two special days). No "servile work" (v. 25) is to be done, and special offerings are made at the tabernacle (Numbers 29:1-6). Importantly, the day is to be a "memorial" and "holy convocation." Thus there is a *calling of the assembly* so that all Israel would gather for the purpose of (1) together *remembering* what the Lord had done for them; and (2) together they might *consider their holy walk* (moral, ethical, and spiritual conduct) before God.

On the tenth day of this month there is to be the most important event in Israel's annual calendar, the Day of Atonement. Today's passage gives details on how the ordinary Hebrew is to conduct himself on this day. The details of how the priests and Levites are to conduct themselves are written elsewhere (Leviticus 16:1-28; Numbers 29:7-11). The purpose of the day is summarized here (vv. 26-28): to make *atonement* for sin (from a Hebrew root, "to cover"). The Day of Atonement pictures the concealing of sin so that a sinful person (and nation) could approach his Holy God!

Jesus Christ made atonement for our sins *once*, when He died upon the Cross. Thus, there is no annual repeating of Christ's Day of Atonement! Yet the emphasis of these two feast days still brings application to us: there should be time set aside from normal work to meditate on Christ's perfect sacrifice. Take some time and (1) remember what God did to save you, and then (2) consider your own holy walk before God.

Leviticus 25:1-17

What is the writer saying?

How can I apply this to my life?

pray *Slovakia – For the church planting to be successful in bringing the Good News to many unbelievers.*

Beginning on the fifteenth day of the seventh month, the children of Israel are to observe the Feast of Tabernacles (called the Feast of Ingathering in Exodus 23:16 and 34:22). The Feast of Tabernacles is an eight-day memorial to God's work of redeeming Israel from slavery in Egypt (v. 43). When the new nation of Israel left their bondage, the Lord led them through the desert, from oasis to oasis, by a pillar of cloud or fire (Exodus 13:21). For temporary dwellings, they made *shelters* or *booths* of tree branches. The word "tabernacles" (v. 34) and the word "booths" (v 42) are the same in the Hebrew text. Note that this Hebrew word is different from the word used to describe the "tabernacle" (*a portable shrine*) which Moses was instructed to build in Exodus 25-40.

The details of the work of the priests during these three feasts of the seventh month are given in Numbers 29:12-38. The response of the people to the priestly ministry of those three observances is seen in Nehemiah 8. There we have the *gathering* (Nehemiah 8:1) and the *mourning for sin* (Nehemiah 8:9), followed by rejoicing over *sins covered* (Nehemiah 8:10-12).

Rejoicing is a characteristic of the Feast of Tabernacles: while families are camping out in their temporary stick-booths, there is much singing and rejoicing. Men, while bringing their branches to build their "booths," would be singing psalms such as Psalm 118:15, 25, 26, "the right hand of the Lord doeth valiantly," "Save now, I beseech thee, O Lord," and "blessed be he that cometh in the name of the Lord."

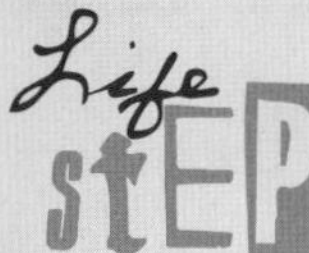

Since the Feast of the Tabernacles follows the Day of Atonement, it is proper for the Feast to be a day of *rejoicing*. Israel has been both saved from *slavery in Egypt* and from *slavery to sin*! Perhaps you could *camp out* for a couple of minutes and sing your own songs of rejoicing to the Lord! How can you rejoice in your Lord?

Leviticus 25:1-17

What is the writer saying?

How can I apply this to my life?

pray *Netherlands Antilles – For a well-staffed body of believers on each of the five islands.*

The subject of Leviticus 25 is "the land which I give you." We call it The Promised Land because God promised it to the descendants of Abraham (Genesis 15:18), Isaac (Genesis 26:3) and Jacob (Genesis 35:12). It is called "the glorious land" (Daniel 11:41), "the holy land" (Zechariah 2:12) and "the pleasant land" (Zechariah. 7:14). However, throughout Scriptures, God declares, "the land is mine" (v. 23). God's complaint with the nations of the world is that they have "parted my land" (Joel 3:2).

Every seven years the land is to have a Sabbath Year of Rest. In verse 21, God promises to miraculously make the sixth year so fruitful that the supply would last until the harvest of the eighth year. In Deuteronomy 15:1-18, Moses explains the reasons and procedures concerning the seventh year to the second generation, just before their entry into the land. The observance is to begin when God chooses the place in the land where Israel is to worship (Deuteronomy 31:10-13).

Years later, when God removes Israel from His land because of Israel's blatant idolatry (2 Chronicles 36:14-16), Jeremiah prophesies that their captivity would last seventy years (Jeremiah 25:11). That is the number of years of rest they owe the land because they have failed to observe the land's Sabbath Year of Rest.

In order to preserve the integrity of the land and the dignity of the poor, there is to be a Year of Jubilee every fifty years (vv. 9-11). All land that has been sold or in any way lost by it original owners during the fifty years, is to be returned to its original family. All debts are canceled and all bondsmen are released.

Two principles: (1) All land is God's land and (2) All people have rights as people created in God's image. How can you honor God's creation and not "oppress" (v. 17) God's creatures?

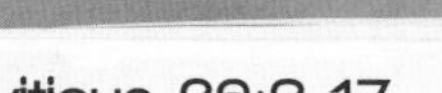

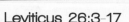

9 Thursday

Leviticus 26:3-17

What is the writer saying?

How can I apply this to my life?

pray *Joe Jordan, Executive Director of Word of Life, for a consistent pursuit of holiness and God's direction for the ministry.*

The "statues" and "commandments" referred to in (v. 3) are an outgrowth of the "covenant" (v. 42) that God made with Abraham, Isaac, and Jacob. This "covenant" concerns their descendants and the land (vv. 4, 5, 6) God unconditionally promised to give to them. However, the possession and enjoyment of *the land* by each generation is dependent upon each generation's conduct in *the land*.

It was a matter of "if ye ... do" (v. 3) then "I will give" (v. 4), and "if ye will not" (v. 14) then "I will set my face against you" (v. 17). The result of performing God's commandments (v. 3) would result in plentitude from God (vv. 4-5), peace from God (v. 6), power from God (vv.7-8),progenyfromGod(v.9),provision from God (v. 10), the presence of God (v. 11), and possession by God (v. 12)!

Verse 14 begins a warning that there will be consequences for failure to hear and heed God's commandments. If there is rebellion (vv. 14-15), there will be retribution (vv. 16-39) until there is repentance (vv. 40, 41) which brings restoration (vv. 42-45).

The three-part theme in verse 12 runs through the entire Bible. It begins in Genesis 17:8 – "I will be their God." The second element is added in Exodus 6:7 – "I will take you to me for a people." The third part is in Exodus 25:8 – "...I may dwell among them." The theme is applied to Israel as part of the promised new covenant (Jeremiah 31:33; Ezekiel 37:27). The theme is applied to Christians in 2 Corinthians 6:16. The theme reaches eternal completion in Revelation 21:3.

As the New Testament *people of God*, we Christians in the church do not have a promise of a land, rather we have a promise of eternal life. Our conduct as Christians determines the abundance of that life in Christ (see 2 Peter 1:11). God wants to bless His people as they choose to live for Him. So then, are you *walking with God* or *walking against God*?

Leviticus 26:18-31

What is the writer saying?

How can I apply this to my life?

pray *Uruguay – For God to reveal truth in a land where spiritists and cultists outnumber true believers.*

In today's passage Moses is continuing his warning to Israel. Moses uses the unusual phrase, "walk contrary," five times. It simply means, *to walk in the opposite direction.* While Israel has been promised great privileges from God (vv. 4-6), if Israel chooses to "walk contrary" (vv. 21, 23, 27) to His righteous laws, then He would "walk contrary" to them (vv. 24, 28). Israel must choose to live so that their walk (conduct) is such that God would be pleased to *dwell* (v. 11) and *walk* among them (v. 12).

The warning, "I will punish you seven times..." (v.18) is a picture of the continuous chastening that will come until their *pride is broken* (v. 19). If *distress of heart* (vv. 16-17) is not sufficient, the Lord God will bring chastisement by *drought* (vv. 18-20). If that doesn't break their rebellion, He will bring *destruction* and *desolation* (vv. 21-22). Then He will bring *death, disease* and *dearth* (vv. 25-26). Finally, He will bring (vv. 29-31) an intensifying of the dearth until people will actually eat their own children (2 Kings 6:25-29). Their seven-fold judgment will become complete.

Moses is telling the people they have a choice. They may have the three-fold blessing of plenty, peace and the presence of God; or they can suffer the seven-fold chastisement of distress, drought, destruction, desolation, death, disease and dearth. Bible history records that Israel chooses to disregard the righteousness of God and walk a "contrary" path of pride and unrighteousness. They will experience all of the calamities about which they were warned.

Since our holy God, who desires to bring us blessings, has not changed, the warning of Moses still applies to Christians today! We must consider if our conduct can be pictured as a *walk in the same direction as God's walk* or a *walk in the opposite direction of God's walk.* Ask God help you walk compatible with His walk!

Leviticus 26:32-46

What is the writer saying?

How can I apply this to my life?

pray *Honduras – For a compassionate outreach by churches to the more than 8,000 exploited street children.*

If God's people will not respond to the chastisements He brings upon them in the land (vv. 16-31), dispossession (their possession of the land will be forfeited), dispersion (scattered amongst the nations) and despair (vv. 32-39) will follow. The reasons for the dispossession are summarized in 2 Chronicles 36:14-21. Psalm 137:1-4, along with several other psalms, poetically describe the despair of the people while they are dispossessed of the land.

Old Testament history tells us that after Israel is dispossessed from their land for seventy years (they were in exile in Babylon), there is *repentance* expressed by *confession* which brought *restoration*. See Daniel chapter 9 for the prayer of confession. We could outline Leviticus 26 as follows: Reverence (vv. 1-13), Rebellion (vv. 14-15), Retribution (vv. 16-39), Repentance (vv. 40-41), and then Restoration (vv. 42-46).

At the end of seventy years, the nation is given the opportunity to return to the land. However, only a remnant of less than fifty thousand respond. The majority remains in dispersion. Almost six hundred years later at Pentecost, Israelites are scattered all over the civilized world (Acts 2:5-11). When the leaders of the nation reject Jesus as their Messiah, God does something new. He calls out the believers from the nation of Israel to lay the foundation for the building of an earthly habitation for Himself from among both Jews and Gentiles (Ephesians 2:19-21).

Although the majority of Israelites are still in dispersion, in recent years there has been a growing regathering to their Promised Land. God will remember His covenant with Abraham (26:42-45).

In God's mysterious ways (Ephesians 3:3-6), Christians are now privileged to be a part of His holy habitation on earth (1 Corinthians 3:9-11). You are thus privileged to have a great spiritual *possession*! Be sure to stay away from a walk that is "contrary" (vv. 40-41)! Perhaps you also have a need for *repentance* by *confession* which brings *restoration*.

When you read the Gospels, you must understand that there are four different views of the Lord Jesus Christ – like four different kinds of photographs presented in one portrait. While each Gospel presents Christ accurately, the emphasis of each is different.

For example, Matthew presents Christ as King. It is written primarily for the benefit of Jews as they consider the claim of Jesus to be their Messiah. Luke, writing to educated Greeks, carefully presents Jesus for people who would want to *measure* this Man's life and character carefully as they consider whether they would become disciples of Jesus. John presents Christ as the Son of God, emphasizing His deity and eternality. The Gospel we are now considering, Mark, emphasizes the Lord as a servant, since Mark is writing primarily to the common Roman citizen or slave. While the shortest Gospel, stories in this book are given with much vivid detail. Rather than emphasizing the sermons and discourses of Jesus as does Matthew and Luke, the Book of Mark focuses in on events that display the actions of Jesus. Mark wants his readers to be convinced of the identity of Jesus as they consider His deeds.

With this in mind, it is easy to understand why Matthew and Luke would include His genealogy. A careful genealogy would be important to Matthew and Luke as they are either introducing a King to be *received*, or a man to be *measured*. John begins with an unusual genealogy involving just Jesus and his heavenly Father, "In the beginning was the Word, and the Word was with God, and the Word was God" (John 1:1). Obviously, John is presenting Jesus as the *eternal Son of God*. On the other hand, since Mark is writing to common Romans citizens and Roman slaves who themselves, would not have known their ancestry, Mark skips the genealogy of Jesus and His childhood and begins with Jesus as an adult, who is beginning his service to mankind. Thus, Mark, knowing his readers, is more interested in presenting what Jesus *does* rather than presenting the *heritage* of Jesus or what Jesus *says*. Hence, the Gospel of Mark is the Gospel of *Action*.

Repeatedly, we read words like, "straightway" and "forthwith" and "immediately." Such English words are the translation of a Greek word found over forty times in Mark, about the same as in all the rest of the New Testament. It has been pointed out that the Romans, to whom the book is primarily written, are impressed by men of action and power. And so, Mark uses words like "straightway" to present a series of events in the life of Jesus that display His power, actions and character. The purpose of the Gospel of Mark is to show the Roman world the active love of God as displayed in the life of the Lord Jesus Christ.

The human writer of this book is Mark, who is also the John Mark that journeys with Paul and Barnabas. Mark is the son of Mary, a wealthy widow, who knew and loved the Lord. It is in her house that the disciples meet after Pentecost (Acts 12:12). So, Mark is familiar with many important Christians of the first century.

We are first introduced to Mark himself in the book of Acts, after he has been included on the missionary team of Paul and Barnabas. Sadly, Mark leaves the *team* in the middle of their ministry and goes home to Jerusalem. Apparently, Mark has become discouraged or even afraid. Paul is disappointed with this, and when Paul and Barnabas start planning for their next ministry, they have a disagreement. Barnabas wants to give Mark another chance, but Paul refuses. The division is so great over Mark that they split up. Barnabas, Mark's uncle, takes Mark with him and Paul links up with Silas. However, Mark continues to grow in his walk with the Lord, and in the end, Paul acknowledges the value of Mark to Paul's ministry. Mark proves to be a great servant of the Lord (see Acts 12:25; 13:13; 15:37-39; 2 Timothy 4:11; 1 Peter 5:13).

The lesson from Mark's life is clear to us today. Sometimes we too get a poor start, but God desires to give us a second chance to be strengthened and grow in our Christian walks, so that we might serve Him. Often, learning by our mistakes, we prove to be of real worth to the Lord. Yes, for the believer, He is the God of the second chance.

While the Holy Spirit leads Mark in the selection of the very words used in Mark's Gospel (we call it *verbal inspiration*), it is true that in this leading and direction, Mark could draw from several reliable sources. The major source of information used in Mark's Gospel apparently comes from Mark's close relationship with Peter. Peter calls Mark his son. It is interesting that Peter is mentioned by name in several connections in this Gospel, while omitted by the other Gospels (vv. 1:36; 11:21; 13:3). We will see that, while Mark is the shortest Gospel, some incidents are conveyed to us with greater fullness and detail.

The Gospel of Mark is a series of little stories connected together. This makes it interesting to read. Be sure to notice the tender touches also presented in the stories. For instance, only Mark, when speaking of Christ blessing the children, tells us that Christ took them in his arms (vv.10:13-16).

You will enjoy reading this book, called by one scholar, *the most important book in the world.* Try and remember as you read it, that it was written between A.D. 60 and 70, when many Christians were being persecuted.

An outline (taken from Gaebelein) of Mark can be summed up like this:

1. The Servant; who He is and how He came. vv. 1:1-13.

2. The Servant's work; not to be ministered unto, but to minister.
vv. 1:14-10:52.

3. The Servant in Jerusalem. Presented as King and rejected. Chapters 11-13.

4. The Servant gives His life a ransom for many. vv. 14:1-15:47.

5. The Servant highly exalted, raised and ascended; His commission to His servants and working with them. vv. 16:1-20.

Mark 1:1-13

What is the writer saying?

How can I apply this to my life?

pray *Pray that the married couples of your church will nurture and protect their relationships by a dependence upon God's Word.*

Please keep in mind that Mark, from the very start of his Gospel, emphasizes Jesus Christ in His work as a servant. This explains why Mark omits details found in the other Gospels; Mark gives nothing concerning the genealogy of Christ, the parents of Christ, the birth of Christ, nor the early years of Christ. This would be in keeping with a servant (or slave) in New Testament times. A wealthy Roman, perhaps an owner of a large farm, would buy a slave because the slave could *immediately* begin to serve in the fields of the farmer. The concern is *how will this slave be able to serve me now*?

The Gospel of Mark begins by quoting two Old Testament passages. In verse 1:2, Mark quotes from Malachi 3:1. Mark declares that John the Baptizer is the promised "messenger" who would prepare the way for the coming of the Lord. Then Mark 1:3 quotes from Isaiah 40:3. Here, John is identified as the "voice" who would announce the coming of the Lord. So we are left with a question of what message is John to deliver? And similarly, what is the "voice" proclaiming about the Lord?

The answer is provided in the next verse when we hear that John is preaching about the "remission of sins" (v. 4). The Greek word for "remission" literally means *to cause one to stand away from something*. Mark understands that the most important thing that Jesus would do is to serve us by providing a way for us to *stand away* from our sins! The preaching of John the Baptizer is to this end – announcing Christ's coming to serve the world as the Servant-Savior, who's greatest deed is to save people from the sin to which they were bound!

Have you ever asked Jesus to give you this free gift of "remission of sins" that will cause you to *stand away* from your sin? If you have, take a few moments to consider the great privilege you have to *stand apart* from your old life of sin and *stand near* to God.

Mark 1:14-28

What is the writer saying?

How can I apply this to my life?

pray *Germany – For godly public officials who will use their influence for the furtherance of the Gospel.*

Note the call of the Lord's first disciples. The call is simple: "Come ye after me, and I will make you to become fishers of men." The response is immediate (v. 18). First, there are Simon and Andrew, then James and John, sons of Zebedee. The sons of Zebedee are in business with their father (we would say, *Zebedee and Sons*). Apparently, it is a thriving business, as there are hired servants present. But, they "straightway" forsook all to follow Jesus!

This is indeed the Gospel of *actions*, especially *actions of the Servant, Jesus Christ*. Note the word "straightway" found three times in these verses (vv. 1:18, 20, 21) and forty-two times throughout Mark's Gospel (the word is translated as "anon," "by and by," "shortly," "as soon as," "straightway," "immediately," or "forthwith"). "Straightway" originally meant *straight down the road* and came to mean *next along the path of time* and thus *immediately afterwards* is intended. Scofield calls this a "servant's word" in that servants are to immediately respond to commands from their masters. Delay is not tolerated; as soon as a task is assigned, the obedient servant is expected to straightway attend to the task. So then, we see throughout Mark's Gospel that Jesus is the obedient Servant of God the Father, who straightway carries out His task of serving mankind.

Obviously, Mark would have also wanted us to notice and mimic this attitude of straightway service of others as a part of our task in our new life as obedient servants of Jesus Christ, our Master.

"Straightway" service adds an insight to Paul's urging us, in Philippians 2:4-8, to have "this mind" of Christ as we look "on the things of others." Just as Christ took on the manner of a servant in His service, so Paul says we are called to be straightway servants to others. Is yours a life of straightway service or an *I'll-get-to-it-maybe-tomorrow* service? What is the character of your life of service?

Mark 1:29-35

What is the writer saying?

How can I apply this to my life?

pray *Finland – For immigrants to encounter Jesus in a real and attractive way.*

In today's passage, we are again directed to see the work of the Lord as a servant. Here, He heals Simon's (later called Peter) wife's mother. Only Mark tells us "he took her by the hand." Tenderly, compassionately, he heals her. The healing is immediate and complete. Afterward, she ministers unto Christ. Imagine the surprise to see this woman, so afflicted, busy again as though she had never been sick.

Of course, Mark would want us to see this pattern given to us by Peter's mother-in-law. Once His hand (in salvation) has touched us, we need to respond with service of gratitude!

In verses 32 and 33 we read that by evening, "all the city" was gathered at Peter's door and "they brought unto him [Jesus] all that were diseased." Isn't this our responsibility – to live a life so that *all around us* see that Jesus has healed us from the *disease of sin* that used to cripple us. What an example! It is so simple, but so important.

Remember that Mark, in his Gospel, only gives his readers a few incidents of the healings done by Jesus. Be sure to notice Mark here describes one healing during a day when Jesus healed dozens and probably hundreds of others in need of His healing touch (see v. 34).

Obviously, the day has been long and constantly busy. Yet Christ, the next morning, arises early and departs into a solitary place to pray (v. 35). Jesus doesn't neglect His personal time alone in prayer with His Father. We are not to forget how important it is to have our own daily *quiet time* with God. Notice also the Lord's choosing a quiet time in the first moments of the day. Jesus understands that power in service is the result of time in prayer. Yes, He is a man of action; His days are full, but He is never too busy to be in communion with His Father!

Two spiritual life principles: (1) Service as the result of gratitude to the Lord and (2) Quiet Time with the Lord resulting in power to serve.

QT Wednesday 10

Mark 1:36-45

What is the writer saying?

How can I apply this to my life?

pray *Italy – Pray for godly officials in a government believed to receive 23 billion annually from extortion.*

Note in our passage how the Lord, in His busy work, handles interruptions. His disciples said, "All men seek for thee" (v. 37). Notice that the Lord takes time for these interruptions. Interruptions are often opportunities to minister to others. Lepers are ostracized in Bible times. No one dares touch them. One such leper approaches the Lord and asks for help. The Lord's first response is to be "moved with compassion" (v. 41). How this should speak to us in our dealing with *the banished, the outcast, or the excluded,* who come into our world. Then, Jesus does the *unimagined thing,* He touches the man! And then He heals the man of the dreaded disease of leprosy. Ah, the touch of the Master's hand that makes the difference! That's the way it needs to be in our service as well! How can we touch another's life by our compassionate service to them?

It is interesting to look at the words "next towns" in verse 38, found only here in the Bible. It is the Greek word *komopoleis,* which is the combination of two common words: *Komo,* used twenty-eight times in the Bible, meaning "a country village" and *polis,* used 164 times, often referring to major population centers, meaning "cities with walls." Thus, *komopoleis* would refer to something bigger than a village but smaller than a city. Jesus is not just concerned with the big cities, but the little out-of-the-way, insignificant places as well. Perhaps God has placed you in a little place to serve Him. Be assured that Jesus is pleased with your faithful service to your small country town! Also, be assured that Jesus sees your faithful, compassionate service in your little place.

Has the Lord Jesus Christ "touched" your life? Has He healed you from the crippling effects of your sin? Take a few minutes to review the amazing story of His "compassion" for you. Then would you take another couple minutes and write a little thank-you note to Him?

10 Thursday

Mark 2:1-12

What is the writer saying?

How can I apply this to my life?

pray *Czech Republic – For continued and increased growth and depth within Bible-believing churches.*

This is the second visit of the Lord to Capernaum. Note how the crowds come to hear him. We read that He first preaches to them before He performs a miracle. This order points out the true purpose of the miracles. The miracles are intended to confirm the message. Keep this in mind as you see the miracles of action in Mark. Certainly, there is compassion on the part of the Lord for the man with palsy, but the purpose of the miracle is not simply the alleviation of pain. The miracle has a greater purpose: the attestation and confirmation of his message about His person.

The picture given is a vivid one: four people bring one sick of the palsy (a paralysis in some part of the body – here, likely rendering the man unable to walk). Surely, these four men believe that if they only could get their friend to Jesus, He would heal their friend! When they find the way to Jesus blocked, they make a new and unexpected way to Him. Note that Christ's first response is that "Jesus saw their faith." Don't miss the point here! Yes, Jesus is going to heal the physical malady of the palsied man, but Jesus is also healing the spiritual lives of these five men of faith; the one on the bed and the four carrying him!

Naturally, the scribes criticized. Actually, their problem is that they see the Lord acting like God, since only God can forgive sins. They are right, but they miss the point; he is acting like God because He is God! Their problem is that they would not concede the point of the miracle of the man's healing, which is: since Jesus is the "Son of man," He can both heal the physical needs of people and He can also heal the spiritual needs caused by sin.

Be confident that Christ's power and His love are frequently connected in the Lord's quiet workings in your life. Ask Him to apply His power to that *crippling* personal need in your life.

Mark 2:13-28

What is the writer saying?

How can I apply this to my life?

pray *Bulgaria – Pray for reconciliation among believers concerning past conflicts and compromises.*

This is the fifth time (1:14-15; 1:22; 1:38-39; 2:2, 10; 2:13) Mark says Jesus is preaching or teaching. Yet Mark has not given us the content of even one the Lord's sermons! Instead, Mark has given us an insight into the intent of the messages given by Jesus. Notice:

- 1:14-15, The Gospel of the Kingdom of God, which is "at hand" and which is summarized by "repent ye, and believe the gospel."
- 1:22, Jesus "taught them as one that had authority"; they were "astonished."
- 1:38-39, Jesus "came…forth" to preach in many places, thus a foundation for a coming Gospel Message to the entire world.
- 2:2 with 2:10, Jesus preached the "word" that the Son of Man has power on earth to forgive sin.
- 2:13 with 2:17, Jesus came to call "sinners to repentance."

Obviously, as Mark tells his Gospel Story, we are to see that each event is an illustration of the Lord's teaching. This would account for the story of Jesus coming to Levi (Matthew), who is "sitting at the receipt of custom" (v. 14). Since Matthew is collecting tolls at Capernaum's harbor at the Sea of Galilee, he is likely taxing the fishermen as they bring their fish to Capernaum's market. Tax collectors, like Matthew, are considered traitors (in service to the Gentile government) and thieves (since they over-charged people and then kept the extra!).

Mark notes the intent of the messages being brought. Even the lowest can be forgiven of sin as Jesus, the *spiritual physician* (v. 17), heals him of his *disease of sin.*

The application is clear, Jesus wants us, who have been cured of our *disease of sin*, to be the *stretcher bearers*, who bring other "sick … sinners" (v. 17) to Jesus, so that He might make them "whole" too.

Mark 3:1-12

What is the writer saying?

How can I apply this to my life?

pray *Pray for those in your church who are seeking employment.*

Again, in today's passage we see the issue of Jesus doing "good" on the Sabbath (v. 4). In this case, the Lord enters a synagogue where there is a man with a paralyzed hand. Jesus sees that there are people who are hostile toward Him in the synagogue's audience. It is apparent that these men desire evidence that could be used to "accuse" Jesus (v. 2) of violating their law of not working on the Sabbath. They miss completely the point that Jesus is demonstrating that He is the true Messiah who possesses the power to heal!

Jesus is filled with anger mixed with grief due to "hardness of their hearts" (v. 5); not having any interest in the man's need and being more interested in preserving their rules. Rather than praising God for the man's healing (v. 5), they want to use the man's plight to trap Jesus!

Apparently, the Pharisees see that they are aligned against a powerful foe for, after the man's healing, they go to their normal rivals, the "Herodians"! This is the first mention of the Herodians (v. 6). The Herodians of our passage are a sort of political and economic party, being Jewish supporters of the ruling family of the Herods. This means that they are in favor of Roman control in Judea and Jerusalem, since the Romans brought with them trade, roads, and markets [and money!].

The surprising thing here is that the Pharisees, who think of themselves as the *Separated Ones* who live apart from contact with worldly people, are joining with the worldly Herodians! Since the Pharisees have become a religious-political party who are threatened by Jesus, it is not surprising that they choose to ally with a competing political party so that together they "might destroy Him" (v. 6).

The Lord's purpose and program will be accomplished. When the Lord brings some needy person into your life, will you respond with a Christ-like concern or with the *hard hearted* indifference of the Pharisees?

QT

Sunday 11

Mark 3:13-21

What is the writer saying?

How can I apply this to my life?

pray *France – For American missionaries to overcome stereotypes and prejudices by reflecting Christ's love.*

Today we have the twelve disciples selected by Jesus. This is a rather strange group; two have formerly been followers of John the Baptizer. Two are known as the "sons of thunder." At least four are fishermen. Most seem to have come from working class, literate backgrounds. None are from royal or privileged families. None are presented as men of genius or outstanding talents.

There are several contrasts. For instance, Peter is the impetuous one, while Thomas is the cautious one, who needs verifiable evidence. Matthew, the former tax collector, is an agent of Rome who is likely sympathetic to the position of the Herodians. Opposite of him is Simon the Zealot, who is a part of a political group who desires to overthrow the hated Romans.

But these men do have something in common; they are all "ordained" to a new purpose in life, (1) to be with Jesus; and (2) to be sent forth to preach the Good News about Jesus (v. 14). Over time, Jesus trains them, molds them, and teaches them. Christ takes weakness and developes strength. Christ takes ordinary men and makes them extraordinary. It is not their natural talent, but the infusing of His power that brings transformation to these men.

If we are to be used of the Lord (and He can and will use us regardless of our limitations), we must also (1) spend time with Him; and (2) be the recipient of His divine touch that transforms us into the Christ-like person He desires of us. Then we, too, will become people who are ready to proclaim the Good News about Jesus.

You can anticipate God using the same pattern in your life. As you spend time "with him," in things like daily devotions and attending a Bible-teaching church, then God will be at work molding and developing your spiritual life.

Mark 3:22-35

What is the writer saying?

How can I apply this to my life?

pray *Pray that God will give your church a greater burden to reach the lost in your community.*

Can you imagine that people actually attributed the Lord's power to demon power? In our passage, we read that they claim He has Beelzebub. The Jews use this name as an expression of contempt. It means *dung-god* or *filth-god*. Further, they ascribe his work to Satan.

Christ's answer is clear. Since Jesus has just cast out demons, if Jesus is empowered by Satan's demonic world, then Satan's "house" would be "divided against itself" (v. 25). So, how could Satan cast out Satan? Such a kingdom would not "stand" (v. 24). Jesus is pointing out that their accusations make no sense.

He then mentions a man entering a strong man's house. Binding the strong man refers to the power of Christ over Satan. Satan has been judged at the Cross (Hebrews 2:14), the full execution of that judgment will take place after the millennium (Revelation 20:10).

How important it is for us to recognize the program and power of Satan. It is formidable, but it is defeated and is awaiting final judgment. We, in turn, have been provided the "whole armour of God" (Ephesians 6:11, 16), which enables us to defend ourselves against all his "fiery darts."

The *unpardonable sin* is now referred to (vv. 28-29). The words "eternal damnation" would be better translated *guilty of an eternal sin*. This is a sin that lasts forever. People commit that sin by persisting in their unbelief and dying in that condition. Continual denial, to a person's death, of the truth of the work of the Holy Spirit, in spite of the evidence, is an eternal sin.

Finally, note the new relationship established by Christ (v. 35). When we stop denying the truth about the Lord's work as our Redeemer and by faith accept the redemption from sin He has provided us, we become His "brother, and my sister"!

Mark 4:1-12

What is the writer saying?

How can I apply this to my life?

pray *Brazil – Outreach to youth as over 9,000,0000 children work the streets to earn a living.*

What a beautiful picture is displayed in this chapter. Christ is in a boat on the Sea of Galilee, the people on the land are listening as He teaches them many things. He is teaching in parables. A parable is *a placing of one thing beside another,* thus the idea is an *analogy* or *comparison* or *illustration.*

The reason for Jesus using parables is given in verses 10-13. Those earnest hearers who wanted to "know" (v. 11) could come to understand and remember the vivid illustration. But, those who didn't want to know, being casual and indifferent, would not "understand" (v. 12). Matthew's Gospel adds, "their eyes they have closed" (Matthew 13:15). Notice the progression given here if only they would be willing to "see" and "hear" the meaning of this parable: (1) They would gain understanding which would lead to (2) conversion, *a turning about,* which would result in (3) "their sins" being "forgiven" (v. 12). Jesus tells His disciples that the subject here is "the mystery of the kingdom of God" (v. 11). A "mystery" in the Bible is something that is given to many but understood only by a few. We believe Christ is talking about the character of *true Christianity* which now exists upon the earth while our *King* is gone. He is speaking of present conditions in the world. Remember, in the future, there will also be a millennial kingdom coming into the world which is different, since Jesus will be present on earth to rule as the *King* of the Jews.

This parable speaks of the sower (Christ) who is sowing seed, some of which fell on the "way side" (old English for *a traveled way or road*), some on stony ground, some among thorns, some on good ground with differing results. The explanation of this parable is given later (vv. 13-20).

We understand that we are to be the "sowers" who are sowing the *seed* of the Gospel Message.

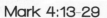

11 Wednesday

Mark 4:13-29

What is the writer saying?

How can I apply this to my life?

pray *For others as they go on short term mission trips to share the gospel.*

The explanation of the *Parable of the Sower* is in our present passage. It speaks of the sower (Christ) who is sowing seeds. As the seeds fall to the ground four kinds of results are obtained. The first seeds are sown by the way side (v. 4). This describes one who hears the Gospel, but the truth of the Gospel never even begins to grow in his life before it is taken away.

Next, the seeds which fall on stony ground (v. 5), speaks of one who hears the Gospel, but it is simply intellectual and surface. There is no root – no genuine conversion.

Then some seeds fall among thorns (v. 7), which are the cares of life and the deceitfulness of riches. The word is choked after initial interest, but true faith does not become rooted in the person's life. Again, there is not a genuine *conversion* which leads to the *forgiveness of sins.*

Only the last seeds mentioned are successful in growing to mature plants that yield fruit. The reason for the growth of these seeds is the "good ground" (v. 8) of a person's faith when he: (1) first understands the truth of the gospel; (2) then allows the truth to become rooted in his life; and (3) after that, allows the *seed of faith* to transform his life so that spiritual fruit is produced!

Have you observed this as the Word has gone forth? The ratio here is one out of four. This suggests that most who hear will not allow the true faith of *conversion* to grow in their lives. Yet we are also assured that there will be some true believers, who are the "good ground" upon which the seed falls and grows. These hear the Word, receive it, and show the reality of their conversion by bearing fruit. While they do not all bear fruit equally, there will be *fruit* and a *multiplying* of the seed.

As you consistently live for the Lord, you will see the seed of His new life growing in you. Over time, there will be marvelous results as He transforms your daily life as a Christian.

Mark 4:30-41

What is the writer saying?

How can I apply this to my life?

pray *Fiji – For ministries to the University of the Pacific in Fiji, which impacts students from each island.*

Jesus begins this next parable with an oratorical question to focus the attention of His audience on His new illustration. He compares the Kingdom of God to a mustard seed, which is generally the smallest seed that would be planted in a garden (see Luke 13:19). Thus, also is the Kingdom of God, very small in its beginnings – a small band of true believers compared to the *garden* of the Roman Empire. Yet the mustard seed sprouts and grows to become, at first, a shrub (similar in appearance to a tomato plant). Yet it continues to grow until it is taller than all the other "herbs" (v. 32, garden plants) that are grown in a gardener's plot. The plant sends out branches and commonly reaches a height of ten feet and perhaps twelve feet. When the plant has grown, the stalks of the plant become rigid so that the plant looks like a small tree. Its branches are strong enough for birds to land upon and rest. Here the birds find safety and shade from the sun. Similarly, the Kingdom of God, from its small beginnings, would expand with new branches going out until it had *shaded* all the Roman Empire by the end of the first century! People from many races and professions are attracted to the *shade* of the expanding church.

Jesus is telling his audience that they are to be patient, trusting in God, as He, like a gardener, tends the *plant* of His church, which would become a great and prominent *tree* in the *garden* of His world!

The next paragraph is refreshing. Christ's humanity is clearly seen in that He falls asleep. The Servant is tired in serving. When the storm comes, the disciples waken Christ. He sleepily arises and as God, rebukes the wind. So, in one little paragraph, we see both the humanity and deity of Christ. The Lord then rebukes them for their lack of faith.

We also have storms in life. How wonderful that our Savior calms the storms. He is in full control. How can Jesus care for you in your storms?

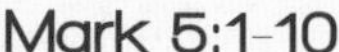

Mark 5:1-10

What is the writer saying?

How can I apply this to my life?

pray *Cuba – Protection for those making undeclared mission trips into this country.*

We begin today with Jesus and His disciples coming by boat to the eastern shore of the Sea of Galilee, a Gentile territory called Decapolis, after the *ten cities* in it. They are met by a man who comes "out of the tombs" (burial caves cut into hillsides). The history of the man (vv. 3-5) is supplied later by the local people who tell of their long experience with him. They know him as a man that no one could "tame" (used of taming wild animals). Men have repeatedly tried to bind his feet with "fetters" and his hands with "chains," but he broke all restraints with demonic strength (v. 4). The man is heard shrieking wildly and seen cutting himself (v. 5). Everyone knows that he is *beyond the help of men*, and only able to be helped by the Lord Jesus!

As the man runs to Jesus, we see three things happen that show that the demons in the man know Jesus is divine and superior in power (v. 6):

(1) First, when he comes to Jesus, he "worshipped" Jesus, which means the man has to *bow down* as the demons pay homage to the One who will be their Judge. They are terrified of His judgment!

(2) Then they speak to Jesus through this man to plead for mercy from the "Son of the most high God." The name "most high God" is used in the Old Testament, often by Gentiles, to refer to the superiority of the true God of Israel, (see also: Genesis 14:18-24; Numbers 24:16; Isaiah 14:14; Daniel 3:26, 4:17).

(3) Thirdly, the demons beg Jesus not to "torment" the man by sending him (and the demons that possess him) to his final judgment (Matthew 8:29; Luke 8:31; see similar response from demons in Mark 1:24).

Sin grips and controls; Satan binds and destroys. But the Lord is the great emancipator; He and He alone can free the sinner. Spend some time praising the Lord today for what He has done for you.

Mark 5:11-20

What is the writer saying?

How can I apply this to my life?

pray *Costa Rica – Pray for the Holy Spirit to break the bonds of materialism, apathy, and ritualism.*

Christ, always in control, commands the demons to come out of the man. When asked, the man says, "My name is Legion: for we are many" (v. 9). Jesus allows this powerful band of demons to enter into a herd of some two thousand (v. 13) pigs, which in turn run wildly down into the Sea of Galilee and are drowned.

Then the herdsmen "fled" into town (probably the town of v. 1) to tell what has happened (v. 14). Many come to see for themselves. The transformation of the man is so complete (he is sitting, clothed and in his right mind; see Luke 8:35), that they become afraid of Jesus. Surprisingly, the people, who have for so long been terrorized by the man, are not pleased to hear he has been freed of his tormentors. They also saw that the herd of pigs (likely intended for the Gentile markets of Decapolis) has been destroyed by the demons. And they are more interested in their business than they are the man who is now liberated. Unhappy about their great economic loss, they *urge* Jesus to leave their territory. No thanks is ever given for removing the terror from their midst! They have witnessed a miracle and have seen the full display of the power of God, but they show no interest in Him.

On the other hand, as Jesus enters the ship to leave, the man begins to *beg* Jesus to allow him to continue with Him as one of His disciples. What a contrast between this man and the townspeople! He uses the same Greek word ("prayed" – *a strong request*) (v. 18) as had been used by the demons (v. 7), and then by the townspeople (v. 17).

The Lord instructs the man, "Go home to thy friends, and tell them how great things the Lord hath done for thee" (v. 19).

Some respond with a fear of Jesus Christ. Some want to distance themselves from Jesus for His presence will cost them. Some desire to be with Jesus, since He alone is their source of freedom.

Mark 5:21-34

What is the writer saying?

How can I apply this to my life?

pray *Pray that the President of the United States would be sensitive and obedient to the leading of the Holy Spirit.*

Today Mark gives us the stories of two people, at the two extremes of status in their society, who approach the Lord for help and healing.

First, Mark presents "one of the rulers of the synagogue, Jairus" (v. 22). He is like a *president of the board of elders.* In New Testament times, men in such powerful positions often became proud, haughty, and pompous in their dealings with others. Jairus has to condescend to the level of common men by coming to Jesus to ask for help. This would have been a surprise to everyone, thus the story begins with the word, "behold" (v. 22). Jairus sets aside his arrogance, when his own daughter is in danger. In his desperation, he approaches the Lord. God is interested in people even though they are filled with self-importance.

On His way to the girl, Jesus is interrupted! This is not new; Christ had often allowed interruptions. The irony is that the interruption of a lowly woman delays His attending to the proud civic leader!! The woman is disheartened after years of *trying everything* only to see the problems grow worse (v. 26). Her condition is one of which she is ashamed. According to the Law of Moses, she is declared unclean and shut off from the public. (Leviticus 15:25-27). The woman desires only to touch the hem of Jesus' garment so that she might be healed (v. 28). The Lord honors her faith and heals her.

There is a contrast here for us to see. We see the proud ruler, and the humble woman. The ruler highly esteemed, the woman looked upon with shame. Both are needy, yet both are loved. Both find healing, yet the proud one waits as Jesus first ministers to the humble one!

Did you notice that the Lord loves both people from the two extremes of society? Ask the Lord to allow some needy person to interrupt your day so that you might show them the love of Jesus! How can you get ready for your response to a divinely-appointed interruption?

Mark 5:35-43

What is the writer saying?

How can I apply this to my life?

pray *Romania – For building materials and skilled laborers to meet the demand for new church construction.*

Today's passage picks up the story of Jairus after the Lord deals with the interruption of the needy woman. Jairus must have wondered why the Lord doesn't go directly to His daughter, since the poor woman's condition was not crucial. You can see the crushing of hope when he receives word of the death his daughter (v. 35). There is now no possibility of help from Jesus; *she is now dead, not just sick*. There must have been a harsh mixing of sorrow and disappointment. But God specializes in things thought impossible!

When Jesus arrives at the home of Jairus, He declares that the child only sleeps (v. 39). The response of those at the house to Jesus is "they laughed him to scorn" (v. 40). This English phrase translates a compound Greek word that means *an open laughing at with disrespect*. Yes, she is dead, but the Lord is declaring first of all that death is not the end of a person. And secondly, Jesus, as Lord over life and death, is going to awaken her out of her death-sleep. By doing so, He is also declaring His deity, since only God has such power over death.

We, too, must learn the lesson of not questioning the timing of God! Christ's words speak to us in our impossible situations, "Be not afraid, only believe" (v. 36). Two purposes are in view: (1) that we learn that God specializes in things thought impossible; and (2) that God allows difficult things in our lives, so that He might teach us a deeper confidence in Him.

Do you worry about death – either your own death or that of someone you love? Remember, all those who have placed their trust in Jesus to save them from their sins also receive the gift of eternal life. This means death for you is now only a sleep from which you will awaken with Jesus in Heaven! Ask Him to give you peace of mind.

Mark 6:1-13

What is the writer saying?

How can I apply this to my life?

pray *Pray for the salvation and protection of those serving in the United States military around the world.*

Our chapter today records the Lord's second visit to the synagogue at Nazareth. The first visit (Luke 4:1-30) resulted in those at the synagogue seeking to kill Jesus (Luke 4:29-30). How the Lord must have loved these people to go back, even when they had been so hostile. These are people of his home town who had known him all his life. As a boy, Jesus had worked as the apprentice of Joseph, the town's carpenter. He is known as the son of Mary (thus Joseph had died).

They begin to ask themselves two things: (a) How did the town's carpenter's son gain such "wisdom" (v. 2) to teach these things? And (b) Where did He acquire the power to do such "mighty works" (v. 2)? When it says "they were offended at him" (v. 3), Mark is telling us that they disapprove of and are angry about His boldness in coming, seeking to teach them. (The English word, *scandalized*, is derived from the Greek word for "offended"). They are refusing to acknowledge his right to proclaim God's truth. They are saying, *This Jesus, a mere carpenter, is not qualified to say or do anything special to us!* Notice the result; "because of their unbelief," not many miracles are done (vv. 5-6).

Don't miss the point: You have the same kind of tools as Jesus. Thus, you too can have a great impact upon your friends at home:

1. You have the written Word of God, the Bible, which is your source of great "wisdom" about God's truth about life.
2. You have the Holy Spirit with you, and it is He who will use your words to do "mighty works" in the hearts of those to whom you speak! By His power, people will be "astonished" by your words!

Don't be surprised when friends who have known you as that *troublesome child* find it difficult to acknowledge your "wisdom" to declare to them God's truth about life. Follow the example of Christ and make that extra effort to proclaim the Good News to your friends!

Mark 6:14-29

What is the writer saying?

How can I apply this to my life?

pray *Peru – For local Christian television programs, which are able to reach the inaccessible upper classes.*

Today we have a *flashback* in time concerning the death of John the Baptizer (vv. 17-29). The "Herod" here (v. 14) is one of the sons of Herod the Great, who was king when Jesus was born (Matthew 2:1). Herod is married to Herodias (v. 17), who had been the wife of Herod's brother, Philip. The intermarrying in the Herod family is a tangled mess. Herodias is the niece of Herod. So, her former husband, Philip, and her present husband, Herod Antipas, are her uncles. There is, therefore, incest, adultery, and political intrigue involved.

John had rebuked Herod for marrying Herodias. Herod knew his marriage was wrong and as a result, he feared John (He even confuses the later reports about Jesus, worrying that John has "risen from the dead (v. 16)!). While Herod had respect for John and "heard him gladly" (v. 20), Herodias hated him. When her daughter danced before Herod, he impulsively offered her any request. Herodias coached her daughter to ask for John's head. Herod reluctantly agreed and had John beheaded.

Herod is plagued by his own *guilty conscience*. Herod "feared" John because he knew John was a *just* and *holy man* who spoke the truth (v. 20)! It is here that we see the point of the flashback paragraph. Notice, at the end of the previous paragraph, the disciples are to preach the truth so that "men should repent" (v. 12, "repent" means to *turn from* their sin and *turn towards* God!). Notice that Herod knows the truth about his own sin, but he would not "repent" from his life of sin. While he is "exceeding sorry" (v. 26) for his sinful deed, he never repents or turns towards God!

Let us be people of God like John the Baptizer, declaring both a message of hope: "Behold the Lamb of God, which taketh away the sin of the world" (John 1:29), alongside a message of repentance! Likely, you have a friend who knows that he needs to repent, but is refusing to do so.

Mark 6:30-44

What is the writer saying?

How can I apply this to my life?

pray *Nigeria – Pray for salvation among the more than 30 people groups that have no known believers.*

Notice that today's paragraph begins with the disciples *reporting in* (v. 30) after an extended mission of going from town to town teaching and preaching that people need to "repent" (see 6:7-13). Now the disciples, who are weary after doing many wonderful things, need to rest. So the Lord takes His own to "rest a while" in a desert place (v. 31). But, the people "ran afoot ...out of all cities" (v. 33) and came to Christ. Instead of being annoyed, He has compassion on them "as sheep not having a shepherd" (v. 34). So He allows the interruption and He compassionately cares for the people. What a lesson for us!

Now this day is coming to a close and the people haven't eaten. The disciples come and advise Jesus to send the people away. Instead, the Lord tells His disciples to feed the people. Apparently, they do some quick figuring and conclude that even if they spent two hundred denarii to buy bread (perhaps this was the amount they had with them), that even that amount would be of little use. One denarius is equivalent to a day's wages. From their vantage point, this is an impossible assignment.

A key point of the miracle is to reveal to the disciples that they have a narrow vision of what the Lord could do through them! To expand their vision, the Lord takes the limited supplies available, the five loaves and two fish, and He multiplies these in a manner that requires the disciples to handle the miracle of the replenishing food supply as they distribute it to the five thousand. The basket each carries does not empty!

Just as he has his disciples handle the multiplying of the food, so He intends for us to handle the spiritual bread that is given out in our service to people. The common pattern of our Lord is to multiply this *spiritual bread* as we are giving out the Word of God.

Jesus often intends to use our hands to distribute His blessings to others! What has Jesus given to you to distribute to those spiritually hungry people around you? How will He multiply it?

Mark 6:45-56

What is the writer saying?

How can I apply this to my life?

pray *Jamaica – For effective gospel outreach within schools and an increase in children's Bible clubs.*

Today we find the Lord sending His disciples onto the sea toward the other side. He then dismisses the crowd and retires into the hills to pray. Let us consider two reasons for His actions. First, note that prayer is the very foundation of the Lord's walk with the Father. By sending the crowd of thousands away, Jesus has rejected a great temptation of a crowd who wants Him as their king. In part, because Jesus here fails to *seize the moment* to become their earthly king, many of these soon turn away from Him and "walked no more with Him" (John 6:66)! By clearly knowing the Father's will for Him, Jesus refuses the glory of the moment and accepts the path that leads to the Cross.

Secondly, the disciples are being influenced by the multitude that wants to take Jesus "by force, to make him a king" (see John 6:15). Jesus would later teach that He is to be a different kind of king! So then, Jesus also wants time alone to *pray for his disciples*, that they might see the true *way* of the Lord! The contrast of verses 47-48 supports this idea; with the disciples *alone* "toiling" against the head winds of a storm, the Lord, on the hillside, is *alone* "toiling" in prayer for them!

In the midst of their distress, the Lord comes to His disciples. At first, they think it is an apparition. Then He speaks to them; "Be of good cheer: it is I; be not afraid" (v. 50). Just as He had met the needs of the multitude in the "desert place" (v. 35), so now He meets their need.

Isn't this the way of life today? We find ourselves toiling without progress on life's "contrary" seas (v. 48). Yet Jesus knows our need and is praying for us. Also, He intends to help us in our *stormy places.*

The point of the story is that we need to consider the miracle of the loaves (v. 52). Jesus sees and meets the needs of the hungry multitude. Jesus sees and meets the needs of the toiling sailors. How about telling Jesus all about your present toils and trusting Him to meet your needs?

12 Saturday

Mark 7:1-13

What is the writer saying?

How can I apply this to my life?

pray *Dominican Republic – For believers to be godly, impartial witnesses to the oppressed Haitians.*

Today we see the opposition which Jesus faces. It is interesting to note that Mark, who is writing primarily to Gentile Romans, provides an explanation of the Jewish customs (vv. 3-4) that gives rise to the issues of this paragraph. The scribes here have become more than just *copiers of Scriptures*; they saw themselves as the teachers of Jewish tradition. The Pharisees have become proud in their keeping of the Jewish rituals; they are the defenders of the rituals that they believe make them holy.

So we see them offended when they find some of the disciples of Jesus eating bread with "unwashen" hands – not that their hands are dirty. Rather, the scribes and Pharisees are upset that the approved hand washing rituals are not being followed.

Christ rebukes these men, calling them "hypocrites" (v. 6). This word means *an actor on a stage who, from behind a mask, would pretend to be someone he is not.* These men are not genuine; with their "lips" (v. 6) they are saying the correct lines but with their "heart" (v. 6) they are far from God. Thus, these *keepers of tradition* are not real in their devotion to God, but are like actors who deceive people through the mask of their traditions and the words from their "lips."

So it is today. There is much tradition and ritual in religion that is used to mask the truth about the sinful hearts of people who are really far from God. How important it is to be real – genuine – not an actor with costume and lines to repeat. Remember, the Bible also declares that "the Lord looketh on the heart" (1 Samuel 16:7), He is not fooled by actors!

It is a terrible thing to masquerade as a follower of the Lord using your Sunday actions as your costume to hide a heart that is far from Him (v. 6). What aspect of your life is only acting and not a true walk in the Lord?

Mark 7:14-23

What is the writer saying?

How can I apply this to my life?

pray *Australia – Pray for churches to understand the post-modern society in Australia and reach out to others who increasingly see God as irrelevant.*

In this paragraph, the Lord continues to rebuke the Pharisees and Scribes for their emphasis on the traditions of Israel, including abstaining from certain kinds of foods (vv. 18-19). For instance, Jews are allowed to eat meat from animals with cloven hooves – two toes – like a cow or deer, but they are not to eat from animals with paws, like a bear or lion. While Israel gains physical benefits from these Old Testament *dietary laws,* their purpose is to set Israel apart as a special nation that is different from the nations around them. The Pharisees and Scribes have twisted the meaning of Scripture so they could say their hearts are pure, since they work at keeping away from impure things.

In contrast, Jesus here presents God's diagnosis of the human heart. Several words, like "hearken" and "understand" (v. 14), "perceive" (v. 18), and he that has "ears to hear, let him hear" (v. 16), are used to stress what Jesus is saying. His words need to be first heard, then considered, next accepted, and finally applied to one's life. Jesus begins by making it clear that external things, like foods, are not the source of impurity in a person's life. Rather, a person's own heart is the actual source of all the "evil things" (v. 23) that "defile" a person. He then gives a list of the kinds of things that "proceed" from a person's evil heart!

The point Jesus is telling us to thoroughly "hear" is two-fold: (1) First, external things, like *dietary laws,* cannot make hearts pure. These *externals* cannot change the character of one's heart; (2) The real problem is "the heart is deceitful…and desperately wicked" (see Jeremiah 17:9). This is seen by the great number of evil things that begin in a person's heart (v. 21) and come out in his life to "defile" (*corrupt, pollute*) him (v. 23).

Are you at the business of applying His words to your life? Jesus wants to make your evil heart pure, how can you let Him do so?

13 Monday

Mark 7:24-37

What is the writer saying?

How can I apply this to my life?

pray *El Salvador – For more Bible schools and funds to meet the needs of the staff and students.*

Jesus now leaves Jewish lands and begins the first *missionary trip* to Gentile lands. This would become the pattern for the missionary trips of Peter and then Paul. Jesus goes to Tyre and Sidon, which are part of the old nation of the Phoenicians (vv. 24-30), thus establishing that the Good News of His coming is to be declared to the Gentile nations.

Even though Jesus is far away along the Mediterranean coast of Lebanon and Syria, His fame has so spread (see 3:8) that "he could not be hid." This time, a Gentile woman begs the Lord to cast out a demon from her daughter.

At first glance, the response of our Lord seems harsh when He said it isn't right to take children's bread and give to the dogs. Yet, a closer inspection reveals that Jesus is not being derogatory but rather is deliberately leaving ajar the *door of hope* when He compares her situation to that of house dogs (not wild, scavenger dogs). Also, we see her faith when she, being a Gentile who has no right of access to the Jewish Messiah (see Matthew 15:27), claims the right of the house dog to the scraps that fall "under the table"! Matthew also adds that the Lord recognizes and rewards her faith; "O woman, great is thy faith: be it unto thee even as thou wilt" (Matthew 15:28).

Obviously, Mark's Gentile readers would have treasured this story, for it declares, to all people, that Jesus is interested in the needs of even the lowest of people from distant places.

Perhaps you feel like an inferior person who is unworthy of the Lord's attention to your problems. Just remember, the Lord leaves ajar the *door of hope* for you too! If you will put your faith in Jesus, then He is quite willing and able to *cast a few scraps under the table* to meet your needs too! Take a minute and write out a request to Him for help!

Mark 8:1-10

What is the writer saying?

How can I apply this to my life?

pray *Pray that the leadership of your church might be able to take a time of rest with their families.*

It seems that it is almost impossible for people to leave Jesus' presence! Consequently we again see a "multitude" desiring to be with Jesus (Mark 1:33; 2:2-4; 3:7-10; 4:1; 5:21). This results in a second miracle of a feeding of a gathering of hungry people (see 6:34-44).

In the first feeding of multitudes, the people had been with Christ for one day. Here they have been with Him for three days (v. 2). Five loaves and two fish are used in the first; seven loaves and a few fish in the second. There are also different amounts of *leftovers*!

Now notice the comment of our Lord to His disciples, "I have compassion on the multitude" (v. 2). A key purpose of Mark in including this event in his Gospel, is to point out that Jesus desires for His disciples to learn to share in His compassion for people.

The Greek word (*splagchnon*) for "compassion" is the source of our word spleen. It is a small organ that helps the body fight infections. While now an obsolete English definition, this organ was viewed as the seat of emotions and passions, for example, *to vent one's spleen.*

In Bible times, the spleen referred to the inner organs, the gut, or bowels and they thought of these as the seat of both violent passions, such as anger, and tender affections, especially compassion. They had noticed that strong emotions were often accompanied by an agitated spleen! So to be *moved with compassion* was saying something like, *I am so angry, my spleen is moving*! Thus, Jesus is saying, *I have such affection for these people, my spleen is throbbing for them!* Today, we would say something like, *my heart goes out to these people.*

We must recognize that Jesus wants us to have compassion for people around us. Jesus wants us to have an *aching spleen* that causes us to be *moved to compassion* by the needs of others. How can you today meet the need of someone around you?

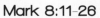

Mark 8:11-26

What is the writer saying?

How can I apply this to my life?

pray *India – For the 800 million who are blinded by Hinduism, to find true spiritual fulfillment in Christ.*

The Lord and the disciples now come to Dalmanutha (likely a village near Capernaum and Tiberias on the west side of the Sea of Galilee). Mark says the Pharisees "came forth" (v. 11) to meet Jesus, which would imply they came from the local capital of Tiberias. Again, the Pharisees seek to test Him. What a surprise that they would ask for a sign when Christ had performed so many miracles; healing lepers, multiplying food, stilling the storm, and raising the dead! Yet, they are full of pride, wanting a special miracle "from heaven" (v. 11) just for them so they could evaluate for themselves these claims about Jesus being their Messiah. It is likely that they have decided that the earlier miracles, like the feeding of the five thousand and the feeding of the four thousand, were just a providing of earthly bread which did not measure up to what Moses had done by providing "bread from Heaven" (Exodus 16:4).

We are told that the disciples have forgotten to bring bread (v. 14). The Lord uses this to give what we might call a *riddle*. The Lord tells them to "beware of the leaven of the Pharisees." Leaven usually speaks of that which is evil (Exodus 34:25; Leviticus 2:11). The leaven of the Pharisees and the leaven of Herod speaks of their conduct and their doctrine. Both groups despise the Lord and are openly opposed to Him.

Jesus then questions His disciples concerning their lack of perception and understanding (v. 17). He asks them about the feeding of the five thousand, and then the four thousand: *How much was left over?* (v. 19). He is asking, *Why do you not see that I am able to meet this need too?* The disciples are acting like the Pharisees!! They too are affected by the "leaven" of lack of faith!

We must (1) remember past blessings from God so that we can (2) trust God to meet our needs during present times of *lacking*.

Mark 8:27-38

What is the writer saying?

How can I apply this to my life?

pray *Romania – For Romanians who will go as missionaries to countries inaccessible to other foreigners.*

There is still speculation as to who Christ is. Christ asks His disciples, "Whom do men say that I am?" The disciples give four answers:

(1) To be like "John the Baptist" (v. 28) would mean that Jesus too is a preacher of repentance from sin.

(2) To be like "Elias" (v. 28, Greek form of Elijah) would mean Jesus is also a fearless wonder-worker and a powerful man of prayer.

(3) To be like "Jeremiah" (included in Matthew's Gospel, 16:14) would mean that Jesus too is a heartbroken prophet of love.

(4) To be like "One of the prophets" (v. 28) means that Jesus is a messenger sent from God who speaks against sin and for holiness.

This discussion is the introduction to the main subject. Now Jesus asks a most important question, "But whom say ye that I am?" Peter answers rightly, "Thou art the Christ" (v. 29, Matthew 16:16; Luke 9:20). Peter's statement divides the two halves of the public ministry of Jesus Christ!! Everything Jesus had done up to this was *to reveal the true Messiah*. Everything after points *to the Messiah completing His work*, that is to "suffer," (v. 31) die, (v. 31) so He might "save" (v. 35) the souls (vv. 36-37) of all who "come" (v. 34) to Jesus.

For the first time, Christ speaks of His death and resurrection. The disciples have difficulty harmonizing this statement with His being their promised King. Clearly, His kingdom would come later.

When Peter protests, he is rebuked. Christ says, "Get thee behind me, Satan" (v. 33). Central to the coming of Christ is His dying for the sins of men. Anything against that purpose is Satanic and not of God.

This most important question remains for each of us to answer today. Do you believe that Jesus suffered for you so that your soul might be saved from the coming judgment of your sin?

13 Friday

Mark 9:1-13

What is the writer saying?

How can I apply this to my life?

pray *Taiwan – For renewed minds, committed discipleship, and humble service to characterize the church.*

Today's account of the transfiguration of Christ is a defining moment in the Gospel story. The story begins with Jesus traveling to a "high mountain" with Peter, James, and John to be "apart" (v. 2), meaning that He is going to spend time in prayer.

Luke tells us that, after they have been on this mountain for some time, the disciples fall asleep (Luke 9:32). Then, as the disciples awaken, they watch His appearance change so that Jesus is enveloped in a heavenly brilliance of exceeding whiteness (v. 3). They also notice two *glorious* companions, Moses and Elijah, talking with Jesus (Luke 9:31). The disciples listen for a time as Moses and Elijah are "talking" (v. 4, *to engage in a conversation with someone*) with Jesus. So exciting is the occasion that Peter gets carried away and interrupts Jesus and His heavenly guests. Peter suggests that they build three tabernacles. Apparently, Peter wants to accommodate these great guests and their conversation with Jesus. But, Peter speaks without thinking (Luke 9:33). These heavenly guests need no earthly comforts! Obviously, this is a time when Peter needs to listen and not interrupt!

At this moment, God's voice is heard from the cloud, "This is my beloved Son: hear him" (v. 7b). While the disciples have for months been listening to Jesus, they still have misunderstandings (5:30-31), incomprehension (8:15-16), and even open rejection (8:32). So we might say that they are not *getting the message* that Jesus is presenting. So, God, Himself, interrupts Peter with the exhortation, "hear him."

What a lesson for us! There are many things about the Christian life that we see as "good for us" (v. 5). Yet, how often do we allow those *good things* to become interruptions of the true message of Jesus; the message of His suffering and death to bring salvation to those that come to Him (8:34-37)?

Mark 9:14-29

What is the writer saying?

How can I apply this to my life?

pray *United Kingdom – For revival in Strathclyde, Scotland's most densely populated, non–Protestant area.*

We begin with Jesus returning with three disciples to the nine disciples. No doubt the scribes and the local people who have gathered are taunting the nine disciples for being unable to cast out a demon from a boy.

As Jesus approaches, a desperate man runs to Him and tells of his son with a demon, which the disciples could not cast out. Certainly, the man has heard of the marvelous powers of this man, Jesus, and has brought his son to the disciples of Jesus hoping to find help.

Notice that Jesus desires not just to help the needy boy but also to assist the father to come to full faith in Jesus. The man says, *If you can do anything* (v. 22). Now Jesus turns the responsibility back upon the man with *If you can believe, all things are possible* (v. 23).

When they first bring the boy to Christ, the evil spirit, being filled with terror that he is being brought before the Divine Judge, who will be his future Tormentor, makes an effort to kill the boy.

Surprisingly the Lord ignores the spirit and talks to the father; "if thou canst believe" (v. 23). The *need* of the boy would wait until the *need* of the father is dealt with! The father "cried out" (v. 24), recognizing this truth; the answer to his request rests not on Jesus but upon his own faith. The man sees his own need (v. 24). He struggles between distrust and true faith when he says, *Strengthen my faith. Distrust still remains. I wrestle with it! Fortify me against my weak faith. Help mine unbelief.*

Only after the Lord heals the man's true but weak faith, does He turn to heal the afflicted boy. The Lord commands the evil spirit to come out of the boy and enter no more (v. 25).

Jesus will often allow your troubling situation to continue as He first heals your struggle with unbelief. Well then, what trouble are you presently dealing with? How is God going to grow your faith through this trouble?

Mark 9:30-41

What is the writer saying?

How can I apply this to my life?

pray *Slovakia – Sensitivity among those ministering to Gypsies, as they are suspicious of outsiders.*

The Lord is now seen traveling and not wanting others to know of his presence as He and the disciples travel through Galilee!

Time is short, coming events demand that Jesus prepare His disciples. He is seeking time to instruct the twelve (v. 31) concerning His coming death and resurrection (in about six months), so that they might be prepared. This is the second of three occasions in which Jesus instructs His disciples on these matters (see also v. 8:31 and vv. 10:33-34). On all three occasions, we see the mental state of the disciples as *confused* over the Lord's statement and *preoccupied* with their own plans and schemes!

We also read that, as close as they are to Him, they are still *afraid* to ask details. Dr. A. T. Robertson suggests that their fear is due to the Lord's stern rebuke of Peter on the first occasion (v, 8:33, "Get thee behind me, Satan!"). Matthew's Gospel adds (17:23) that they are *deeply distressed* and *greatly saddened* by these impenetrable teachings of Jesus.

What is their frame of mind as they argue after each occasion? Implied on the first (v. 8:33) and clearly displayed after both the second (9:33-34) and third occasions (10:35-41), the disciples are concerned about their own ambitions and self-serving desires. They are distracted because they want Jesus to reign as King, not die by a betrayer's actions (v. 31). What a contrast between the self-sacrificing submission of the Master and the self-promoting ambition of His servants!

Sometimes, we find ourselves not hearing the Lord because we too are distracted by personal ambition! In your walk as a Christian, is personal humility your priority or is personal promotion?

QT

Monday 14

Mark 9:42-50

What is the writer saying?

How can I apply this to my life?

pray *Pray that the youth of your church will know the Word, grow in Christ, and live out their faith.*

The word "offend" (v. 42) originally referred to the *tripping stick* in a trap. For example: a rabbit would *stumble* over the stick and the trap would fall upon it. It was used metaphorically of a stumbling block placed in a path to cause others to fall into the trap of sin. Christ warns about doing or saying a thing that becomes a tripping stick of a spiritual trap that *snags* young believers, like the child in their midst (v. 36).

The punishment for such evil deeds is presented in vivid but figurative language (verses 43, 45, and 47, "cut it off" and "pluck it out"). Jesus is teaching that, while you can't deal with sin by mutilation, you must deal with the *root of sin* which is the heart (see Mark 7:21). Christ is saying that sin is serious business and must be dealt with. We must also be careful that we are not a tripping stick to others.

The punishment of "hell… fire" (vv. 43, 45, 48) is vividly presented as a warning! Don't dismiss His warning; for those who will not turn to Jesus to deal with their evil hearts, a literal hell fire does await them!

The reference to salt is interesting. The disciples relate to *salt talk*, as salt is a necessary ingredient in such a hot climate and is a means of preserving food. Didn't Christ say, "Ye are the salt of the earth" (Matthew 5:13)? What does salt do in a believer's life? Salt, among other things, retards decay. So a part of our responsibility to our world is that we must oppose the prevalent rotting that corrupts our world. We are to be salt shakers that add a godly flavor to our world.

So Christ says, *Have salt in yourselves.* A Christian must guard his actions and words so that they do not lose their saltiness. We stay salty by maintaining a relationship with the Lord while in the world.

So then, does your life add a *godly saltiness* to your work place, your home, and your neighborhood? Perhaps you have bad habits or a *hot tongue* that can become *tripping sticks* for other believers around you.

Mark 10:1-16

What is the writer saying?

How can I apply this to my life?

pray *Bahrain – Bahrain has more freedoms than most Arab states. Pray that there would be more political and religious freedom to help the spread of the Gospel.*

We begin with "he arose from" there (v. 1, Capernaum by the Sea of Galilee, 9:30, 33). Likely after a few of months, He came to the "the farther side of Jordan." This is called the Lord's Perean Ministry (that is, the province of Perea, east of the Jordan River). Again, we see an open character in the Lord's ministry; He allows the multitudes to gather so that He might teach (v. 10:1) and heal many (Matthew 19:2).

Soon adversaries arrive. They ask questions about divorce. They are convinced that any answer will offend some of those who are present! The *libera* faction holds to a loose interpretation of the Law (Deuteronomy 24:1); a man could get divorced for insubstantial reasons, such as a wife talking loudly or burning a meal. The *strict* faction holds that "bill of divorcement" is allowed only to protect the innocent party from "uncleanness" or adultery.

The hardness of their hearts shows that they are insensible to the principle that a husband and wife must remain one. Rather, they are looking for concessions that allow for their wicked ways. Christ leaves no doubt that marriage is a divine institution established by God, and that divorce is not the will of God (vv. 8-9). He clearly says that a man should leave his father and mother and cleave to his wife (meaning *to stick to*). It is presented here in a Greek passive voice which means God Himself glued them together in marriage for life!

Christ goes on to explain that putting away one's partner and marrying another is committing adultery (vv. 11-12). Jesus is saying that a man or a woman who needlessly divorces his mate, thereby separating what God had glued, is committing a serious sin of the heart.

We must also reject the hard-hearted life style of the Pharisees! Choose to live by the clear teachings of God. How can you avoid *ungluing* what God has *glued* to your life?

QT Wednesday 14

Mark 10:17-31

What is the writer saying?

How can I apply this to my life?

pray *Philippines – Funding for the staff and supplies needed to continue Bible correspondence courses.*

The paragraph before us involves a rich young ruler. Matthew tells us that he is a young man (Matthew 19:22). Luke tells us that he is a ruler and very rich (Luke 18:18, 23). He addresses the Lord, asking what he could do to inherit eternal life. First, the Lord rebukes him for using the word "good." Christ says that only God is good. This does not teach that Christ is not God. Rather, the Lord is showing the young man that he is implying, by this title, that Christ is God. However, the young man does not really believe it. It is as though Christ is saying, "Either, by this title, you acknowledge me as God, or else you deny in your thinking the expression of your lips. Either I am God, or I am not good – for God alone is good." (E. S. English.)

The Lord probes his heart as He tells the young man to keep the commandments. The young man claims that he kept them all from his youth. When the Lord responds that he must sell all he has and give it all to the poor, the young man is sad and "went away grieved." The Lord would not declare that this young man is on his way to heaven because he had kept the Law!

The Lord has applied the *divine scalpel* and he has probed the *diseased spot* in the man's life. It is probable that the young man has properly tithed a part of his riches and has given alms to the poor from his riches, but he is not willing to give up all his riches. His riches are greater to him than the Lord; the riches are his true god! The first commandment says, "Thou shalt have no other gods before me" (Exodus 20:3). He surely knows that if he breaks even one commandment, then he is guilty of breaking all the Law.

The Lord goes on to explain that it is a hard thing for rich people to give up their *gods of riches* and come to the true God. Has the love of riches kept you from being a true follower of Jesus Christ?

Mark 10:32-45

What is the writer saying?

How can I apply this to my life?

pray *Let us come before His presence with thanksgiving; let us shout joyfully to Him with psalms (Psalm 95:2).*

The Lord now begins His last trek to Jerusalem. Note that the Lord "went before them" (v. 32). In a real sense, He is spiritually alone on this decisive journey, none could fully comprehend what He is purposing to do or what He is going to endure!

The disciples are content to follow behind Him since they are "amazed" and "afraid."

- Follow means *to follow one who goes before*. It is commonly used to signify the relationship of a student who "followed" a teacher.
- "Amazed" means *to experience astonishment by seeing some unusual event* (see also Mark 9:15). There are things about the manner of His walking ahead in solitude that causes their astonishment.
- "Afraid" means *to be put in a state of terror by some force*. It is from a root word, *to flee* or *to run*. Apparently, His unwavering determination is the foreboding force that makes them want to run!
- "Took again" After a time, Jesus *admits the twelve again into His company* (v. 32). Jesus knows they are near panic. So He, for a third time, tells His disciples to take a close look at the soon-arriving sufferings of the Lord. Sadly, they still could only behold their own hopes of reward as victors in the coming Kingdom of their Lord (v. 35).

So we see an incompatible dilemma here: (1) We see followers of Jesus who are not accompanying Jesus; (2) Disciples, committed to a relationship with Jesus, wanting to flee-in-terror from Jesus! (3) When commanded to look carefully at the plan of God for His Suffering Servant, the disciples instead look to their own plan of advancement; (4) While they are plotting to get their share of the glory, Christ says, "Whosoever of you will be the chiefest, shall be servant of all" (v. 44).

How can you follow the pattern of Jesus and not seek a profit by just accompanying Jesus?

Mark 10:46-52

What is the writer saying?

How can I apply this to my life?

pray *Nicaragua – Outreach to youth in a land where broken homes, poverty, and secularism are the norm.*

As Christ re-crosses the Jordan River, on His way up to Jerusalem, He passes through Jericho. That a "great number of people" (v. 46) are following Jesus is not surprising, since He and many others are on their way to Jerusalem for the Passover. Likely, others from Jericho are scurrying to see the Lord, about whom they have heard much.

And so, as the Lord is leaving Jericho, we encounter a blind beggar named Bartimaeus. Luke tells us that he inquires as to what the excitement is all about (Luke 18:36). When he discovers that Jesus is passing nearby, he begins to call out, "Jesus, thou Son of David, have mercy on me" (v. 47). Others begin to order him to "hold his peace" (v. 48). But he would not listen and cries out the more.

Jesus, in the middle of the great crowd, now stops and commands that the blind man be called to Him. With great enthusiasm he *throws away* his garment and jumps up to respond to the Lord's call. This outer garment is likely his *everything*; his bed, shelter, warmth and protection. One might ask: how does he ever expect to find it again? Well, he just knows Jesus is going to give him his sight back!

When Christ asks, *What will you that I should do unto you?*, the man knows his answer, "that I might receive my sight" (v. 51). It is clear that he has faith that Jesus, as the Messiah, could heal him. Christ says, "Thy faith hath made thee whole." Upon receiving his sight, he follows Christ. Luke adds, that he follows, "glorifying God" (Luke 18:43).

In Isaiah we read, "And in that day shall the deaf hear the words of the book, and ... the blind shall see out ... of darkness" (Isaiah 29:18).

Of course, as believers, we know we were blind, but our eyes have been opened. We see ourselves as blind and helpless. Dear friend, thank Him that, like the blind man, He drew us to himself and saved us. Now then, how can you today, like this man, follow the Lord and honor Him by living with a keen desire to glorify Him?

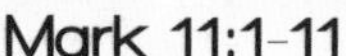

Mark 11:1-11

What is the writer saying?

How can I apply this to my life?

pray *Hungary – For new workers to have a burden for Hungary and the funds to support them.*

This is a beautiful scene. Christ is approaching Jerusalem from Jericho: first to Bethany, about two miles out, then to Bethphage, about one mile. At the Mount of Olives, Jerusalem can be seen. Here He stops and waits for the arrival of a colt, which would be a young donkey. Riding in on a colt is a recognized symbol used by new rulers to declare that they intend to bring peace not war (after all, He is not riding a war horse!). Perhaps the colt's owner is a believer who somehow knows that Jesus would need the colt, and so has sent word to Jesus to arrange for the use of this *unused* colt. John's Gospel tells us that many within the city, who have already arrived for Passover, now add to the commotion by running out of the city, spreading palm fronds before Him.

As Christ approaches the city, the people with Him are casting their garments and masses of leaves on the road before him, and are crying "Hosanna; Blessed is he that cometh in the name of the Lord" (v. 9). These acts are a traditional welcoming of a new ruler.

It is important to note what is meant by the people's shouts. "Hosanna" (v. 9) means *save now* or *save us, we pray*! Also, the words "he that cometh" is a traditional title for the Messiah who is to come. "In the name of the Lord" means they recognize that Jesus is coming by God's authority to fulfill God's promises to Israel! To this they add "blessed be the kingdom of our father David," which clearly indicates that they understand that Jesus is a prince of Israel, a descendant of their great king, David. In effect, they are saying something like, *We welcome You, Son of David! We urge You to save us now, granting us victory and prosperity. Since God has blessed You, bring these blessing upon us! Set up the promised kingdom of David!*

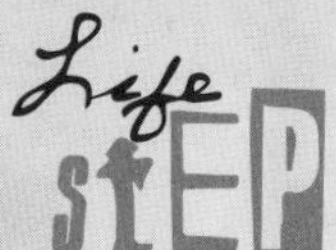

As Christians, we too recognize the *Kingship* of the Lord Jesus. How can Jesus be "King" in your life today?

Mark 11:12-24

What is the writer saying?

How can I apply this to my life?

pray *Argentina – For the salvation of the president and the stabilization of this country's economic and judicial systems.*

The story of the tree is told in two parts, before and after the Lord's visit to the Temple. For an unknown reason on this Monday morning of the *Passion Week*, Jesus leaves Bethany hungry, without breakfast (certainly Martha would not have wanted this lapse of hospitality!).

As the Lord approaches a fig tree, it gives an appearance of being an exceptionally healthy tree since it is full of leaves so early in the spring (April). Figs are unusual trees. They first grow their fruit and then they fill out with foliage later in the spring. For this tree to be full of leaves gives promise that it is an *early bloomer*, which should have had well-developed fruit! Christ approaches the tree and sees it has no fruit at all. Nothing but leaves! Being disappointed with the tree, He curses it.

The actions of the Lord Jesus are best understood as His acting out a parable which has a lesson to be learned. The fig tree is a picture (or type) of Israel. Other passages also tell us this (Hosea 9:10; Joel 1:7, 12; 2:22; Nahum 3:12; Zechariah 3:10). He sees Israel with *leaves of profession* but bearing no fruit. Thus, it is useless. The nation of Israel would be laid aside (hence the curse) and she would become a dead tree. Today, the Lord is calling out a people for His name – called the church. Someday, he will restore the fig tree – and it will flourish (see Romans 11). When Peter, the next morning, sees that the fig tree is dried up from the roots, the Lord responds, "Have faith in God" (v. 22). Jesus is declaring that God would one day restore the nation of Israel. Then, he explains that if we have faith in prayer – mountains can be removed. God specializes in things thought impossible. Don't underestimate His divine ability.

Are you a fruitful Christian? Do you *profess* to be a Christian but lack all evidence of *possessing* the fruit of the Christian life? How can *spiritual figs* grow in your *tree*?

Mark 11:25-33

What is the writer saying?

How can I apply this to my life?

pray *Pray for many salvation decisions to result from the Christmas presentations being presented in many churches.*

Christ has a great deal to say about forgiveness. He makes it clear that we should forgive as the Father forgives. If we refuse to forgive, our refusal will have, says the Lord, an effect on our being forgiven (v. 25).

"If we confess our sins, he is faithful and just to forgive us our sins, and to cleanse us from all unrighteousness" (1 John 1:9). Do you have a forgiving spirit? Or, do you, like many others, hold grudges?

After passing the dead fig tree on this Tuesday morning, the Lord comes again, for a third day, into the temple area. As he is "walking" and likely teaching groups of people as they stroll in the courtyard, the rulers of the Jews, the chief priests, the scribes, and the elders, "come to him" (v. 27). They, being angry over the disruption He has caused on the previous day, challenge Him. They ask "by what authority" (v. 29) does Jesus do what He has done and who gives the authority. Obviously, they are also declaring that Jesus is one who has no official "authority."

Actually, these leaders have a mechanism for granting authority. A man has to attend their rabbinical schools and be ordained. Only then, after graduation, would he be allowed to speak or act as an authority. The point is this; these *blind* spiritual leaders are refusing to *look* at the deeds of Jesus and the teachings of Jesus, for then they would know that His authority comes from God Himself, and not from their schools.

But the Lord sees their hearts. They are less than honest, and He knows it. So he asked a question regarding John the Baptist. Was John's baptism from heaven or men? The text explains that if they say "from heaven," Christ would ask why John wasn't believed. If they say "of men," they fear the people. So they chose not to answer.

The Great Commission begins with, "All power is given unto me ..." (Matthew 28:18). This is the word "authority" in today's passage. By what right can you *cause a disruption* while witnessing for the Lord?

Mark 12:1-12

What is the writer saying?

How can I apply this to my life?

pray *El Salvador – For believers willing to commit to the discipleship of new converts.*

Today we have the Lord speaking with the religious leaders of Israel who have come to Jesus to challenge His authority (see 11:27-33).

His parable reflects an ancient practice: Far-away landlords owned large farms which they leased to local farmers. The farmers worked the land and paid, as rent, a portion of the crop to the landowner's stewards.

The parable is a review of Israel's failure to repay their *rent*. God has always desired a *return* from His vineyard, which He has planted through the *fruits of repentance and righteousness* (see also Luke 3:8).

The "certain man" is God Himself, the landowner. The servants are the Old Testament prophets (see Jeremiah 25:4-7). The "one son" is the Lord Jesus (see also 1:11; 9:7). The "husbandmen" are the religious leaders of Israel. After three servants have been refused, the son is sent (v. 6). Sadly, the husbandmen kill the son, thinking to gain from their evil deed.

Jesus concludes with, "What shall therefore the lord of the vinyard do?" History tells us that by 70 A.D., Israel had been destroyed (v. 9) with the Jews being either killed, enslaved, or scattered far from God's "vineyard"!

Jesus now uses a metaphor to close this parable (v.10). The "stone" that is "rejected" is "become the head of the corner." As before, the Stone is the Lord Jesus. Jesus, quoting from a Messianic text (Psalm 118:22-23), gives an unexpected twist to the parable:

- The Rejected Son will become the Retrieved Stone.
- The Dead Son will become the Exalted, Living Cornerstone!

Jesus, in the metaphor, is declaring, not only His coming death, but also His coming *retrieval from the dead* to become the Exalted Cornerstone of a new and living temple, the church (see 1 Peter 2:5-6).

What profit does God expect from His investment in you?

Mark 12:13-27

What is the writer saying?

How can I apply this to my life?

pray *Costa Rica – Pray for the salvation of youth enslaved by drugs and bound to secularism.*

Again today, the enemies of Jesus seek to "catch him in his words" (v. 13)! There are several groups in Christ's day which dislike and compete with each other for influence in Judea. The surprise in today's passage is that two political-opposites, the Pharisees and the Herodians (v. 13), are now united against their more-dangerous enemy, Jesus. They ask whether it is lawful to pay taxes to Caesar, obviously a pre-planned trap, for no answer would satisfy all.

Jesus begins His response by asking for a Roman denarius, a small silver coin likely having the image of Tiberius Caesar (14-37 A.D.) and these words, "Tiberius Caesar Augustus, Son of the Divine Augustus" (The inscription says much about the imperial cult of emperor worship!)

Christ's answer is, "Render to Caesar the things that are Caesar's, and to God the things that are God's." Clearly, Christ recognizes the state is ordained by God (see Romans 13:1-7). Since Jews are benefiting from Roman presence in commerce, roads, and safe travel, they are obligated to pay taxes as a debt they owe Caesar. In fact, the word "render" (v. 17) means *give back* what belongs to Caesar.

Notice that Jesus extends his answer beyond their question: "and to God the things that are God's." This declares a rejection of the emperor's claim to deity. Thus, Caesar is not to be given the divine honor and worship he demands; those taxes are God's alone! More importantly, all men, including the Romans, owe a *tax debt* to God! This is the greater tax upon a person's life! God, due to His blessings, demands a tax of our time, talents, money, service, and worship!

First of all, are you an honest, tax-paying citizen? Jesus would expect you to be one! But more importantly, do you pay your *divine taxes* as you give "to God the things that are God's"? Perhaps you need to have a little talk with the Lord about *back taxes* owed to God!

Mark 12:28-44

What is the writer saying?

How can I apply this to my life?

pray *United Kingdom – For a harvest of souls in Aberdeen, Scotland's largest area of non-church-goers.*

Today's passage introduces a new law expert, a scribe, who is grouped as "one of the scribes" seeking to trap Jesus by their questions. This law expert, who has been impressed with the Lord's answers (v.28), takes a surprisingly friendly attitude towards Jesus. Yet, as Matthew 22:35 points out, his purpose, at least at first, is to tempt Jesus. He asks, which is "the first commandment of all"? Jewish custom is to divide the Law into 365 prohibitions, one for every day of the year. They also list 228 commandments, one for every part of the body. So then, this law expert is asking which of these six hundred is "first" in importance!

Christ starts by quoting Deuteronomy 6:4-5, "Hear, O Israel; The Lord our God is one Lord: ...love the Lord thy God with all thy heart,...soul,...mind,...strength: this is the first commandment." Then Jesus gives a *second most-important commandment* by summarizing a part of the Law (v. 31) — quoting from Leviticus 19:18, "... Thou shalt love thy neighbour as thyself."

By these two statements, Jesus summarizes the whole of a Jewish believer's moral and spiritual responsibility to God. Further, the two statements can be further summarized by one word, "love"! Loving the Lord completely and loving one's neighbor summarizes the whole law.

After the scribe's response, Christ adds, "Thou are not far from the kingdom of God." Not far, but not yet in! Many are almost persuaded and not far, who have not trusted Christ. Remember, being a Christian begins with a personal commitment, "Ye must be born again" (John 3:7).

Next, the Lord poses a question: Since they believe the Messiah would be the son of David, Jesus asks, how could the Messiah also be the Lord over David? The Messiah is both! He is *David's Son* and *David's Lord*! Jesus is both wholly man and wholly God.

How do you show your love for God and others?

Mark 13:1-13

What is the writer saying?

How can I apply this to my life?

pray *Spain – For godly men to write, develop, and produce more Christian literature in the Basque language.*

The Olivet Discourse is a result of two questions posed by the Lord's disciples. When the Lord speaks of the destruction of Jerusalem, they ask when these things would be and what would be the sign that these things are starting. The Lord answers and gives us much detail as to the coming tribulation that will take place here on the earth.

Remember that the next event on God's *future calendar* is the Rapture of the church (according to Scripture, the Lord's coming at the Rapture can happen at any moment). This will begin a seven-year time of God's judgment known as the Tribulation.

Mark 13:5-13 describes the first half of the Tribulation. First, many will come claiming to be Christ (v. 6; including the Antichrist, 2 Thessalonians 2:1-12). Note also, that there will be bloodshed (v. 7). This seems to correspond to the first two horsemen of Revelation 6:2-4 – the white horse (a false messiah) and a red horse (wars and rumors of wars). Next, there will be famines and troubles (corresponding to the third horseman on a black horse with a pair of balances in his hand, Revelation 6:5).

At the end of the Tribulation, the Lord will come in power and glory to the earth (Revelation 19:11-16). He will have three purposes in coming: (1) to rescue His chosen people, Israel; (2) to destroy the evil world system; and (3) to establish His thousand-year reign as King of Israel and, from Israel, over the whole world.

All of these are the "beginnings of sorrows" (v. 8), which is another name for the first half of the Tribulation. Praise the Lord, "God hath not appointed us to wrath" (1 Thessalonians 5:9).

The hope of the believer is the soon coming of Christ. Knowing the future should influence how you live now! Is your hope in Christ's return influencing how you live today?

Mark 13:14-23

What is the writer saying?

How can I apply this to my life?

pray *Angola – For medical missionaries laboring in a nation where landmines outnumber people.*

Our present passage deals with important future events. After the Rapture of the church (1 Thessalonians 4:13-18), the Tribulation will take place. The first half is called "the beginnings of sorrows" (v. 8). The "abomination of desolation" (v. 14) is a reference to Daniel's prophecy (Daniel 9:27). It refers to the desecration of the temple when the Antichrist will sit in the temple and demand to be worshiped. This will take place in the middle of the seven years (middle of the prophetic week). It is then that the Lord says they should flee (v. 14). Those on the housetop should not go down into the house; those in the field should run and not turn back. It will be difficult at this time for a woman with child (v. 17). This is a brief description of the last part of the Tribulation (also called The Great Tribulation). Christ says that it will be the worst of all times. The "elect" in verse 20 speaks of *elect Israel.*

Some may ask: why does God allow the Tribulation? Among other things, it will be the crucible through which God will deal with Israel and bring them back to a place of repentance and salvation. Remember, the church will not be here. But, during this period, 144,000 Jews will be God's evangelists and will preach the Gospel of the kingdom in all the earth. This is clear from verse 10, "And the gospel must first be published among all nations." They will do in seven years what the church has been doing for two thousand years. People will be saved from all parts of the earth (Revelation 7:9-14).

Reader, if you are not born again and the Lord should come, you would be left behind to experience all this. What an awful prospect. To those of us who know Him, we await His return. Maranatha (*Come Jesus*)! Spend some time reviewing in your mind how you came to know the Lord Jesus as your Savior.

Mark 13:24-37

What is the writer saying?

How can I apply this to my life?

pray *Slovakia – Slovakia, as a nation, needs a sense of direction. Pray for these people to seek God as they search for identity and meaning.*

The coming Tribulation has been the primary subject of this chapter. Beginning with verse 5, we have had a rather vivid picture of that time, following the Rapture of the church, called the "time of Jacob's trouble" (Jeremiah 30:7). It will last seven years; the last three-and-one half will be the most intense. Our present paragraph speaks of that which is "after that tribulation" (v. 24). The description refers to the coming of Christ in *great power and glory*. Again, this is not the Rapture that will take place seven years earlier – there are no such signs identified with that appearing. This is often called *The Revelation of Christ,* as described in Revelation 19:11-16.

It is fitting that the Lord would give a parable of the fig tree – referring to Israel (v. 28; see also 11:12-14). You will recall that the Tribulation will bring elect Israel to their knees as they look on Him whom they have pierced (Zechariah 12:10). Is the fig tree budding today? While Israel is returning to the land, and cherishes the land greatly, they are not doing so *in belief.* The primary reference here is what God does in bringing Israel to Himself during the Tribulation.

We believe the reference to "generation" (v. 30) refers to the *race of the Jews,* meaning that Israel will have an identity as a nation until these things be fulfilled. Israel is the miracle nation preserved by God as His chosen people. The command to "watch" (v.33) clearly refers to a looking toward that wonderful day of His glorious appearing. Of course, the church knows that before these events, He will come. We too are "to wait for his Son from heaven" with expectancy (1 Thessalonians 1:10).

This *hope* of Christ's return is a *purifying hope*. Remember, "Every man that hath this hope in him purifieth himself even as he is pure" (1 John 3:3). Perhaps you need to add a prayer request about some area of your life that needs God's help to make it truly "pure"!

QT

Monday 16

Mark 14:1-11

What is the writer saying?

How can I apply this to my life?

pray *Praise God for his work as Creator (Psalm 8).*

Today's passage is *sandwich structure* story-telling. The conspiracy of the religious leaders is presented in vv. 1-2 and again in vv. 10-11. This is divided by the story of the anointing of Jesus by Mary (vv. 3-9).

The chief priests are plotting Christ's death (see John 11:47-53) but are being careful to minimize public uproar; thus they are willing to wait until after the feast. "Craft" means a *cunning strategy* (v. 1). The unexpected offer of Judas (v.10) gives them reason to act during the feast.

Jesus is the honored guest at the home of Simon the leper (v. 3), who is likely the man healed by Jesus in 1:40-41. A woman enters and anoints the head of Jesus with spikenard from an alabaster jar (containing up to a pint). John 12:3 identifies this woman as Mary, sister of Martha and Lazarus. He adds that she also anoints Jesus' feet!

Since it is a custom to pour a few drops of this on the heads and the feet of guests (still done in India and considered a compliment), why does Mary pour out far more than needed? Likely she has another custom in mind. When a person dies, it is also a custom to anoint, with spikenard, the cloth burial bandages. She understands that soon Christ is to die as he gives Himself as a ransom on the Cross.

Note that some considere this a waste. The ointment is worth three hundred denarii, about three hundred day's wages. Instead of a rebuke, the Lord says she has done a good work. Here is love in action!

How can you apply one or two of the lessons of Mary's good deed?

1. When serving the Lord, no cost is too great! Serve despite the cost!
2. Serve the Lord, despite the criticism that your service is a "waste."
3. Love for Christ transforms the humblest service for Him into honor.
4. When you cannot do everything needed, do what little you can.
5. Notice Mary goes away carrying the same *fresh scent* as Jesus!

16 Tuesday

Mark 14:12-21

What is the writer saying?

How can I apply this to my life?

pray *Uganda – Praise – Due to steps taken by churches and the government, the rate of the spread of AIDS has been cut in half.*

The *Passover* (v. 12) is a looking back to Exodus 12, where the death angel *passed over* the homes of those who had placed blood from a sacrificed lamb on their entrance door posts.

But, more importantly, *Passover* was also intended to be a looking forward in anticipation of God sending His perfect substitutionary Lamb, the Messiah, who is Jesus Christ (John 1:29, see Isaiah 53:4-7).

We note that the Lord gives specific instructions about the man carrying water and about the upper room in which they are to meet (vv. 13-15), indicating that Jesus has made an advance reservation for a private place for this *Last Supper*.

Finally, that evening, the Lord solemnly declares beforehand that one the twelve disciples would betray Him (v. 18). We should note that a Messianic Prophecy speaks about the Lord's statement; Psalms 41:9 says, "Yea, mine own familiar friend, in whom I trusted, which did eat of my bread, hath lifted up his heel against me."

It is not obvious to the disciples who this betrayer is to be. Each is aware of his own weakness of character. All are asking, "Is it I?" (v. 19, Greek: *It is not I, is it?* – which expected a response, *No, it is not you*). At this point, the Matthew account adds that Judas asks, "Master, is it I?" to which the Lord responds, "Thou hast said" (Matthew 26.25; *Yes, it is as you have said*). One commentary writes, "But every one of them recognized his weakness of character, whereby he might be guilty of this deed. And so, any one of them might have been the betrayer."

To begin with, has the blood of God's Lamb caused God's judgment to *pass over* you? Has the Lamb's blood freed you from slavery to sin? Do you, as did the disciples, recognize your own bent towards sin? Knowing your own weakness of character, how will you find strength from God this week so that you might remain true to your Savior?

Mark 14:22-31

What is the writer saying?

How can I apply this to my life?

pray *France – For an impact to be made on the core French population.*

In today's passage, we have details from the second of the several courses of the elaborate Jewish Passover Feast.

Jesus, now at his last Passover Meal, institutes the first Lord's Supper (Matthew 26:26-29 and Luke 22:19-20). Within a few hours, Christ would fulfill God's Old Testament Covenant to Israel which had been pictured year by year at the Passover Feast. As God's *Old Covenant* is being fulfilled, Jesus establishes a *New Covenant* (v. 24, Hebrews 10:9-10).

Here, Jesus speaks of literal things; bread, wine, His body and blood, to introduce figurative things. The *bread* is an emblem of His flesh, and the *wine* an emblem of His blood. The verb "is" is used by Jesus (vv. 22-23) with an intended meaning of *represents*.

Paul says that the Lord's Supper is to be a table of *examination* (1 Corinthians 11:27-28), where we search our own hearts. It is also to be a table of *anticipation*; we are to regularly observe it "until that day" (v. 25; 1 Corinthians 11:26) we fellowship with Jesus when He bodily brings us to His "marriage supper of the Lamb" (see Revelation 19:9).

Let us take a look at one other little word, "my blood ... shed for many" (v. 24). The word, "for," here means *on behalf of* and speaks of His sacrificial death where He vicariously (*to take the place of another*) dies for our sin! This takes us back to His declaration, "the Son of man came ... to give his life a ransom for many" (10:45).

As they leave the upper room (v. 26), the Lord tells of the shepherd being smitten and the scattering of the sheep. Peter claims that he would be the exception. The Lord speaks of Peter's future denial of Him. Peter protests and is joined by the others. How wrong they are.

What in your life needs to be transformed by the crucified Lord?

Mark 14: 32-42

What is the writer saying?

How can I apply this to my life?

pray *Saudi Arabia – For Saudi believers to have the ability to meet together in safety and have access to God's Word.*

Jesus and the eleven disciples leave Jerusalem and walk to the mount of Olives. The Lord asks eight disciples to sit near the entrance to Gethsemane (literally *Press of Oils*). During the harvest, it is a very busy, outdoor, olive-processing factory, but now it is a quiet spot for prayer. Then Jesus takes Peter, James, and John with Him into the garden-like enclosure.

Jesus then became "amazed" (v. 33, *distressed, astonished*) and "very heavy" (*a mind saturated with loathing*). Likely He is distressed by their lack of faith. Also, Jesus is anticipating the Cross where He would bear the sin of the world (John 1:29). He then says that He is "exceeding sorrowful unto death" (v. 34), meaning He is so overwhelmed with *deep grief* that it threatens to kill Jesus! So He asks the three to "watch" on His behalf, as those who are burden-bearers.

Jesus moves off and cries out, if it is possible, take away this coming hour of separation (*from His Father*) and judgment (*by His Father*) (v. 35). He knows the "cup" of suffering (v. 36) which He must drink as the sin-bearing substitute for lost men. Jesus is facing His greatest temptation to turn away from doing the will of His Father. Yet we see Him triumph as He calmly places His trust in His Father. From this point on Jesus "thought no longer of Himself or his sufferings, only upon the all-holy, all-wise will of the Father" (Geikie, *Life and Words of Christ*).

After His prayer, Jesus returns and finds the three asleep. Remember as they are coming, Peter (and then the others) have emphatically declared that he would not be "offended" (*to fall away*) from Jesus. Yet Peter fails to support the Lord through an hour of watching in prayer.

How might you "watch" over a fellow Christian whose sorrows have become overwhelming?

Mark 14:43-52

What is the writer saying?

How can I apply this to my life?

pray *That God would increase your awareness of the lost and your boldness in sharing Christ's love.*

In this paragraph Judas, "one of the Twelve," betrays the Lord. We see that while he has been close to the Lord, he has remained far away. We are told that as "a great multitude" comes to the Garden, Judas calls Him "Master" and kisses Him. He thus, by prearranged signal, identifies Jesus as the one to be taken. Then Peter (per John 18:10) draws a sword and smites a servant of the high priest, cutting off his ear. Even though the Lord had told the disciples that He was to be arrested, tried, and killed, Peter, impulsive in his flesh, acts. Peter attempts to *start a war* by cutting off an ear! (Jesus then heals the man's ear, Luke 22:51.)

Consider this: Jesus had just successfully arranged (14:13-14) to hold the Passover Meal within the city of Jerusalem, a city controlled by those seeking to kill Him. Why then has Jesus not arranged for a secret spot for this prayer meeting? Since He knows Judas is to betray Him, why does Jesus go to an expected location? Why not one of the many other enclosures? Jesus must have chosen this spot, knowing Judas would come. Jesus is presenting Himself as a Lamb to the slaughter, "No man taketh it [my life] ... I lay it down" (John 10:18).

A sad word comes next, "And they all forsook him, and fled" (v. 50). They had confessed Him as the Christ – yet all now flee!

Who is the young man that flees (vv. 51-52)? Mentioned only here, it really does not contribute to the story. This *side* detail only makes sense if this man is Mark, author of this Gospel! He is pointing out that he also becomes frightened and flees! Since a theme of his Gospel is discipleship, this minor detail is offering a vital lesson; when *any disciple* fails, the Lord will be faithful to recover His *friend* who has faltered!

Do you struggle with the guilt of having "fled" from a responsibility God gave to you? Well, so did Peter and likely Mark. Now is a good time to ask the Lord Jesus to forgive you.

Mark 14:53-65

What is the writer saying?

How can I apply this to my life?

pray *Peru – For the continued work of the Holy Spirit among the Quechua and Aymara people.*

Christ is brought before the four groups that comprise the Jewish Sanhedrin, the ruling body of Jews at Jerusalem.

This is the first of two main trials (Jesus faces six judicial authorities; John 18!]. Rome has granted local, judicial authority to the Sanhedrin. Thus, this religious body rules on secular matters by leveling fines, punishments, etc. The Romans have retained responsibility for the death penalty. Since all here want Jesus put to death (v. 55; 14:1), they need witnesses (v 55-57, 59) for both this trial and then the second Roman review trial, where a death penalty could be issued.

There is "no intention of giving Jesus a fair hearing to discover if the charges were just" (Hendrickson, p. 607). The entire trial is invalid:

(a) No trial for life could be held at night or begin on the eve of a major Jewish festival like the Passover.

(b) Jewish law requires two or, better, three supporting witnesses to bring a conviction. Yet, the many false (*or lying*) witnesses (v. 56) could not satisfy the two supporting witnesses rule.

(c) Their best evidence is the misapplied statement of Jesus about "destroy this temple" (v. 58; He never said, *made with hands,* see John 2:19). But no witnesses for the defense are called to clarify that Jesus is speaking of His own death and resurrection.

(d) The high priest's question, "Are thou the Christ?" (v. 61), is an invalid question since it requires Jesus to incriminate himself (rather than have supporting witnesses whose testimony incriminates Him).

(e) Note that the high priest makes his own ruling (v. 63), rather than allowing the required twenty-four hours before all vote to determine a ruling.

When wrongly treated or falsely accused, do we react with patience like Christ or in anger like the world?

Mark 14:66-72

What is the writer saying?

How can I apply this to my life?

pray *Uganda – For new missionaries to adapt quickly, live the Word, and persevere amidst opposition.*

We begin with Peter "without" (Matthew 26:69) and "beneath" (v. 66) the elevated courtroom where Jesus is being tried (Luke 22:54-55).

A servant girl, the courtyard's doorkeeper (John 18:16), "looked upon" Peter, then declares "thou also wast with Jesus of Nazareth!" Peter denies with a legal expression, "I know not, neither understand I what thou sayest" (v. 68). Events are getting *hot* by the fire, so Peter backs off to the entranceway. During this quiet pause, the rooster crows.

Then, others (Matthew 26:71; Luke 22:58; John 18:25) begin saying, "This is one of them." He denies it again (literally, *kept denying*; likely, he has to respond to the several people who accuse him here).

After an hour (Luke 22:59), others "that stood by" (v. 70) accuse Peter, *...you are one of them!* Peter has spoken enough for them to know he was not from Jerusalem. He is from Galilee, *up north*!

Peter has to *up* his defense so he "began to curse and swear" (v. 71); placing himself under God's judgment if he is lying to them. The word "curse" means *to declare condemned*. The word "swear" means *to take a solemn oath*. At this point "immediately, ...the cock crew" (Luke 22:60)! The rooster's crowing interrupts Peter, causing him to remember the earlier words of warning from Jesus (14:30).

We must ask: (1) Why has Peter come to the courtroom after fleeing in the Garden (14:50)? (2) Why doesn't Peter leave after his first denial? (3) Why does he only back off to the entranceway (He could have fled)? (4) During those two hours, what doubts and fears are going through his mind? (5) How could he still deny the Lord Jesus?

As the rooster crows, the Lord "looked upon Peter" (Luke 22:61). Likely a look that mixed grief, sorrow, and compassion, for the Lord still loved him. How about you? Does the Lord grieve over your sin? Will you repent and allow Him to cleanse you of your sin (1 John 1:9)?

17 Monday

Mark 15:1-15

What is the writer saying?

How can I apply this to my life?

pray *Pray that believers will exercise their privilege to vote for their government officials.*

This paragraph begins with the "whole council" agreeing to take Jesus to Pilate (v. 1) since they are restricted by Roman law; all death-penalty cases have to be brought before the Roman magistrate.

Pilate already "knew" they had delivered Jesus "for envy" (v. 10), so we see a series of maneuvers by him and by the Jews, who want the Romans to execute their sentence without a Roman re-examination. Pilate is being maneuvered to use his power for judicial murder.

Mark's brief account focuses on Pilate's examination of the crucial, central charge, "Art thou the King of the Jews?" (v. 2a). The answer of Jesus, "Thou sayest it" (v. 2b), does not translate to a clear answer. Yet, Jesus, using a common legal confirmation of His day, is declaring a clear-cut, legal affirmative. In a court room today, he would say something like, *Yes, that is what I am; I am the King of the Jews!*

Yet, Pilate finds "in him no fault at all" (John 18:38). As a result he continues to maneuver to avoid judicial murder (that is, Luke 23:6-12, Herod). Yet, as the *review judge* of the *higher court,* his responsibility is to do one of two things: (1) to demand the witnesses be brought before him for a retrial; or (2) he should enforce his verdict of innocence!

At this point, his cowardice shows as he attempts one last maneuver: He brings Barabbas (v. 7), a murderer, and Jesus, who left Pilate convinced that He had done no evil (v. 14), before the people. But the chief priest keep Pilate *boxed in* with the people's cries to "Crucify him" (vv. 13-14). Then Pilate allows that which he tried to avoid, judicial murder, as he orders Jesus away to be crucified.

Let us not forget Jesus died for us! What happened here was no accident, nor was it simply the hatred of the Jews or Romans. The purpose of His coming was to die for the sin of the world (John 1:29). Thank the Lord for the love He displayed in coming to take our place.

Mark 15:16-26

What is the writer saying?

How can I apply this to my life?

pray *Venezuela – For the despair caused by poverty, crime, and violence to cause people to seek Christ.*

The Roman soldiers have just finished scourging Jesus (v. 15). Likely Pilate, the Roman governor, would have watched from his raised judgment-seat as his order is carried out. The soldiers then lead Jesus back into the Praetorium (v. 16), which is *army headquarters* as well as Pilate's living quarters. (The Praetorium is a magnificent palace built by Herod the Great forty years earlier, now occupied by the Romans.)

We note that the "whole band" or *cohort* of soldiers is called together. These soldiers are going to have great sport with this Jesus and none wants to miss out on the mistreating of a man they consider to be a fake claimant of the Jewish royal throne. Thus, the entire garrison is present; officially, about six hundred soldiers.

Likely, a faded "purple"-hued soldier's outer cloak (crimson red when new) is placed on Jesus (v. 17; Matthew 27:28). A crown of thorns is placed upon His head and a reed (Matthew 27:29), as a *king's scepter*, in His hand to accent the image of a despised Jewish king. They then salute, "Hail, King of the Jews!" (v. 18) as they struck Jesus with the reed and spit upon Him to complete their torment of their prisoner.

The physical agony is indescribable. Remember, although He is God, He is suffering as a man. The scourging and abuse leave Him exhausted. Simon of Cyrene is *compelled* to bear His cross. At Golgotha, where He is crucified, He is offered myrrh to deaden the pain, but he refuses. The soldiers then cast lots to divide his garments, not realizing they are actually fulfilling Scripture (Psalm 22:18).

While incredibly sad, this is not a defeat! Look beyond the hate and the ridicule. The greatest pain here is not physical, but the spiritual pain of *bearing our sins* "in his own body on the tree" (1 Peter 2: 24). As you think of that hour, thank the Lord Jesus for winning a victory for you!

Mark 15:27-38

What is the writer saying?

How can I apply this to my life?

pray *Panama – Increased educational opportunities for those in or considering full-time ministry.*

Again, we approach the Crucifixion with a sense of the marvelous grace of God. While the crucifixion of Jesus is a gross violation of justice, both Jewish and Roman, it is also the greatest victory of the Lord Jesus! When viewed from God's plan for man's redemption, the Crucifixion is the completion of Christ's purpose on earth. He came to seek and to save the lost (Luke 19:10). This, as we have said, is not tragedy, but triumph. Prophecy is also being fulfilled (Isaiah 53:9-12).

The mocking of Jesus intensifies, "they that passed by railed" on Him about destroying the temple! This was the misapplied charge that brought his conviction in the trials of the night before. The chief priests join with, "He saved others; himself he cannot save." The criminals being crucified add their insults (v. 32). Even the Roman soldiers join in (Luke 23:36).

Suddenly the setting changes, for now the "sun was darkened" (Luke 23:45). It is high noon (the sixth hour of daylight, v. 33), yet the sun is dark for three hours. It would seem that the hand of God in the Heavens has quieted the mockers. No doubt fear has replaced boldness.

The "darkness over the whole land" is linked to the words of Jesus, three hours later, "My God, why hast thou forsaken me?" (v. 34). Has the Father forsaken His Son? Yes! Is the darkness a visible indication of God's judgment upon sin? Yes! (See Isaiah 5:30; 60:2; Amos 5:18, 20; etc.) But the important question is, why did this happen? The answer is: because Jesus was a *sin offering* for us. God judged His own Son as the Son bore our sins. "He hath borne our griefs, and carried our sorrows: yet we did esteem him stricken, smitten of God" (Isaiah 53:4).

Our greatest joy comes from knowing that Jesus was *made sin* for us (2 Corinthians 5:21). Write out a thank-you prayer to the Lord for being the substitute for God's judgment upon your sin.

Mark 15:39-47

What is the writer saying?

How can I apply this to my life?

pray *South Africa – For churches to commit financial aid to those seeking to attend Bible school.*

Our passage deals with those who are at the foot of the cross. There are two Mary's, (Mary Magdalene, and Mary, the mother of James the less as well as Joses and Salome).

We read that they had followed the Lord and ministered unto Him along with many others. Another person is Joseph of Arimathaea, who boldly approaches Pilate asking for Jesus' body. Joseph brings fine linen and lays him in a sepulcher. A stone is rolled over the door.

This writer has been to where it is thought Christ was crucified. A few yards from Golgotha was the empty tomb. When I first visited Calvary I was so moved, I went aside and wrote the following words:

Behold the hill, grotesquely shaped
The skull, the brow, in bold relief
Against the sky, a testimony to
His anguish, agony and grief.

How different now the open sky
So bright and blue, How darkened then
When God forsook His precious Son
Bearing my guilt, my awful sin.

Behold the hill, Golgotha's hill
And now, look back – review that day
See Him, outstretched, bridging the gap
What access here through Christ – the way!

On the cross Christ defeated Satan (Hebrews 2:14). There He bore our sins (2 Corinthians 5:21), and there He opened the way of salvation for you! Praise the Lord!

17 Friday

Mark 16:1-8

What is the writer saying?

How can I apply this to my life?

pray *Australia – Pray for those who have had less opportunity to hear about God: Muslims, those in isolated rural areas and immigrants.*

The resurrection of Christ! Let the words of the angel echo loud and clear: "He is risen; he is not here: behold the place where they laid him." Yesterday, I told of going to Calvary and later writing a poem expressing my thankfulness for the cross. The second stanza, written at the same time follows.

Behold and see the empty tomb
What victory in its vacancy
What triumph in its emptiness
And sure receipt of victory

No towering shrine erected here
No gaudy work of men, to spoil
Its sweet and plain simplicity
No worship of its stone and soil

Empty! One word makes it unique;
Empty! One word explains our joy;
Empty! One word rings loud and clear;
Empty! One word our tongues employ.

Annulled are all satanic powers
By Son of God and God the Son,
Behold the tomb! Hear now this word,
Empty! Praise God, the victory's won!

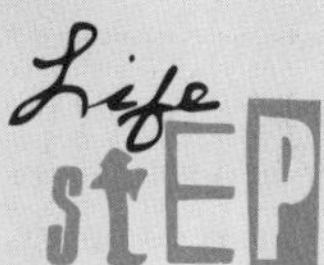

There is *victory in that tomb's vacancy*. Take time to see the victory of the *Cross* and the *Open Tomb*. They declare that you will not face a judgment for your sin and you will be with the Lord forever!

Saturday 17

Mark 16:9-20

What is the writer saying?

How can I apply this to my life?

pray *Harry Bollback, Co – founder of Word of Life, as he and his wife Millie travel and minister.*

While we accept the genuineness of this paragraph, we also note that this paragraph is, for unknown reasons, missing from many ancient manuscripts, or copies, of Mark's Gospel. We do want to insist that the Gospel of Mark, without this paragraph as some would insist, fails to be *Good News*, because without the paragraph, Mark would leave his Gospel with Jesus still in the grave and the disciples scattered.

When we started this study of Mark, we emphasized that the thrust is to be one of the actions of the servant. He, the Lord, is the greatest servant. Now, we have Him risen and appearing to several, including the eleven. He reprimands them for not having believed those who have seen Him earlier after His resurrection.

Then, the *Servant* says, "Go ye into all the world, and preach the gospel to every creature" (v. 15). The *Servant of Action* is now seeking to activate His own and send His disciples as servants bearing the Gospel. This is Mark's declaration of Christ's Great Commission here. Go and preach. We note that variations of this Great Commission are found at the ends of all four Gospel accounts and at the beginning of Acts! Obviously, the Lord Jesus wants us to take seriously this commissioning! While there are many ways of serving the Lord, the greatest is this: *getting out the message of salvation.*

The signs mentioned here are characteristic of signs in the early church before the completion of the Word – the Bible. Today these are no longer operative, as they are not needed. We authenticate our message by God's revealed Word.

Crucifixion, Resurrection, and Ascension. *Yesterday* he died for me – *today* He lives for me – ascended into glory ever living to make intercession for us (Hebrews 7:25). But the picture is not complete. *Tomorrow* He comes for me, and for that wonderful event we all watch and wait. Write the Lord a note telling Him why you wait for Him!

Any time believers take up sides and battle other believers, it hurts. It hurts even more when the adversaries are long-time friends. That is exactly what is happening in the churches to whom John is writing. A new philosophy has infiltrated the church body and believers are finding themselves in a quandary. They want to know which side is right. They want to know if both sides are believers. They wanted to be sure that they are believers.

The situation is not all that unique. The church is rather new. The believers are striving to serve the Lord. Some so-called believers from another area come and begin to teach new ideas. They have a new view of sin, a new view of revelation, a new view of Christ. A number of church leaders soon embrace this teaching and ... Presto! ... a church split is in progress.

The genuine believers are caught in the *love-versus-doctrine* snare. They want to love these men because they claim to be Christians, but their presence in the assembly is causing young believers to be led astray due to false doctrine. Some are even unsure about who is right and who is wrong. They want direction. They want assurance. And that is exactly why John writes this epistle.

Things are not all that different today. It would be nice if we lived in a homogenized church where everybody believed exactly the same way. It would be nice if we could just let everyone believe whatever they wanted and not have to worry about it. Unfortunately, we don't and we can't.

The struggle is not for us to decide who is saved and who is not saved; the struggle is with fellowship. When John wrote this epistle, his purpose was exactly this: to guide us in the area of fellowship. He wants us to be in fellowship with God and with all other believers who are in fellowship with God. He wants us to know that we are saved.

This is not a book about what salvation is or the doctrine of eternal security. It is a book about assurance—a book about feeling saved. How do we know that our religion is the right one? How do we know that Heaven is our home? It is one thing to know the doctrine of eternal security; it is quite another to know for sure that we are saved. John has written this book for exactly that reason: so that we can know that we have eternal life.

John sees four relationships that affect how we feel about our salvation: Our relationship to the Word of God (1:1-2:6), our relationship to the people of God (2:7-3:24), our relationship to the Spirit of God (4:1-4:21) and our relationship to faith in God (5:1-5:13). The last few verses of the book review the confidences that we have as believers.

1 John 1:1-4

What is the writer saying?

How can I apply this to my life?

pray *Thailand – Salvation and deliverance for the millions of men, women, and children working within the tourist driven "sex industry".*

One writer comments, "John wrote his Gospel to prove the deity of our Lord, assuming His humanity, and his first epistle to prove His humanity, assuming His deity." John accomplishes the latter by stating, "…we have heard [Him], which we have seen [Him] with our eyes, which we have looked upon, and our hands have handled, of the Word of life" (v. 1). Using three different means of evidence – hearing, seeing, and touching – John establishes his proof of our Lord's humanity.

John has to do so, for heretics called "gnostics" are challenging that truth. There are Docetic Gnostics (*dokeo-* "to seem," these argued that the Lord *only seemed* to have a body; that is, a *phantom*, so to speak); and Cerinthian Gnostics (after Cerinthus, who distinguished between the physical-man, Jesus, and the divine-spirit, Christ). They claim that the Christ came upon Jesus at His baptism and left Him at the cross.

John identifies Jesus as "the Word of life" (v. 1). He then details his fellowship with Him and expresses his desire that his readers might experience the same. The Greek word for "fellowship" is *koinonia*, and carries with it the idea of one person having a joint participation with another in *something possessed in common* by both. He wants to share with his non-eyewitness readers his first-hand knowledge of the life of the Lord gained through the senses of sight, hearing, and touch.

You can *possess in common* with John a fellowship with God the Father and His Son, Jesus Christ! As the Spirit of God guides you in your study of the Word, you can see/hear/touch the Lord Jesus through John's eyes/ears/hands witness to you! Take a minute and write out a favorite aspect of your "fellowship" with Jesus. What part of your walk with Jesus brings an overflowing joy (v. 4) to your life?

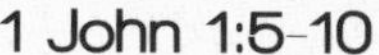

1 John 1:5-10

What is the writer saying?

How can I apply this to my life?

pray *For missionaries who will be separated from family and friends this Christmas season.*

John now begins his first subject (1:5-2:11), the truth that God is light. John tells us that those who want to have fellowship with God must *live in that light.* Christ taught this same truth (John 1:4 3:19; 8:12; 9:5; 12:46). Light is contrasted with darkness (v. 6) as a picture of the absolute nature of God. God is *all light* – thus completely holy – "in Him is no darkness at all" (v. 5).

Having identified God's character, John develops a series of "if" statements that alternate between right and wrong responses to God:

1.) First, some are saying they "have fellowship with him [God]," while they continue to *walk in darkness.* This is ridiculous and untrue: just as you cannot carry a light into a room and claim that it is still completely dark, so you cannot be carrying the *light from God,* while still walking in darkness (v. 6). Light and darkness cannot *share* the same space!

2.) A second "if" statement begins at verse 8. Some are claiming to have a character *free from a sin nature.* Not only are those folks liars, but they are self-deluded. Their claim demonstrates that the truth is not in them. Conversely, the believer who recognizes he is a sinner, and confesses his sins, will experience God's forgiveness (v. 9).

3.) A third group is claiming to have *never sinned* (v. 10). This is a claim that makes God out to be a liar, since the entire Gospel message rests on the fact that man is sinful and needs a Savior.

So then, we cannot walk in darkness, it destroys fellowship. But then, neither can we walk perfectly in the light (that is why God offers His forgiveness if we confess our sins to Him!). Thus, we learn that a part of our fellowship with God is to (1) seek a walk in the light, and (2) to confess our sins when we fail to walk as children of God's light. Well then, how can you have a better walk with God in the light? And what do you need to confess to God so that He might forgive you of it?

1 John 2:1-6

What is the writer saying?

How can I apply this to my life?

pray *Slovakia – For believers to overcome apathy and be consumed by a passion to please Christ.*

Chapter two brings a change of tone. John moves away from the confrontational instruction of the first chapter where he deals with the "if" situations involving doctrinal error. Now, using an affectionate tone, he is addressing his believing family members, referring to them as my "little children," a title he uses often (2:12, 28; 3:7,18; 4:4; 5:21).

He begins by offering a warning (v. 1) and a promise (v. 2). The warning: *Don't sin. That's why I'm writing.* The promise: *But if you do, God has provided a way for you to respond, so don't lose heart.* It is found in "Jesus Christ the righteous" who serves as the believer's "advocate" (v. 1), coming alongside as his defender and to plead his case in God's courtroom. There, He acknowledges the believer's guilt and presents His work on the cross as grounds for acquittal.

John makes it clear that what Christ did at Calvary was for all mankind, not just believers (v. 2). There He became man's "propitiation," where He removed the cause of separation between God and you, the sinner. The death of Jesus made it possible for a holy and righteous God to bestow mercy upon you, a believing sinner, on the basis of satisfied, divine justice upon your sin. Wow, think of it! A divine sacrifice provided by the Divine One, Jesus Christ the Son of God! Please understand: if there are those who do not experience the benefit of Christ's payment, the fault lies not in the sacrifice, but in the sinner who fails to accept it.

John then answers the question, *How can I be assured that Christ is my propitiation and my advocate?* in verses 3-6. It is found in a lifestyle of obedience to His commandments, and in walking as He walked.

Does your daily life reflect the truth that Jesus is your propitiation and your advocate? How is your obedience and daily walk? His great sacrifice should bring about a lifestyle pleasing to Christ. So then, what has changed in your lifestyle since you asked Jesus to save you?

1 John 2:7-11

What is the writer saying?

How can I apply this to my life?

pray *Papua New Guinea – For wisdom and God's guidance for the many Christians working in Parliament.*

John has been emphasizing "fellowship." A component of fellowship is love. A believer in fellowship with God, who is walking in the light of that fellowship (1:7), is walking in love toward his *brothers in Christ* (v. 10). Conversely, the believer out of fellowship with God will find that he cannot get along with God's people. John's point is that members of God's family are to love one another. To that end John writes an "old" (v. 7) and yet "new" (v. 8) commandment about Christian love.

God's command to love goes back to earlier books of the Bible (Leviticus 19:18, Deuteronomy 6:5), where man is commanded to love God and his neighbor. Jesus combined those in Matthew 22:34-40, stating that they summarized all the Law and the Prophets (thus, all the rest of the Old Testament). But now the "old" commandment is also "new," for Christ gave new meaning to and example of the word "love."

Notice also that love becomes "new" to believers as they exercise it in their own lives (v. 8). As Christ loved sacrificially, so should we. The darkness that enveloped us prior to salvation is "past" (v. 8), and "the true light [of Christ] now shineth" in our lives (v. 8).

John is giving us another way to evaluate the genuineness of our fellowship with God! The person, who claims to exist in God's light yet hates his brother, is in the dark (v. 9). However, the one who loves his brother (in actual actions, not merely in words) is in the light. Conversely, the brother-hater exists in darkness, and is in danger of stumbling over unseen obstacles, for he cannot see where he is going (v.11).

Take time to check out your *love-quotient.* How have you demonstrated a Christ-like, others-minded love to your brothers and sisters in Christ in recent days? This *love from God* seeks to serve others without demanding anything in return! Ask God to show you someone in need of some help. How can you be of service to them?

QT Thursday 18

1 John 2:12-17

What is the writer saying?

How can I apply this to my life?

pray *Praise God for sending "Emmanuel," God with us, to be our precious Savior (Matthew 1:23).*

A demonstrable love relationship is to exist among members of God's family. John now addresses these members, and does so by grouping them according to their spiritual status. He lists his instructions to them according to where they are in their Christian walk:

1.) "Little children" (2:12,13b). The COMMENCEMENT of the Christian Life. These are the newborns in the family of God. Their sins have been forgiven.

2.) "Young Men" (2:13-14). The CONFLICT of the Christian Life. Moving on to manhood does not come without a struggle. Learning how to handle the Word of God gives victory over the wicked one.

3) "Fathers" (13a). The CONSUMMATION of the Christian Life. These have now progressed to the level of spiritual fathers. They are people of spiritual maturity, having grown in their knowledge of Him.

Having identified their spiritual-growth status, he gives to all three groups this caution: "Love not the world, neither the things that are in the world" (v. 15). This is not the "world" for which Christ died, but the *world system* that is hostile to Christ. While this evil *world system* will *pass away* (v. 17), it continues to be deceptive and dangerous, using as its tools both "lust" and "pride" (v. 16).

So the caution is given that the believer must *abide* in his walk with God (abiding means to continually be *camping out* with God),, for it is always possible for him to be defeated by this evil system. The believer's defense is to continue to "doeth" of the "will of God" (v. 17).

At what *level* is your Christian walk? Since at every level the *world system* is a danger to you, are you doing that which brings spiritual victory? Are you abiding in the will of God and doing as commanded by the Word of God? What do you need to *do* today to *abide in God's will*?

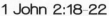

1 John 2:18-22

What is the writer saying?

How can I apply this to my life?

pray *Nicaragua – For a mighty work of salvation to occur among this country's military forces.*

In these verses John contrasts true and false teachings about Jesus. Those who claim fellowship with God are to pursue truth, not false teaching. One cannot believe lies and have fellowship with God.

John reminds his readers that the one called "antichrist" is coming (see Revelation 13:1-10; Matthew 24:5, 24). While that Antichrist has not yet appeared, John wants his readers to understand that they are in the beginnings of the last time period (v. 18) which ends when he appears. John says that since there are those with the *spirit of antichrist* already on the scene, that the "last time" has begun (essentially, this is the time period between the First Coming and the Second Coming of Christ).

John warns that many with *against-Christ* attitudes and doctrines are already on the scene. These "antichrists" are dangerous, for, though not believers, they are to be found in the visible church. They have characteristics like Christians ("they went out, that they might be made manifest that they were not all of us," v. 19) which is saying they were *church members* but not Christians!

They also are denying the deity of Jesus. They are saying that the man, Jesus, is not the Messiah of the Old Testament (v. 22, "Christ"). Their deviant teaching clearly brands them as liars (v. 22).

If Jesus is not God and the promised Messiah of the Old Testament, then His death could not pay the infinite price of our sin. In the same way, if Christ had not become a flesh-and-bone man, then He could not become our substitute when He died upon the Cross. Jesus had to be both God and man in one person to become our Savior!

Thank Jesus Christ, God the Son, for His great love for you, for it was His love that led Him to become a man so that He might also be your eternal Savior!

1 John 2:23-27

What is the writer saying?

How can I apply this to my life?

pray *Japan – For the Holy Spirit to help believers overcome ancestral influences by the study of God's Word.*

John's stress on the foundational doctrine of Christ continues. Error here, i.e. denying that Jesus is the Son of God, would invalidate one's claim to be a part of God's family. The point: the Son and the Father are inseparable, and must be accepted together (v. 23).

John offers some advice: when confronting the false claims of these antichrists, simply abide in the truths already learned (that is, Christ's incarnation, holy life, death, and resurrection). These great truths provide that which is vital for ongoing fellowship and communion (v. 24).

John then adds this: having embraced these great truths, you have the sure promise of eternal life (v. 25), which is far more than ongoing existence. It is a quality of life (not simply quantity) that can be experienced now. It is a promise Christ made repeatedly (John 3:15-16; 6:40; 17:3). Later John writes: "He that hath the Son hath life" (1 John 5:12).

John is reminding them of these truths due to the seductive nature of these false teachers, who are attempting to lead these believers into spiritual adultery – away from the truth into falsehood (v. 26).

Their protection is found in the "anointing" which they have "received" (v. 27). The "anointing" is receiving the Holy Spirit who uses the Word of God to teach them the truth. His indwelling presence provides the necessary spiritual discernment so that no child of God ever needs to be led away by error. The key, however, is found in the word "abide." It is that relationship that successfully counters false teaching.

So then, are you *abiding* in Christ? Abide means *to permanently 'stay-at-home' in your beliefs* about Christ. You too, must be warned by John's instructions. Be sure you have your doctrine of Christ straight. Write out a summary statement of your beliefs in Jesus Christ and then spend some time praising Him for who He is!

19 Sunday

1 John 2:28–3:3

What is the writer saying?

How can I apply this to my life?

pray *Pray for those who teach in your church to be faithful to the word, enthusiastic in their presentation, and compassionate toward the lost.*

John closes chapter two with a challenge, one based upon the certain return of the Savior. In anticipation of that great day, the believer is to live a life that permits him to stand before Christ and not be ashamed! The key: *to be constantly abiding in Him,* a word picture meaning *to stay-at-home with Jesus,* that is, *living in close fellowship with Him.*

With verse 29, John points out that true sonship ("born of him," v. 29) is expressed in Christ-like characteristics such as righteousness, love, and truth.

John excitedly writes "Behold" (3:1) as a command to *Pay Attention! Look at this truth until you have learned its implications!* The love that God bestows upon us in calling us His children is "exotic – foreign to the human heart – love" (Wuest). It is that *agape* love that is given without measure and does not ask for anything in return. It results in our enjoying a new status as the children of God.

In verse 2, John compares the present and future of God's people. Our present reality is the privilege of being His children. While the future is still somewhat dim, one great fact stands out – we will be like Christ, a transformation that will take place at His return. To *be like Him* includes both physical changes – we get a new *resurrection body* – and spiritual changes of purity (v. 3), no sin (v. 5), and righteousness (v. 7).

This future "hope" (v. 3) encourages us to cleanse ("purifieth") our lives as Jesus was "pure" in His life. As "partakers of the divine nature" (2 Peter 1:4), we possess the ability to show the attributes of Christ in our daily lives as we are enabled by the Holy Spirit who dwells in us (3:24).

Check yourself out. Since you are a child of God, does your life demonstrate a *pure life* to a watching world? What area of your life does the Holy Spirit want to further *purify*?

1 John 3:4-10

What is the writer saying?

How can I apply this to my life?

pray *Ghana – For evangelistic outreach in the northern region, which has had less exposure to the Gospel.*

John turns his attention from Christ's future appearing (v. 2), to His past appearing (v. 5). His first coming had two objectives: (1) to take away sins (vv. 4-6), and (2) to destroy the works of the devil (vv. 7-8). The sinning child of God is demonstrating a failure to understand or appreciate what Christ did for Him on the cross.

Carried further, a person born of God (v. 9) lives a habitually righteous life. Thus, a person living in sin is demonstrating that he has not been born into the family of God (v. 6). Both *sin* and *lawlessness* are used here. Sin means *to miss the mark.* Lawlessness implies the more serious offense of *purposely disregarding God's law.*

It is likely that the false teachers are playing down the seriousness of *minor* sins. Thus, John insists that any sin is rebellion against God. John's point: one who abides in Christ does not continually practice sin.

Similarly, one who habitually sins has not come to know God in a permanent relationship (v. 6). In fact, one who practices sin is of the devil (v. 8), the source of sin. From his fall (Isaiah 14:9-17; Ezekiel 28:12-14), Satan has been in revolt against God. We are not surprised that John here declares that it was the "purpose" of God (v.8) to destroy the works of the devil by means of Christ's incarnation.

John concludes that true believers cannot practice sin because God's seed of a new divine nature dwells within them (2 Peter 1:4). From that divine seed comes divine characteristics, which we are responsible to develop to spiritual maturity (vv. 8 & 9). It is this holy lifestyle that distinguishes God's children from Satan's children (v. 10).

So then, to which spiritual family do you belong? If you say you have been born into God's family, do you see the indicators of that new life? Are there divine characteristics of a pure life growing in your life? How about talking to God about an area of your life that needs some growing?

19 Tuesday

1 John 3:11-16

What is the writer saying?

How can I apply this to my life?

pray *Praise God for His faithfulness and protection in your life this year.*

Verse 10 introduces an additional trait of a genuine Christian: love for the brethren. This command is not new. Christ Himself presented it in John 13:34-35. Believers are to have an extra measure of love for other believers, especially when, in John's day, Christians would not worship the Roman emperors as gods, making them deserving of death. Commonly, Christian love for one another is vital for survival.

John develops his point by citing a negative example: Cain's lack of human brotherly love for his brother, Abel (v. 12, Genesis 4). Cain, whose evil works were influenced by Satan, killed Abel because Abel's works were righteous. *Don't be surprised,* John says, *if you experience such hatred,* for the world will always hate Christianity. The world hates Christians because the Christian message is offensive to it (v. 13).

John now contrasts a Christian's love for other Christians with the hate that the world directs toward them. He notes that one of the ways we know that we have passed from death unto life is "because we love the brethren" (v. 14). When this love is not evident in a believer, he needs to consider if he has genuinely been born into God's family!

John continues by observing that hatred is an indicator that one has not been born into God's family (v. 15). Hatred is incompatible with Christianity. John is echoing Christ's words in Matthew 5:21-22, where He equates hatred with murder. Verse 16 gives the positive contrast, i.e., a willingness, if need be, to lay down one's life for the brethren. Such is the extent of sacrifice that may be demanded of a Christian.

Loving sacrifice for one another ought to be the norm among believers. Think back, has there been a fellow Christian who has carried out some deed of sacrificial love on your behalf? Now *think around you,* is there some Christian that needs you to exercise sacrificial Christian love towards them? How can you begin acting as his Christian brother?

1 John 3:17-24

What is the writer saying?

How can I apply this to my life?

pray *Cuba – Increased freedom in the areas of Bible printing, importation and distribution.*

In verse 16 Jesus is presented as our model for true love – a love which is sacrificial. He is contrasted with the individual who claims to possess God's love, but who is unwilling to help a needy brother. He has the means, sees the need, but he *shuts* his heart, choosing not to help ("bowels," "compassion," heart, etc. – all references to the seat of one's emotions). It is a picture of one who has failed the test of love (v. 17).

Such behavior is to be avoided. Love is to be active, not simply verbal. True love is not hypothetical; rather it is demonstrated by "deed" (v. 18). Genuine, self-sacrificial love for fellow believers is proof of the genuineness of one's own position in God's family (v. 19a).

The remaining portion of verse 19 and verse 20 go together, and should be translated: "And we shall persuade our heart before Him, that if our hearts condemn us, God is greater than our hearts, and knows all things" (Hodges). Because the possibility exists that a conscientious believer may be plagued by unjustified guilt feelings, he can rest in John's word of comfort, that God, who is all-knowing, is also all-loving.

Being freed from an accusing conscience allows us to approach God with great boldness (v. 21). Such confidence brings an assurance that God has heard our prayer and will be answering as requested. There are some attached conditions: (1) we must be keeping His commandments; (2) we must be doing that which pleases Him; (3) we must believe in His Name, that is, in all He is; and (4) we must love one another (vv. 22-23).

The chapter closes with a return to the abiding principle that makes keeping Christ's commandments possible (v. 24).

Check out your love life. Negatively, have you recently shut out a fellow believer to whom you could have provided God-enabled, loving assistance? Positively, ask God (v. 22) to help you to see and then do that which is pleasing in His sight as you lovingly serve others today!

1 John 4:1-6

What is the writer saying?

How can I apply this to my life?

pray *Pray that thousands will be reached with the Gospel of Jesus Christ in 2009 all across the world.*

John argues that a person's heavenly sonship can be demonstrated by adherence to truth, especially concerning the Doctrine of Christ. With "many false prophets" in the world (v. 1), John warns that the veracity of a speaker must be checked; is he from God or Satan? Since, in John's day, the New Testament has not yet been completed, John states that true spirits will confess that Jesus is the Christ, the Messiah, while false spirits will not (vv. 2-3, see also 1 Corinthians 12:13). In John's day, it is the Gnostic heresy that fails this test. Today, this doctrinal deviation marks false cults. Heresy in this area affects other areas of Theology. Example: if Jesus is not the Christ, then the Bible is not inspired. Similarly, if Jesus was not the God-Man, then He was not an acceptable sacrifice for our sins, thereby invalidating our salvation.

John assures his "little children" that they have overcome the spirit of antichrist (v. 4). They have withstood the lure of false doctrine because the One in them (a reference back to the Holy Spirit; see 3:24; 4:2) is greater than the one indwelling the world.

In verse 4, John addresses his readers. In verse 5 he focuses on the heretics. They are clearly creatures of the satanic world system; thoroughly in tune with the direction Satan is taking it. They speak the world's language and find ready acceptance by the world.

In verse 6, John turns his attention to teachers of the truth. His claim: "We are of God," and those in tune with God would listen to men like John and the apostles whose message comes from God. Those deluded by the world and its thought patterns would not care to hear the truth.

John would want to warn you about false teachers and the lure of false doctrine. How can you rely on the *One in you* to aid you in *overcoming* the error that comes your way? The Bible is God's Word, the true message from God. Jesus Christ is God's Son and our Messiah.

1 John 4:7-12

What is the writer saying?

How can I apply this to my life?

pray *Pray for the faithfulness of those who evangelize and minister to those in your local prisons.*

This passage, one of the finest things ever written, begins another cycle of John's teaching, focusing on a genuine believer's display of love (see also 2:7-11; 3:10-24). The word "love" (*agape*) is used here, in various forms, thirteen times, plus twelve more times in tomorrow's selection.

John declares that love reveals God's essence: He is love (v. 8); it is His supreme quality. It summarizes all He says and does. Agape marks God's love for the world (John 3:16) and for sinners (Romans 5:8). It characterizes Christ's love for His church (Ephesians 5:25) and for individuals (Galatians 2:20). It is also the manner in which mankind is to love God.

He begins (v. 7) by calling his readers "beloved," for they have experienced God's love. That being the case, they should exhibit the same kind of love. Doing so demonstrates the genuineness of one's relationship with God. Notice that the opposite is also true. If this agape-type love does not exist in a person's life, such a person is giving evidence that a genuine relationship with God does not exist (v. 8).

In verse 9, we see an echo of John 3:16. God sent "His only begotten Son into the world," putting action to His words. His purpose: to provide eternal life for lost mankind. He was sent to be the "propitiation for our sins" (v. 10, that is Christ's death was the satisfaction of God's wrath upon our sin, Romans 3:25, 1 John 2:2). That love of God provides an example for His children. Just as God demonstrated His love toward us through Christ's incarnation and work on the cross, so should His children demonstrate love toward the rest of the family (v. 11).

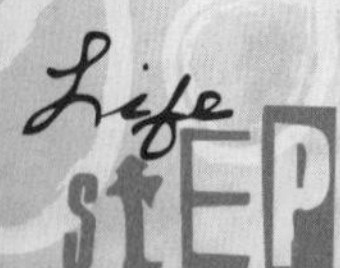

The Father has bestowed great love upon us. His love is a pattern we should follow. How about asking God to bring to mind someone to whom He would want you to bestow an act of this sort of divine love.

1 John 4:13-21

What is the writer saying?

How can I apply this to my life?

pray *Bolivia – Revival for churches who are growing in number but lack commitment in their lifestyle.*

Today John gives an additional test of a believer's relationship with the Father: the presence of the Holy Spirit (1 Corinthians 6:19). The Spirit is given to all believers at their salvation. He lives within the believer producing "fruit" (Galatians 5:22-23). He also "gifts" all believers (see 1 Corinthians 12). It is the outworking of these gifts that proves the Spirit's presence.

In verse 14. John testifies to his personal knowledge that the Father sent the Son into the world to provide God's offer of salvation to everyone. Verse 15 follows with a statement that *throws the doors open* to anyone who will walk through on God's terms: the acknowledgement and belief that Jesus Christ is His Son. Both John and his first readers have done exactly that: "We have known and believed" (v. 16).

Because a believer's relationship with the Father is confirmed by the presence of the Holy Spirit, he can stand before God with great confidence that "casteth out fear" (v. 18). What John is saying is that fear and love cannot co-exist. If fear is present, it is a rebuke to its possessor and an indicator that God's love has not truly captured his heart.

The inner working of the Holy Spirit declares that a true believer's heart has been captured by Christ. The result of the Spirit capturing a person's heart is that love will be put into practice (v. 21). Note that claiming to be a family member and saying, *I love God*, but failing to practice love, brands the claimant as a "liar" (v. 20).

Do you still have lingering fears about your own salvation, your own death, or the final judgment of God upon your sin? A key application here is that the Spirit will witness to your spirit that you are genuinely God's child. As such you now possess eternal life (not a final death!) and you have obtained a Savior from the coming judgment of sin! If these fears persist, ask God to allow His great love to cast out such fears!

1 John 5:1-8

What is the writer saying?

How can I apply this to my life?

pray *Austria – 80% of Austrians have been involved with the occult. Pray that the truth of the scripture would boldly go forth.*

Here John continues to point out that a genuine love for God should result in our love for our brother in Christ. Our brothers would be those who have also come into God's family having responded to "whosoever believeth that Jesus is the Christ" (v.1) (the Anointed One sent by God to be our Savior, 4:14). This same doctrinal test has been used earlier (2:22; 4:2, 3, 15) to distinguish true believers from false Gnostic teachers (see 1:1-4). All believers, therefore, have a common link to the Father through Jesus and a resultant love for one another.

That link is developed in verses 2-3. It looks back to three concepts featured in previous verses: love for God, love for His children, and love for His commands. John declares that one leads to another: loving God leads to loving God's people and obeying God's commands. We must recognize that keeping God's commands is a demonstration of our love for God and our faith in Christ as the Son of God (v. 5).

In verse 6, John begins discussing the person of Christ. He refutes Gnostic error by offering three infallible witnesses. First, the Holy Spirit: He descended on Jesus at His baptism in the form of a dove. Also, Christ Himself said that the Spirit's work was to witness of Him (John 15:26). Second, water: At the beginning of His ministry (His baptism) the Father identified Him as His Son (Matthew 3:13-17). Third, blood: A reference to the conclusion of His ministry (His crucifixion). Jesus did not receive "the Christ" (the anointing) at His baptism and lose it at the cross. Both at Jesus' baptism and crucifixion, the Father spoke as a witness to His Son's Deity.

The evidence has spoken. Jesus is the Christ, the anointed One. He has given us commands to obey, love one another and keep God's commands. Think of how you could practice (1) a love for God, (2) a love for the people of God, and (3) a love for His commandments!

20 Monday

QT

1 John 5:9-15

What is the writer saying?

How can I apply this to my life?

pray *United Kingdom – For God to create a thirst for and a commitment to God's word in the hearts of youth.*

John, continuing on his subject of witnesses to the truth of the Gospel, asks his readers to think through their sources of witnesses. While they have accepted testimony from human witnesses (v. 9a), John declares that the witness of God Himself (v. 9b) is much greater.

John now moves from the objective (a witness has been offered, v. 9b) to the subjective (it is necessary for us to place our faith in Jesus who has been presented, v. 10a). What God has done is of no value until accepted (v. 10b). Once accepted, there is a confirming inner "witness" of the Holy Spirit to support the evidence offered (v. 10a).

On the other hand, the one who rejects the gift God has offered is, in effect, calling God "a liar" (v.10b), thereby *impugning* God or challenging God's character as being false (v. 10).

John next cites the record (v. 11): God has given "us" (those that believe Jesus is the Christ, v. 1) eternal life. We now possess a life that will never end. It is found in a personal relationship with His Son (v. 11); if you have the Son (2:23; 2 John 9) you also have life. Conversely, without believing in Jesus there is no hope of eternal life (vv. 11-12).

Just as the Gospel of John concluded with John stating his purpose (John 20:31), John does the same here (v. 13). The Gospel brings people to faith; this letter helps believers, challenged by heresy, to know with confidence that they have followed the truth about Jesus Christ (v. 13).

Knowing we are in God's family makes it natural for us to pray to God (v. 14). When we pray according to His will, we can be confident that He will answer (see also 1 John 3:22, John 14:14; 15:7).

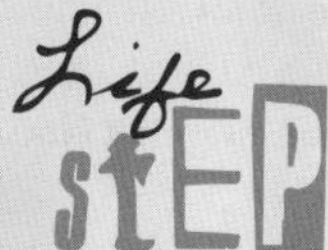

Pause in gratefulness to God, not only for salvation offered and accepted, but also for the wonderful resource of prayer! All because of His Son, the Anointed One, our Savior Jesus Christ!

1 John 5:16-21

What is the writer saying?

How can I apply this to my life?

pray *Argentina – Funding for students with a desire to study God's word at camps and Bible schools.*

Two scenarios are presented (vv. 16-17); a "sin not unto death" and a "sin unto death." Since John emphasizes the first, let us begin there.

A brother seeing another brother in sin, should pray for him, knowing that such is God's will. Since the term "brother" refers to Christians, a "sin not unto death" refers to a genuine believer who has chosen to sin. Note that while God, for a time, will endure his sin, God will not allow him to sin indefinitely! The observant brother should pray for the one sinning, requesting that God restore him to proper fellowship without having to end his "life" on earth by taking him to his eternal home to heaven.

The "sin unto death" does not elicit a request to pray. This is God's business alone. While commentators are divided on this, it quite likely refers to physical death (and not a spiritual, eternal death) and is related to believers. We note that because of sin, Old Testament believers like Moses and Aaron experienced death (Numbers 20:12, Deuteronomy 3:26-27), as did Ananias and Sapphira in the New Testament (Acts 5:1-11). While a child of God cannot commit sin that would nullify his salvation, he can commit sin so grievous to God that God would choose to end his life and call him home prematurely!

John closes with a summary: (1) born again ones do not practice sin (v. 18, see 3:9); (2) we may know with certainty that we belong to God and not Satan's world system (v. 19); and (3) God has given us "eternal life," by means of the coming of Jesus Christ into the world (v. 20).

His final instruction is to "keep yourselves from idols" (v. 21), that is, anything that would remove God from His proper place in our hearts.

Has God made you aware of and then burdened your heart for a genuine Christian brother or sister who is openly sinning against God? Then, would you begin to earnestly pray for this brother requesting that God bring about his restoration to a proper walk with Him?

20 Wednesday

2 John 1-6

What is the writer saying?

How can I apply this to my life?

pray *Cayman Islands – For Christians to continue to hold fast to the Christian values in the midst of wealth and materialism.*

In the introductory verses (vv. 1-3) of this little epistle, John, the author, calls himself "the elder." The emphasis is on age, not office, though in John's case both apply – he is the lone remaining apostle. We also meet the recipient, "the elect lady" which is a title of the church as a whole and "her children" a reference to its membership. Thus, this letter is intended to be circulated to all local churches. That is true of some of Paul's letters. Hence, this letter also applies to our present-day local churches.

John's greeting is similar to other New Testament writers, and includes the triplet of grace, mercy, and peace (v. 3). But it is also different, for it is expressed as a prediction (future tense) and not as a wish, as in many other cases. The church and its members receive these blessings from both Father and Son (v. 3), administered with both truth and love.

John then moves to a word of commendation (v. 4), for he was rejoicing that as he came in contact with her (the church's) children, he found them "walking (continuously) in truth," just as God has commanded. Next he turns (v. 5) to the immediate reason behind his writing. He reiterates his constant *theme song*, "that we love one another." This command has been in place from the beginning and, in fact, was stated by the Lord Himself (John 13:34-35; 1 John 3:11). It must, however, be exercised within the guidelines of obedience. It must be put into action – action that is designed for the good of one another. Thus, John's charge is that they "walk after" this command (v. 6).

How has your conduct with your Christian friends resulted in onlookers rejoicing in your love for one another? What might you plan to do with your friends so that John's "love one another" commandment to you is obvious to an onlooker?

QT

Thursday 20

2 John 7-12

What is the writer saying?

How can I apply this to my life?

pray *Pray for those who teach in your church to be faithful to the Word.*

Behind John's reason for his exhortation to his readers to "love one another" (vv. 5-6) is the presence of false teachers who are spreading heresy in the church. While believers are to love one another, they are not to extend such hospitality (v. 10) to those who would not acknowledge that Jesus came in the flesh (v. 7). John selects this cardinal doctrine of the incarnation as the key test of a false teacher (v. 7). To reject this doctrine, marks a person as a deceiver and an antichrist.

John offers a warning and a command (v. 8): *Watch out! Be on guard.* Why? There are false teachers who have the potential of making useless all the work that has gone into building the Church.

John's explanation for this stern warning is that some are not standing firm on the basic teaching that Jesus is the Christ, the Messiah. They are instead *going beyond* ("transgresseth") that teaching, as are the Gnostics in their *enlightenment.* John declares that these do not have God (v.9). On the other hand, the one who stays within the bounds of that which was originally taught, has both Father and Son (v. 9). *Therefore,* says John, *if someone comes to you with a false teaching, they are not to be helped in any way* (v. 10). If you fail to follow such directions and offer some form of hospitality, you become a partaker of his evil deeds. While love is to be expressed among believers, such love must be withheld from the heretic. The believer should not give even passive or unintended cooperation to the false teacher.

Do you know someone who teaches a false doctrine? First of all, you should be praying that they would come to know the truth. Secondly, while you must continue to have a love for that individual, you must act in a manner that does not assist them in spreading their false teachings.

3 John 1-8

What is the writer saying?

How can I apply this to my life?

pray *Mexico – Protection of believers in Chiapas and Oaxaca who are persecuted for their faith.*

John again refers to himself simply as the "elder" (see 2 John 1). The recipient is Gaius, apparently a prosperous believer who is a leader in a local church. The subject is hospitality and traveling preachers. John expresses his love for Gaius (v. 1), his concern for his health (v. 2), and the joy he experienced in hearing that Gaius, probably one of his converts, is walking "in the truth" (v. 3). There is no greater joy (v. 4).

Verses 5-8 are a review of how traveling teachers are to be cared for, and Gaius is commended for his example. If the traveler is one who shares similar convictions, hospitality is to be generously extended. Such a practice is a demonstration of faithfulness to God (v. 5) and makes the doer a *partner in the enterprise* of Christianity ("fellowhelpers," v. 8)

The text makes it clear (v. 6) that many traveling preachers have come Gaius's way. Later, these testified of his love towards them (v. 6). John encourages Gaius to send them on their way with a generous offering – giving as if you are giving directly to God. By his love, they are motivated to minister for "his name's sake," (v. 7). Their faithfulness is to be supported in every way possible by like-minded Christians, for the pagan world to which they are going has no obligation to do so.

The support of missionaries is not optional. As believers, we are responsible to provide for those who take salvation's message to the lost. Our assistance makes us co-workers with them in "the truth" (v. 8).

How are you doing in this matter? Does your conduct make it evident that you are *faithfully doing whatsoever* (v. 5) you can to *send them forth in a worthy manner* (v. 6)? Gaius's record is clear, and he is commended. What can you do this month (and every month after!) as a "fellowhelper," so that this commendation can be extended to you?

3 John 9-14

What is the writer saying?

How can I apply this to my life?

pray *Pray for the youth of your church to be godly testimonies at school and in their communities.*

In contrast to Gaius (v. 1), whose behavior is commendable, we meet Diotrephes, a man whose behavior is shameful. His love for the "preeminence" (*desiring to be first,* v. 9, meaning he is jealous of the influence of others like John) is causing great difficulty in the church.

John has written earlier to Gaius's church (perhaps a reference to 2 John, likely carried to the churches and then taught through by traveling teachers). This letter has been rejected by Diotrephes (v. 9). Diotrephes's opposition to apostolic authority results in John making it clear that he intends to come and expose his actions as rebellion (v. 10).

John's indictment of Diotrephes is two-fold. First, his words: he spoke maliciously against John and his company. Second, his actions: he refused to accept the traveling Bible teachers that John had sent to the church. He also had acted to prevent anyone else in the church, like Gaius, from helping them, even to the point of excommunication (v. 10).

Diotrephes's actions were so forceful that John feels it necessary to exhort Gaius to continue his practice of genuine hospitality; Gaius is not to give in to Diotrephes's pressure. Rather, Gaius is to "follow [imitate] ... that which is good" (v. 11). In so doing, he would demonstrate his genuine relationship with God (see also 1 John 2:29; 3:9; 4:7; 5:1, 18).

A fourth character is now introduced, Demetrius. He apparently is the carrier of the letter to Gaius and is likely one of John's Bible teachers. John himself gives evidence that Demetrius is worthy of Gaius's hospitality (v. 12).

Gaius, Diotrephes and Demetrius. One is a wealthy, yet generous church leader. One is a self-promoting church problem. One is a worthy teacher of Bible truth. If John were here today, how would he characterize your life? To what evidence would John point to make his case?

Although Ezra is classified with the Historical Books and Haggai with the Prophetic Books of the Old Testament, the two books should be studied together. The principle subject of both books is the *rebuilding of the temple* at Jerusalem (the temple had been destroyed and the Jews taken into exile by the Babylonians in 586 B.C.). Ezra begins his ministry (458 B.C.) as a priest and scribe of Judah some sixty years after Haggai is called as a prophet (520 B.C.) to encourage the Jewish people who have returned to Jerusalem to finish the rebuilding of the temple (516 B.C.) at Jerusalem. Haggai had been with Zerubbabel, the governor, when he is allowed to return to Jerusalem (538 B.C.) by the Persian king, Cyrus. The connection between the two men is clearly seen when we realize that the first half of Ezra's book is Ezra's history of the return of the Jews to Jerusalem (Ezra is recording events from before his time – 538 B.C. to 515 B.C.). Here, he also mentions Haggai's important historical role in helping Zerubbabel; see Ezra 5:1-2.

Almost a century before Solomon's Temple was destroyed by the Babylonians in 586 B.C., the prophet Isaiah foretold that a king named Cyrus would order its rebuilding (Isaiah 44:28). In 539 B.C., Cyrus, king of Persia, conquered the city of Babylon and the Babylonian empire in accordance with the prophecy of Isaiah 45:1-4. Daniel, still serving in the royal court after sixty-seven years of captivity, likely showed Cyrus his name in Isaiah's prophecy (Daniel 6:28; 10:1).

A year or so after Cyrus decreed (538 B.C.) the rebuilding of the Jewish temple at Jerusalem, an expedition of about fifty thousand exiled Jews arrived in Jerusalem under the leadership of Zerubbabel. Zerubbabel was the grandson of the last Jewish king of the independent kingdom of Judah; Jehoiachin (598 B.C.). Jehoiachin was taken into exile by Nebuchadnezzar and remained imprisoned at Babylon for another thirty-seven years! The foundation of the new temple was laid in 536 B.C., about the year Daniel died.

However, there was opposition by non-Jewish, local people to the rebuilding of the temple, which resulted in a decree of a succeeding Persian king that halted the work on the temple for fifteen years. Then the prophets Haggai and Zechariah were raised up by God as prophets who delivered several messages of rebuke and encouragement over a period of four months. Four years later, the second or rebuilt temple was completed just seventy years after the destruction of the first or Solomon's temple.

After a fifty-seven year gap in Ezra's history, Ezra picks up the story in the book of Ezra with his own return (458 B.C.) to Jerusalem with a second group of Jews, perhaps five thousand people (1,500 men identified in Ezra 8). Ezra brings needed supplies as well as leaders who could help reestablish moral, spiritual, and administrative procedures. The book of Ezra then records the history of Ezra's *spiritual reforms* at Jerusalem, and then ends after recording the resulting *revival* that takes place at Jerusalem in 456 B.C.

The story of Ezra's ministry picks up again some sixteen years later in the book of Nehemiah after Nehemiah had completed rebuilding the wall of the city of Jerusalem. Afterwards, Nehemiah the Governor and Ezra the Priest/Scribe together bring a second revival to Jerusalem! Thus, Ezra's own ministry to the returned Jews at Jerusalem extends from Ezra 7 (538 B.C.) to Nehemiah 10 (440 B.C.). Besides his effective ministry of God's word, he led two great prayers of national confession, recorded in Ezra 9 and Nehemiah 9.

Ezra 1:1-11

What is the writer saying?

How can I apply this to my life?

pray *Ukraine – Wisdom and courage for full-time workers hampered by restrictions that limit growth.*

The book of Ezra begins by repeating the last two verses of 2 Chronicles. Thus, the events in Ezra immediately follow 2 Chronicles. This also is the basis for our opinion that Ezra wrote both Chronicles and the book of Ezra. In Chronicles, Ezra gives a summary of the history of the world, beginning with Adam, to the exile of the Jews to Babylon. Chronicles ends with Cyrus the king of Persia decreeing that the exiled Jews could return to their homeland (538 B.C.). The book of Ezra picks up here and continues Jewish history to Ezra's own ministry in 456 B.C.

"The first year of Cyrus" (v.1) is the year that Cyrus, king of Persia, becomes king at Babylon (5:13) by conquest. The decree of Cyrus includes the words, "The Lord God of heaven" (v. 2). This is a Hebrew designation for God. Its use by Cyrus indicates scriptural counsel by a Jewish adviser – probably the aged Daniel (Daniel 6:28).

The proclamation of Cyrus offers all Jewish captives the opportunity of returning to their homeland of Judah (v. 3). Although only a remnant of less than fifty thousand leaves, many others willingly gave of their substance.

"Sheshbazzar" (v. 8) is a Chaldean name for Zerubbabel. Zerubbabel is called "the prince of Judah" (v. 8) because he is of the royal family of King David. Yet he is trusted by Cyrus to be the Persian governor at Jerusalem. He is also listed in the genealogy of Jesus (Matthew 1:12).

Some of the "vessels of the house of the Lord" (v. 7) are taken to Babylon in each of the three attacks upon Jerusalem (Daniel 1:2, 2 Kings 24:13 and 2 Kings 25:13-15).

The comforting message that comes through to us in the return of Israel to the Land is: God always keeps His promises. Since our God continues today, what promise of His do you need to trust in today?

Ezra 2:1, 64-70

What is the writer saying?

How can I apply this to my life?

pray *For safety, salvation decisions, and consecration commitments during Christian winter camps.*

During this period in Israel's history, the twelve tribes are scattered throughout the Persian Empire (Esther 3:8, 8:9). "The people of Israel" (v. 2) and "all Israel" (v. 70) include members of all twelve tribes. Those who return are listed in various categories in verses 2-63. Verse 2 names the leaders. Then in verses 3-19 are the families from Jerusalem. Next (vv. 20-35) are the returnees from other cities. Verses 36-39 name the priests, followed in 40-42 by the other Levites. The "Nethinim" of verses 43-54 are descendants of non-Jews who were appointed by King David to do the maintenance work of the temple area. They eventually became Jews by practice and intermarriage. They are grouped with the children of Solomon's servants (vv. 55-58). Various groups who could not trace their ancestry are listed in verses 59-63.

"Offered freely for the house of God" – This is the third time the givers' willingness is mentioned (2:68; 1:4, 6). Whenever God wants to build a structure for fellowship, there are willing people. When He directs the building of the tabernacle, there are so many givers they have to be ordered to stop giving (Exodus 35:2; 36:5-7)! When King David gathered materials for the temple, he used national funds (1 Chronicles 29:2). But when the people saw him also giving his own goods (29:3), they wanted to have a part (29:6-9). There were also willing givers when the temple needed repairs (2 Kings 12:4). This giving was in excess of their tithe that supported the Levites and was required by law.

New Testament giving for Christians also begins with the *willing heart* (2 Corinthians 8:3, 12) that first *gives oneself* (2 Corinthians 8:5). God desires to use our yielded lives and possessions to build His holy habitation on earth (1 Corinthians 3:9; Ephesians 2:20-22; 1 Peter 2:5). Have you willingly given your *heart* and *life* to God? As a part of your fellowship, how can you financially help other believers in need?

21 Tuesday

Ezra 3:1-13

What is the writer saying?

How can I apply this to my life?

pray *New Zealand – Pray for a great harvest of souls in urban areas where open air teams minister.*

Verses 1-6 tell of the reinstatement of some of the worship procedures prescribed by the Law of Moses. The first day of the seventh month (v. 1) is a special Sabbath that is announced by the blowing of trumpets (Leviticus 23:24). The first order of business is to build the Altar of Sacrifice so that animal sacrifices to God could again be offered. The Altar of Sacrifice is a large fire-box on which the priests place sacrifices. It is to be positioned in front of the temple.

The full observance of the Day of Atonement needs to await the completion of the temple. Only some aspects of the Feast of Tabernacles (v. 4) are observed here. The Feast of Tabernacles is an eight-day time of living outdoors in tents. It is a reminder of Israel's journey, under God's care, in the wilderness and it is to be a preparation of the Day of Atonement when the high priest would sprinkle the blood of their sacrifices on the Mercy Seat in the temple.

It required more than a year (v. 8) to gather all of the materials needed to begin reconstruction of the temple mount area. The laying of the foundation (v. 10) is celebrated by playing instruments and by antiphonal singing (chanting alternating phrases by a choir and an assembly) from the Psalms (verse 11 is from Psalm 136).

The foundation for the rebuilt temple is laid (v. 11) fifty-two years after the destruction of Solomon's Temple. Many of the older men who had seen the first temple recognized that their replacement temple would be far less spectacular (Haggai 2:3). The younger generation refuses to let this dampen the celebration and continues to praise God.

The intent of beautiful music is to enhance the rejoicing of believers as they worship the Lord. Are you allowing disappointments in your life to rob you of your rejoicing in the goodness and mercy of God in your life?

Ezra 4:1-5

What is the writer saying?

How can I apply this to my life?

pray *Bermuda – Pray for unity among believers so that God's agenda can remain the focus of their hearts.*

To understand this passage, we must begin with an explanation of who were the "people of the land" (v. 4). First, note that around 700 BC, the Assyrians had defeated the Northern Kingdom of Israel and forced its people to live elsewhere in their empire. They then repopulated the land to the north of Judah and Jerusalem with heathen people from various other conquered nations (2 Kings 17:24). An exiled, idolatrous priest of Israel was sent back to Israel to teach the new inhabitants "the manner of the God of the land" (2 Kings 17:27-28). The result was a further mixing of the worship of the true God with that of several other gods so that "they feared the Lord, and served their own gods" (2 Kings 17:33, 41).

These people, with their mixture of religions, are the "adversaries" of Ezra 4:1. They had intermingled with and then dominated the few Israelites left by the Assyrians, and later the Babylonians, (Jeremiah 39:10). Since they now outnumber these newly returned exiles of Israel, their plan is to again intermingle with and dominate this new group. Their line is *we sacrifice to the same God that you do, so let's join together in rebuilding the temple* (v. 2). The answer by the Jewish leadership is, *King Cyrus sent us to do this work and we will do it ourselves.* The decree of Cyrus said the re-building of the house of the Lord God of Israel is to be done by His people (v. 3).

Failing at the tactic of infiltration, the "adversaries" set upon a program of intimidation (3:3; 4:4) and political maneuvering (v. 5). They are successful in delaying the construction for about fifteen years.

Satan still uses the tactics of infiltration, intimidation and political maneuvering to disrupt God's program on earth. We work and live in the world, but are we cooperating with it in spiritual matters? When it comes to serving God with righteous holiness, are we separated from the world?

Ezra 4:6-16

What is the writer saying?

How can I apply this to my life?

pray *Philippines – For seminary graduates willing to work among the rural poor.*

Persia, as a world empire, lasted from its defeat of Babylon in 539 B.C. until its own defeat by *Alexander the Great* in 331 B.C. The Persian Empire was ruled by ten kings. The eighty year span of the book of Ezra involves the first five kings. The first, *Cyrus*, dies in battle in 530 B.C. His son, *Cambyses*, commits suicide about 522 B.C. The usurper *Gaumata* seizes the throne for seven months. Then the third, *Darius the Great*, rules until 486 B.C, when his son, *Xerxes* (*Ahasuerus* of Esther), is enthroned. The fifth ruler is *Artaxerxes* who begins to rule in 465 B.C. and reigns forty years. His name is found in Ezra 7:7 and Nehemiah 2:1.

Most Persian rulers have a *throne title* and a *personal name*. Bible and secular history record these designations in Hebrew, Greek, and Aramaic. So there may be two or three designations for any one king.

What then is the identity of the kings to whom the letters of verses 6 and 7 are written? The book of Ezra dates from sixty years after the completion of the temple in 516 B.C. The prominent kings *Ahasuerus* (of Esther) and *Artaxerxes* of Ezra 7 reign during those sixty years. Since Ezra records that these two letters cause the fourteen year delay in completing the temple, then *Ahasuerus* of verse 6 and *Artaxerxes* of verse 7 are alternate names for *Cambyses* and *Gaumata*, who rule during the fourteen year delay. Don't allow the repeated use of these names later cause concern; a later king often used a *court name* of a popular, earlier king!

Since these letters (vv. 6, 7) to the Persian kings are from the enemies of returned people of Israel, then Ezra's purpose is to illustrate the persistence of Israel's enemies in delaying reconstruction of the temple and, afterwards, the rebuilding of the city and its walls.

Satan's very name means *adversary*. So don't be surprised if Satan uses evil people to oppose you. Ask the Lord for deliverance!

Ezra 4:17-24

What is the writer saying?

How can I apply this to my life?

pray *Nigeria – For the HIV/AIDS epidemic in Nigeria. If the epidemic continues, by the year 2020, 60% of Nigerians will have HIV/AIDS.*

The text clearly states that adversaries of the Jewish builders write a letter to the Persian king, Artaxerxes (mentioned four times in Ezra 4). That letter (vv.12-16) makes no mention of "the house of God [the temple] which is at Jerusalem" (v. 24). It speaks of the city and its walls. The king's reply (vv. 21, 22) likewise does not mention the house of God. His reply orders that the city not be rebuilt until the king gives further command. On the other hand, the earlier decree by Cyrus says nothing of the city or its walls, but only authorizes the re-building of "the house of God at Jerusalem" (6:3). By Artaxerxes's answer, we could speculate that he does not completely trust these adversaries of the Jews. We could also conclude that the Jews, had they feared God and not their adversaries, could have continued building the temple! Authorized by the king's reply, the adversaries show the reply to the Jews. The letter motivates the adversaries to stop the work in Jerusalem "by force and power" (v. 23).

There are fourteen years and three changes of Persian kings between the laying of the foundation of the rebuilt temple (3:10) and "the second year of the reign of Darius king of Persia" (v. 24). By letters and by hired counselors, it is the practice of the adversaries to persuade each new monarch to stop the work of the returned Jews. We are not told how much is accomplished on the temple and the city during these fourteen years. Nor do we know how much is destroyed "by force and power." We do know that all "work of the house of God" stops until God raises up Haggai, Zachariah, and Ezra to encourage the people to complete the task.

In the work of the Lord, it often appears that the adversary has the power to stop God's work. Remember that God always foreknows every hindrance and is able to overcome all obstruction! What is hindering you from getting on with God's work?

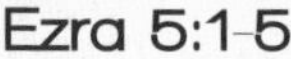

Ezra 5:1-5

What is the writer saying?

How can I apply this to my life?

pray *Thank the Lord for His all-encompassing forgiveness and compassion (Psalm 103:10 – 13).*

The city of Jerusalem, along with its magnificent temple, had been destroyed by the Babylonians in 586 B.C. We are now considering the situation in that city in 520 B.C. There was some past activity of cleaning away rubble in the temple area (3:1-10). The foundation of a new temple (likely the *plaza area* upon which the temple was to be built) and some preliminary construction on the temple itself (4:1-3) were done fifteen years ago. Sadly, there was no further work on rebuilding the temple.

There are now nice homes surrounding the rubble of the city occupied by fifty thousand Jews who have returned to their home land. They have had some good harvest years after their arrival from exile sixteen years ago, but recently there has been drought and dearth.

The leaders are discouraged, and the people are pessimistic. Suddenly, the Lord raises up from among them two prophets, Haggai and Zechariah, who tell the governor Zerubbabel and the high priest Jeshua (alternate English spelling of "Joshua") that they have a word from the Lord (Haggai 1:1). God tells them why they are having poor crops and what to do about it (see Haggai 1:2-11). Zerubbabel and Jeshua recognize that Haggai and Zechariah are God's true prophets, and within four weeks they have the people hard at work rebuilding the temple, while Haggai assures them that the Lord is with them (Haggai 1:12-15).

All this activity arouses the adversaries of the Jews, who promptly report it to Tatnai (Tattenai), the recently appointed Persian satrap (provincial governor). He comes to Jerusalem to investigate the accusations of the adversaries.

Have you become spiritually lethargic and discouraged in doing the work to which God has directed you? What do you need to do to be like Zerubbabel and Jeshua, who began again to work?

Ezra 5:6-17

What is the writer saying?

How can I apply this to my life?

pray *Jamaica – For Jamaican believers to have greater access to and interest in Christian resource materials.*

When Cyrus established the Persian Empire, as much as possible, he utilized the governmental structures in place, demanding homage and tribute by military control. After his death, succeeding Persian kings faced a series of rebellions by the subjugated rulers. Darius successfully quelled these uprisings and removed the leaders. He structured twenty administrative regions and appointed trusted Persian staffs, each headed by a governor (satrap). Tatnai (v. 6) is the governor of a region that extends from the Euphrates River on the East to the Mediterranean Sea on the West. Interestingly, his region approximated the Kingdom of David and Solomon at its height.

The Lord gives Zerubbabel just the right words for answering Tatnai's question. Basically, he summarizes the five hundred year history of the temple at Jerusalem, from Solomon to the present, in a straight forward manner. Note that Zerubbabel uses his Persian name, Sheshbazzar.

Several months would pass in forwarding the recommendations of Tatnai's letter to Darius. During that time, work on the temple proceeds rapidly. Less than a month after building resumes, Haggai receives a second message from the Lord (Haggai 2:1-9). He re-emphasizes that they are doing the Lord's work, and the Lord is with them. A few days later, the word of the Lord comes to the prophet Zechariah. His message is a call to repentance and a warning not to follow the rebellious ways of their fathers (Zechariah 1:1-6).

Perhaps you, like Zerubbabel, can explain God's directing in your life to those unsaved people of importance around you! How can they be shown the good hand of God who has been a help to you?

22 Monday

Ezra 6:1-12

What is the writer saying?

How can I apply this to my life?

pray *Germany – For new and effective ways of reaching the youth for Christ.*

Darius, king of Persia, follows the suggestion of Tatnai, one of his governors, and has the Persian government record checked. Records are found (v. 3) that confirm the explanation given to Tatnai by Zerubbabel is true. In verses 3-5, Darius quotes from the decree of Cyrus, furnishing details that add to our knowledge of that decree.

In his decree to Tatnai, Darius goes further than Cyrus. First, the Jewish leaders are to have no governmental interference (vv. 6-7). Next, the decree makes Tatnai responsible for supplying everything needed to build the temple (v. 8). The funds are to be supplied from the tribute collected from the inhabitants of Tatnai's province. The very adversaries who have been obstructing its progress must now pay to have the temple completed. Further, they must furnish the animals for sacrifice and sustain the builders with wheat, salt, wine, and oil (v. 9).

Why is there such urgency in the decree of Darius? Verse 10 indicates that he believes the success of his dynasty depends upon the prayers that will be offered at the temple. Darius wants to be certain that the God of Israel is on his side! By pronouncing the precise manner in which an obstructer of the building of the temple will be executed, Darius adds power to the warning. Anyone who would even consider obstructing can clearly envision his fate. The decree even invokes the wrath of God upon future kings who "alter and to destroy this house of God which is at Jerusalem."

A principle reason why Satan is infuriated against God and His people is because he is the perpetual loser. As we see in today's passage, his apparently successful strategies eventually end up furthering the program of God on earth! Be careful, for Satan will never stop being the adversary our adversary! Are you facing barriers? How can God turn these barriers into milestones of progress?

Ezra 6:13-22

What is the writer saying?

How can I apply this to my life?

pray *Czech Republic – For the organization and funding needed to start a national Christian radio network.*

Here we see Ezra giving a historical account of the *team-ministry* of the two prophets, Haggai and Zechariah. The book of Haggai consists of the four messages he prophesies (v. 14) to Israel. The first message is to get the construction started. The next three messages are delivered during the first three months of building. He likely continues ministering during the four years of construction. Zechariah brings a message between Haggai's second and third. Then shortly after Haggai's fourth, he begins a series of prophecies about God's future purposes for Jerusalem. His theme is, "...the Lord... shall yet choose Jerusalem" (Zechariah 1:17; 2:12; 3:2). Later, Zechariah prophesies of the first and second comings of Messiah.

One might ask, *Why is Artaxerxes named in the sequence at the end of verse 14?* He doesn't become king until fifty years after the temple is completed. Perhaps the answer is found in "the commandment of the God of Israel" (v. 14) prophesied in Isaiah 44:28. He charges Cyrus to build the city of Jerusalem and its temple, which God considers to be one project. God would always use Jerusalem and the temple together. Neither Cyrus nor Darius mentions the city in his decree. But the Artaxerxes of chapter 4 does. He orders the building of the city to cease "until another commandment shall be given from me" (4:21). That may be why God brings Artaxerxes into the picture before his time.

The temple is completed in 516 B.C., exactly seventy years after the destruction of Solomon's temple, in 586 B.C. Worship resumes, but complete observance awaits the building of the city (Nehemiah 8:17).

Like King Cyrus and King Saul (1 Samuel 15:13), we think we please the Lord when we perform the parts of His directives that we choose. We have difficulty learning that in His eyes, partial obedience is total rebellion. Are you completing all that God wants you to do?

Ezra 7:1-10

What is the writer saying?

How can I apply this to my life?

pray *Bolivia – For boldness and integrity as national leaders attempt to shut down the cocaine industry.*

We have now moved ahead in time to the days of Ezra. We begin at Babylon, controlled by Persia, and proceed to Jerusalem in the year 458 B.C. The temple, completed fifty-eight years ago, sits among the rubble of the city, destroyed 128 years before. The adversaries have thwarted efforts to rebuild the city. The leaders who brought fifty thousand returned captives here seventy-eight years ago are now gone. Worship is mechanical and half-hearted. The Jewish people are in a serious state of spiritual decline.

Therefore, the Lord God of Israel has sent His next choice servant, Ezra the priest, "a ready scribe in the law of Moses" (v. 6), to Jerusalem. Ezra brings with him priests, Levites, singers and temple workers (v. 7).

Darius, the Persian king who authorizes the completion of the temple, is succeeded by his son Xerxes, who then reigns twenty-eight years. Xerxes is King Ahasuerus of the book of Esther, who took beautiful Esther for his queen, twenty-one years before. Her kinsman and adoptive father, Mordecai, saved the king's life and became prime minister of the Persian Empire. Mordecai and Esther were then major influences upon the government of the king of Persia (Esther 8:15; 9:4, 29).

When Artaxerxes (grandson of Ahasuerus), of today's passage, becomes king about seven years before, likely there remained a favorable influence for the good of the Jews. This results in Artaxerxes sending a beneficial decree (v. 6) with Ezra to the Jews at Jerusalem.

Verse 10 tells of the steps Ezra takes to be a teacher of God's Word. First, he applies his heart to seeking out what God has to say. Second, he makes certain that he is *doing* in his own life the things he was going to teach. Third, he teaches others what God has said. Are you seeking to know God's Word? Are you also endeavoring to *do* it?

QT

Thursday 22

Ezra 7:11-28

What is the writer saying?

How can I apply this to my life?

pray *Aruba – Praise the Lord for this country's full religious freedom. Pray for a harvest of souls.*

By royal decree (vv. 12-26), Artaxerxes offers an *all expense paid* trip back to the Promised Land to all the "people of Israel" (v. 13). Sadly, only a few, about five thousand, respond. Amazingly, the king, his counselors, and any of the people of Babylon who also chose to participate, "freely offered unto the God of Israel, whose habitation is in Jerusalem" (v. 15). The priests are especially noted for their generosity.

Artaxerxes displays unbelievable confidence in Ezra. He gives him a *blank check* with authority to fill in the amount (vv. 18-23)! Ezra is even given authority to appoint magistrates and judges (v. 25) and is specifically directed to teach the Word of God (v. 25). Ezra is given authority to confiscate, banish, imprison and even to execute (v. 26)!

The king's purpose is to have an offering brought "unto the God of Israel." Artaxerxes mentions "God" sixteen times! He calls Him "the God of heaven" four times (vv. 12, 21, 23), indicating he acknowledges that the "God of Israel" (v. 15) is supreme Ruler over all other gods and over all judgment upon earth (v. 23). Eight times he speaks of "thy" and "your God" (that is, Ezra's) but, sadly, never does he say *my* God (that is, Artaxerxes's).

Artaxerxes's purpose is also to ensure the blessing of the "God of heaven" upon his realm and his sons (v. 23). In accordance with God's promise to Abraham (Genesis 12:3), God does bless Artaxerxes! Artaxerxes reigns forty years. His realm prospers more than one hundred years.

In verses 27 and 28, we have Ezra's response as he praises God by acknowledging that all the king had bestowed was from "the Lord God."

When we understand that each of us is on a divine mission and that the "hand of the Lord" is also upon us, how can we not be encouraged and overflowing with thanksgiving? How is the "God of heaven" guiding you?

22 Friday

Ezra 8:1, 15-23

What is the writer saying?

How can I apply this to my life?

pray *Panama – Removal of obstacles for those translating the scriptures and Christian literature.*

We note that Ezra has begun using first-person pronouns (I, my, me, we, and us) from Ezra 7:27-9:15, indicating his personal involvement from this point on and also his authorship of the book of Ezra. In chapter 8, we see that he recently arrived in Jerusalem (7:8) as he tells of events that happened in Babylon several months earlier (8:15-31).

In verses 2-14, he lists the family groups who assemble to come with him. He gathers them at a place called Ahava, beside a river he designates by the same name (vv. 21, 31). The trip is delayed because there are no Levites to perform the duties at the temple, as required by the law.

God gives him the wisdom to solve that problem (vv. 16-20), and another problem arises. Evidently, the king has brought up the matter of the perils of the journey.

It would take almost four months to travel the one thousand miles. They are transporting great wealth in gold and silver (7:15). They have little children and other possessions (8:21). In all, they would present a very desirable prize for marauding robber bands. The obvious answer is a military escort. But Ezra has assured the king that God would protect them. So he chooses to delay the trip and take time for a concerted prayer effort. He testifies of the Lord's faithfulness in verses 23 and 31.

Notice the four factors of Ezra's success: (a) Ezra brings together the right people (vv. 2-24); (b) Ezra has a right beginning – fasting and prayer (v. 21); (c) Ezra has the right perspective concerning problems – the "hand of our God is upon all them" (v. 22); and (d) Ezra gives the right attention to care for the holy things of God (vv. 24-29).

Ezra's successful journey is a model to us concerning the preparation for and execution of his plan. Do you seek to follow Ezra's *four-step plan for success?*

Ezra 8:24-36

What is the writer saying?

How can I apply this to my life?

pray *Czech Republic – For godly public school teachers who will use their religious freedom to evangelize.*

In Ezra's account of the trek from Babylon to Jerusalem, he says nothing concerning the rigors of the journey. There is no mention of sickness, injuries or death. There are no words telling of storms, heat, or weary days. He makes no comments about fears or dissension among the people. There are no words of complaining!

On the other hand, Ezra goes into great detail concerning his care for "the offering of the house of our God" (v. 25). He makes certain that no one handles the sacred things for the temple, except the Levites. He divides the precious items among twelve Levite leaders. He selects the right individuals for this important responsibility. "Ye are holy unto the Lord; the vessels are holy also" (v. 28, see Numbers 8:14-16). This entire operation is rather remarkable considering that the gold, silver, and metal objects for the temple and its service weigh more than twenty five tons!

"Twelve bullocks for all Israel" (v. 35) – one for each tribe represented by the exiles who return. Since the returnees, first with Zerubbabel and now with Ezra, contain members of all twelve tribes, there would no longer be a divided nation with the return of these exiles (v. 35).

Ezra has his priorities right! He takes care of his duties as spiritual leader (vv. 34-35); that is, he accounts for all the temple valuables and he directs the giving of thanks to God. We have here a fifth step in Ezra's plan for success; namely, Ezra ends right by the giving of thanks.

Then he deals with matters of political authority. He visits the political leaders to let them know of the king's letters of "commissions" (v. 36).

Two New Testament verses give us our application: (a) We Christians are all called by God to be a "holy priesthood" (1 Peter 2:5), and (b) we are also to be "ambassadors for Christ" (2 Corinthians 5:20). A true disciple makes it his priority to focus on God's program. Do you?

Ezra 9:1-5

What is the writer saying?

How can I apply this to my life?

pray *Uganda – For believing Ugandans living abroad to be called back to minister among their people.*

When Ezra returns to Jerusalem from delivering the king's decree to the governors (7:21; 8:36), he is informed that the priests, Levites, and the princes of Israel have led the people into intermarriage with the idolatrous "people of the lands" – the Gentiles living in the area (v. 1). They have also begun to practice the immoral idolatry of these Gentiles.

"I rent my garment and my mantle, plucked off the hair of my head and of my beard, and sat down astonied" (*astounded and stunned with amazement*). The magnitude of their sin can be judged by Ezra's reaction in verse 3!

Isaac and Jacob were forbidden to marry Canaanites (Genesis 24:3, 28:1). It was found in the Law of Moses for all Israelites (Exodus 34:11-16). Moses repeats the order to the second generation (Deuteronomy 7:1-6). The sins of the Canaanites had become so abhorrent that God ordered Israel to destroy them and to possess their land. Joshua warned succeeding generations to heed this command (Joshua 23:12-13).

However, Israel never eradicated these heathen from the Promised Land (Joshua 15:63; 16:10; Judges 1:28-35). The pagan people around Israel were a continual snare to Israel, leading them into intermarriage and idolatry. The Hittites, Jebusites and Amorites were descendants of Canaan (Genesis 10:6). The Ammonites and Moabites were descendants of Lot, living east of Canaan.

Notice that all the Israelites "trembled" at the proclaiming of the "words of the God of Israel" (v. 4). They became full of fear as they reflected back upon God's righteous judgments on such faithless conduct in their past.

If Ezra came to you today, would he be pleased that you fear the *words of God* and have *separated* yourself from the evil things in the world around you?

Ezra 9:6-15

What is the writer saying?

How can I apply this to my life?

pray *Jamaica – Effective medical ministries in a land where half the male population abuses drugs.*

Today we hear Ezra pray a great prayer of national confession. As a ready scribe, Ezra would have known that former leaders of Israel had prayed such prayers (Exodus 32:11-14, Numbers 14:13-19, Daniel 9) and that God had mercifully responded to the confessions of Moses and Daniel on behalf of Israel. Although Ezra personally is guiltless of the sins confessed, four times in his prayer (vv. 7, 10, 15) he identifies himself with the sinful nation by use of the first-person-plural, "we." This is the pattern set by Moses when he returned from Mt. Sinai and beheld his people dancing before a god/idol shaped as a golden calf.

Ezra begins by confessing "our iniquities" (v. 6). He acknowledges that Israel's past woes were caused by the trespasses and iniquities of the nation (v. 7). In verse 8, he credits God's grace for their release from their exile. In verse 9, he credits God's mercy in allowing them to rebuild the temple. In verses 10-12, he confesses that their present sins defile the Promised Land that God gave His children forever. He then recalls God's gracious conduct, for God had given them past punishments that were "less" than what they "deserve" (v. 13).

Ezra concludes with three truths: (1) as the "Lord God of Israel," Ezra knows God still loves His people; (2) God's righteousness still demands judgment upon their sin; and (3) to Ezra's amazement, God is patiently withholding judgment upon their present sin (v. 15). Since Ezra knows they deserve to be completely destroyed on "this day," he could only bow before God praying for God's continued mercy.

A long time has past since Ezra prayed confessing the sins of Israel, but God still has not changed! God is still gracious, kind, patient but also righteous and the Judge of our sin. In all His dealings with you, He loves you. So then, are there sins in your life that you need to confess to God (see 1 John 1:9)?

Ezra 10:1-9

What is the writer saying?

How can I apply this to my life?

pray *Praise God for sending His Son to be our Savior.*

Whereas Daniel prayed his prayer of national confession alone before God, Ezra's prayer is very public. When the people see his reaction upon discovery of their sins (9:3), they are convicted and assembled around him (9:4). As he prays with great intensity, the congregation weeps in repentance. Shecaniah, one of the more discerning among the guilty ones (v. 2), joins in the confession and introduces a ray of hope. He believes that God would respond favorably to the outpouring of remorse. He also perceives that the only recourse is to proceed according to God's law, regardless of the cost.

In his speech, Shecaniah acknowledges Ezra's authority (v. 4). He encourages Ezra to give the orders for them to follow. Ezra commands the leaders to swear publicly that they would do according to God's Word. Then he retires into a chamber of the temple to fast and pray (v. 6).

The leaders order all of the Jewish men to assemble in Jerusalem within three days or lose their possessions and citizenship (v. 8). The assembly is held in December, the cold, rainy season, in the open. Facilities for this gathering are very restricted in Jerusalem. Trembling from both cold and guilt, they wait on Ezra to confess their sin.

Let us note their *Steps to Restoration*:

- They are genuinely ashamed of their sin (v. 1).
- Their confession is specific, "We have trespassed ..." (v. 2).
- They confidently place their "hope" in God's mercy (v. 2b)
- They are willing to take action to correct the situation (v. 3).
- They are guided in repentance by the Word of God (v. 3b).
- They commit themselves to "do" right after this matter (v. 5).

Is there a sinful "matter" (v. 9) in your life that needs your confession? Do you need to work through these same *Steps to Restoration* with God?

Ezra 10:10-19, 44

What is the writer saying?

How can I apply this to my life?

pray *United Kingdom – For many teens to be saved through Christian camping and outreach events.*

With a cold, December rain falling, thousands of men stand before the temple, waiting for Ezra to speak. They are well aware of the matter upon which he would speak. As he arises, his grim countenance matches their concerned demeanor. He does not begin with a funny story to ease their discomfort. His subject is sin – their sin. He immediately points out the specific transgression and tersely states the painful solution.

The congregation understands his solution and agrees to act upon it. However, they are fearful that the rulers don't comprehend the magnitude of the problem, nor the extent of the complications involved. They plead for a thorough investigation and an orderly procedure over a period of months.

According to the list given in verses 18-43, there are 113 families to be dissolved. Some involve children. Seventeen priests and ten Levites are among those married to pagan wives. There are four men, including two Levites, who oppose the dissolutions (v. 15). We are not told what subsequently happens in their cases.

The congregation is sent home and a council, headed by Ezra, sets an appointed time in which each case could be examined. The council first deals with the sinning priests. Each brings a sacrifice in accordance with Leviticus 5:17-19. Next come the Levites, and then the rest of the guilty ones. It takes about three months to accomplish the task.

Though forgiveness is available from our merciful God (1 John 1:9), the consequences often remain (2 Samuel 12:10-12) and often take considerable time to make right. Do you have a sinful practice in your life? Begin now to deal with it. Perhaps you could find a godly person to assist you and counsel you in making "an end" (v. 17) to the evil habit.

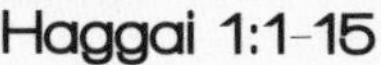

Haggai 1:1-15

What is the writer saying?

How can I apply this to my life?

pray *Slovakia – For an attitude of spiritual optimism and activism to explode among Slovakian youth.*

As you will recall, Ezra, in the first part of his book, writes about four events: (1) Israel's return from their exile away from the Promised Land; (2) Israel's start at the rebuilding of the temple (Ezra 3, 538 B.C.); (3) opposition that causes the work to stop (Ezra 4); and (4) the role of the prophets Haggai and Zechariah in encouraging the people of Israel to restart and then finish its construction (Ezra 5:1, 520 B.C.). Today we begin a brief look at Haggai's four messages of encouragement.

Haggai begins with a criticism from God to the Israelite leaders. They have decided that the temple is not going to be rebuilt in their day; "The time is not come" (v. 2). So they turn their attention to their *own personal concerns* (while others go hungry, v.6), finding "time" to build their own "cieled houses" (meaning *paneled walls and ceilings*) so they could *dwell in comfort and luxury*! Apparently, they have decided to use in their own homes, the expensive wood brought from Lebanon, which was intended for use in building the temple (Ezra 3:7)!

As a result, God has brought repeated crop failures and other business failures that results in the loss of their money (v. 6). Haggai points out the reason for their difficulties is their selfish-focus. God is declaring that it is time to set aside their selfish pursuits and "Go up to the mountain, and bring wood, and build the house" of the Lord. Then God would take pleasure in it and bring blessings to His people.

Zerubbabel, the governor and Joshua, the high priest receive the words of Haggai as the voice of God. With a further word of encouragement from Haggai (v. 13), they stir up the people so much, that within the month, the work on the temple is in full force.

Are you *seeking first the kingdom of God and His righteousness* so that He might *add unto you* (Matthew 6:33)? Or, is your life all about you and yours? "Consider" (v. 7) your use of your "time"!

QT

Friday 23

Haggai 2:1-9

What is the writer saying?

How can I apply this to my life?

pray *Peru – A God-honoring end to animosity and division between Quechua and Spanish-speaking believers.*

Haggai's second message from the Lord comes about seven weeks after his first, and about four weeks after the rebuilding of the temple resumes. Since the temple they are rebuilding is obviously less magnificent than Solomon's, some have become discouraged (v. 3, also Ezra 3:12). Haggai's second message is to encourage the builders to "be strong" (v. 4) by giving them a vision as to how their endeavor fits into God's future program.

Haggai first assures all that the Lord is in charge and that His Spirit is among them as He promised their fathers before them (Exodus 29:45). Next, he gives them a look into the future (vv. 6-9).

Since verse 6 is quoted and explained in Hebrews 12:26-29, we know that this prophecy is still future to us. He is speaking of the Great Tribulation (Matthew 24:29). Some interpret "the desire of all nations" (v. 7) to mean the Messiah. Certainly, all nations desire peace (v. 9) which will come only when Jesus, the Prince of Peace, sits on His throne.

"Latter house" in verse 9 speaks of the temple, then being rebuilt. "Former" (v. 9) refers to Solomon's first temple that was destroyed. Haggai is saying that the builders need not be concerned that the temple they are rebuilding is less spectacular than one which had been destroyed. They are involved in a work that would end in a "glory ... greater" than the first temple. In particular, we note that Jesus, who is the glory of God (2 Corinthians 4:6), would enter this second temple, and by doing so, would adorn it (see also Matthew 12:6; John 2:13-22) with glory.

Today, we too can "be strong" (v. 4), in that we know that God will use our work as Christians, in witnessing and ministering to others, to build a living, "spiritual house" (1 Peter 2:5), which is the "temple of the living God" (2 Corinthians 6:16), that God, in our times, now dwells in.

Haggai 2:10-23

What is the writer saying?

How can I apply this to my life?

pray *Cuba – Godly and moral men of integrity to be placed in key leadership roles of any future government.*

Between Haggai's second message and third message, Zechariah brings a call to repentance (Zechariah 1:2-6). The people respond by acknowledging that their sin has brought God's judgment upon them.

Before the captivity, Jeremiah reminded the nation that they were the Lord's special people, who had so defiled themselves that God could not use them (Jeremiah 13:10, 11). This brought about the seventy years of *desolation* of Jerusalem (Jeremiah 25:11) and exile of its Jewish people.

In three places, the Bible dates the beginning of the *Desolation* (2 Kings 25:1; Jeremiah 52:4; Ezekiel 24:1, 2); that is, when the Babylonians laid siege to Jerusalem. Haggai tells, three times, when the seventy years of Desolation end (vv. 10, 18, 20); "From this day will I bless you" (vv. 15, 18, 19).

In his third message, Haggai confronts the priests (v. 11) with a principle – *dirty hands* defile holy sacrifices, but holy sacrifices do not cleanse *dirty hands. Clean hands* can only come from *clean hearts.* The blood of Christ alone *cleanses the heart.* His blood is represented by the blood of animal sacrifices until His perfect sacrifice is offered. Therefore, the priests need a washing of their *dirty hearts* before their *dirty hands* could be made pure, and thus ready for offering sacrifices.

Haggai's fourth message is to Zerubbabel, the Jewish prince appointed by the Persians as governor of Jerusalem. Zerubbabel needs encouragement as he leads this little work on the far edge of Persia's vast empire. Zerubbabel is a prince of Israel because he is a descendant of King David. Haggai prophesies to him that his descendant would be the future Messiah, who would "overthrow the throne of kingdoms" (v. 22).

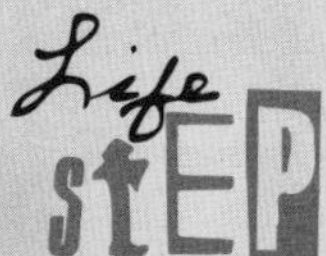

If our hands are *dirty* from being involved in sin, our dirty hands render our lives unfit for holy service to God. Do you need cleansing for service?

The Book of Nehemiah picks up the story of the Lord's dealings with His people, Israel, twelve years after the close of the Book of Ezra. The two books are presented as one book in early Hebrew texts but, in the 15th Century, Hebrew Bibles begin to re-introduce the original division of the two into separate books, as is customary in Bibles today.

"The street shall be built again, and the wall, even in troublous times" (Daniel 9:25). "Jerusalem lieth waste, and the gates thereof are burned with fire; come, and let us build up the wall of Jerusalem" (Nehemiah 2:17). Ninety-three years transpired between the above prophecy by Daniel and the cited challenge by Nehemiah to his followers. At the time of his prophecy, Daniel has been a captive in Chaldea for sixty-seven years, and is anticipating an end to the seventy years of "desolations of Jerusalem" (Daniel 9:2). The very year he prophesies, King Cyrus permits the return of the captives to the Holy Land. In Nehemiah's time, the rebuilt temple has been completed by the returned remnant seventy years previously (see Ezra, Haggai and Zechariah), but the city walls are still a pile of rubble.

When God's time comes to do a work on earth, He selects a leader of resolute purpose. It must be a person who is willing to set aside any plans he may have and yield his whole being to God's program. He must do God's work God's way, regardless of how unreasonable it may seem. We have a noteworthy list of such people in the Bible: Noah, Abraham, Moses, Joshua, Daniel, John the Baptist, and Paul. Today, we begin a study of another who needs to be added to this list, Nehemiah.

The book relates how the Jewish man, Nehemiah, who has been at the Persian palace at Shushan (Greek *Susa*), serving as the king's cupbearer, is afforded the opportunity to travel to Jerusalem to oversee the rebuilding of the walls of the city of his ancestral home. The book thus provides a chronology of Nehemiah's ministry in Jerusalem. His first tenure as the Persian governor at Jerusalem covers twelve years (445-433 B.C.). He then returns to Shushan to take up his duties there. He returns to Jerusalem for a second tenure in about 430 B.C. (Nehemiah 13:6). Tradition says that Nehemiah remains governor after this second trip to Jerusalem until he obtains great age.

There are small groups of Jewish exiles that return with Nehemiah on his two journeys to Jerusalem. These would have been the third and fourth returns of exiles in 445 BC and 430 BC.

While the book focuses on the account of the rebuilding of the walls at Jerusalem (the words, "build" and "walls," are used fifteen and thirty-six times), the book also provides the reader with an understanding of how political control of Jerusalem and the surrounding area is returned to Jewish hands with the approval of the Persian King, Artaxerxes. Note that Nehemiah has come to Jerusalem with official instructions to rebuild the city (2:5-6) and *not just the walls* around the city. In the ancient world, a *fortified city* would also become a *center of influence* to the territories surrounding. Thus, all of the Persian province of Judea is in view!

Nehemiah's concern is primarily for the people of Jerusalem; the rebuilding of the walls and city of Jerusalem are only the symptoms of this greater concern. Note that Nehemiah's *initial concern for the people* who "are in great affliction and reproach" (Nehemiah 1:3) becomes the basis for his being seen as "a man to seek the welfare of the children of Israel" (Nehemiah 2:10). Thus, we are not surprised that while the first half of the book (chapters 1-6) is the story of the *rebuilding of the walls,* the last half (chapters 7-13) is about the *spiritual rebuilding of God's people* into a proper relationship with their God.

The Book of Nehemiah also provides us with several additional sets of lessons throughout the book that support these themes:

1. God puts the story of Nehemiah in the Bible so that we could better understand how to be godly, effective leaders or good followers in doing His work His way.

- The principle lesson for us concerns the importance of a leader's dedicated *prayer life,* in seeking God's mind to do His work in a manner pleasing to Him.
- Characteristics of the godly leader that God uses includes: (1) a God-pleasing willingness to act upon a God-directed burden; (2) a ready heart that moves beyond one's comfort zone; (3) a God-honoring plan to accomplish a God-given task; and (4) a trustworthy character that pleases one's superiors.

2. The providential care of God is an evident theme of the book (Nehemiah 1:5-7; 9:7-37). God would want us to see that He is both *steadfast* and *faithful* to His covenant with Israel based upon His election of Israel as His people.

- *Divine blessing and care* is shown (Nehemiah 5:19; 6:9; 13:14, 22, 31) as coming to those that bring their invocations to God (*a formal prayer calling on God for blessing, help, inspiration, protection*)
- *Divine help* is shown (Nehemiah 2:4-5; 4:9) as coming to those that *pray* and then *set out by faith* to accomplish the deed for which they pray.

3. The Book of Nehemiah shows us that the Scriptures are *essential to a righteous walk* with God.

- The Scriptures are *read*, *interpreted* and *applied* to regulate the community's life (Nehemiah 8:1-18; 9:3).
- The proclamation of the Scriptures *brings conviction* to the priests, Levites, and people (Nehemiah 8:9; 9:2-3).
- The Scriptures are the *basis for reform* (Nehemiah 13:1-3, 17-27).

24 Sunday

Nehemiah 1:1-11

What is the writer saying?

How can I apply this to my life?

pray *Ecuador – Pray for church growth to continue to increase and for a renewed emphasis on evangelism.*

The book opens in the year 445 B.C. with Nehemiah as the king's cupbearer at the Persian palace of Artaxerxes, who has reigned for twenty years. It is here, some thirty-five years before, that Esther had been chosen queen by this king's father (Esther 1:1, 2). Ezra, thirteen years before, had been commissioned by Artaxerxes (Ezra 7:11-26) to return to Jerusalem.

Nehemiah's story begins when a delegation of Jews arrives from Jerusalem. He inquires concerning the people and the city. Their answer causes him deep distress. He weeps, mourns, fasts and prays (v. 4).

We can find great benefit in closely considering Nehemiah's prayer (v. 5-11). He addresses his prayer to the "Lord God [Yahweh Elohim] of Heaven" (v. 5). As Elohim, God is the great and awesome Supreme One of Heaven. As Yahweh (or Jehovah), Nehemiah is recognizing that he is speaking to the Holy One who has personally reached down to people on earth. Similarly, we should begin our prayers by acknowledging just how great God is to us (Matthew 6:9).

Next, Nehemiah confesses who he is before this Holy God – an undeserving sinner (v. 6)! Also, like Moses, Daniel, and Ezra in their intercessory prayers, he identifies himself with the sinning nation. He specifies the particular sins that have been committed.

Before making his petition, Nehemiah brings before God a promise from His own Word upon which to base his request (vv. 8-9). He then recalls God's past actions on behalf of His people. Now he is ready to present a specific request. He wants God to arrange a favorable audience with the king as he fulfills his duties as cupbearer (v. 11).

It is common for even dedicated Christians to have deficiencies in their prayer lives. To begin to strengthen your own prayer life, how about writing out a sentence or two of your own prayer prologue!

Nehemiah 2:1-8

What is the writer saying?

How can I apply this to my life?

pray *Bolivia – For caring youth ministry in a land where 80% of children are living in extreme poverty.*

Nehemiah has been mourning, fasting, and praying for four months ("Chisleu" v. 1:1 [December] through "Nisan" v. 2:1 [April]). The king notices the effect this has upon his countenance and questions him. The king correctly deduces that Nehemiah is afflicted with "sorrow of heart" (v. 2) rather than bodily ailment. Nehemiah is struck with fear because it is a serious affront to appear before a Persian king with a sad face. After all, so the thought goes, who could possibly be sad when in the presence of such a powerful man?

Nehemiah discloses the reason for his sadness. The king is sympathetic, rather than offended, and offers to be helpful. Again, we are surprised by the king's response, after all, so the thought goes, who would want to leave the king's presence?

After sending up a quick, silent prayer (v. 4), Nehemiah asks the king to be sent to Jerusalem with all that he would need for the rebuilding of the city. The king issues written orders to all concerned. Nehemiah then gives God the credit (v. 8)

The Persian kings, Cyrus, Darius and Artaxerxes have all previously issued decrees for rebuilding the *temple.* However, the only one commanding rebuilding the *city* is this one by Artaxerxes. It is of prime importance in understanding the prophetic Scriptures, especially Daniel's prophecy concerning sixty-two weeks of years, from the commandment to restore Jerusalem unto the time when the "Messiah the Prince" shall be "cut off" (Daniel 9:24-27).

Like Nehemiah, we need to learn that God answers prayers on His time schedule, not ours. Like Nehemiah, we often need to be persistent in our prayer requests for an extended time. Only then can we properly offer up quick *now God* prayers! So then, what prayer needs are in your life that call for daily prayer? How can you prepare for the part that God will require of you when He chooses to answer your persistent prayer?

Nehemiah 2:9-20

What is the writer saying?

How can I apply this to my life?

pray *New Zealand – For Bible schools and churches to convey a mission emphasis among their people.*

Leaving the Persian capital of Susa, Nehemiah journeys west, likely passing through the capitals of the Satrapy (Persian provinces) of Babylon and Syria, and giving each governor the king's letters (v. 9). Sanballat (v. 10) is an administrator of Samaria, immediately north of Jerusalem. Similarly, Tobiah is an administrator of Ammon, to the east. Both are under the control of Syria. Both are unhappy to receive the decree from King Artaxerxes, so they join together to oppose the work of God.

Three days after his arrival, Nehemiah takes a few men on a nocturnal survey of the conditions surrounding the rebuilt temple area (v. 12). He doesn't share with the others what he intends to do (v. 16).

Next, he gathers the leaders together to confront them with the reproachful situation (v. 17). He tells them that God Himself is directing him (v. 18a) and that King Artaxerxes is very supportive of his intended project (v.18b). He challenges them with, "let us build" (v. 17), and they respond with, "let us rise up and build" (v. 18c).

When Sanballat and Tobiah hear of the plans to rebuild Jerusalem, they ally with Gesham, the leader of the Arabian tribes to the south. To the north, east, and south, Israel faces opposition that not only ridicules Israel but accuses Nehemiah of rebellion against the king (v. 19). Nehemiah's response: "The God of heaven, he will prosper us; therefore we his servants will arise and build." He lets them know he is doing God's work!

A detail we do not want to miss is that God not only answers Nehemiah's prayer (1:11), but also, God goes beyond his requests and blesses Nehemiah with a powerful contingent of Persian "captains... and horsemen" (v. 9)! Remember God knew ahead of time of the opposition Nehemiah would face upon his arrival at Jerusalem.

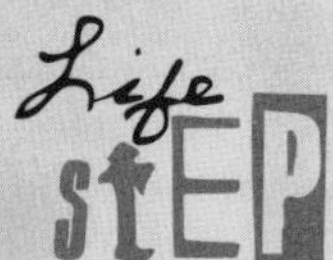

Are you facing opposition? How can you declare your faith that God will bless your efforts? For what blessing do you need to ask God?

Nehemiah 3:1-16

What is the writer saying?

How can I apply this to my life?

pray *Australia – Sensitivity and skilled communication for those sharing the gospel in Aboriginal areas.*

Nehemiah loosely organizes the wall builders into forty-two groups, each of which possesses homogeneity within its group. Most groups are from a common family. Some of these labor near their homes. Other groups are formed from certain occupations. Some are *commuters* from surrounding cities who tend to work with their own leadership. Some groups are small. One is so large that it not only rebuilt a gate, but also almost one-third of a mile of wall. All have proportional assignments!

Be sure to note that everyone participated with the exception of a few "nobles" (v. 5). These "put not their necks to the work of their Lord," since they feel that such menial work is below their position!

Now note that the priests have set a good example and undertake the first assignment (v. 1). They build the sheep gate on the northeast corner of the city and extend the north wall westward. The sacrificial sheep are brought through that gate into the temple area. The assignments proceed counter-clockwise around the city.

Expositors have made spiritual applications from the ten gates of Jerusalem. One of these applies each gate successively to stages of a Christian's life. The sheep gate represents the doorway to salvation (John 10:9, 11). After one is saved, he is to be a witness, pictured by the fish gate (Matthew 4:19). The old gate speaks of the Christian's walk in the old paths of the faith (Jeremiah 6:16). The valley gate tells of trials and afflictions (2 Corinthians 4:17). The dung gate represents confession that cleanses and disposes of spiritual refuse (2 Corinthians 7:1; 1 John 1:9). The fountain gate is the Spirit-filled life (John 7:38).

Are you a person of some importance in your world? Do you model your attitudes and service for the Lord after the *nobles* (v. 5) or the *priests* (v. 1)? Are you *neglecting your duties* to your Lord? Or are you among the *first who go to work* in service of the people of God? Remember, God has not asked you to do everything, but He does expect you to work on your section of the "wall" of the ministry of Christ!

24 Thursday

Nehemiah 3:17-32

What is the writer saying?

How can I apply this to my life?

pray *Serbia – For forgiveness between ethnic groups that have been at war for so long. Pray that people would be able to rebuild trust and cooperation.*

The water gate (v. 26), when applied to the Christian life speaks of "the washing of water by the word" (Ephesians 5:26). See also Nehemiah 8:1 and Psalm 119:9.

The horse gate (v. 28) symbolizes warfare. The Christian life is a war against the forces of evil (2 Corinthians 10:4). Therefore, we "put on the whole armour of God" (Ephesians 6:11) and "fight the good fight of faith" (1 Timothy 6:12).

When Jesus entered Jerusalem (Zechariah 9:9; Matthew 21:5), He came through the east gate. When He comes to reign, He will come as the "bright and morning star" (Revelation 22:16), which rises in the east just before day.

Historians have concluded that the "Miphkad" gate (v. 31) is the appointed place for soldiers to muster for inspection, for the Christian this corresponds to the Judgment Seat of Christ.

So a summary of the ten gates would be as follows:

- Sheep gate (v. 1) – salvation – John 10:9, 11
- Fish gate (v. 3) – witness – Matthew 4:19
- Old gate (v. 6) – walk – Jeremiah 6:16
- Valley gate (v. 13) – trials – 2 Corinthians 4:17
- Dung gate (v. 14) – confession – 2 Corinthians 7:1
- Fountain gate (v. 15) – spirituality – John 7:38
- Water gate (v. 26) – word – Nehemiah 8:1
- Horse gate (v. 28) – warfare – Ephesians 6:11
- East gate (v. 29) – rapture – 1 Thessalonians 4:17
- Miphkad gate (v. 31) – inspection – 2 Corinthians 5:10

Notice that this long list ends where it began (see vv. 1 and 32). The work goes all the way around the city. God wants to *go all the way around* to build up every area of your life. What section of the walls of your life does God want you to work on next?

Nehemiah 4:1-9

What is the writer saying?

How can I apply this to my life?

pray *India – Protection and boldness for believers facing persecution by Hindu extremists.*

When they learn of the rapid progress of the rebuilding of the wall, the adversaries intensify their campaign of ridicule and mockery. They try to convince the workers that their toil in the oppressive midsummer heat is futile. Sanballat also attempts another tactic. He makes a speech to the political and military leaders of Samaria, accusing the Jews of building a fortress.

Nehemiah answers the attempts at intimidation with public prayer (v. 4). The result is a workforce with a mind to work (v. 6), a heart to pray and an eye to watch (v. 9). They are doing God's work, God's way (Luke 21:36). Within a few weeks, the wall is joined together, built to half the intended height.

The adversaries are incensed beyond measure and recruit a new ally. Ashdod is the principal city of the Philistines and is located directly west of Jerusalem. These four groups of people surrounding Jerusalem normally fought each other. The one thing they have in common is antagonism against the true God and His program on earth. So they "conspired all of them together to come and to fight against Jerusalem" (v. 8). This is precisely what will happen again at the end of the Tribulation, when the nations around Israel will again conspire to destroy it. To examine the comparison, see Zechariah 12:2, 14:2 and Revelation 16:14.

Have you faced adversaries to your work for the Lord Jesus? Have you been accused of being weak, defenseless, unable to worship, slow, without resources, and having questionable ability? Israel and Nehemiah certainly are! Notice some of the accusations are true! These people are not stonemasons, but shepherds, priests, and shop keepers! Remember Nehemiah's response! He prays for God's assistance, then Israel takes courage and does what God wants of them.

24 Saturday

QT

Nehemiah 4:10-23

What is the writer saying?

How can I apply this to my life?

pray *Bulgaria – For believers to have the wisdom and discernment to avoid doctrinal error.*

A wave of discouragement overflows the builders. They complain, *Our strength is gone – the task is too great – and we are afraid of our adversaries.* Day after day, the Jews living nearest to the adversaries come to the builders and warn, *If you don't stop the work, the adversaries will swoop down upon all of us and kill us.*

Nehemiah halts the work long enough to assemble the workers and see that each family is supplied with weapons. He knows that the local leaders opposing him wouldn't defy the edict of King Artaxerxes. He also knows the weapons would overcome their sense of helplessness and at the same time send a message to the adversaries. Nehemiah reminds the workers of two responsibilities: (1) they are doing God's work and He would not fail them; and (2) they are fighting for their own families.

The arming of the workers convinces the adversaries that their campaign of fear has failed, so the work resumes. The servants of verse 16 are probably a company of Jews who are supplied to Nehemiah when he comes to Jerusalem. He places half in charge of the work, and half become a military guard. Trumpeters are posted at intervals along the wall to summon everyone with weapons to the trumpeter's position when an attack threatens.

Nehemiah encourages his people with the cry of Moses, "The Lord shall fight for you" (Exodus 14:14; Deuteronomy 1:30). When faith in God is replaced by fear of men or frustration over circumstances, one's effectiveness in God's work comes to a halt. Faith is the victory over fear, frustration, or failure. The builders of the wall do their work comforted by their weapons, because God causes them to be encouraged in spite of the weakness of their faith.

Have you allowed a fear of people or a frustration with circumstances to cause your service for God to come to a halt? How can you, like these Israelites, stay on focus to do the task God has assigned to you?

Nehemiah 5:1-13

What is the writer saying?

How can I apply this to my life?

pray *United Kingdom – Over 40% of evangelical churches have no one under the age of 20. Pray for a harvest of souls amongst young people.*

Having successfully allayed the hindrances from without, Nehemiah now faces new problems that emerge from within. This time Nehemiah faces selfishness and greed! The poorer people are being oppressed by their wealthier brethren. During a famine, some have to borrow to feed their large families (v. 3). Some have to borrow to pay the king's tax (v. 4). Since the lenders control the mortgaged property's harvests (v. 5), the debtors have no means to pay the high interest. Some of the people resort to selling their children into slavery (v. 5) to pay their debts.

The law concerning these matters is clearly presented in Leviticus 25:35-42. A Hebrew with means is required to relieve his poor Hebrew neighbor. He is prohibited from charging interest on loans and must treat a debtor as a hired servant – not as a slave. God's reason is that when they were all slaves in Egypt He had redeemed them all. Thus, they are obligated to obey God's principles of business and are not to follow the *more profitable* practices of the nations around them. The oppressors are deliberately ignoring their obligations to God.

Nehemiah has the unpleasant task of confronting the oppressors with their sin. He calls an assembly and charges: *As we have the ability, it is our duty to redeem Jews who are enslaved to heathens – not to enslave our own brothers! You need the fear of God in your hearts.*

Nehemiah tells them what must be done. They recognize their sin and Nehemiah's God-ordained leadership by complying. The Lord is glorified!

Christians are also under obligation to God. Christians were slaves to sin. We were bought by the blood of Christ and given a new life in Christ. Now we are to live according to God's principles for that new life. Several of our obligations concern money and business practices too. How can you be of service to your fellow-Christians in spite of the economic cost to you? Similarly, how can you, for God's glory, forgive a debt owed to you?

Nehemiah 5:14-6:9

What is the writer saying?

How can I apply this to my life?

pray *Germany – For the salvation of those in key areas of leadership so that they can influence public policy.*

In 5:14-19, Nehemiah gives personal testimony of his conduct during his twelve years of governorship. God wants this account in His Word for the Lord's people to read through the years. The Apostle Paul makes it clear that it is proper for spiritual leaders to receive material recompense from their followers (1 Corinthians 9:7-14). However, like Nehemiah, Paul chooses not to receive compensation from those to whom he ministers. Nehemiah and Paul want to emphasize that they are bound to their ministries by God's call and they look to Him for future reward (5:15, 19; 1 Corinthians 9:15-18). Their desire in no way lessens our obligation to support those who minister spiritually to or for us (Romans 15:27).

"I am doing a great work, so that I cannot come down" (6:3). Nehemiah would have "come down" both physically and spiritually if he had left his mountaintop to counsel in their valley of deceit. In more ways than one, they "thought to do me mischief" (v. 6:2).

After having his request rejected four times, Sanballat tries a new tactic. In effect, he says, *If you don't come down and counsel, we will report to the king that you are planning to set up your own kingdom* (v. 6:5-6). To this threat and accusation, Nehemiah replies, *your accusation is false and therefore we are not afraid of your threat* (v. 6:8).

Nehemiah knows the purpose of this continuing opposition is to weaken the effort of the builders through fear. Therefore, he again prays to God for strength (v. 6:9).

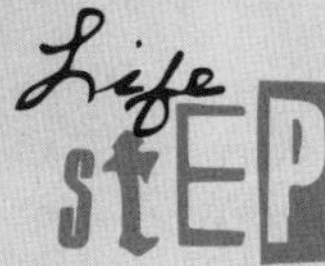

"Blessed is the man that walketh not in the counsel of the ungodly" (Psalm 1:1). In our day-to-day life, we receive instruction, direction and counsel from unsaved people. Like Nehemiah, it takes courage on your part when people in your world use subtle diversions to cause you to stop doing the work God has called you to build. Take a minute and ask yourself two questions: What great work does God want me to do? and What have I allowed into my life as a distraction from God's work?

QT Tuesday 25

Nehemiah 6:10-19

What is the writer saying?

How can I apply this to my life?

pray *Pray for your church to have wisdom and integrity in dealing with the finances entrusted to it.*

When the wall is nearing completion, Nehemiah visits in the house of Shemaiah, who is a leader among those Jews who oppose the building of the wall. He informs Nehemiah of a plot to assassinate him. He advises that the only safe place for Nehemiah to escape death is the sanctuary of the temple and he offers to take him there. Nehemiah knows the warning is not from God (v. 12) because the law forbids any but priests to enter the sanctuary of the temple. For him to flee there would discredit him as upholder of the law and as leader of God's people (v. 11). Actually, Shemaiah is a hireling of the adversaries, Tobiah and Sanballat (v. 12), who are also in league with the false prophetess Noadiah and her cohorts (v. 14).

As the plot against Nehemiah unfolds, it developes that Tobiah the Ammonite and his son have married daughters of prominent Jewish leaders. These traitors have been circulating letters from Tobiah against Nehemiah. When that fails to stop the work, they attempt to convince Nehemiah that Tobiah is a friend who has been very helpful to the Jews.

In spite of all the delaying tactics, the wall is completed in just fifty-two days! It is interesting that the completion of the walls of Jerusalem is a testimony to all those who live around Jerusalem, that the God of the Israelites has done a great work in their midst (v. 16).

The Scriptures speak of the building of the church in terms of building a habitation for God on earth (Ephesians 2:19-22; 1 Peter 2:5). God is also at work building a new person in your own life. What great projects has God built in your life? How are these testimonies of God's love, care, and design for you?

Are there threats to your safety that cause you to want to run and hide? How can you, like Nehemiah, take courage and trust in God?

25 Wednesday

Nehemiah 8:1-12

What is the writer saying?

How can I apply this to my life?

pray *Canada -- For youth living in a country with the third highest youth suicide rate in the world to find hope in Christ.*

The walls of Jerusalem are completed just five days before the beginning of the four feasts of the seventh month (Leviticus 23:24). Immediately, Nehemiah prepares for the influx of people who would respond to the blowing of the trumpets (7:1-4). Next, he consults the register of those who arrived with Zerubbabel ninety years previously (7:5-73). He needs to determine the eligibility for service of the Levites and priests. Some are rejected because their genealogy couldn't be proven.

So the people gather to hear the reading of the law by Ezra the scribe. Nehemiah stations Levites throughout the congregation to explain the Scriptures as they are read. The reading is in Hebrew, and most of the people by this time speak only Aramaic. Ezra 7:10 tells how a teacher of the Word should prepare to teach. Nehemiah 8:8 gives the proper methodology: (1) Scripture is read to people, (2) Scripture is explained to people, and (3) people are made to understand how to apply the Scripture to their lives.

Because most of the people have never before heard and understood the Word of God, they are overcome with emotion (Hebrews 4:12). It is obvious to them that their lives do not conform to God's requirements. They weep with remorse.

The Levites go through the crowd telling the people that this is a day for rejoicing – a day to celebrate the hearing of the Word; "for the joy of the Lord is your strength." The people respond joyously!

The Word of God is a two-edged sword in Nehemiah's time as it is in our time. It gives life to those who receive it and condemns to death those who reject it. What application of Scripture does God want you to make in your life? Put it into practice so that you might know the "joy of the Lord"!

Nehemiah 8:13-9:3

What is the writer saying?

How can I apply this to my life?

pray *Costa Rica – For continued growth in missionary outreach, which has doubled over the last 10 years.*

On the first day of the seventh month, Ezra reads the Word of God all morning to "all that could hear with understanding" (8:1-3). On the second day, the leaders study the Word in more depth (v. 13). They discover that beginning the fifteenth day of the seventh month they are to observe the Feast of Tabernacles according to Leviticus 23:33-44. The sacrifices of the festival were observed when the altar was first set up years before (Ezra 3:3, 4), but the Israelites have not dwelled in tabernacles (booths) since the days of Joshua. This is a necessary part of this observance because it memorializes the deliverance from Egypt to their children (Leviticus 23:41-43).

All the while they are making preparations and observing the Feast of Tabernacles, they keep reading and studying the law of God. On the twenty-second day of the seventh month, they observe the last of the special annual Sabbaths that begins with the Passover in the first month. These annual Sabbaths are called holy convocations and "solemn assemblies."

Two days after the end of the seventh month festivities (9:1), instead of going home, they continue to assemble for reading, confession and worship.

This brings about the longest prayer in the Bible (9:5-37). Along with Daniel's prayer of Daniel 9 and Ezra's prayer of Ezra 9, it is a prayer of national confession.

As you study and apply the Word of God to your life, similar responses will come to your heart and soul. There should be new insights into how God expects you to live. There should be a step of obedience as you choose to practice the Word of God. There should be some first *doings* of the things of the Word of God. There will be great gladness and joy as your life is brought into closer fellowship with God.

25 Friday

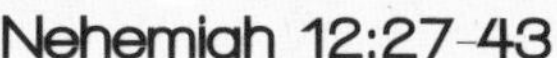

Nehemiah 12:27-43

What is the writer saying?

How can I apply this to my life?

pray *Bolivia – For youth outreach activities to the 53% of the population that is 19 or under.*

The effectual ministry of the Word as described in chapter 8 produces the repentance and confession of chapter 9, "thou hast done right, but we have done wickedly" (9:33). The evidence of godly repentance is the covenant of chapter 10 signed by the governmental and spiritual leaders (9:38). They promise, "to observe and do all the commandments of the Lord" (10:29). More specifically, they promise no intermarriage with the heathen (10:30), to keep the weekly and annual Sabbaths according to the law (10:31), and to tithe for the support of the Levites and their work (10:32-39).

Nehemiah 11:1-12:26 lists the people involved in the governmental and religious procedures and to an extent describes their functions.

The stage is now set for the dedication of the wall of Jerusalem (12:27-43) and the restoration of the temple procedures (12:44-47). The Levites are brought to Jerusalem from all parts of the Land for leading the festive occasion. The singers with their musical instruments are brought to center stage. After a purification ceremony, Nehemiah organizes two great choirs of singers. One choir leads a procession around the wall. The other choir and its procession march in the other direction until they meet. The rejoicing of the men, women and children is heard for a great distance.

In this world, God's people often face toil, trials, and heartache. For those Christians who faithfully stay focused upon the tasks God has given them to do, there can also be much rejoicing "with great joy" (v. 43). Are there any *for-God-has-made* events in your life? What has God done in your life that can be seen by those people around you?

Nehemiah 13:1-14

What is the writer saying?

How can I apply this to my life?

pray *Japan – Holy Spirit to help these people see their sinfulness so that He can call them to repentance.*

Nehemiah governs the land of Judah twelve years (5:14), according to the time previously set with King Artaxerxes (2:6). Chapter 13 takes us to a time several years later, when the king permits Nehemiah to return a second time to Jerusalem.

Beginning at verse 4, Nehemiah tells of events that transpire while he is away from Jerusalem. The people are disobeying the law precisely in the three areas in which they have covenanted to obey (10:30, 31, 37).

First, they stop tithing and that forces the Levites to leave their temple duties to find other means of support. The storerooms in the temple are empty. Tobiah, the Ammonite, who is married to the daughter of a Jewish leader (6:18), makes a deal with Eliashib, the high priest. Further, Eliashib's grandson marries a daughter of Sanballat, the Samaritan (Horonite refers to a city in Samaria)! That utterly corrupts the high priesthood, which is hereditary.

When Nehemiah arrives on the scene, Tobiah is comfortably living in the temple storerooms. Nehemiah throws Tobiah and all of his furnishings out and commands the building to be physically and ceremonially cleansed. He then appoints faithful leaders to collect, safeguard, and distribute tithes.

The remainder of the chapter tells how Nehemiah corrects the observance of the Sabbath and the practice of intermarriage.

The maneuvering of Tobiah results in this unholy man living in the holy temple. Perhaps you have allowed sinful practices or things to maneuver themselves into your life until they are contaminating your life, which should be set apart as a holy habitation for God, a living temple! Just as Nehemiah "cast forth" all the *stuff* of Tobiah, what *stuff* is making your life unholy before God? What do you need to "cast forth"?

The Book of Acts is a study in transitions. It shows the transition from Law to Grace; from a focus on Israel to a focus on the church. Acts is also the only historical sequel to the Gospels.

The author of the book is Luke, a close associate of the Apostle Paul. The book is written as a companion volume to the Gospel of Luke, as seen by comparing the opening verses from both books (see Luke 1:1-4, Acts 1:1-3).

There are a number of important transitions in the book. The most important, however, is the transition from the Kingdom to the Church. The church, which began in Acts 2 on the day of Pentecost, is not instituted abruptly. In fact, it is not until the arrival of the Apostle Paul that the *mysteries* of this church age are revealed to us. In Acts, chapters 1-12, Peter is the prominent apostle and his preaching, for the most part, is geared to the Jewish people. In Acts 3:19-21, Peter makes an authentic re-offer of the Kingdom, which the Jews had rejected.

The last chapters of Acts focus primarily upon the ministry of the Apostle Paul and thus, it can accurately be said that Acts is an apologetic for his ministry.

The Apostle Paul, in these few years, was said to have "turned the world upside down" (Acts 17:6). Clearly, the doctrines of the church age are unfolded before our eyes and the kingdom fades into the background. Acts was written in approximately A.D. 60-62.

We generally outline the book based on Acts 1:8, "But ye shall receive power, after that the Holy Ghost is come upon you: and ye shall be witnesses unto me both in Jerusalem, and in all Judaea, and in Samaria, and unto the uttermost part of the earth."

I. The Witness to Jerusalem (Acts 1-7)
II. The Witness to Judaea and Samaria (Acts 8-9)
III. The Witness to the Uttermost Part (Acts 10-28)

Because the Book of Acts is a book of transitions, we need to be careful that we do not consider all the things that happen as normal. For example, Ananias and Sapphira are not examples of the normal way to handle people in the church who lie about their giving. Many of the spectacular events are transition elements and did not continue, even to the end of Acts itself.

Acts 1:1-11

What is the writer saying?

How can I apply this to my life?

pray *Portugal – Pray that saved teens will be encouraged to reach their unsaved friends through evangelistic outreach programs.*

The "former treatise" referred to in verse 1 is the Gospel of Luke (see Luke 1:1-4). As the author of both this book and of the gospel that bears his name, Luke sought to arrange his material in as orderly a fashion as possible (Luke 1:3). Theophilus, literally *friend* (philus) *of God* (theos), was more than likely a wealthy Gentile who could have financed all of Luke's research and writing.

This first section brings us up to date as to where we are in the account of Christ's life. Luke summarizes the events that took place during the forty days that Christ spent on earth, from His resurrection to the ascension. Clearly, Luke wants to focus our attention on Christ's promise to send the Holy Spirit from the Father. Jesus asks them simply to wait in Jerusalem until the Spirit is given.

The disciples, realizing that Jesus is about to depart, ask Him how they would know when He will restore the Kingdom to Israel. They are still thinking in terms of the physical, earthly kingdom as described in the Old Testament. Jesus is noncommittal in His answer. They do not need to know when the Kingdom will come. They only need to know what they should do in the meantime. In verse 8, the word for *witness* is a word we have transliterated *martyr*. All of the apostles, with the possible exception of John, will be martyred for the sake of the Gospel.

We live in a world of instant access and waiting has almost become a lost art. If we are ever going to experience everything God has for us, we will need to learn to wait. Jesus asks the disciples to wait in Jerusalem. Their obedience is rewarded with an empowerment from God.

26 Monday

Acts 1:12-26

What is the writer saying?

How can I apply this to my life?

pray *Praise God that He supplies all our needs according to His riches in glory by Christ Jesus (Philippians 4:19).*

The distance from the Mount of Olives to Jerusalem is not that far. When Luke describes it as the Sabbath Day's journey, he is speaking of the distance that a Jew was allowed to walk on the Sabbath (just over ½ of a mile). This does not imply that these things happened on a Sabbath; in fact, it is a Thursday, forty days after the Resurrection.

The group that is meeting in the upper room includes the remaining eleven apostles, the women who had regularly supported Christ's ministry (cf. Luke 8:2-3), Jesus's mother, Mary, and Jesus's half brothers. (According to Matthew 13:55, they are James, Joseph, Simon, and Judas.) Jesus's brothers are not saved during Christ's ministry (John 7:5), but become believers sometime after the resurrection. James and Jude are both authors of New Testament books.

Some have concluded that the decision to replace Judas is a mistake, a rush to judgment. However, in order to fulfill Matthew 19:28 a replacement "must" (see v. 22) take place.

The uniquely Jewish practice of casting lots is last seen in the New Testament here, at the end of this chapter.

Luke states that they were all of one mind, devoting themselves to prayer. These are two characteristics of the early church: unity of purpose and dependence upon God.

The early church was a dynamic church that turned the world upside down for Christ. The key elements in their success were simply this: they depended totally on God and were incredibly focused. These two elements are always necessary for spiritual success.

Acts 2:1-13

What is the writer saying?

How can I apply this to my life?

pray *Mexico – For outreach to teens as churches tend to gear all programming to adults.*

Pentecost is fifty days after the Feast of Passover. The word *pentecost* actually means fiftieth. This Feast is a celebration of the wheat harvest. It is also the traditional date for the giving of the Law to Moses on Mount Sinai. This day would mark the beginning of a great harvest. It would also mark the birth of the Church.

That Pentecost was "fully come" (v. 1) is the indication that this day fulfills all that the feast had pointed to for over 1,400 years. The symbols that appear in this section all relate to the Holy Spirit. Jesus uses wind in John 3:8 and fire in Matthew 3:11 and Luke 3:16. Wind reminds us of the mystery of the Spirit's ministry and fire speaks of His judgment.

This event marks the beginning of the Church. All believers since that time have been baptized into the body of Christ, which is the Church, at the moment they are saved. This is the first occurrence of tongues in the Book of Acts. Throughout Acts, each time tongues are seen (chapters 2, 10 and 19), both Jews and an apostle are present. Also, that which is spoken in tongues is heard and understood as a known language.

Today, much confusion surrounds the issue of tongues. However, the Bible is clear that tongues are a foundational sign to authenticate the work and messengers (Hebrews 2:3, 4) of God. A foundation is only laid once (Ephesians 2:20).

Acts 2:14-21

What is the writer saying?

How can I apply this to my life?

pray *Bolivia – That redeeming love will break the long-held bondage to idolatry and superstition.*

The response of the unbelievers to the sign of tongues is divided. Some are amazed while others dismiss it as drunkenness. Peter takes advantage of the situation to address both groups.

Peter challenges the accusation of drunkenness by pointing to the time. Verse 15 indicates it is only the third hour (9 a.m.), far too early for drunkenness.

The men Peter addresses are devout and respect the Scriptures. Peter wants to be sure they realize that what they are seeing is a Biblical phenomenon.

His quote from Joel is interesting. Clearly the first portion of the passage is fulfilled in Acts 2, but if we read down through verse 21, we see some elements that are not fulfilled in Acts. Verse 19 is clearly referring to the tribulation period. The fulfillment of the remainder of Joel's prophecy is contingent upon the repentance of Israel, which will not occur until the end of the Tribulation (see Matthew 24:27-30; Zechariah 12:10).

Almost every day we are presented with opportunities to speak out about the Lord Jesus Christ. Peter tells us to be ready to give an answer for the hope that we have. If you were there at Pentecost, would you have seized the opportunity? What about the opportunity you may get today?

Acts 2:22-36

What is the writer saying?

How can I apply this to my life?

pray *Poland – For the exposure of all false doctrines. Jehovah's Witnesses outnumber followers of Christ.*

This is just over fifty days since the Crucifixion of Christ and since Peter denied his Lord beside a courtyard fire, but what a difference. Peter's message is one of victory, not one of defeat. He did not need to prove that Jesus had performed miracles, for they had seen Him.

The miracles of Christ verify that He is Whom He said. When the disciples of John the Baptist came asking if He really is the Messiah of Israel, Jesus, Himself, points to His works saying, "The blind receive their sight, and the lame walk, the lepers are cleansed, and the deaf hear, the dead are raised up, and the poor have the gospel preached to them" (Matthew 11:5). These are the very works the Prophet Isaiah said that Messiah would do (Isaiah 35:5, 6).

Notice Peter's perspective in verse 23. The cross was not a mistake. It was a part of the plan of God. They had nailed Him to the cross, but it had always been a part of God's plan. It is the Resurrection that Peter emphasizes in this sermon by referring to Psalm 16:8-11 and 110:1.

These Messianic Psalms are clearly not referring to David, for he saw death and experienced the corruption of the grave. Clearly they foretell the resurrection of Christ, whom God would not abandon to the grave.

Isn't it great that God's blessing does not depend on our faithfulness? In the face of our rebellion, God was faithful to atone for our sins. You may have rejected Him yesterday, but He is willing to receive you today.

26 Friday

QT

Acts 2:37-47

What is the writer saying?

How can I apply this to my life?

pray *Pray for your pastor and his family to grow in God's grace and maturity and to pursue righteousness.*

The response of the people to Peter's message is dramatic. They immediately ask what they should do. Peter's answer is a little difficult to understand. Repentance is clearly a requirement for salvation. Faith and repentance are two sides of the same coin. To turn to God (faith) is to turn from going your own way (repentance) and vice versa. However, baptism is not a requirement for salvation. We can safely say that Peter is not making baptism a part of being saved.

Let's notice a few things. The people did not ask Peter what to do in order to be saved. They asked him what they should do next. His answer is they should be saved (involving repentance) and then be baptized. It is the next phrase that is so controversial. It has been misinterpreted to say that baptism is *for* the remission of sins. Here, the word *for* would be better translated *with respect to.*

Clearly Peter is not attempting to give a definitive statement regarding the requirements for salvation. Considering the large number of clear passages concerning salvation that do not include baptism, it would be a poor interpretation to reach such a conclusion based on this one difficult passage.

This passage concludes with a casual report in verses 46-47, summarizing the book up to this point.

One rule of hermeneutics is that clear passages must interpret those that are difficult to understand. This is just such a case. *Always interpret the obscure in light of the clear teachings of Scripture.*

Acts 3:1-11

What is the writer saying?

How can I apply this to my life?

pray *Canada – Pray for Bible institute ministry teams to have a lasting impact in local churches.*

The account in this section is of the lame man who is healed by Peter at the gate called Beautiful. Peter and John are on their way to the temple at about three o'clock in the afternoon, when a man who has been lame from birth approaches them for alms. The man does not know Peter and is not even thinking about being healed. Peter clearly has the gift of healing. When he commands the man to get up and walk, the man is immediately healed.

A few facts about this healing are worth noting in comparison to today's so-called *healers*. Peter heals instantly and fully. Peter heals by his own faith, not by the lame man's. Peter goes to the sick and heals in the streets, not at a place where he can control the environment. Peter asks for no remuneration. So-called faith healers today do not follow the Biblical pattern. When Peter heals this man in Jesus's name (v. 6), this is the same as saying by Jesus's authority. In many ways this lame man is a picture of unbelieving Israel. He is outside the temple; Israel is outside of fellowship with God. The answer for this man is to meet Jesus Christ. In the same way, Israel will never be whole until they turn in repentance to Christ (Zechariah 13:9).

The love of Christ compels us to reach out to those in need. Peter did not need to stop to help the lame man, but he did. We need to be of the same mind. Find needs and strive to meet them. There will never be a shortage of needs, but there is always a shortage of workers.

Acts 3:12-26

What is the writer saying?

How can I apply this to my life?

pray *Portugal – Pray for more open doors with local churches and for more workers to help teaching and discipling students.*

Peter uses the circumstance of this healing, and the crowd that gathers in response, as an opportunity for the Gospel. He begins by giving glory to God and proclaiming that this miracle is done through the power of the resurrected Christ. He then lays the blame for Jesus's crucifixion squarely at the feet of Israel. This man stands whole, through faith in the Holy One they had denied.

When Jesus came presenting Himself to Israel, He came offering Himself as their Messiah. Had they repented and responded to His offer, He then would have instituted the literal earthly Kingdom (see Matthew 4:17). Israel's rejection of Christ was through their ignorance, but was a fulfillment of that which the prophets had foretold (v. 18). Having said this, Peter then gives an authentic re-offer of that literal earthly kingdom.

The phrase in verse 19, "when the times of refreshing shall come from the presence of the Lord," is clearly a reference to the Millennial Kingdom which will be established at His second coming. The construction of this verse relates this clause and the preceding clause to the condition, "repent ye therefore." The repentance of Israel will signal all future blessings that await God's chosen people. Israel's continuing rebellion does not take away from the legitimacy of Peter's re-offer of the Kingdom.

The nation of Israel's present state of unbelief does not change the fact that a glorious future awaits God's chosen people. The promise God made to David of an everlasting Kingdom has not been taken away or revoked. During the Tribulation period Israel will again take center stage in the program of God.

Acts 4:1-12

What is the writer saying?

How can I apply this to my life?

pray *United Kingdom – To exchange their passion for political correctness for one of biblical correctness.*

This is the beginning of persecution in the book of Acts, and it is the religious leaders who initiate it. The Sadducees are particularly angry because they do not believe in a resurrection. Jesus had defeated their best lawyers in public debates (Matthew 22:23-33) and now His disciples are preaching that He was resurrected from the dead. They are able to put the messengers in jail, but they cannot stop the message. Peter and John stand before the Sanhedrin the next morning. Most of the men present are the same ones who had condemned Jesus. Caiaphas is presently the high priest (see Matthew 26:3, 57; John 11:47-53:, 18:13,14,24-28), but Annas, his father-in-law and former high priest, is still the power to be reckoned with.

As Peter stands up to speak, he is filled with the Holy Spirit. The Greek word used for *filled* (v. 8) is often used in Acts to speak of a supernatural empowerment that enables the person filled to act or speak for God. Again Peter uses this opportunity to present Jesus Christ as the only way of salvation.

Verse 11 is a quote from Psalm 118:22. The phrase, "head of the corner," or "cornerstone" was an allusion to the most significant stone of the foundation (see Ephesians 2:20).

The Gospel is the power of God unto salvation and can never be silenced. Sinful man may be able to imprison or kill the mouthpiece, but the message will continue to move forward. Opposition has never weakened the Church it has always strengthened it.

27 Tuesday

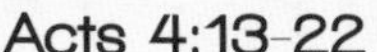

Acts 4:13-22

What is the writer saying?

How can I apply this to my life?

pray *Honduras – For godly businessmen to establish enterprises to employ and evangelize the poor.*

The Sanhedrin find themselves in a real bind. They want to punish Peter and John, but they are speechless because of the healed man who is standing there before them (v. 14) and because of the crowd. They are glorifying God because of the healing that had taken place. Because they waited until morning (they prosecuted Jesus at night), they have to consider the people who gather to watch the proceedings.

Unable to physically punish the preachers, they warn them to stop preaching and teaching about Jesus. Peter's reply (v. 19) in no way advocates civil disobedience. Believers ought to obey their human authorities in all things, except when they are asked to do something that is a direct violation of God's Word.

Verse 20 is the perfect basis for giving your testimony. You simply are to share what God has done in your life (see 1 John 1:1-3).

The man upon whom this miracle is performed is over 40 years old. He had lain in this spot often and surely, the Lord Jesus Himself had passed by this man. The miracles of God are always done according to God's sovereign will and are designed to authenticate the work or workers of God.

Human nature being what it is, we often find ourselves looking for a reason to disobey the authorities that God has placed in our lives. This is not the norm. Generally, human authorities are not a hindrance to the Gospel. Very seldom will we find ourselves in a position where we have to ignore the law to serve God.

Acts 4:23-37

What is the writer saying?

How can I apply this to my life?

pray *Mexico – That the Mexicans find their identity in a personal faith in Christ.*

Upon their release, Peter and John return to the company of believers and relate all that has happened. As a result, God is glorified in light of His sovereignty over the affairs of men.

Verses 25 and 26 are a quote from Psalm 2:1-2. This royal Psalm will ultimately be fulfilled at the end of the Tribulation when Christ establishes His Millennial Kingdom. Later in Acts 13:33, Paul again references this Psalm, stating that the promise of Psalm 2:7 is fulfilled in the Resurrection of Jesus Christ. The phrase in verses 27 and 30, "thy holy child Jesus," is better translated *thy holy Servant Jesus*. Here the Greek word translated *child* is the same word translated *servant* in verse 25, in reference to David.

The persecution that the infant Church faces does not cause discouragement, but rather has a great unifying effect on the believers. Their prayer (v. 29) is not a prayer for deliverance, but rather a prayer for boldness. God is pleased to answer this petition, and does so with power. The place is physically shaken and the disciples are filled with the Spirit of God. The signs and wonders (v. 30) validate that the message and ministry of the Apostles is truly from God.

Verse 32, "all things common," is not advocating Christian socialism but rather is an indication that the early Church is bound together with great concern for one another. Many who placed their faith in Christ would be cut off from the resources of their unbelieving family.

Unity is always a mark of the Church that is walking in the Spirit. The unity seen in the early Church is not just a first century exception, but rather should permeate the Church today. Where the Spirit of the Lord is, there is unity!

Acts 5:1-11

What is the writer saying?

How can I apply this to my life?

pray *Papua New Guinea – Rural church work is being weakened by church hopping. Pray for committed members.*

The story of Ananias and Sapphira is one of the most sobering in the New Testament. Here is a couple caught up with outward appearances. In Acts 4:36-37, Barnabas sells his land and gives the proceeds to the Church. Ananias and Sapphira want to appear just as spiritual; but they are not willing to give all their money. They want to give the appearance that they have. The result of the lie is graphically described in this passage.

Without a doubt, many people since that time have lied about how much they have put in the offering. Why is it only this one time that a death sentence is imposed? Several answers are proposed. The fact that an apostle is present makes the situation different for today's local churches. Local pastors do not have the same authority as Peter did. This event is early in the life of the church and is given as a warning to all who would follow. Or, perhaps, God wants to maintain a high level of purity within the early church. Whatever the answer, we probably do not need to worry that this will happen at a Sunday service today. But neither should we think lightly of our sin.

We know very well that God is a loving God and is the Father of all mercies. This does not mean that we should impose upon His goodness. Ananias and Sapphira thought they could sin and get away with it.

Acts 5:12-23

What is the writer saying?

How can I apply this to my life?

pray *Argentina – Increased scholarship funding to enable foreign students to attend Bible colleges.*

We should not expect that each and every event that occurrs during the early days of the church will re-occur in this day and age. Verse 12 gives a summary that generally describes what is happening at this point in the history of the church. Just as the deaths of Ananias and Sapphira are unique to the early church, so are the miraculous healings that are taking place.

As God continues to work through the apostles, the people hold them in high esteem (v. 13). Some even believe that Peter's shadow held healing power (v. 15). However, the text does not say that any are healed in this manner. Although we do see that many of those who are sick or demon possessed, who come to the apostles, are made whole again. As a result of the attention that these miracles are bringing to the apostles, the religious leaders become envious (v. 17) and throw them into prison. God, however, had other plans and sent his angel to open the prison doors; a fact which escapes the notice of their keepers (vv. 22-23).

Sometimes it is those who know the least about the Gospel who are most open to it. It seems there are always those who stand on the edge. They know that Christ is the answer, but they just aren't ready for a commitment. They stand at the gate, hesitating, while others pour in. Don't get caught standing at the door, which may not be open tomorrow.

27 Saturday

Acts 5:24-32

What is the writer saying?

How can I apply this to my life?

pray *Costa Rica – For the growth and strengthening of Bible schools that train leadership.*

The high priest and captain of the temple are still trying to figure out what has happened to the apostles, when the report comes that they are standing in the temple (v. 25) teaching the people. Because public sentiment is on the side of the apostles, the religious leaders handle the situation with great care.

Once again, before the Sanhedrin, they are asked why they disobeyed the command to not preach "in this name?" That the high priest will not name the name of Jesus shows the contempt he holds for Him.

Peter again presses the same response he had given earlier – they must obey God rather than men. The religious leaders are more concerned for their reputations (v. 28) than they were for the truth. Their statement, "filled Jerusalem with your doctrine," is an indication that word about the apostles' ministry and message had filled the city. Peter again uses this opportunity to preach the Gospel – the death, burial, and resurrection of Jesus Christ – and to call those who hear unto repentance and forgiveness. They personally are witnesses of the events they proclaim, and the Holy Spirit bears witness that they speak from God by signs and wonders.

Those who are overly concerned about their reputation will find difficulty being rightly related to God. The world does not understand what it means to follow Christ and will often exhibit great hostility toward those who choose to live a godly life. Acceptance by the crowd will be meaningless in eternity.

QT

Sunday 28

Acts 5:33-42

What is the writer saying?

How can I apply this to my life?

pray *Brazil – Pray that Christians in high profile positions would keep a moral and ethical testimony.*

As the Apostles find themselves before the Sanhedrin once again, the council wants to put them to death (v. 33). Gamaliel gives the council some very wise advice. Since the Apostles are put outside, how does Luke know what is said in the room? It is very possible that Paul, a student of Gamaliel, is present during this council. It is also possible that Nicodemus and Joseph of Arimathea are on this council.

Using a couple of examples from recent history, Gamaliel suggests that they ought to wait and see what comes from this new teaching. If what is happening is from mere men, it would soon fade, just as the examples he cites had (vv. 36-38); but if it is of God, they will not be able to stop it (v. 39). The council takes his advice but has the apostles beaten before setting them free.

The reaction of the apostles is beautiful. They rejoice that they are counted worthy to suffer for Christ. Not a complaint is heard.

This is unjust, unfair, and unconstitutional, yet James would later say, "count it all joy when ye fall into divers temptations" (James 1:2). He speaks from experience.

A little opposition has never been bad for the Church. It may seem harsh for the short term, but it will always purge out the dross and improve the testimony of the Church.

28 Monday

Acts 6:1-15

What is the writer saying?

How can I apply this to my life?

pray *Praise the Lord for His sovereignty over details of your life.*

At the beginning, the Church is in "one accord." This does not last long, however. What cannot be accomplished from the outside is often done with ease from the inside. Today's passage deals with the first Church business meeting and the first dispute.

The dispute is over how relief is distributed. Believers from outside of Judea complain that their widows are not being taken care of properly. The apostles feel that leaving the ministry of prayer and preaching to serve tables is not the answer. Therefore, they choose from among the congregation seven men, whose responsibility it is to make sure that these kinds of things are handled properly. This is the model upon which the office of deacon is based today. These men are chosen because of their integrity and their spiritual qualifications, not because they are trained in food service.

Stephen is one of the seven men chosen. Other than that, we know very little about him. Most likely, he is a Hellenistic Jew, not from Judea. His defense before the Sanhedrin in chapter 7 marks him as a well educated man. Apart from this, we know that he was full of grace and spiritual power.

The word deacon simply means *to serve* and really goes back to this idea of serving tables. No task should be considered menial and no task should be assigned apart from spiritual requirements. Neither should any task be beneath a believer. The apostles are not above waiting on tables, but are conscious of ministry constraints they face.

Acts 7:1-16

What is the writer saying?

How can I apply this to my life?

pray *Czech Republic – Pray for the establishment and growth of Christian institutes and seminaries.*

Although not much is known about Stephen (Luke introduces him in the list of men chosen to serve in 6:5) he stands to deliver one of the most powerful messages in Acts. As this chapter begins, Stephen is given an opportunity to defend himself against the accusations made at the end of the previous section (see 6:11-14). Just as Jesus is falsely accused so Stephen is slandered before the religious leaders.

Stephen's reply is the longest message in the Book of Acts, but his focus is not on defending his own reputation. The main point of Stephen's message is found in verse 51, "as your fathers did, so do ye." Earlier, Jesus made the same criticism of this generation (Matthew 23:31-32). Stephen's message illustrates this history of hard-heartedness and rebellion against God's guidance.

Stephen begins with the historic account of Abraham, who is the father of the nation of Israel. He traces the working of God from Abraham's call in Mesopotamia to his sojourn in Egypt. Stephen rehearses the promises of a son (seed) and the land, which he pointed out to his hearers, was where they were now dwelling (v. 4). He then reviews the deliverance from the bondage of Egypt, through Joseph.

Stephen carefully details the life of Joseph, which has many parallels to the life of Christ. Their brothers reject both. Also, when Joseph's brothers first come to him in Egypt, they do not recognize him, but they do on their second visit. Likewise, Christ Jesus is not received upon His first coming but will be at His second coming.

God is faithful to His promises and longsuffering. However, He will not always continue to extend His grace in the face of continual rejection. If you have never accepted God's gracious offer of salvation make today that day.

Acts 7:17-29

What is the writer saying?

How can I apply this to my life?

pray *Hungary – Pray that many Bible school students here from central Europe will become leaders at home.*

Stephen, continuing his message before the religious leaders of Israel, moves from Joseph to God's working through Moses. One of the accusations leveled against Stephen is that he spoke blasphemous words against Moses. The sons of Israel, upon his first attempt to be their deliverer, reject Moses, like Joseph and Jesus. Surely those who heard Stephen's message would have been able to see the parallel to Christ.

Throughout his message Stephen skillfully develops the pattern that Jews historically reject the deliverers that God raises up for His people, according to His promises to them. Now, just as then, God provides the ultimate Deliverer, One who has come to deliver them from their sin; and they act consistently in rejecting Him. Stephen's point is that his hearers are doing what the nation always does whenever God works in their midst.

It is significant to note that up until this point his hearers are patiently listening to what Stephen has to say. They are quite willing to hear how their forefathers had missed God's will and persecuted God's man; however, that would all change when Stephen turns his message upon them and holds them responsible for the rejection and death of Christ.

Often we have no problem hearing and being sympathetic to the fact that others fall short of God's will. However, when we are the ones being confronted with our own sin, then that is a whole other matter. Let us be quick to hear and quick to respond in repentance when our sin is made known unto us. "He, that being often reproved hardeneth his neck, shall suddenly be destroyed, and that without remedy." (Proverbs 29:1).

Acts 7:30-43

What is the writer saying?

How can I apply this to my life?

pray *Portugal – For the churches to raise up full–time workers of the Gospel.*

Continuing on the subject of Moses, Stephen forges his case against the nation of Israel.

Moses is the one that God calls at the burning bush (v. 30), sends to deliver the people from bondage – and they refuse him (v. 35). Through Moses, God shows His power unto Pharaoh by great signs and wonders. He continues to work signs and wonders through the parting of the Red Sea and throughout their time of wandering in the wilderness. This is the same Moses who prophesied that God would raise up another deliverer from among them, and yet even while he is on Mount Sinai receiving the commandments of God, the people's hearts are turning, in rebellion, back to Egypt. The word translated *church* in verse 38, is better translated *assembly*. At no time is the Church seen in the Old Testament.

Stephen's point again is that Israel has a history of missing God's man and rebelling against God's program. Even though God has worked mighty miracles through Moses, so quickly their fickle hearts are ready to turn away from Him, back into the bondage they had just left. In the same way, Jesus Christ comes, attesting by signs and wonders just as Isaiah (Isaiah 35:5-6) had prophesied He would. Yet Israel does not receive Him, but clings to their bondage.

As a result of their fathers' sins, God sends them into captivity in Babylon (v. 43). Would they now get off without punishment?

Jeremiah wrote, "The heart is deceitful above all things, and desperately wicked: who can know it?" (Jeremiah 17:9). The worst kind of deception is self-deception. Let us be quick to examine our own hearts and turn from any hint of rebellion that God reveals.

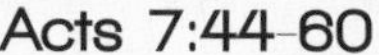

28 Friday

QT

Acts 7:44-60

What is the writer saying?

How can I apply this to my life?

pray *Nigeria – For the many godly businessmen who use their influence to witness in every area of society.*

After a long recitation of Israel's rocky relationship with God and his messengers, Stephen, in this passage, applies the message directly to those who are present. He calls them "stiffnecked" (v. 51). This word comes from the agricultural methods of that day. An ox or beast of burden, that refuses to obey the reigns and turn its neck, is called stiffnecked. It does not respond to direction.

To be "uncircumcised in heart and ears" is an even greater insult. Circumcision is a sign of the Abrahamic covenant. Stephen is telling them that they are Jews by outward signs, but Gentiles on the inside, and traitors of the heart.

In verse 52, his accusations become more specific. Their fathers, disguised as God's people, murdered the prophets. They, wearing the same disguise, murdered the Messiah.

In response to his words the Jews rush upon Stephen and murder him with their own hands. The events surrounding his death mark it as special. He is given a vision of God's glory and of Jesus Christ (vv. 55-56)! He calls out in a way similar to Jesus, "receive my spirit" and also, like Jesus, he requests forgiveness for his assailants.

This also marks the formal introduction of Paul, the Apostle to the Gentiles. He is still called Saul at this point, but from here on in the Book of Acts, Peter begins sharing the spotlight with Paul. Soon Peter will all but disappear from the pages that Luke writes.

A religious exterior can often hide a treacherous heart. Christianity is not a matter of outward form; it is a personal relationship with Jesus Christ. Put your focus on the inner man and the outer man will be fine.

Acts 8:1-13

What is the writer saying?

How can I apply this to my life?

pray *Pray that God would save many of the teachers and administration of your local public school.*

Once Stephen is stoned, a full-scale persecution breaks out in Jerusalem. This begins the second major section of the book as the Gospel moves into Samaria. Samaria is a region located directly north of Judea. The people who live there are of Jewish and Gentile blood. As such, the Jewish establishment despises them. However, Samaria is included in Acts 1:8.

Verse 3 gives a quick update on the activities of Paul/Saul. He becomes a leader, if not *the* leader of the persecution that breaks out.

Philip, like Stephen, is one of those chosen by the early church to serve the church and aid the apostles. When Philip preaches the Gospel to the Samaritans, it marks a new phase in God's program.

The word for miracles in verse 6 is *semeion* and refers to a *sign*. A sign miracle is one that is used to authenticate a message or the messenger.

The apparent conversion of Simon is included in Luke's account as an example of how some will try to use the Gospel to their own advantage. There is some question as to the genuineness of this conversion. Peter, in verse 23, seems to say that Simon is still lost.

It is persecution that triggers this spread of the Gospel. It was the jolt that got these missions started. God intends that we be missions-minded and if we don't get about that business, He may use some undesirable means to get us moving.

29 Sunday

Acts 8:14-25

What is the writer saying?

How can I apply this to my life?

pray *United Kingdom – Wisdom for those ministering among the 900,000 college and university students.*

This is a key passage to our understanding of miracles and sign gifts in the New Testament. Philip has been ministering in Samaria for a while now. Many are saved and baptized, but only Philip is filled with the Holy Spirit and performing miracles. As word of what was happening among the Samaritans gets back to Jerusalem, Peter and John are sent to Samaria.

In verse 17, Peter lays hands on these converts and they receive the Spirit. Simon, the magician, reveals his true heart by trying to buy apostolic authority.

The sign of speaking in tongues in the Book of Acts only occurs in the presence of an apostle. The significance of Peter and John being there as the Holy Spirit is given is to assure that there is no division in the Body of Christ, thus widening the gap that already exists between Jews and Samaritans.

So often we long for some of the powers that the apostles had. We need to be careful. Simon, who was caught up with a desire for such powers, was far from God in his heart. The gifts have their place in church history but that time is past. Let's not get the mindset of Simon who let the gifts blind him to the purpose of God.

QT Monday 29

Acts 8:26-40

What is the writer saying?

How can I apply this to my life?

pray *Germany – That opportunities of sharing the Gospel with the unsaved will not be lost.*

The city of Gaza (v. 26) is destroyed in 93 B.C. and is rebuilt closer to the Mediterranean coast in 57 B.C. The deserted desert road of this passage passes through ancient Gaza, which more than likely, is in the Judean desert along the road that leads to southern Egypt.

In Acts 1:8 Jesus tells His disciples that they would be His witnesses in Jerusalem, Judea, Samaria and unto the uttermost parts of the earth. Following the stoning of Stephen, we immediately see the Gospel moving out from Jerusalem. Clearly, the transition of the Gospel has begun and will not stop until it has gone to the uttermost. God leads Philip to leave the *many* of Samaria and go to the *one* in the Judean desert. The eunuch that Philip is led to (v. 27) is a high-ranking official of the court of Candace, queen of the Ethiopians. Ethiopia, here, is a reference to all of Africa, south of Egypt. This powerful man is an apparent worshiper of the God of Israel.

As he travels in his regal chariot, the eunuch is reading from the writings of the prophet Isaiah. At the urging of the Spirit, Philip joins the man's chariot and engages him concerning what he is reading. Verse 31 indicates that he does not understand the interpretation of what he is reading (Isaiah 53:7-8), but is eager to learn. Philip, beginning at that passage, proclaims Christ and the way of salvation. Responding in faith to what he had heard, the eunuch believes and desires to be baptized. Again, his baptism is not a part of being saved, but an evidence of his faith and subsequent desire to obey the Lord.

Paul tells Timothy to be instant (ready) in season and out of season to preach the Word (2 Timothy 4:2). We, too, need to be ready at all times and prepared for opportunities that God brings our way to share Christ. Are you studied up and prayed up so that God can use you?

29 Tuesday

Acts 9:1-9

What is the writer saying?

How can I apply this to my life?

pray *Philippines – Safety of missionaries working within the reach of Muslim extremists in Mindanao.*

Saul's conversion is one of the most dramatic accounts in Scripture. This is a man whose life is transformed – completely turned around in a moment – as he encounters Jesus on the Damascus road. Paul would share his incredible testimony before both great and small (Acts 26:22).

Saul is not looking to find salvation as he sets out for Damascus that day; he is looking to destroy the church that he sees as a threat to Judaism. This is a man consumed by his desire to destroy Christianity, like a fuming volcano uttering murderous threats. He is a fulfillment of Christ's prediction, "that whosoever killeth you will think that he doeth God service" (John 16:2). To suppose that such a man could change without the intervention of God is unthinkable. Saul is convinced that he is serving God; but now, as he comes in contact with Heaven, he is shocked to find out that he is persecuting God. His whole theology is blown apart. If Jesus is God, and Saul now realizes that He is, then his whole life to this point has been misdirected. Those who accompany Saul could hear the voice, but could not understand what was being said.

Saul was a most unlikely candidate for salvation just as many of us were. Never underestimate the power of the Gospel. There is no life that it cannot transform.

Acts 9:10-22

What is the writer saying?

How can I apply this to my life?

pray *Papua New Guinea – Rural church work is being weakened by church hopping. Pray for committed members.*

At this point, God has Saul's full attention. His sight is gone and he doesn't know if he will get it back. His entire reason for living has just been overthrown. As he sits in Damascus awaiting direction from God, he has no idea what lies ahead, but God does. God has a plan (v.15).

God does not have one of the apostles come to Saul. He could have, but He doesn't. This conversion is to be special, because Saul is going to be an apostle. We know little of Ananias. He has a common Jewish name and he is a resident of Damascus. When Jesus asks Ananias to go to Saul, his immediate reaction is fear. He has heard of Saul's reputation. Jesus reassures Ananias and tells him of His plans for Saul, a chosen instrument. He has been prepared for the task ahead. His theological training, his fluent Greek, his familiarity with Greek culture and his Roman citizenship all make him a perfect choice to carry the Gospel to the Gentiles. Verse 20 tells us that Saul wastes no time in getting busy for God.

What we see and what God sees are often different. The early church saw Saul as a threat; God saw his potential for good. In fact, it is when we are most useless in our own eyes that we are most useful in God's. See yourself and others the way God sees.

29 Thursday

Acts 9:23-31

What is the writer saying?

How can I apply this to my life?

pray *Korea – For godly Chinese businessmen to use their easy access to North Korea to share the Gospel.*

The zeal with which Saul had persecuted Christ is now turned to serving Him. His reputation gives him an immediate opening into the synagogues in Damascus. This might look like the same old Saul, but he sure doesn't talk like him. Galatians 1:17-18 makes it clear that at some point Saul spent three years in seclusion in the desert. It appears this stay in the desert occurrs between verses 22 and 23 of Acts 9.

Saul chooses not to go immediately to Jerusalem. These three years would help believers in Jerusalem forgive his mistreatment of them. This also gives Paul time, under the guidance of the Holy Spirit, to formulate his theology, which would bring a new emphasis to the church.

Verses 22-25 bring us full circle. Paul is now "increased the more in strength." This does not refer to physical but mental strength. His reasoning skills have become so sharp that he confounds the Jews in Damascus. Unable to refute Saul's teaching, they try to kill him. The trip to Jerusalem related in verses 26-29 corresponds to Galatians 1:18-21.

Although most of the disciples are fearful, Barnabas reaches out to Saul (Paul). This section ends with another of Luke's summary reports (v. 31).

As soon as Saul was able, he began to share his faith in Jesus Christ, but he also realized that he needed more preparation. The three years that Saul spent in the desert were essential to his effectiveness as a minister. If a man of Saul's caliber needed time to prepare, it is not surprising that we too need to take time.

Acts 9:32-43

What is the writer saying?

How can I apply this to my life?

pray *Austria – Austria has amoung the highest suicide, abortion and alcoholism rates in Europe. Pray that these people will turn to Jesus to meet their needs.*

The emphasis once again shifts to Peter. Paul is prepared by the Lord to carry the Gospel to the Gentiles, but just as Peter opens the door to Samaritans in Acts 8, Paul opens the door to Gentiles.

A church already exists in Lydda, but Peter's visit and ensuing miracles serve to strengthen and expand the congregation. The healing of Aeneas is one of the more prominent miracles performed there.

At Joppa, one of the saints, a godly woman named Dorcas, dies. The believers there send for Peter. Peter comes immediately to Joppa and, sending everyone else out of the room, he prays and the woman is raised from the dead.

We sometimes forget the power that accompanies the ministry of an apostle. Luke is trying to give us an overview of the status of the church in the areas it reaches. The Gospel fills Jerusalem, spreads to Judea and Galilee, and reaches into Samaria. The apostles are able to travel from city to city and find believers. The church is ready for its next wave of expansion. Peter takes up residence at the home of Simon the tanner. Most Jews will not go near a tanner because of the ceremonial uncleanness associated with the trade. Peter's presence at this home sets the stage for Chapter 10.

The early church does not have the resources that we have. Travel is slow and arduous. The needs of the people are great. In spite of that, they get the job done. With all of our comforts how are we doing at reaching our world for Jesus Christ?

29 Saturday

Acts 10:1-8

What is the writer saying?

How can I apply this to my life?

pray *Venezuela – For the defeat of any legal proposal to end or restrict evangelism in any way.*

To this point in the Book of Acts, all conversions are either Jews, half-Jews (Samaritans) or Jewish proselytes (the Ethiopian eunuch). Cornelius is the first recorded occasion of a Gentile being converted directly to Christianity. The amount of space accorded it by Luke in the Book of Acts stresses its importance.

Cornelius is called a "centurion" and a member of the Italian band. This designation means that he is a Roman soldier and leader of 100 men. A *band* equals 1/10 of a Roman legion. He is called "one that feared God" (v. 2).This phrase is used by Jews to refer to a Gentile who is unwilling to fully convert to Judaism, but who worships the true God of Israel. For the most part Cornelius follows Jewish practices but remains uncircumcised. The "ninth hour" (about three o'clock according to an historian of that time), is when the afternoon sacrifices are offered at the temple. It is also a traditional time of prayer for devout Jews. Note how clear the details of his vision are, even down to a specific person named Peter at a specific house of Simon the Tanner located by the sea. Apparently, there is more than just Cornelius who fear God in this household. He sends one of his "devout" soldiers to find Peter.

Cornelius may at times have wondered if his commitment to the God of the Jews was known. But his piety did *not* go unnoticed. God does not miss even the smallest sacrifice made in His name. Let us be diligent to serve God out of a heart of love and gratitude.

QT

Sunday 30

Acts 10:9-22

What is the writer saying?

How can I apply this to my life?

pray *Indonesia – For Muslim's (80% of India) hearts to be open to the truth of Jesus Christ.*

The next day, as Cornelius's delegation approaches Joppa, Peter has a vision. The "vessel" that is lowered is not defined for us. The word is used in Scripture for various containers. The vessel is spread out in the same fashion as a sheet drawn at the four corners. Contained in the vessel are a large variety of mammals (four-footed beasts and wild things), reptiles (creeping things) and birds (fowls). The common tie between all these is the fact that all are unclean, that is, forbidden by the Mosaic dietary laws (Leviticus 11).

The immediate lesson that God is teaching Peter clearly has reference to the delegation that is about to arrive from Cornelius. God wants Peter to realize that He has the right to change certain aspects of His program. The Gospel is about to make an incredible leap, so that in a few short years the church would become largely Gentile.

While Peter is trying to understand the vision, the delegation from Cornelius arrives. The Spirit instructs Peter that their arrival is in conjunction with the vision. From verse 22, it would appear that one or both of the servants are Jewish.

The phrase "doubting nothing" in verse 20 is very instructive. Under normal circumstances, Peter would have doubted about taking the Gospel to Cornelius. Peter is still in the *go only to the lost sheep of Israel* mode (Matthew 10:6). Had the vision not come to him, he would have most likely dismissed Cornelius's vision as some cruel hoax. But now, through the eyes of faith, Peter is beginning to get a glimpse of just how the Gospel is to go to the entire world.

In a similar fashion to Peter, we sometimes underestimate the extent to which God wants to work in our lives. We are happy with the little we have. Pray that God enlarges your vision so that you might strive to do great things for Him.

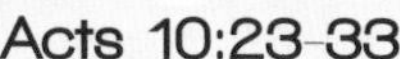

30 Monday

Acts 10:23-33

What is the writer saying?

How can I apply this to my life?

pray *Praise the Lord for the faithful believers who have had the greatest positive impact on your life.*

As Peter departs for Caesarea with the men from Cornelius, he takes along Jewish brethren from Joppa. This fact will be important later (v. 46), for any time the gift of tongues occurs in Acts, it is always in the presence of an apostle with Jews witnessing the sign (1 Corinthians 1:22).

Cornelius shows great faith (v. 24) by assembling his family and friends in anticipation of Peter's arrival. Peter's refusal of his worship (v. 26) underscores the pure motive with which he serves God.

Both Peter and Cornelius are still a little uncertain about exactly what is about to happen. Peter knows that God has given him a mandate to meet with Cornelius, and only Cornelius knows that Peter has an important message for him. Notice verse 29. It is clear that Peter is wondering exactly why God has sent him to Cornelius.

In verse 33, Cornelius expresses a similar sense of expectancy. It is very important to note God's participation in this event. Clearly, God instructs Peter to go to Cornelius, just as He instructs Cornelius to send for Peter. However there is one thing that God does not do. He does not preach the Gospel to Cornelius.

An emerging principle of the church age is that men are to reach men with the Gospel. Angels do not preach it. God does not supernaturally deliver it. It is the believer's responsibility to share the Good News of eternal life. This does not mean that God is not involved. It is God who empowers the Gospel. It is God who directs His saints. But it is the church's responsibility to take the Gospel into all the world.

The person most often prepared to share the Gospel is *someone else.* It seems that most church work falls on *his* shoulders too. Let's recognize that it is *our* responsibility to go and to share the Good News with all of mankind.

Acts 10:34-48

What is the writer saying?

How can I apply this to my life?

pray *Dominican Republic – For believers to be godly, impartial witnesses to the oppressed Haitians.*

Peter, in verses 34 and 35, sets forth a new and powerful truth: that the Gospel is in no way limited to the Jews. It is available to all men without any connection to the nation of Israel. The phrase in verse 35, "and worketh righteousness," in no way implies that salvation is by works. Works are an evidence of salvation, not its basis.

Notice the components of Peter's message. First, he establishes the deity of Jesus. He is called "Jesus Christ" and "Lord of all" (v. 36). Next, he emphasizes Jesus's humanity. His death and resurrection are described (vv.39-41). Because of these things, salvation is available to all men by faith (v. 43). Notice that according to the opening phrase of verse 43, all of these things are according to the Scripture. Peter, who is given the keys to the kingdom, opens the door for a truly international Gospel.

God always validates times of great change through the use of signs and wonders. So it is when Cornelius and the other God-fearers respond in faith to Peter's message that there is an outpouring of the Holy Spirit similar to that on the Day of Pentecost. Peter correctly accepts this as God's seal of approval on the preceding events.

Based on God's acceptance of these Gentiles, Peter suggests that they should be baptized. By baptizing them, Peter is accepting them into the visible church, thus recognizing what God has already done.

The Gospel has never changed. Salvation has always been by faith. In the Old Testament, God chose to spread this message in conjunction with the nation of Israel. In the Book of Acts, God makes a transition from using Israel to using the Church. The Gospel has not changed, only the methods used to make it known.

Acts 11:1-15

What is the writer saying?

How can I apply this to my life?

pray *Philippines – For seminary graduates willing to forsake ambition and work among the rural poor.*

The word of Peter's ministry in Caesarea travels quickly to Jerusalem. He arrives to a firestorm of accusations concerning the fact that he has spent time in a Gentile home. The phrase, "of the circumcision," (v. 2) is a reference to Jewish Christians. The fact that they are Christians, and not just Jews, is evident from the phrase, "as on us at the beginning," (v. 15) and the fact that he feels compelled to answer their concerns.

Verse 4 indicates that Peter gave them a *from the top* sequential accounting of what has happened in Caesarea. In verse 12 the near demonstrative, "these," used in conjunction with the six brethren, indicates that they came up to Jerusalem with Peter and are ready to certify all that he says is true.

Peter's recounting of the angel's message to Cornelius (vv. 13-14) appears to conflict with the initial account given in chapter 10. However the phrase, "he shall tell thee what thou oughtest to do" (10:6), is a variant not found in the oldest Greek manuscripts.

The phrase, "as on us at the beginning" (v. 15), signifies that the Gentile believers in Caesarea manifest the same sign of speaking in tongues as the believers in Jerusalem did in Acts chapter 2.

The initial reaction of the Jewish believers is not based in the Word of God, but in their tradition. Saving the Gentiles has always been a part of the plan of God. Let us be careful not to elevate our traditions higher than they merit.

QT Thursday 30

Acts 11:16-30

What is the writer saying?

How can I apply this to my life?

pray *Czech Republic – For increased growth and depth within Bible – believing churches.*

One of Luke's purposes in writing this book is to demonstrate how God brings the Gospel to the Gentiles. Even though a Gentile *God-fearer* named Cornelius has already become a believer, there is still no attempt to reach out to the Gentiles as a whole. Verse 19 makes this very clear. The Gospel is still considered to be for the Jew, and even as the message spreads out into Gentile cities, such as Antioch, the message is restricted to Jews, proselytes and perhaps a few God-fearers. All of this is about to change.

Barnabas is sent by the church in Jerusalem, in response to the report that Grecians at Antioch have placed their faith in Christ. As he ministers in Antioch, God continues to add to the believers (v. 24). Verse 25 indicates that Barnabas leaves Antioch to go in search of the Apostle Paul. This is probably due to the rapid growth of the church at Antioch and the need for reinforcement. This proves to be an important development in the life and ministry of the Apostle Paul, for this church would become the home base for much of his ministry. For one year, Saul and Barnabas minister in the church in Antioch (v. 26).

A prophecy about a famine and subsequent relief effort (vv. 28-30) corresponds with Paul's visit to Jerusalem recorded in Galatians 2:1-10. Details of this visit are recorded there that are not found in the Book of Acts.

As we read the Scriptures, we sometimes get the impression that all the events are taking place within a short period of time. Not so! The Apostle Paul spends many years in preparation for his role as an apostle. Always seek to do the Lord's will in the Lord's time.

30 Friday

Acts 12:1-11

What is the writer saying?

How can I apply this to my life?

pray *Bulgaria – For freedom from the media and local government's constant attempts to obstruct evangelical outreach or growth.*

The Herod mentioned in this chapter is Herod Agrippa I, a grandson of Herod the Great. His attack on believers in Jerusalem is most likely an attempt to win and retain the good will of the Jews. Under this persecution, James, the brother of John, becomes the first apostle to be martyred. Jesus alludes to his martyrdom in Matthew 20:23. This is not the same James who becomes the leader of the Church in Jerusalem and is the author of the Book of James. Verse 3 gives a good picture of the general response of the Jews to Christianity.

The reason Peter is not immediately executed is the Feast of Unleavened Bread. This takes place during the seven days immediately following Passover. Because these are holy days, the Jews do not look favorably on any execution during this time. The word translated *Easter* in verse 4 is actually *Passover*.

Peter's miraculous rescue from prison is a story often recounted. It does, however, raise a question. Why does God engineer such a miraculous escape for Peter, but let James die? The answer is not one of knowledge but one of faith. God's plans for each person are individually designed for that person.

We often look at a brother or sister in Christ and see God doing something tremendous in their lives. We then are disappointed when He does not do the same for us. This is a wrong response. Rejoice that God's plan for your life is uniquely tailored for you and cannot be compared with His plan for anyone else.

Acts 12:12-25

What is the writer saying?

How can I apply this to my life?

pray *Ghana – For the liberation of those women being forced to live in bondage to the fetish system.*

As has been his pattern through the book, Luke quietly introduces John Mark through a reference to his mother's house. John Mark will later accompany Paul and Barnabas on the first missionary journey.

Peter now finds himself alone and free on a Jerusalem street. The responses to this escape are very revealing. First, Luke describes the response of the believers who have been praying for his release. In fact, a prayer meeting is taking place at that very moment. A young girl, Rhoda, responds to Peter's knock at the door and is so excited that she runs to tell those who are praying what has happened. In her excitement, she forgets to open the door. Peter stands outside while she tries to convince those inside that Peter has actually been released. What a shock they have when the door is opened and there stands Peter. It is probably a good thing that Peter's release is not dependent upon their faith.

The second response we see is Herod's. Unable to accept the supernatural, he assumes that this is an inside job and has the jailors executed. His failure to execute Peter so shames him that he leaves Jerusalem and goes to Caesarea. While there, the people of Tyre and Sidon flatter Herod by calling him a god. Because he fails to correct them and give glory to the True God (v. 23), he is immediately judged and eaten by worms. Now this is truly an inside job!

It is probably a good thing that the work of God is not dependent upon the faith we display in our prayers. God answers even when we doubt. And yet we cannot help but ask ourselves: How much goes undone because we fail to ask or because we ask without faith?

Acts 13:1-13

What is the writer saying?

How can I apply this to my life?

pray *Cayman Islands – For the wealth of the island to be used to extend God's kingdom.*

The church at Antioch is quite a place. Verse 1 gives a list of some of the prominent men who minister there. This church is a great model as it moves out under the direction of the Holy Spirit. The decision to send out Paul and Barnabas does not come as they sit around looking for something to do, but while they minister. The laying on of hands (v. 3) is a sign of ordination into the work to which they have been called. This begins the first missionary journey of the Apostle Paul.

Their journey takes them first to the island of Cyprus. At Salamis, Paul starts a pattern that he follows in all his missionary journeys; he first announces the Gospel in the synagogue. Why Paul chooses to do that probably has more to do with practical matters than theological. Members of the synagogue know much of the background material necessary to give the Gospel context. Furthermore, the God-fearing Gentiles associated with the synagogue give Paul an open door into the non-Jewish community.

A second pattern that emerges is that of opposition to the Gospel. Moving westward, the missionaries come to Paphos, the provincial capital. The proconsul at this time was Sergius Paulus, a wise man who wants to hear this good news. A sorcerer named Elymas attends him and opposes their ministry. This contest ends very quickly with a powerful miracle: a seeing man became blind. Things become a little too intense for John Mark, who returns to Jerusalem (v. 13).

Prayer can easily be put on the back burner. The church at Antioch sets a beautiful pattern of prayer prior to and throughout the moving of God. Let us be known as people of prayer and of the Book.

Acts 13:14-25

What is the writer saying?

How can I apply this to my life?

pray *Angola – For the establishment of a righteous government to put an end to over 25 years of civil war.*

Antioch in Pisidia is not to be confused with Antioch of Syria, the location of the church Paul and Barnabas are sent out from. Pisidian Antioch is east of Ephesus and geographically located in Phrygia. Politically it is considered to be part of the Roman province of Galatia.

While at Pisidian Antioch, Paul continues his pattern of first visiting the Jewish synagogue. The custom is to allow visitors to make a comment to those gathered after the Scripture has been read (v. 15). Paul takes this opportunity to share the Gospel.

Beginning with God's choice of Israel, Paul progresses through the rich history of the Jewish nation. The message he proclaims progresses through verse 41. Paul sets about to show that the coming of Christ Jesus is not an anomaly in God's program, but rather the fulfillment of His righteous plan. Toward the end of this section, Paul speaks of king David and his Promised Heir, for which the nation is looking (v. 23). Paul presents Jesus Christ as their Messiah and reminds them that as John the Baptist was closing out his ministry, he was proclaiming that One was coming after him, whose shoes he was not worthy to untie.

Up to this point Paul's message is a rehearsal of the past, but he soon moves to a stern warning for all who hear his voice.

In sharing Christ with a lost and dying world, we must be careful to present a balance of God's love, grace, justice and holiness. We must speak the whole truth and do it in love.

Acts 13:26-41

What is the writer saying?

How can I apply this to my life?

pray *Thailand – For pastors to accept their responsibility to lovingly confront believers engaging in sin.*

This passage contains the heart of the Good News that the Apostle Paul preaches. Three times (vv. 27, 29 and 33) Paul emphasizes that the things that happen to Jesus Christ are not mistakes. Rather, they all happen according to the prophetic plan of God. This is an important point to Paul and ought to be with us. God has always intended that Jesus should die. It is part of God fulfilling His promise. Paul shows continuity between the Old Testament and the events of the New Testament, bolstering his case by quoting from Psalm 2:7 and 16:10.

Verses 38 and 39 clearly present Paul's distinctive emphasis on justification apart from the works of the Law. Forgiveness of sins is available because of the death, burial and resurrection of Jesus Christ. This forgiveness is accessed through faith. What the Law of Moses is unable to do, Jesus does.

Paul concludes the sermon with a warning. No doubt he could see resistance to the Gospel on the faces of the Jews present, therefore, he quotes to them Habakkuk 1:5. Paul chooses this passage by design, to include the Gentiles in his offer. God again uses the Gentiles to arouse His people to jealousy. Why? Because they accept the Gospel while the Jews do not.

Without Old Testament history, we would have no way to understand the significance of the many things which are presented in the New Testament. The Jewish leaders, who are in the best position to see the truth of the Gospel, are the most resistant to it; while the Gentiles, who are less versed in the Old Testament, are the most responsive.

QT Wednesday 31

Acts 13:42-52

What is the writer saying?

How can I apply this to my life?

pray *Give thanks for all God has given to you.*

Spiritual blindness is a cruel master. It not only blinds a person's heart and mind but it seeks to impose this blindness on others as well. So it was with the Jews in Antioch of Pisidia. They not only reject the Gospel themselves, but they do not want anyone else to accept it.

The Jews, as with Jesus, use the courts and civil authorities to do their dirty work. Their concerns are not for the souls of men, but for their own pocketbooks. The response of Paul and Barnabas is to turn their efforts to the Gentiles, who are open and receptive to the Gospel.

The commandment in verse 47 is that which Paul is called unto (see Acts 9:15), and that to which the Holy Spirit had set apart Paul and Barnabas (see 13:2). The quotation, "a light of the Gentiles," is from Isaiah 49:6 and is spoken of the Messiah. Simeon uses the same quote as he blesses the young boy Jesus at His dedication in the Temple (Luke 2:32). The phrase, "ordained to eternal life" (v.48), is a look from God's prospective. Our responsibility is to proclaim the Gospel.

The act of shaking the dust off their feet is instituted by Jesus in Luke 9:5 and 10:11. The act is directed toward the Jewish community, rather than the city as a whole, and is a symbol of excommunication, tantamount to calling a man a heathen. The believers who remained behind are not discouraged by this turn of events, but filled with joy and the Holy Spirit (v. 52).

The Gospel is as much a tool of division, as it is of union. To those who believe it, it is the tie that binds our hearts together in Christian love. To those who reject it, it is a stone of stumbling and a matter of much resentment (see 1 Peter 2:8).

Acts 14:1-13

What is the writer saying?

How can I apply this to my life?

pray *Italy – For youth ministries to have an effective outreach among the 1,600,000 university students.*

Although Luke writes that Paul and Barnabas spend a great deal of time in the city of Iconium (v.3), in only a few verses he covers their time and ministry there (vv. 1-5). Luke writes that signs and wonders accompany their ministry, yet no specific details are given of how God is working.

The plural form of "apostles," referencing Paul and Barnabas in verse 4, is used of Barnabas in the sense that he is divinely sent, being set apart by the Holy Spirit. However, he does not share the apostolic authority of Paul and the Twelve.

Verse one states that there is a great response to the Gospel from both Jews and Gentiles alike. However, the city is divided and the resulting opposition comes from both groups (v. 5).

Paul and Barnabas flee Iconium, having learned that they are about to be stoned. At this point in history, their flight to the region of Lycaonia puts them beyond the jurisdiction of the authorities in Iconium.

Paul, at Lystra, heals a man crippled from birth. This great miracle causes the people to think that the Greek gods are paying them a visit. They call Barnabas, "Jupiter," and Paul, "Mercurius." Jupiter and Mercurius are the Latin equivalents of the Greek names, Zeus and Hermes. The priest of Jupiter (Zeus) prepares offerings for the two at the gate.

In all that is happening, Paul and Barnabas never lose sight of what their ministry is about (v. 7): preaching the Gospel. Let us be careful that we not lose sight of what God wants us to focus our lives upon.

QT

Friday 31

Acts 14:14-28

What is the writer saying?

How can I apply this to my life?

pray *Kenya – Continued growth for Kenya, which has the highest percentage of believers in all of Africa.*

At Lystra, things take an ugly turn. Verses 14 to 18 detail the great difficulty Paul and Barnabas have in repelling the crowd's desire to worship them as pagan gods. All of this comes to an end as Jews from Antioch and Iconium arrive. Upon winning over the crowd, they incite them to stone Paul. Miraculously, Paul is dragged out of the city as a dead man, only to stand on his feet and return to the city. One can only imagine the impression this leaves on the disciples who stood around Paul thinking he was dead (v. 20).

The ministry in Derbe is not described in great detail. Luke only writes that many disciples are made in that city. Amazingly, Paul and Barnabas return right back through the cities where they had faced such opposition, purposing to encourage the disciples there. The "kingdom of God" (v. 22) is a reference to the coming millennial kingdom.

Upon returning home to Antioch in Syria, they gather together the church that has sent them out and give a full report of how God has used them to reach the Gentiles. During the time that Paul spent in Antioch of Syria (v. 28), he writes the letter to the Galatians, which is addressed to the churches where he and Barnabas have just ministered on their first missionary journey.

Paul and Barnabas experience the highs and lows of serving Christ and yet remain faithful through them all. When the crowds try to exalt them, they refuse to take the glory that belongs to God. When they are abused, they continue in fearless and faithful service. Let us be quick to learn from their godly examples.

Acts 15:1-12

What is the writer saying?

How can I apply this to my life?

pray *Romania – Need for trained leadership in a land where the average pastor oversees five churches.*

As the Gospel spreads to the Gentiles, an inevitable controversy begins to arise. Do the Gentile believers need to be circumcised? While the Gospel is being proclaimed among the Jews, this is not a problem. As more and more Gentiles enter the church, there arises a group that insists the Gentile believers must be circumcised. This is probably not the same group that Paul writes about in Galatians 2:12. Why not? The decision to send Paul and Barnabas to Jerusalem comes immediately, and Paul would not have taken the time to write Galatians before this decisive meeting. However, the issue is the same with both groups.

While in Jerusalem, they meet with the elders of that church and the apostles to resolve this matter. The group within the Jerusalem church, who are advocating Gentile circumcision, are converted Pharisees that have a hard time letting go of their legalistic past. Peter, as the foremost of the apostles, is the first to speak. It is Peter who opens the door to Gentile conversion in Acts 10, when he ministers to Cornelius, an uncircumcised Roman centurion. Peter's point is that if the Holy Spirit accepts Gentiles apart from the Law and circumcision, why should we, as men, try to require it? Peter's characterization of the Law as a "yoke" (v. 10) is very appropriate, seeing that the legalists are trying to use the Law as a means of working for sanctification and salvation (Galatians 3:3).

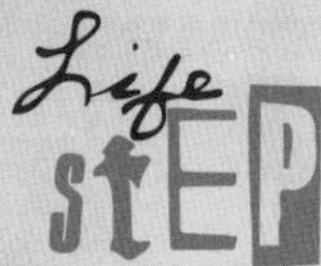

Rules and regulations, whether in the Old Testament or the New, are always meant to be a diagnostic tool. They are never empowered to make anyone righteous. Righteousness via law is a burden we can never hope to bear.

Acts 15:13-29

What is the writer saying?

How can I apply this to my life?

pray *Praise Him for giving us a living hope through the resurrection of Jesus Christ (1 Peter 1:13).*

After an unrecorded speech by Paul and Barnabas, James addresses the council. This James is the *brother* of Jesus and the author of the book of James. He appears to be the chief elder in the Jerusalem church. The fact that he makes the final decision is very appropriate, seeing that the men who bring the trouble to Antioch (Galatians 2:12) came from James (although it is doubtful that their teaching has his support). The believing Pharisees hold James in high esteem, since he is one of them. Finally, since he is the chief pastor, it is only appropriate that as a matter of respect, he be given the last word.

James's conclusion is a great victory for Paul and Barnabas, and the *apart from the law* Gospel they are preaching. The three restrictions that James places on the Gentiles are included to address some practical problems that may result from this ruling. If Jews and Gentiles are to live harmoniously in the church, it is imperative that the Gentiles be sensitive to the Jewish believers. James suggests two ways that Gentiles could help their Jewish brothers feel more comfortable. They are to abstain first from food offered to idols and second, from blood, whether by itself or in the meat. Both of these issues are particularly offensive to the Jews. For a longer discussion of this matter, see 1 Corinthians 8 to 10. Morality is also an issue. The Jewish community is used to a high standard of morality, but Gentile believers are not. James includes a prohibition against fornication, asking the Gentiles to adopt a godly standard of sexual conduct.

To make circumcision a part of the Gospel places keeping the Law into the equation. The standards of the Law are given to show man his shortcomings, not to establish his righteousness.

Acts 15:30-41

What is the writer saying?

How can I apply this to my life?

pray *Dominican Republic – Praise – For a major increase in the planting of evangelical churches.*

As Paul and Barnabas return to Antioch with the verdict of the Jerusalem council, they bring with them Judas and Silas. The church at Antioch is greatly encouraged by the decision in Jerusalem and also by the ministry of Judas and Silas. Verse 33 states that after some time they both return to Jerusalem. The apparent conflict with verse 34 does not exist in the oldest manuscripts and may be an addition in light of verse 40. However, ample time exists for Paul to send for Silas from Jerusalem.

After some time of ministry, Paul suggests to Barnabas a second journey to strengthen the churches established on their first trip. Even though they are in agreement about going, there is a disagreement about whether or not to take Mark. Paul's objection to Mark is because Mark quit the team during the first journey. With the disagreement at a stalemate, the decision is made to have two missionary teams instead of one. Paul, to his credit, later commends Mark in his epistles (Colossians 4:10, Philemon 24 and 2 Timothy 4:11).

Silas is chosen as Paul's new partner. This benefits Paul when the false teachers claim that they are officials of the Jerusalem church. He also, like Paul, is a Roman citizen, a fact that provides much legal protection and could open many doors.

As believers, it should be our policy to avoid contention as much as possible. There are times, however, when we must agree to disagree. If done in the right spirit, as with Paul and Barnabas, such confrontation can have positive results.

Acts 16:1-13

What is the writer saying?

How can I apply this to my life?

pray *Uruguay – For God to move in the hearts of those living in the coastal region of Montevideo.*

Timothy is a young man whose reputation precedes him (v. 2). Paul's decision to circumcise him is a practical matter to avoid offending the Jews. Because Timothy's mother is a Jew, he too is considered Jewish. It is obvious from verse 3 that Paul made it his business to promote the decision of the Jerusalem council, including not requiring Gentiles to be circumcised. At verse 5, Luke gives another of his summary reports concerning the progress of the work of God.

Paul and Silas, after enlisting Timothy in Lystra, are planning to continue their work in Asia Minor. Twice they attempt to enter regions that they did not formerly visit, but are forbidden by God. The exact manner by which God communicates His desires to Paul is not known. At Troas, Paul receives what is known as the Macedonian call. God uses a vision to communicate this call to Paul and immediately the apostle makes plans to cross over to Macedonia. Notice Luke's use of the word "we" in verse 10. It is assumed that Luke joins Paul at Troas. This is the first of several *we* sections, as Luke intermittently joins the missionary team. Paul, with his usual approach, heads to the major city of Macedonia, Philippi. Apparently, there is not the required number (10) of Jewish men to form a synagogue at Philippi.

Clearly, Macedonia is not Paul's first or second choice for missionary service. We need to be a light where God has placed us and allow Him the freedom to use us where He sees fit. Grow where you are planted.

Acts 16:14-24

What is the writer saying?

How can I apply this to my life?

pray *Netherlands Antilles – Praise God for faithful radio staff that keep the gospel accessible to many.*

Lydia, a God-fearer, turns to the Lord quietly as she converses with Paul at the riverside (vv. 13-14). Lydia's occupation is to sell purple dye and fabric. Thyatira is located in Asia Minor. She responds to Paul's message as God opens her heart. Her conversion is marked by an immediate desire to minister to the needs of Paul and those that accompany him.

A young slave girl, who is possessed by a "spirit of divination," takes it upon herself to advertise for the apostle. Her supposed ability to tell the future is a very marketable commodity in that city. The word translated "divination" is *pythoness,* and is used to indicate a person who is inspired by Apollo, the *god of the oracles* worshipped at Delphi or Pythia. The Septuagint uses this word to describe one who has a familiar spirit, such as the witch at Endor (1 Samuel 28:7). In an obvious case illustrating that the ends do not justify the means, Paul rejects this woman's endorsement and casts out the demon that has been afflicting her. Her freedom from this demon does not impress her masters. They only see the loss of income that this will cause and bring Paul and Silas before the magistrate, who orders them to be beaten and cast into prison. Their feet are made "fast in stocks" (v.24), which are designed not only to hold prisoners but also to make their imprisonment as painful as possible.

Some have questioned why the Apostle Paul did not approve of the endorsement by this young slave girl. The answer seems clear: When we accept an endorsement, we also endorse those from whom we accept it.

Acts 16:25-40

What is the writer saying?

How can I apply this to my life?

pray *Papa New Guinea – For the leaders of this land to seek righteousness and guidance of God in the affairs of their nation.*

Paul and Silas may have been hurting on the outside from the beating they receive as well as their cruel accommodations, however, spiritually they are rejoicing. At midnight, they are still singing praises to God. At that point, an earthquake shakes the prison, every door is opened, and all the restraining devices come off the prisoners. The jailer, assuming that the prisoners have fled, is about to kill himself when Paul calls out from the cell. Not only are Paul and Silas still there, but all the other prisoners as well. The jailer, who is most likely a retired soldier, has probably been listening to the songs of Paul and Silas and immediately asks how he can be saved. Upon hearing the Gospel, his response is immediate. He takes the missionaries into his home, shares the Gospel with all who are there, cares for their wounds, and then he and his household are baptized.

The jailor's home was most likely a part of the prison complex, and he does not shirk his responsibility to produce the prisoners in court the next day. The magistrates want to send Paul and Silas away quietly, however, Paul wants no part of that. They have been publicly flogged, and now want an official release, as it is unlawful to treat a Roman citizen as they have been treated.

We sometimes cry out to God for an explanation when we find ourselves in trying times. We need to be reminded that God is God of the prison cell just as much as He is God of the winner's circle. Wherever He leads, He can supply.

32 Friday

Acts 17:1-9

What is the writer saying?

How can I apply this to my life?

pray *Dominican Republic – For church leaders and their congregation to be good witnesses in tense and inequitable situations.*

The next major city that Paul visits is Thessalonica. This is the capital city of Macedonia. As usual, Paul begins his ministry in the synagogue. He ministers there for three consecutive Sabbaths, showing from the Old Testament Scriptures that Jesus must be the Christ. Paul's sermons convince only a few of the Jews, but many of the Gentile proselytes and God-fearers turn to Christ.

This brings an immediate action from the synagogue officials. They enlist the help of some unsavory characters from the area and start a riot that proceeds to the house of a Gentile named Jason. We can assume that the missionaries are using this as a place to live, for worship services, or both. Since Paul and Silas are not present, Jason is dragged before the courts and a security deposit is taken from him. Exactly what Jason forfeits if any more trouble occurs is not clear. Money, his home, or his life, are all possibilities.

Because Paul does not want to jeopardize his friends, this effectively ends his ministry in Thessalonica.

While the Gospel is bringing peace and joy to the lives of the individuals who believe, it is bringing turmoil to the community. The Thessalonians accuse the believers, calling them, they "that have turned the world upside down" (v. 6). If the Gospel is not rattling anyone, maybe it is not being heard.

Acts 17:10-21

What is the writer saying?

How can I apply this to my life?

pray *Chile – For future church leaders to be called from among those saved at evangelistic activities.*

From Thessalonica, Paul proceeds to Berea, which is a little to the south and west. As both Jews and Gentiles are responding to the Gospel, the unbelieving Thessalonian Jews soon follow, having heard that Paul is preaching in Berea. As a result, Paul is forced to leave there and move on toward Athens.

In Athens, Paul is provoked by the prevalent spiritual blindness. His ministry in the market place draws the attention of a number of philosophers. The stoics lay a great emphasis on the rational faculty of man and teach a high moral standard and sense of duty. The Epicureans, on the other hand, teach that pleasure is the chief end in life. The greatest pleasure is to live a life of tranquility, free from pain, detrimental emotions and fear of death. Both of these groups, although diametrically opposite, philosophically could agree on one thing: The Gospel is not suited for intelligent men. They refer to Paul as a "babbler," literally a *seed picker*. The idea is that Paul is like a bird picking up fragments of philosophy here and there without belonging to any discernable system.

Verse 19 says that Paul is brought to the Areopagus. This court is made up of local *approved* lecturers and is to hear more fully his teaching; however, he is not on trial.

The Gospel is without friends in this world. Whenever alliances are made, the true Church will always find itself alone. As believers, we should neither expect, seek, nor enlist the allegiance of worldly philosophies.

33 Sunday

QT

Acts 17:22-34

What is the writer saying?

How can I apply this to my life?

pray *Uganda – For God to call witnesses to the Karamojong, Pokot, and Jie, nomadic people.*

Paul's sermon before this Athenian crowd is much different than the one he preaches in the synagogues. The message remains the same but is packaged in such a way that it retains the interest of the crowd. His opening remarks are a classic example of how one should go about presenting the Gospel. He starts where his listeners are. The statue with the inscription "TO THE UNKNOWN GOD" is a vivid and concrete illustration that opens the door for Paul to speak about Jesus. They cannot summarily reject Paul's God for they, by erecting this statue, admit that there are gods that they do not know. If such gods exist, it would be unethical not to listen, seeing that perhaps this stranger knows just such a god.

Throughout the sermon, Paul uses this same technique. He does not quote the Old Testament but rather their philosophers (v. 28). By using thoughts and concepts that are known to them, Paul is able to unlock and illustrate new truths that are unknown to them. The message Paul proclaims shows God's greatness as Creator, goodness as Provider, sovereignty as the One in control, and His grace in salvation.

The response is three-fold: Some mocked, some wanted to hear more, and some believed (see vv. 32-34). This too, is what we can expect as we present the Gospel to a lost world.

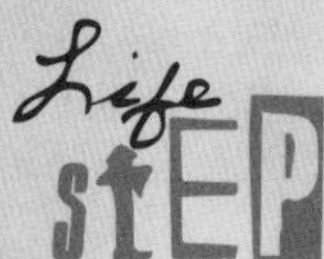

When presenting the Gospel we must ask God to give us great wisdom to present the truth in a way that is best grasped by our audience.

Acts 18:1-17

What is the writer saying?

How can I apply this to my life?

pray *Chile – For the Chilean church to overcome its spiritual isolation and develop a missionary zeal.*

From Athens, Paul moves southward to Corinth. There, Paul stays with a Jew named Aquila and his wife Priscilla, who are fellow tent makers. While their conversion is not mentioned, they have recently come from Rome where a church already exists.

Corinth is renowned for its carnality. Being located on a narrow neck of land between the Peloponnesian peninsula and Northern Greece, it is both a seaport and land route. Ships are actually pulled by land across the isthmus from the Aegean to the Adriatic Sea. This means that thousands of travelers pass through this city each year. With this volume of visitors, it is easy to see why prostitution and other such activities abound.

Just as Corinth is an ideal location for Satan to market his poison, it is also an ideal location for Paul to reach the maximum number of people with his Gospel. As usual, he starts in the synagogue and, true-to-form, he is soon expelled. This time, however, the angry Jews are not able to chase Paul from their city as Paul is commanded by God to stay there and minister. He does so for the next eighteen months. When Paul shakes his cloak before leaving the synagogue, it is a symbolic act similar to shaking the dust from one's shoes (see 13:51).

The Gospel does not always have its greatest impact where we think it will. The moralistic philosophers in Athens resist the Gospel; but in Corinth, a city renowned for all forms of wickedness, there is a great door open to the apostle.

33 Tuesday

Acts 18:18-28

What is the writer saying?

How can I apply this to my life?

pray *Pray for an unsaved friend or family member.*

As Paul returns to Syria, he leaves Aquila and Priscilla in Ephesus and travels on alone. God has a work for them to accomplish there in Paul's absence. Verse 22 marks the end of Paul's second missionary journey. After a brief time of refreshing at the church in Antioch, he begins his third journey (v. 23).

Very few people, apart from the apostles, are singled out for individual attention in the Book of Acts. One such person is introduced in this passage: Apollos. It seems clear that this man becomes very influential in the early church. Paul makes multiple references to him in the Book of 1 Corinthians and places him in very elite company: Jesus, Peter and Paul (see 1 Corinthians 1:12).

Apollos had only known the message preached by John the Baptist: a message of repentance and preparation for the coming of the Messiah (v. 25). When Aquila and Priscilla hear him teach in the synagogue, they take him aside and share with him the full message concerning Jesus Christ. His conversion only serves to make him a more powerful witness for Christ. With the church's blessing, he crosses over from Ephesus to the region of Achaia, and there powerfully preaches Jesus as the Christ (v. 28).

Aquila and Priscilla are faithful to share Christ with Apollos. He in turn is a man powerfully gifted by God in speech and reasoning from the Scripture. Let us be faithful in our witness. We do not know what link in the chain God may use us to forge.

Acts 19:1-10

What is the writer saying?

How can I apply this to my life?

pray *Paraguay – For committed Christians to occupy positions of leadership and influence within society.*

As Paul comes into Ephesus on his third missionary journey, he meets up with twelve men that are disciples of John the Baptist. More than likely, they are the residual fruit of the early preaching of Apollos; before Aquila and Priscilla share Christ with Him. As Paul comes to understand that they have only embraced the message of repentance that John has taught (vv. 3-4), Paul preaches Jesus unto them and they believe. As they place their faith in Christ and are baptized, Paul lays hands upon them and they receive the Holy Spirit. For the third and final time in the Book of Acts, the receiving of the Holy Spirit is manifested by the sign of speaking in tongues. Note that every time speaking in tongues occurs in Acts, it is always in the presence of an apostle and Jews, and is for the purpose of validating the man and the work of God.

According to verse 8, Paul teaches in the synagogue for three months. The words "hardened" and "believed not" in verse 9 are both in the imperfect tense, implying a continuing process. In other words, the more Paul teaches, the more resistant they become. Taking his followers with him, Paul continues his teaching in the lecture hall, belonging to a man named Tyrannus. Some early manuscripts indicate that Paul teaches from the fifth to the tenth hour (11 a.m.-4 p.m.). This would be during the mid-day break for the businesses of Ephesus.

Doctrinal error often enters because of a system developed upon a single passage or verse. Throughout the Book of Acts, tongues have followed a consistent pattern of only occurring in the presence of an apostle. This could not occur today (Ephesians 2:20).

33 Thursday

Acts 19:11-22

What is the writer saying?

How can I apply this to my life?

pray *Argentina – Outreach among the 500,000 Jews living here. Pray that they would accept their Messiah.*

God is doing miraculous things by the hand of the Apostle Paul, validating his ministry. Verse 12 tells us that people are even healed through a handkerchief or an apron taken from Paul to the afflicted person. Paul, however, never promotes such practices.

The incident of the seven sons of Sceva (v. 14) serves as a warning about dabbling in the supernatural. Evidently, these men are trying to use the name of Jesus like a magic formula. Quite possibly, they do not even know the Lord. The demon they encounter, seeing they have no authority, gives all seven at once a good thrashing. The result of this event serves only to settle a godly fear over Ephesus and magnify the Lord Jesus. Following this, many come to the faith and show evidence of genuine repentance by turning from their former evil practices (v. 19).

Verse 20 is the sixth of seven summary reports on the work of God that Luke gives in the Book of Acts.

With the phrase, "I must also see Rome" in verse 21, a turning point in the Book of Acts occurs. Paul's primary focus is to get to Rome. This city would be used as a strategic sending point to Spain (Romans 15:22-24). Paul sends Timothy and Erastus ahead of him into Macedonia to help collect an offering to be taken to Jerusalem. Of Timothy much is known, but of Erastus, nothing more can really be said other than his name appears two other times – Romans 16:23 and 2 Timothy 4:20. Evidently, he remains a faithful servant to the Apostle Paul.

We cannot expect God's work to go unchallenged and without opposition. The attack comes without warning and should remind us to always remain on guard.

Acts 19:23-41

What is the writer saying?

How can I apply this to my life?

pray *Spain – For the Holy Spirit to remove religious cynicism, the lasting stain of the Spanish Inquisition.*

The silver shrines for Diana (Greek = Artemis) are probably representations of her sitting in her temple (one of the Seven Wonders of the World). Devotees purchase these shrines and present them at the temple as an act of worship. Demetrius is the leader of the silversmith's guild. The Gospel has such an impact in the three years of Paul's ministry that thousands of people forsake the worship of the goddess. As a result, the market for these shrines falls. Not only that, but the influence of Ephesus (the center of worship for the goddess) diminishes and the profits plummet.

The theatre into which Gaius and Aristarchus are taken is a structure more like a stadium and could hold upwards of 25,000 people. The officials, "chief of Asia" in verse 31, are known as *Asiarchs*. Only one holds the title at a time, but the title, once held, is kept for life. That these men are friends of Paul, shows they do not regard Paul or his message as criminal.

It is only the good sense of the unnamed "townclerk" (v. 35) that brings this near mob action to a close. He appeals to the crowd, stating that they have no real basis of accusation against Paul and his associates, and that Demetrius and his fellow artisans have the courts in which to make their appeal.

When sin abounds, there are always those who are making a profit off of the misery of others. When lives are gloriously changed by the power of the Gospel, then the money spent on vices stops. That is the right kind of recession!

Acts 20:1-12

What is the writer saying?

How can I apply this to my life?

pray *Ukraine – For believers willing to translate biblical resource material into the Ukrainian language.*

These verses are packed with events and locations. It appears, however, that Luke rejoins Paul in Philippi as verse six begins the second of the *we passages*: passages that indicate Luke accompanies Paul. The trip across the Aegean Sea to Troas takes five days. More than likely, they encounter strong tail winds, as the crossing only takes two days.

The passage, starting in verse 7, presents the clearest evidence of the early church meeting for worship on the first day of the week, Sunday. This is done because it is the day of Christ's Resurrection. One commentator has noted several reasons why Scripture does not require Christians to observe the Saturday Sabbath: 1) The Sabbath is the sign of the Mosaic Covenant, and Christians are under the New Covenant; 2) There is no New Testament command to keep the Sabbath; 3) The first command to keep the Sabbath is not until the time of Moses (Exodus 20:8); 4) The Jerusalem Council (chapter 15) does not order Gentile believers to keep the Sabbath; 5) Paul never cautions Christians about breaking the Sabbath; and 6) The New Testament explicitly teaches that Sabbath keeping is not a requirement.

Eutychus, the young man of verse 9, is probably 7 to 14 years old. Luke gives us the probable cause for the fall and death of the young man: stuffiness from the smoke of many oil lamps and the lateness of the hour. These contribute to Eutychus's fall. Luke, as a physician, would be very qualified to declare him dead. Paul performs a miraculous resuscitation, which gives great comfort to the church.

The events of this passage could have been a great discouragement to Paul and to this young church. However, God uses this as a means of encouraging them all. We must trust that God always does what is best no matter what the circumstance.

Acts 20:13-24

What is the writer saying?

How can I apply this to my life?

pray *Venezuela – For missionaries to overcome the obstacles that make obtaining a visa a difficult process.*

This section begins by tracing Paul's movement down the west coast of Asia Minor. Paul's desire is to be in Jerusalem by the feast of Pentecost. Pentecost is the middle feast of the seven major feasts which Israel celebrates. For the Jews, this feast marks the giving of the Law, but is significant to believers because it marks the birth of the church.

So as not to be detained in Ephesus, Paul sailed on to Miletus and called for the Ephesian elders to join him there (v.17). He reviews the character of his ministry among them (vv. 18-21) and begins to reveal that his present course would lead him to bonds and affliction. In verse 22, Paul makes a statement that he is going to Jerusalem, bound in the spirit. There are those who would say that Paul is out of the will of God by going. However, in 23:11 Jesus Himself confirms that the trip is part of His good and perfect will.

It is while Paul is in a Jerusalem prison that Jesus appears to him to tell him to take courage. Just as Paul has been a testimony in Jerusalem, he will also be one in Rome. The terms Paul uses to address the elders of the church at Ephesus are noteworthy. The Greek term for "elders" (v. 17) is *presbuteros*. This is a term that is borrowed from the Jewish synagogue. The term "overseers" (v. 28) is the word *episkopos*. This word is translated "bishop" in Titus 1:7.

It has been well observed that there are always two threats to the church, one from the outside and one from the inside. Praise the Lord if you have a pastor who cares for you and teaches you the Word!

34 Monday

QT

Acts 20:25-38

What is the writer saying?

How can I apply this to my life?

pray *Slovakia – For Slovakian and Hungarian believers to overcome cultural animosities and embrace unity in Christ.*

As Paul summarizes his ministry, he has no regrets. He has not held back anything either in his preaching or in his personal sacrifice. Now as he faces what is looking like the final leg of his journey, he is resolved to finish well.

Paul's call to self-examination, "take heed therefore unto yourselves," is the same admonition he gives Timothy in 1 & 2 Timothy. Timothy serves as pastor of the Ephesian church. Paul, in using these words, stresses the leader's responsibility to watch over and protect his congregation. Paul's metaphorical use of "grievous wolves" (v. 29) underscores the danger that false teachers bring to the church. Note, too, that Paul makes it clear that the attacks likely come from men inside the church. Paul commends these leaders to that which could see them through anything that lay ahead: God and His Word.

One of the ways to discover a false teacher is to observe their love for money. Although Paul could have demanded the right to earn his living from the Gospel, he chooses to work with his hands to provide for his own necessities. There are times in his ministry, however, that he accepts support (see 2 Corinthians 11:8 and Philippians 4:10). The term in verse 37, "fell on Paul's neck," is a common Biblical phrase of expressing extreme emotion and affection. The sorrow is from the realization that it is doubtful they would ever be united again this side of Heaven.

Paul lives his life for the Lord. He has a deep love for people and as a result they love him back. Caring for people the way Paul does takes sacrifice. Yet the sacrifice yields great dividends. Do the people around you sense your care for them?

Acts 21:1-14

What is the writer saying?

How can I apply this to my life?

pray *Uruguay – For men and women committed to bringing more Christian radio programming to this region.*

The words "were gotten" in verse 1 really mean *to tear away* and again show the difficulty Paul and the Ephesian Elders are having in parting their relationship. Upon landing at Tyre, Paul finds some disciples. Here the Spirit reveals to the believers that Paul would face persecution at Jerusalem. Paul apparently already knows this to be true (20:23). The believers at Tyre (v. 4) and later the friends at Caesarea (v. 12) try to convince Paul not to go up to Jerusalem, but he is resolved to go. Paul's mission is given to him by the Lord (20:24) and he is ready to die if necessary at Jerusalem.

At Caesarea, Paul and the disciples stay with Philip. The designation, "one of the seven" (v.8), is a reference to the seven men chosen to wait on tables (6:2-5). Philip's virgin daughters are said to have the gift of prophecy. During the infant days of the church, many miraculous sign gifts are in operation. This gift is obviously not limited to men (see 1 Corinthians 11:5).

The prophet Agabas gives a visual illustration of what awaits Paul. This, however, does not alter his course. Note that he does not suggest God is saying don't go, but rather, this is what is waiting when you do go. Seeing Paul's resolve, the disciples commit this to God's will (v. 14).

How many of us, if we knew that we would suffer persecution upon arriving at a location (as Paul did) would still be willing to go. When God's direction is sure, nothing should keep us from following God's direction.

Acts 21:15-26

What is the writer saying?

How can I apply this to my life?

pray *Columbia – Outreach to the 700,000 women and children displaced by drug wars and violence.*

The arrival in Jerusalem ends Paul's third missionary journey. Throughout the Bible, it is said one goes "up to Jerusalem" (v.15). This is because Jerusalem is elevated on a plateau. Paul is well received by the brethren, undoubtedly, because of the much-needed offering he brings (24:17).

James, the brother of Jesus and head of the Jerusalem church, is well respected by all the Jews around Jerusalem. By this time, the church in Jerusalem numbers thousands of Jewish believers. While truly believers, they are still very committed to their heritage (v. 20), also recognizing Christ as their Messiah.

The Judaizers are spreading false reports that Paul is teaching Jewish believers to forsake their heritage. This accusation is proven to be false, simply by observing 16:1-3 and 18:18.

The Jerusalem elders propose a way by which Paul could demonstrate his loyalty to the traditions (vv. 23-25).

Paul's decision to follow their suggestion is not a mistaken compromise. However, it is during the process of these men completing their vows that Paul is mobbed in the Temple.

While men naturally cling to their traditions followed from birth, many have come to believe that Jesus is their Messiah and only Savior. There is no other way by which man can be reconciled unto God.

QT

Thursday 34

Acts 21:27-40

What is the writer saying?

How can I apply this to my life?

pray *Guatemala – For the growth and maturity of the churches in the nation.*

Jews from Asia bring three accusations against Paul: (1) That he teaches people to forsake their heritage; (2) That he opposes the law; and (3) That he defiles the temple by taking Trophimus, a Gentile, past the Court of the Gentiles. This last charge is absurd, as the Romans have given the Jews permission to execute any Gentile so defiling the temple.

To guard the purity of the Temple, the Jews remove Paul and close its doors. Paul is rescued from the frenzied crowd who are trying to beat him to death, by the Roman tribune. This is the highest-ranking official stationed at Jerusalem. The garrison is comprised of 1,000 men. The use of the plural "centurions" suggests that 200 men are dispatched to rescue Paul. Each centurion would command 100 men. Paul is taken back to the barracks at Fort Antonia that overlooks the temple complex.

The Egyptian (v. 38) is a false prophet who, several years earlier, had promised to drive out the Romans. Before he could do so, however, his forces were attacked and routed by Roman troops led by Governor Felix. Though several hundred of his followers were killed or captured, he managed to escape. Lysias assumes he has returned and then is captured by the crowd.

Paul identifies himself as a Jew from Tarsus. Tarsus is an important cultural city, with a university rivaling those at Athens and Alexandria.

Here we see God's hand of preservation upon Paul. According to God's will, Paul has a date in Rome and nothing is going to short-circuit that end. Praise God for His sovereignty in the affairs of men.

34 Friday

Acts 22:1-16

What is the writer saying?

How can I apply this to my life?

pray *Italy – For missionaries working in a culture that is spiritually ritualistic, apathetic and cynical.*

This is the first of six defenses offered by the Apostle Paul. The other defenses come at 22:30-23:10; 24:10-21; 25:1-12; 26:1-29; 28:17-29. This section also contains the second of three accounts of Paul's conversion. The other two occur in Acts 9:1-19 and Acts 26:2-18.

As Paul addresses the false charges brought by the Asian Jews, he speaks to the people in their own language. The first accusation is shown to be false, as Paul was born among the Hellenistic Jews of the Diaspora, but has been brought up in Jerusalem. The second accusation is shown to be ridiculous, as Paul has been a student of the most celebrated rabbi of the day, Gamaliel. Paul would have received extensive instruction in the Old Testament Law and rabbinic traditions. One thing Paul does not mention is that he has also been a Pharisee. In verse 4, Paul shows that he really has more zeal than the ones listening to him, as he has been the leading persecutor of the Way.

Verse 16 has caused concern to some, but grammatically the phrase, "calling on the name of the Lord," precedes "arise, and be baptized." Salvation comes from calling on the name of the Lord (Romans 10:9-13), not from being baptized.

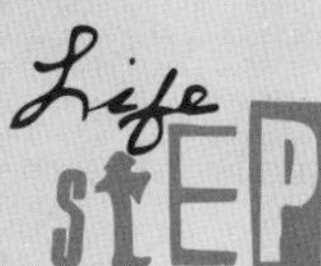

In the midst of a hostile crowd, Paul proclaims Jesus as the "Just One" (v.14), and claims to have seen the resurrected Lord. We, too, should be as quick to take our stand for the resurrected Christ.

Acts 22:17-30

What is the writer saying?

How can I apply this to my life?

pray *Mexico – For an end to the national media's portrayal of believers as enemies of Mexican culture.*

Paul's return to Jerusalem, mentioned in verse 17, comes after his ministry in Damascus (9:20-25) and, according to Galatians 1:17, 18, after the three years in Arabia. Paul also claims to have received direct revelation (in his trance) from Jesus Christ. The "trance" experience is unique to the apostles. Only Peter in Acts 10:10 and 11:5 and John in Revelation 1:10 have similar revelations. Paul's insistence that the Lord has sent him to minister to the Gentiles is too much for the crowd. Because of racial prejudice, the Jews cannot accept the teaching that Gentiles can be saved without first becoming Jewish proselytes.

The crowd returns to its uncontrollable rage. They show great and intense emotion by tearing off their clothes, in preparation for stoning, and throwing dust. This act of dust throwing can also be seen in 2 Samuel 16:13.

Lysias rescues Paul again and determines that he should be examined under scourging. The flogging would be done with a flagellum, metal/barb-tipped leather thongs attached to a wooden handle. Many never survive. According to Valerian and Porcian laws, Roman citizens are exempt from this punishment. Paul exercises his rights as a citizen (false claims to Roman citizenship yielded the death penalty), thus saving his life as well as Lysias's life and military career.

We see Paul exercising his earthly citizen rights. As believers, we are citizens of Heaven, but we are also citizens of an earthly nation. As such, we should exercise our rights that have been granted to us.

35 Sunday

QT

Acts 23:1-10

What is the writer saying?

How can I apply this to my life?

pray *Pray that God would increase your awareness of the lost and your boldness in sharing Christ's love.*

Paul's opening statement before the Sanhedrin shows that his conscience is completely clear (see 24:16; 1 Timothy 1:5; 3:9; 2 Timothy 1:3). In verse 2 we are introduced to the high priest, Ananias. This man is one of Israel's cruelest and most corrupt high priests; his actions so alienate him from the Jewish people, that at the revolt against Rome in A.D. 66, the people murder him. The illegal act (see Deuteronomy 25:1-2) of striking Paul would be in keeping with Ananias's character. This is a vicious blow, not simply a slap on the face.

The reactions to the blows in Jesus's trial (John 18:22-23) and Paul's here are interesting. Jesus reacts by calmly asking the reason for the blow. Paul, in an outrage, flares up in anger. Understand, Paul's action is wrong, but being sensitive to the Holy Spirit (clear conscience from v. 1) he admits his error in verse 5. Even though Ananias is an evil man, he still holds a God-ordained office, and as such is due the respect that comes with the office.

The issue of the resurrection is so intense between the two sects that the Pharisees are willing to defend Paul against the Sadducees. The Pharisees are more closely aligned with Christian doctrine and as such, we find many coming to know Christ. This is not true about the Sadducees. Nowhere do we find a Sadducee coming to Christ.

The Resurrection of Jesus Christ is a major dividing point. Indeed one cannot be saved without belief in the bodily resurrection of Christ.

Acts 23:11-22

What is the writer saying?

How can I apply this to my life?

pray *Nigeria – For committed Christian leaders that will follow through with real preparation of Bible lessons and true discipleship.*

Verse 11 introduces us to the fifth of six visions Paul receives in the Book of Acts. This vision comes at a crucial point in Paul's ministry, as they all do, and centers around confirmation that Paul's desire to go to Rome is granted.

The men of verse 12 bind themselves under a curse. If they really are men of integrity, they signed their own death sentence. In verse 14, they approach the chief priests and elders. It is significant that the scribes are not mentioned here, as the scribes would be mostly Pharisees. They have already demonstrated their willingness to defend Paul. Verse 16 is one of the few clear indications in Scripture that Paul had a family. 1 Corinthians 7:8 indicates that Paul never took a wife, or at a minimum is widowed. Much is left to speculation concerning why Paul's nephew is in the right place to learn of this plot. By God's grace, this information reaches Paul who is only under protective custody and not under arrest. As such, he is able to receive visitors.

Upon hearing of the plot, Paul sends him to the commander who takes this threat seriously. The commander asks the nephew not to reveal their conversation so Paul could be moved without incident.

It is comforting to know that nothing can happen to us apart from God's approval. Man may plan, but only God can make provisions for it to happen. No matter how wicked or vile the men, nothing, *absolutely nothing* can happen in our lives without God's approval.

35 Tuesday

Acts 23:23-35

What is the writer saying?

How can I apply this to my life?

pray *Korea – For the salvation of North Korea's leadership.*

Lysias, with knowledge of the planned assassination, realizes his need to get Paul out of Jerusalem and to his supervisor, Felix. Felix is residing at Caesarea. The fact that Lysias sends half of his garrison shows just how serious the plot against Paul must have been.

The entourage leaves at the third watch, or 9 p.m. In the letter Lysias writes to Felix, he tries to portray himself in the best possible light. In doing this, several facts are omitted: Paul's near scourging, as well as the omission that Lysias, at first, thought Paul was "that Egyptian" (21:38). Lysias fails to mention any crime that Paul committed. As such, he is declaring Paul's innocence.

The trip to Antipatris is about forty miles from Jerusalem. To travel there in one night would have been an exhausting trip. Being in the largely Gentile region of Samaria, the foot soldiers are no longer needed, and thus are sent home. Yet Felix needs to determine if Paul's case falls into his jurisdiction. Upon learning that Paul is from Cilicia (at that time Judea and Cilicia were under the legate of Syria), Felix knows he has the authority.

While waiting for the accusers to arrive from Jerusalem, Felix commands that Paul be detained at Herod's Praetorium. This is also Felix's official residence.

It's amazing how God orchestrates our every move. Paul is protected. The Gospel is defended. And now, Paul has a greater opportunity to share the Gospel with some major political figures.

Acts 24:1-16

What is the writer saying?

How can I apply this to my life?

pray *Nigeria – For the staggering growth of the church to continue and for the body to become mature.*

Acts 24 is the account of Paul before Felix. Coming with the Jews from Jerusalem to present a case against the Apostle Paul, is the orator, Tertullus. Tertullus is a common name in the empire and more than likely a Hellenistic Jew.

Felix is governor of Judea from A.D. 52-59. He is never very influential in the Roman government. According to the Jewish historian Josephus, he is noted for his defeat of a rebel from Egypt, but because of his brutality, angers the Jews. Verse 27 tells us his office is given to Festus two years after the incident before us.

In keeping with the day's legal practices, Tertullus opens with the customary flattery and a promise to be brief. Noteworthy is his use of "clemency" (v. 4) with regards to Felix. This term is singularly inappropriate to one whose ferocity is attested by the historians Josephus and Tacitus.

Paul is accused of violations against Roman law and Jewish law. The first is the most serious before the court, as the Romans would not tolerate rebellion or those who incite it. Had the Jewish leaders been able to substantiate this charge, Paul would have faced severe punishment, possibly even execution. The second charge against Paul is that of being a ringleader of the Nazarenes and a desecrator of the temple. This is the only place in the New Testament the word "Nazarenes" (v. 5) is used to describe believers. It is probably used here in the hope that Felix might look upon its followers with disfavor.

The real dispute between Paul and his accusers centers upon the resurrection. The natural (unsaved) man will always have a problem with the supernatural. The resurrection is a historical fact but must be received by faith.

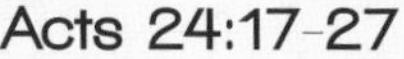

Acts 24:17-27

What is the writer saying?

How can I apply this to my life?

pray *Columbia – Pray for the safety and accuracy of those participating in Bible translation projects.*

Verse 17 is the only reference in Acts to the delivery of the offering Paul has been collecting for the poor saints in Jerusalem (see 1 Corinthians 16:1-2).

Paul sets the record straight – he is not coming to stir up discord, but rather to ease the burden of many of his countrymen. The fact that the Asian Jews are not at this court (vv. 18-19) is another plus for Paul's defense. If the accusations are true, they should have been there.

The real point for this trial is given in verse 21. The dispute is between the Sadducees and Pharisees, who stand theologically opposed on the issue of the resurrection. Obviously, Paul's belief in the resurrection is not a crime under either Jewish or Roman law. The court is adjourned pending more information from Lysias, but there is no evidence that Felix ever summons him.

Felix and his wife, Drusilla, come to Paul to learn more of *the Way*. Drusilla (a pre-twenty year old daughter of Agrippa, who Felix lures away from her husband) is the third wife of Felix. Paul's message to Felix is that God demands righteousness and self-control. Clearly Felix is under conviction as he listens to Paul's words (v. 25). His fear of judgment is real, for he has failed on both counts.

Felix foolishly rejects the Gospel hoping for a more convenient time. Our world is full of people like Felix who foolishly believe there is abundant time to receive Christ. Our responsibility is still the same as that which Paul felt – to proclaim the Gospel of Christ.

Acts 25:1-12

What is the writer saying?

How can I apply this to my life?

pray *New Zealand – For missionaries to capitalize on this nation's love of sports as a means of outreach.*

This passage contains Paul's fourth of six defenses (see 22:1-21; 22:30-23:10; 24:10-21; 26:1-29; 28:17-29). It is given before the new procurator, Festus. Where Felix was a cruel, greedy and manipulative official, Festus is very just and a capable ruler. He rules from A.D. 59-62.

Verse 3 introduces us to a second ambush plot (see 23:15). The difference between the two is that in this incident, the Sanhedrin are the plotters and not the accomplices. As a Roman citizen, Paul has every right to be judged in Caesarea. The fact that this is an official trial is seen in the phrase "judgment seat" in verse 6. The prosecution states its accusations again and Luke is quick to point out that (v. 7) none could be proved. Two years have passed since Paul has been arrested. Festus wants to do the Jews a favor and asks Paul to go to Jerusalem to be judged. It is doubtful that Paul would have ever made it alive. Paul rejects the compromise and reminds Festus that he has every right to be judged and have a sentence declared right there in Caesarea. After hearing Paul's appeal to be judged in Rome (a right he has as a Roman citizen), Festus confers with his advisors and grants Paul his request. By granting the appeal, Festus removes himself from responsibility and transfers it to the emperor. The Caesar, to whom Paul is being sent, is Nero.

By God's grace, Paul is now on his way to Rome at Rome's expense. Why is it that we often fail to trust God and His direction for our lives? Let us be quick to follow and trust that God always knows best.

Acts 25:13-27

What is the writer saying?

How can I apply this to my life?

pray *Austria – Each student receives their own free copy of the Bible at school. Pray that they would study it and accept its truths.*

Agrippa is the last of the Herods to play a prominent role in New Testament history. Bernice is not Agrippa's wife, but his sister (their other sister is Drusilla). Agrippa and Bernice have an incestuous relationship. Bernice, for a time, becomes the mistress of Emperor Vespasian, and then of his son, Titus. However, she always returns to her brother. The occasion of their visit is simply to greet the new procurator. King Agrippa has no authority over Festus, but is an expert in Jewish affairs and has wanted to hear Paul for some time (v. 22).

Festus speaks, relating the events that led up to this present occasion. Also, he includes how Paul refuses to go up to Jerusalem to be judged, choosing rather to appeal to Caesar. Augustus (v. 21) is another way of referring to the Roman Emperor Nero. Festus's dilemma is what to write as an explanation for sending Paul. In reality, to send a prisoner to the emperor without proper charges is not only foolish but could be very dangerous. Festus is hoping that with King Agrippa's vast knowledge in Jewish affairs, he can help to formulate the charges.

The commanders mentioned here are the five tribunes commanding the five cohorts stationed in Caesarea.

One might not think that someone such as King Agrippa would want to hear about religious matters. Yet, some of the most unlikely people we meet may be the most receptive to hearing the Gospel. Be prepared at all times to give an answer for the hope within you (1 Peter 3:15).

QT Sunday 36

Acts 26:1-18

What is the writer saying?

How can I apply this to my life?

pray *For many to accept Christ at summer camps around the world.*

Paul is permitted to speak in his defense. The gesture "stretched forth the hand" is a common way of beginning a speech. Paul appeals to Agrippa's knowledge and expertise of Jewish customs. It must be remembered that Paul is not on trial here, but is being given an unbelievable opportunity to give his testimony. In fact, Paul's purpose here is to see Agrippa and others converted (vv. 28-29). Paul gives account of his pre-conversion, his upbringing and the fact that he lived as a Pharisee. He speaks of the hope of the promise, and that of the resurrection. Paul then tells of his zeal in persecuting Christian believers. The last phrase of verse 10 literally means, *I threw my pebble.* This is a reference to an ancient custom of recording votes by means of colored pebbles.

In tomorrow's passage Paul goes on to tell of his obedience to the commandment given him by the Lord. In verse 18 he begins a thought that carries through to verse 23. In this section he defines "the gospel." It starts in verse 18 with a) illumination then b) repentance and c) forgiveness which provides d) adoption into the family of God with e) sanctification while all of this is accessed through e) faith. He then argues that these details of the gospel message were predicted in the Jewish Scriptures in verses 22-23.

What liberty! Many would love to give their testimony before a group like this. However, not many would like the process it took to get there. Lest we forget, Paul has been imprisoned for over two years, even though basically declared innocent by three leaders: Lysias, Felix and Festus.

Acts 26:19-32

What is the writer saying?

How can I apply this to my life?

pray *United Kingdom – For God to raise up a new generation of vibrant, doctrinally sound Bible teachers.*

Festus, astonished that anyone could actually believe that the dead would live again (certainly no Roman would accept this), interrupts the testimony of Paul and declares that all of his learning has driven him mad. Paul, with gentle tact, shows himself not to be mad. He informs Festus that what he has said about Christ and His resurrection is common knowledge in Palestine, and that he believes King Agrippa fully understands the validity of what he has been saying.

Paul's assertion to Agrippa: "King Agrippa, believest thou the prophets? I know that thou believest" (v. 27). This places Agrippa in a dilemma. To believe in the prophets would be tantamount to believing in the resurrection and would put him at odds with his Roman friends. To not believe the prophets would put him at odds with the Jews. To avoid the dilemma he answers with a question. The phrase, "Almost thou persuadest me to be a Christian," could be better understood as, *Do you think you can convince me to become a Christian in such a short time?*

The conclusion that Festus and Agrippa reach privately must have become known to Paul, for as he discusses his case, later with the Jews in Rome, he relates that only his appeal kept him from being set free (v. 32, see also 28:18-19).

Paul's appeal to Caesar is not a mistake, but rather the way the will of God unfolds for him. When we walk with God by faith and are obedient to all we understand, there is never a need to look back and second-guess our decisions. Trust God and don't lean on your own understanding.

Acts 27:1-13

What is the writer saying?

How can I apply this to my life?

pray *Hungary – Praise God for a peaceful transition from Communism to democracy and for religious freedom.*

The return of the pronoun "we" marks the return of Luke as a traveling companion to Paul. More than likely, Luke has been staying near Caesarea so he could minister to Paul. Luke, and perhaps Aristarchus (see 19:29), look and act the part of Paul's servants. This would help explain the good intentions and liberties they are offered by their escorts during the trip.

There is secular historical evidence of a cohort named Agustans Regiment being stationed in Palestine at the time of Agrippa II. The centurion, Julius, is more than likely part of the corps of officer-couriers attached to the regiment. These officers are assigned for communication between the emperor and the provinces.

Who the other prisoners were, we can only speculate. Regardless, a Roman citizen who appeals to the emperor would be treated better than most prisoners. Stopping at Sidon, Paul is permitted to visit his friends. The friends are part of a church that is probably established during the persecution following the death of Stephen (11:19).

The Alexandrian ship (v. 6) is more than likely an Egyptian grain ship taking grain as an export to Italy.

The "fast" mentioned in verse 9 is probably the Day of Atonement, based upon the turn in the weather that is about to take place.

Paul's vast ministry gives him many friends in many places. A life of service unto the Lord may not be the fast track to financial success, but will yield dividends that money cannot buy.

Acts 27:14-29

What is the writer saying?

How can I apply this to my life?

pray *Fiji – Pray for the Indians of Fiji of whom only six percent profess Christ as Savior.*

Not heeding Paul's warning in verse 10 of impending danger, Julius continues the trip. Verse 14 says they are surprised by a violent storm. The tempestuous wind is called "Euroclydon." The word is really two words together meaning *east wind* and *north wind*. It is a strong and dangerous wind and, although common in these seas, is greatly feared by those who sail. This wind is part of the divine purpose to fulfill Jesus's words to Paul that he should testify of Him as Lord before Caesar.

Luke in detail recounts that they are able, with great difficulty, to secure the ship's boat, speaking of the dingy that is probably hauled behind the ship. The undergirding of the ship refers to the use of cables wrapped around the hull and winched tight. This procedure is known as frapping and helps the ship endure the battering of the storm.

The lightening of the ship in verse 18 is the throwing overboard of all unnecessary gear and cargo to lighten the ship and enable it to ride higher on the waves (see Jonah 1). Verses 23 and 24 give the last of Paul's six recorded visions (see 9:3-6; 16:9-10; 18:9-10; 22:17-18; 23:11). In this vision an angel reaffirms the promise he has received from Jesus that Paul would get to Rome (see 23:11). Paul encourages the crew that not only would he appear before the emperor, but also they would all survive for his sake. The world has no idea how much it owes to the presence in it of righteous men.

Nothing keeps God from His promises. Man may plan, but God disposes of the matter. In the midst of the storm, God is still pleased to let His servant know that all is going according to plan.

Acts 27:30-44

What is the writer saying?

How can I apply this to my life?

pray *Panama – For discipleship that encompasses family dynamics, as over 70% of births are illegitimate.*

As they took soundings by lowering a weighted rope until it hit bottom, the sailors confirm the nearness of land. Paul watched as they prepared to launch the dinghy "under colour as though," meaning *under the pretext of,* dropping additional anchors. In reality, their plan is more than likely to flee (v. 31). But there are duties to perform (vv. 39-40) and the sailors need to stay. This time Julius heeds Paul's advice and the dinghy is cut loose and set adrift.

Paul encourages all the men to eat. With the storm and inherent difficulty in food preparation, little or nothing has been eaten in the previous two weeks. The phrase, *there shall not a hair fall from your head,* denotes absolute protection from harm. Luke adds that there are 276 people on board – this is not a small ship.

In the morning, land is spotted and an attempt is made to get to the beach. The ship, however, is run aground on a reef and commences to break apart from the pounding of the surf. Before jumping overboard, the soldiers plan to kill all the prisoners. Knowing Roman law, they fear for their lives. If a soldier loses his prisoner, he would lose his own life or face the same punishment as intended for his prisoner.

Fortunately, Julius opposes the plan and takes command. He orders those who can swim to go first, and the others to follow on planks or other items that would float. The result: 276 survive and arrive safely on shore.

Since Paul is going in the right direction, why is he shipwrecked? The focus of the Bible isn't on the *who* or *why* of our pain, but on the *how* of our response.

36 Friday

Acts 28:1-16

What is the writer saying?

How can I apply this to my life?

pray *For young people in your church to see the need and commit to full time Christian service.*

The island of Malta, in Paul's day called Melita, is located some fifty to sixty miles south of Sicily and is roughly seventeen miles long and nine miles wide. Paul and crew stay there until it is safe to travel, approximately three months.

A snake bites Paul while gathering sticks for the fire. That the snake was deadly is obvious from the response of the natives watching to see when Paul would die. Certainly, Paul's survival is due to God's miraculous intervention. God uses this incident once again to validate Paul as His messenger. During the next weeks, God works many miracles at the hands of Paul. This is certainly done so the people of Melita might come to believe the Gospel.

The trip to Rome continues on an Alexandrian ship that bears a figurehead of the sons of Zeus, called the Twin Brothers, Castor and Pollux. Sailors revere these mythological figures as protectors on the sea.

The brethren hear of Paul's arrival and come to welcome him to Rome. Three Inns is about thirty miles from Rome. Ten miles farther down, the Appian Way is the market of Appius. This greatly encouraged him.

Their arrival in Rome is almost as a footnote when Luke mentions it, "And when we came to Rome."

Through many hardships, Paul serves God and now, at last, he is at Rome. God has given him this desire and now it is being fulfilled. What passion has God given you for serving Him?

Acts 28:17-31

What is the writer saying?

How can I apply this to my life?

pray *Germany – Pray for theologically sound Bible schools and staff to emerge for the training of workers.*

Paul, under house arrest, can't leave to go to the people; so God has the people come to him! The interesting thing here is that the Jewish leadership willingly comes to hear Paul. Evidently, the grapevine of accusation has not spread as far as Rome, for the leaders are predisposed concerning Paul. They are inquisitive about what Paul has to say about "this sect" (v.22). Paul's explanation is his sixth and final defense recorded in Acts (see 22:1-21; 22:30-23:10; 24:10-21; 25:1-12; 26:1-29).

Paul's defense of the Gospel goes from morning until evening. Paul proclaims the Gospel by explaining, testifying and persuading. In so doing, he appeals to the intellect, emotions and will. Verse 24 gives us the typical response: some are persuaded but others would not believe.

The best explanation for the rather abrupt ending of the book is that Luke writes Acts before Paul's release from his first Roman imprisonment. Helped on by his fellow workers and with a confidence in God that is unshakeable, Paul evangelizes Rome (see Philippians 1:13; 4:22).

The Book of Acts is a critical link between the Gospels and the Epistles. Without Acts, much would be left to the imagination concerning how the great transitions of the Bible occur. Thank God for His grace in preserving His Word.

Today God is still building His Church. We, too, have an opportunity to be a part of the work of God by our faithful and dependent service. This book should encourage us to follow God wherever He leads.

This fourth book of Moses derives its title from two numberings (censuses) the Lord tells Moses to take for the purpose of determining the manpower available for warfare. The first numbering occurs a little more than a year after the children of Israel are delivered from slavery in Egypt. The second takes place about thirty-eight years later, when all but two men of the first census are dead. There are 603,550 in the first census and 601,730 in the second.

Chapters 1-9 tell the story of how the Lord prepares the Israelites for the journey to the place of warfare. Chapters 10-12 tell of the march and the delays that cause an eleven-day journey (Deuteronomy 1:2) to take several months. Chapters 13 and 14 tell of lost opportunity to enter into warfare, victory and blessing because of unbelief and rebellion. Chapters 15-20 record selected occurrences during the thirty-eight years that the Lord waited for a new generation to do His work on earth. Chapters 21-36 tell of the Lord's dealings with that new generation in preparing them to enter, conquer and possess the Promised Land.

The importance of the Book of Numbers to believers today is indicated by the many references in the subsequent books of the Bible. Some of these are: Nehemiah 9:19-22; Psalms 78:17-32; 95:8-11; 106:13-32; 1 Corinthians 10:1-11; Hebrews 3:7-19.

The warfare of God's people in the Old Testament is against those opposed to the fulfillment of His purposes and program on earth. Our warfare is against "spiritual wickedness in high places" (Ephesians 6:12). We are equipped with spiritual weapons (Ephesians 6:13-17). Like God's people of old, some of us who have been delivered from the slavery of sin, evidence no desire to enter the war against the *giants* of opposition. We therefore *wander in the wilderness* while others enter into the fight to victory over the powers that oppose God's program on earth.

Numbers 1:1-4, 44-46

What is the writer saying?

How can I apply this to my life?

pray *Bosnia-Herzegovena – 1.3 million refugees fled Bosnia during the war. Many that remained are still homeless. Pray for those struggling to rebuild their lives.*

When the Lord delivers Israel from Egypt on the fourteenth day of the first year, they are only a few days journey from the Promised Land. Instead of leading them directly there, He turns them away from the Land into the wilderness. First, they need to learn to look to Him for the necessities of life. He sends them bread from heaven (Exodus 16:4) and water from the smitten rock (Exodus 17:6). Second, they need rules by which to live. He gives them the law (Exodus 24:3). Third, they need a way of approach to a Holy God. He gives them the tabernacle, which is completed one year after the departure from Egypt (Exodus 40:17). Fourth, they need instructions in observing the laws and in approaching God. He gives them the words contained in the book of Leviticus.

The Book of Numbers begins almost thirteen months after Israel leaves Egypt, with an order to Moses from the Lord. Moses and Aaron are to take a census of the men available for warfare.

In verses 5-16, the Lord Himself selects the leader of each of the twelve tribes, who will assist in the task. Verses 17-43 tell in great detail exactly how many fighting men are available from each tribe. The total adds up to 603,550 who are at least twenty years old and "able to go forth to war in Israel" (v. 45).

To do His work on earth, the Lord uses dedicated individuals organized for a common purpose. He appoints the leaders, determines the procedures and empowers (Acts 13:1,2).

I am delivered from slavery to sin through faith in the blood of Christ, my Passover Lamb (1 Corinthians 5:7), applied to the doorposts of my heart. My food is "the true bread from heaven" that came down from God (John 6:31-33). I drink of the water that flows from the smitten Rock (John 7:37-39). Now I have access to the Holy God for instruction in worship and in service (Hebrews 10:19-22).

37 Monday

QT

Numbers 1:47-2:2

What is the writer saying?

How can I apply this to my life?

pray *Costa Rica – That the church's vitality will not be sapped by secularism, materialism, and the influence of the New Age mindset.*

In the numbering of the twelve tribes of Israel (vv. 20-43), only ten of Jacob's twelve sons are named. Joseph is omitted because Jacob made his sons, Ephraim (v. 33) and Manasseh (v. 35), equal to their uncles, thereby giving Joseph two tribes (Genesis 48:5-6; Numbers 1:10). Levi is missing because the Lord has a special assignment for his tribe that makes it ineligible for warfare.

Much of the Book of Numbers is concerned with the Levites. Their relationship with the tabernacle is summarized in verses 50 and 51 and is greatly expanded upon in chapters 3, 4, 8 and 18.

Verses 52-54 are about the positioning of the tribes around the tabernacle while they are encamped. The details of the encampment of each tribe, except Levi, are covered in 2:1-16 ("...every man by his own camp, and every man by his own standard..." 1:52). Among the multitude of God's people, each individual is important. Each has his own place in God's overall plan and program "...with the ensign of their father's house..." (2:2). Family structure and heritage is very important in God's program for His people (2:34).

Beginning with verse 17, the remainder of chapter 2 gives details concerning the order of march when the Lord leads them from one encampment to another. "Let all things be done decently and in order" (1 Corinthians 14:40).

"And the children of Israel did according to all that the Lord commanded Moses, so did they" (1:54). God's people are making preparations to embark upon an assignment from the Lord. He knows how to accomplish the desired results. It is for them to pay close attention to His instructions and to trust His leadership. Trust will overcome tedium as well as fear. Unbelief and impatience will produce failure (Proverbs 3:5, 6).

Numbers 3:1-16

What is the writer saying?

How can I apply this to my life?

pray *Ukraine – For the teachers, textbooks, buildings and scholarships essential for leadership training.*

Levi, the third son of Jacob, has three sons – Gershon, Kohath and Merari. Moses' sister, Miriam, and brother Aaron descend from Kohath. The Lord chooses Aaron and his four sons to serve as priests in the tabernacle (Exodus 28:1). Their consecration ceremony is described in detail in Leviticus chapter 8. Aaron's two older sons, Nadab and Abihu, "died before the Lord" for offering "strange fire before the Lord, which He commanded them not" (Leviticus 10:1-2).

All of the legitimate priests of Israel for the next 1,500 years have to prove descent from one of Aaron's two younger sons, either Eleazar or Ithamar. The term "Levites" designates all of the descendants of Levi except Aaron and his progeny who are called "priests."

Pertaining to the tabernacle, the priests are charged with the ceremonial, sacrificial and spiritual duties. The Levites assist the priests, having their duties confined to the material aspects of the tabernacle. They erect it and dismantle it for travel. They transport it and maintain it. The specific duties of each family are described in detail in chapter 4. Basically, the Gershonites care for the coverings, the curtains and the hangings of the court. The Kohathites are responsible for the furniture and its accessories. The duties of the Merarites involve the structure itself, including the boards, pillars, sockets and cords.

"God is a Spirit; and they that worship him must worship him in spirit and in truth" (John 4:24). The sin of Nadab and Abihu is akin to that of Cain and King Saul. They were willing to worship the true God if they could do it their way. That is *will worship* instead of Spirit directed worship. If such impedes the advancement of God's program, it may result in immediate death (Acts 5:5). Otherwise it results in removal from service (1 Samuel 13:13-14; 15:26).

Numbers 3:38-51

What is the writer saying?

How can I apply this to my life?

pray *Panama – For the increased quality and impact of Panama's Christian television and radio broadcasts.*

The subject of verses 14-37 is the numbering of the Levites and their placement around the tabernacle during encampment. The male Levites are counted from one month old upward, whereas the other tribes included only those twenty years upward who were able to go to war. This difference is because they are numbered for a different reason, as will be seen. The Levites encamped on three sides of the tabernacle (west, south and north) between the other tribes and the tabernacle, "that there be no wrath upon the congregation of the children of Israel" (1:53). They are to see that there is no profane encroachment upon the sacred sanctuary. The families of Moses and Aaron encamp on the east, in front of the entrance, to guard the way of approach (v. 38).

When the Lord brings the tenth plague upon Egypt, all of the firstborn of Egypt, men and cattle, are slain (Exodus 12:29). The firstborn of Israel are spared, and the Lord claims them for His own possession (Exodus 13:2, Numbers 3:13). After the Levites are numbered, the Lord tells Moses to count the firstborn of Israel; those born since He hallowed them as His own. There are 22,000 numbered Levites (v. 39) and 22,273 firstborn of Israel. Then the Lord exchanges 22,000 of the firstborn for the Levites. Thereby, the Levites become His own hallowed possession. The remaining 273 firstborn are redeemed for five silver shekels each. Henceforth, every firstborn male is brought before the sanctuary at age one month and redeemed for five shekels (Numbers 18:15-16).

Presenting the firstborn to the Lord is an acknowledgment that all life is from the Lord and for the Lord. Even though we are His by right of creation, we are "sold under sin" (Romans 7:14) and must be redeemed (Romans 3:24). If we are to be of use in His work on earth, there must be a presentation of the body to Him (Romans 12:1).

Numbers 6:1-8, 22-27

What is the writer saying?

How can I apply this to my life?

pray *Ghana – For trained and spiritually mature men to accept a role in church leadership.*

Chapter 4 tells in detail the procedures to be used by each of the three Levite families in caring for and transporting the tabernacle. In chapter 5, the Lord instructs Moses concerning leprosy (vv. 1-4), neighbor relationships (vv. 5-10) and marriage relationships (vv. 11-31).

Chapter 6:1-8 presents the three requirements of the Nazarite vow. The word means *separated one*. First, the Nazarite abstains from all alcoholic beverages and from any product of the grapevine. The fruit of the vine represents that which is pleasurable in life (Judges 9:13, Psalm 104:15). Second, the Nazarite grows long hair, which is a reproach for a man but a crown of glory for a woman (1 Corinthians 11:14-15). Third, the Nazarite separates himself from anything dead. Death represents the defilement and corruption of sin (1 Corinthians 15:54, James 1:15).

By these outward signs, the Nazarite declares himself to be separated, for the term of his vow, from normal aspects of life and as "holy unto the Lord." The vow is for a specified time, usually one to three months. However, in the case of Samson (Judges 13:5), Samuel (1 Samuel 1:11) and John the Baptist (Luke 1:15), the vow is for life, made by parents before the Nazarite was born.

Verses 9-21 tell the particulars for observance of the vow and the procedures upon termination of the vow. Verses 22-27 present the *Aaronic Benediction*. Verses 24-26 have been repeated at the closing of Christian meetings for centuries.

There is a sense in which every Christian should be a Nazarite for life, but not by outward signs. We should be separated unto the holiness and purposes of God. That will result in separation from much that this world considers necessary for a pleasurable life. Devotion to Him and His Word will keep us from the defilement of sin.

Numbers 7:1-9, 84-89

What is the writer saying?

How can I apply this to my life?

pray *Croatia – Evangelical Christians have cared for many during wartime. Pray that this testimony will have a lasting impact for Croatia.*

When the Lord calls Moses to the top of Mt. Sinai (Exodus 24:18) to give instructions for building the tabernacle, His purpose is to dwell among His people (Exodus 25:8). The tabernacle is the method whereby sinful man could approach a Holy God. His place of abode is behind the second veil, in the Most Holy Place, above the mercy seat between the cherubim (Exodus 25:22). When the tabernacle was completed, the Lord made known the glory of His presence (Exodus 40:34).

Moses anoints the tabernacle and all that pertains to it (Leviticus 8:10-11). The next procedure in readying the tabernacle is the dedication of the great altar of sacrifice located just inside the court. The twelve-day ceremony, recorded in Numbers 7, describes that procedure.

First, the twelve leaders named in Numbers 1:5-15 bring six wagons pulled by twelve oxen for the Levites to use in transporting the tabernacle. Next, on twelve successive days, each leader (prince) gives supplies needed by the priests to perform the ceremony and also the animals to be sacrificed in dedicating the altar.

Verses 84-88 summarize verses 10-83. With the dedication complete, the Lord fulfills His purpose and speaks to Moses from between the cherubim.

If you wonder where the princes obtained all that silver, see Exodus 3:22 and 12:35. It is God's way of paying them wages for their service to Egypt as slaves.

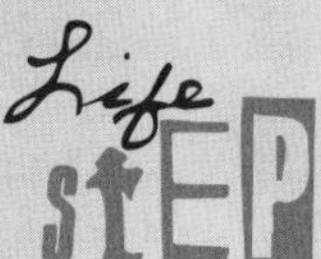

It is difficult for us to understand the complexity of God's method of approach to His presence because of our failure to comprehend the width and the depth of the chasm between His holiness and our sinfulness. Who will tell a sin cursed world of God's grace in sending His dear Son to Calvary to bridge that chasm?

Numbers 8:5-18

What is the writer saying?

How can I apply this to my life?

pray *Ecuador – Praise – In 1967 only 115 Quichua people were believers and today there are nearly 200,000.*

Beginning at verse 5, chapter 8 tells of the dedication and sanctification (setting apart) of the Levites. Their service is entirely under the direction of Aaron, the high priest. They are the Lord's gift to Aaron for service (3:9; 8:19). Every dedicated and sanctified Christian is the Father's gift to the Son for service (John 17:6). As our Great High Priest, "He is the head of the body, the church" (Colossians 1:18).

Before the Levites could serve, they needed to subject themselves to a two-fold cleansing. First, they receive the one-time application of the "water of purifying." Then daily they need to wash their garments. This pictures our need for the once for all "washing of regeneration" (Titus 3:5), to be followed by works "good and profitable unto men" (Titus 3:8). Acceptable service also requires daily "washing of water by the word" (Ephesians 5:26), that we might serve with garments of righteousness (Colossians 3:12).

The sin offering depicts that which Christ did for us in taking away our sin – the innocent dying for the guilty. The burnt offering shows the God-ward aspect of the cross. He fully accepts His Son's death as the just payment for sin; that is, He was propitiated (Romans 3:25).

The Levites are redeemed; bought for a price. The firstborn are God's special property, and He gave one firstborn for each Levite. We are redeemed; bought with a price. God gave his firstborn for each one of us (Hebrews 12:23).

There are many involved in "Christian" work in unwashed garments. They are not "taking heed" according to His Word (Psalm 119:9). God's counsel to such is to get "white raiment, that thou mayest be clothed, and that the shame of thy nakedness do not appear" (Revelation 3:18).

38 Sunday

Numbers 8:19-26

What is the writer saying?

How can I apply this to my life?

pray *Paraguay – For new believers to sever all ties to former religious practices and superstitions.*

According to verse 19, the Levites are given to Aaron to do the service that brings atonement for the children of Israel so they could approach a holy God without being slain in the presence of His holiness. The word "atonement" (a covering) appears about eighty times between Exodus 29:33 and Numbers 31:50 and less than ten times elsewhere in Scriptures.

That the atonement, furnished by animals sacrificed according to the law, does not provide eternal salvation to the offerer is made clear in Hebrews 10:1-4. Justification is not by "deeds of the law" (Romans 3:20). No one has ever been saved by "works of righteousness" (Titus 3:5). Salvation has always been a *heart matter.* It is a gift to those who have a heart to renounce self-will and self-righteousness, to rely upon God's will and His righteousness. "Abraham believed God, and it was counted unto him for righteousness" (Romans 4:3). Asaph (Psalm 50:13-15) and David (Psalm 51:14-17) understand this concept.

What then does atonement by means of animal sacrifice do for the offerer? It provides forgiveness for sins confessed, and thereby a means of approach to a holy God. The emblematic transfer of sin from the offerer to the innocent animal expresses the offerer's confession of sin. He thankfully witnesses the animal's death in place of his own. God forgives the sin and covers it in anticipation of the perfect sacrifice of His dear Son upon the cross, which would blot out the sin forever.

Every day we encounter people who are ignorant of their need of what Christ accomplished on the cross for them. In times like these, people are desperate for good news. How then will we reach them? We can pray for specific opportunities to tell what happened in our own lives. We can more substantially support those who are actively proclaiming God's Word.

Numbers 9:1-5, 15-23

What is the writer saying?

How can I apply this to my life?

pray *Guatemala – Pray for missionaries to develop successful discipleship programs to train rural believers.*

The first annual commemoration of the Passover is observed about two weeks after the tabernacle is completed and about two weeks before the command to number the Israelites, (Exodus 40:17, Numbers. 1:1).

Verses 6-14 give instruction concerning those who are not able to observe the Passover, those who refuse to observe it and non-Israelites dwelling among them.

The primary function of the pillar (or cloud, v. 15) is to guide Israel in the journeys from Egypt to the Promised Land. It first appears in this respect the day they depart (Exodus 13:21) and never leaves them (Nehemiah 9:19). It tells them when to go, when to stop and how long to stay. It leads them step-by-step in the way they should go.

The second purpose of the pillar is for a covering. It moves from front to rear in order to cover the flight from the Egyptians, giving Israel light and the Egyptians darkness (Exodus 14:19-20). When Israel is encamped, the cloud spreads out over all the camp to protect from the desert sun (Psalm 105:39). At night, it is a fiery pillar, giving light and repelling predators.

Thirdly, the pillar gives visual evidence of the Lord's presence in the midst of His people. God speaks to Moses from the cloud before the erection of the Tabernacle (Psalm 99:7). Afterwards, only the high priest, once a year and after very involved procedures, could approach the presence of the Lord between the cherubim (Leviticus 16:2). But the whole congregation could behold the cloud emanating from the Holy Place behind the veil.

The indwelling Holy Spirit is our invisible pillar of cloud. We are led step by step by Him. He guides us into all truth as He illuminates the Scriptures for us, and enhances our prayer life (Romans 8:26).

Numbers 10:1-13, 33-36

What is the writer saying?

How can I apply this to my life?

pray *Pray for your pastor and the leadership of your local church.*

The sounding of trumpets had an important role to play for God's people in the past and will have in the future. The words trump, trumpet, trumpets and trumpeters are found fourteen times in the New Testament and more than one hundred times in the Old. Verses 2-10 tell of six occasions when various sounds of the trumpet direct Israel in the march and subsequently.

1. To call an assembly of the leaders.
2. To assemble the tribes to the door of the tabernacle.
3. To call for the various groups to begin a march.
4. To assemble the able-bodied men to war.
5. To announce a holy convocation.
6. To announce the beginning of a new month.

A few days more than thirteen months after the children of Israel depart Egypt, the pillar of cloud directs them to begin an eleven day journey from Mt. Sinai (sometimes called Horeb) to the Promised Land (vv. 11-13; Deuteronomy 1:2). Verses 14-28 give the details of the order of march.

Verses 29-32 tell of a conversation between Moses and Hobab, his Midianite brother-in-law, who lives in the area. In a lapse of faith in the directing cloud, Moses beseeches Hobab to guide them in finding suitable camping spots. That's precisely what the cloud was given to do (vv. 33-34; Deuteronomy 1:33).

The rousing call of Moses, which he shouts at the beginning of each day's march (v. 35), is repeated as the first verse of Psalm 68. That Psalm is a song of triumph and glory.

For an intriguing personal study, look up "trumpet" (and related words) in a concordance. As used in prophetic Scriptures, see the exciting part trumpets play in your own future, as well as that of Israel.

Numbers 11:4–17

What is the writer saying?

How can I apply this to my life?

pray *Pray for those that work with the youth of your church to have love, wisdom, and perseverance.*

Throughout the first 10 chapters of Numbers, we read words like, "the children of Israel did according to all that the Lord commanded Moses" (1:54). When there is unity in obedience to God's directives, Satan looks for people who will disrupt the harmony (Acts 6:1). He finds them among the "mixt multitude" (v. 11:4).

Seeing the manifestation of God's power on behalf of Israel in Egypt, people of various origins follow Israel out of Egypt (Exodus 12:38). When Moses numbers Israel according to their tribes, these people do not belong under the banner of any tribe. They camp in "the uttermost parts of the camp" (11:1). But the mixed multitude has no appetite for the food of the Promised Land: milk, honey, grain, fruit, olive oil and such foods produced above the surface of earth. They crave the fish, cucumbers, melons, leeks, onions and garlic of Egypt; food produced on or below the surface. They disdain manna, which God calls "bread of heaven" (Exodus. 16:4, Ps. 105:40) and angel's food (Psalm 78:25). Israelites have partaken of Egypt's food for so long, that it is easy to stir up their lust for it. When lust has conceived, it brings forth sin (James 1:15).

Moses complains to the Lord for placing the burden of God's sinning people upon his shoulders. Seven times in verses 11-15, he uses the pronoun "I." He has his eyes upon his own inadequacies rather than upon the power of the Spirit given him. The Spirit has the same power, whether upon Moses alone or upon seventy elders also.

Shouldn't this lesson from God's Word cause us to consider the effect earthly cravings have on our appetite for heavenly sustenance? The world around us is the place of our ministry, yet it has attractions which allure us. Let us pray daily for a spiritual appetite strong enough to protect us from Egypt's delights.

Numbers 11:18-25, 31-33

What is the writer saying?

How can I apply this to my life?

pray *Peru – Apathy, doctrinal error, and cults are crippling churches. Pray for more trained Bible teachers.*

After completing only three days of the eleven day journey to the Promised Land, the progress is halted for a whole month because of the murmuring of the people. They remember the meat they ate in Egypt and insist that Moses give them flesh to eat. The Lord promises to gorge them with meat for a month. This seems incredulous to Moses, considering there were 600,000 fighting men plus their families to feed. The Lord assures Moses that He is able to perform to whatever extent He promises. Approximately a year previously, in response to their murmuring, the Lord promised them flesh to eat and then fulfilled the promise (Exodus 16:8, 12-13).

Translators and interpreters are not conclusive as to what is connoted in verse 31 by "two cubits high upon the face of the earth." However, if a homer in Moses' day is the same as in later Hebrew history, ten homers are about sixty bushels. Considering the geographical extent of the supply, it is more than could possibly be consumed.

The people only need to trust the Lord for guidance. He already has proven to be reliable. In a few more days, the manna would have ceased, and they would have eaten from vineyards and fruit trees they did not plant and drunk from wells they did not dig (Deuteronomy 6:11, Joshua 5:12). Instead, they bring upon themselves the curse of a great plague. There is no cure for unbelief except judgment.

Even among Christians we hear, "That's what I did" or "that's what I bought, because that's what I wanted." Most of our troubles arise from insisting that we get what we want when we want it. We pay very little attention to the consequences. When will we learn that God knows best concerning both what and when? "Rest in the Lord, and wait patiently for him." (Psalm 37:7).

Numbers 12:1-15

What is the writer saying?

How can I apply this to my life?

pray *Costa Rica – That the Costa Rican people will understand that salvation is not by works, but by faith.*

Moses' wife, Zipporah, by which he had two sons, is a Midianite. Sometimes in Scripture, Ethiopia (or Cush) refers to an area in Arabia where Midianites live. Whether the wife of verse 1 is Zipporah or a second wife, she is not a Hebrew; this bothers Miriam and Aaron. Miriam was ten to fifteen years older then Moses. Aaron is three years his senior. They are unhappy because *little brother* is exercising too much authority. After all, Aaron is the Lord's anointed high priest (Exodus 29:5-7), and Miriam is a prophetess (Exodus 15:20). Moses is only a humble servant.

Verses 4-10 emphasize that the Lord has a different perspective of Moses than his older sister and brother do. Moses is the appointed overseer of God's household on earth. Verse 7 is quoted and expounded upon in Hebrews 3:2-5 in order to impress us with that fact.

Leprosy is the penalty for intruding into an office to which God has appointed another; as was painfully experienced by King Uzziah (2 Chronicles 26:16-21). Leprosy is to the body what sin is to the soul. It eats away until it destroys.

In both the Old Testament (Ezekiel 14:10) and the New Testament (1 Thessalonians 5:12), the hearer is responsible for heeding God's chosen spokesman only.

Aaron confesses their sin (v. 11), and Moses intercedes for them. Notice in verse 15 how the sin of two of God's servants affects the forward progress of the whole congregation.

We are entirely too occupied with the shortcomings of other Christians. The Lord will remove some of us from effective service because we just can't resist criticizing those in positions of authority. Although we don't admit it, such criticism is an expression of envy.

Numbers 13:1-3, 16-25

What is the writer saying?

How can I apply this to my life?

pray *Uruguay – For God to save and call a witness among the upper middle-class, which is estimated to be the largest unevangelized group.*

In Deuteronomy 1:20-23, under the inspiration of the Holy Spirit, Moses relates what took place between Numbers 12:16 and 13:33 Moses said to the people, "Behold, the LORD thy God hath set the land before thee: go up and possess it, as the LORD God of thy fathers hath said unto thee; fear not, neither be discouraged." (Deuteronomy 1:21) With one voice the people answer, "We will send men before us, and they shall search us out the land." (Deuteronomy 1:22) The plan pleases Moses.

Keep in mind that God already foreknew that Israel would refuse to enter the land, with or without their plan to search out the land before possessing it. The land is inhabited by "seven nations greater and mightier than thou" (Deuteronomy 7:1). Possession would be impossible apart from a miracle from God, such as He performed in delivering them from Egypt. They need to rely on Him and His promise if they are to do His work on earth.

In order to reach His ultimate goal in the face of their unbelief, the Lord said to Moses, "Send thou men, that they may search the land." By commandment to Moses, the Lord selects the twelve leaders named in verses 4-15. He wants to use two of them for His future purposes.

Moses instructs the twelve in verses 17-20. The extent of the search is described in verses 21 and 22. The evidence of the fruitfulness of the land is presented in verses 23 and 24.

Several psalms interpret the lessons to be learned from Israel's failure to enter the Promised Land. Psalm 78:22-32 teaches that all the "wondrous works" on behalf of Israel do not produce faith to believe His Word. Psalm 95:8-10 says the problem was *heart error.* Psalm 106:10-24 contrasts their belief unto salvation with their unbelief in failure to go on to victory.

Numbers 13:26-14:5

What is the writer saying?

How can I apply this to my life?

pray *Philippines – Evangelistic discernment for Filipinos working abroad in countries hostile to the gospel.*

"We are well able" (v. 30). "We be not able" (v. 31).

Twelve men see and experience the same things during a forty day spying expedition. Their assignment is to evaluate what they see and advise Moses and the people whether or not to enter the Promised Land. The minority report advises: *yes, and immediately!* The majority say: *No!* Who gives the correct advice? They each do according to their perspective.

Caleb considers the miracles the Lord has performed on their behalf over the past two years. Then he considers what the Lord promises, to give them the fruitful land of milk and honey. He sees a God greater than the obstacles. He would see His promise fulfilled.

The majority leave God out of the picture they see. Psalm 106 sums up their perspective. "Then believed they His words; they sang his praise. They soon forgat His works; they waited not for his counsel" (vv. 12-13). "They forgat God their saviour, which had done great things in Egypt" (v. 21). "They despised the pleasant land, they believed not his word" (v. 24).

The people accept the counsel of the majority, fall into deep despair, and rebel against the Lord and His leadership. For the sake of their children, they would go back to the slavery of Egypt.

It is astounding how the Lord's people turn to the devices of Satan's world system *for the sake of their children.* The Lord has great plans for those children. Thirty-eight years later, they would possess the Promised Land. He also has great plans for our children if our first concern is their part in His program for bringing lost people into His fold. Disregard for His purposes in their lives will lead them into this world's slave market.

39 Monday

Numbers 14:6-19

What is the writer saying?

How can I apply this to my life?

pray *Mexico – Effective ministry to youth through Christian camping, outreach activities, and social aid.*

In verse 5, we see the reaction of Moses and Aaron to the rebellion of the people. We see the reaction of Joshua and Caleb in verse 6. These four know that rebellion against God's specific calling is a grievous sin (1 Samuel 15:23). They plead with the rebelling ones who believed those fearful spies who thought that they could not defeat the Canaanites. Joshua and Caleb counter: "They are bread for us." Fighting under the Lord's banner brings strength, not death, by the enemy! "There was no fear of God before their eyes" (Romans 3:18). Rather than fearing God, they feared *what man could do unto them.* In response to the pleading, the people would have stoned Joshua and Caleb, except for intervention by the Lord.

For the second time (see Exodus 32:10), the Lord offers to smite the rebellious people and make a new nation of Moses' own progeny. Moses objects, giving three reasons why the Lord should not do that. First, the Egyptians would discredit the might of the Lord. Second, other nations would say God was unable to complete His purposes for His people. Third, that would leave His promise to Abraham, Isaac and Jacob unfulfilled (Deuteronomy 9:27).

Moses continues his intercessory prayer by proclaiming the Lord's power, His longsuffering, and His great mercy. He recounts the many times the Lord has forgiven the iniquity of His people since they departed from Egypt.

If God's work on earth is to go forward, there is much need for intercessory prayer on behalf of His sinning people. The Holy Spirit put Moses' prayer in the Bible for our instruction (2 Timothy 3:16-17). The emphasis should not be on the sins committed but on the purposes and character of God. We need to point out the reasons He should forgive from His viewpoint.

Numbers 14:20-33

What is the writer saying?

How can I apply this to my life?

pray *Panama – For believing fathers to be committed to following biblical family principles.*

Rebellion by the Lord's called ones does not deter Him from manifesting His glory on earth through human beings. Instead, it changes the recipient chosen to manifest His glory. In this case, the children of the called ones who rebelled will experience the glorious entry into the Promised Land. From human perspective, it appears that the Lord's purposes are delayed thirty-eight years. However, because of His omniscience, He foreknew of the rebellion and planned His eternal purposes accordingly. He was, and still is, right on schedule! The rebels, though pardoned, are disciplined, suffering the consequences of their sin against the Lord's purposes.

The note on verse 22 in the Ryrie Study Bible, lists the ten times the people murmur (complain) against the Lord, beginning at Exodus 14:11-12. The number ten signifies sufficiency. At this point, the Lord pronounces, *This is enough of your rebellion!*

Twice in Numbers, once in Deuteronomy, and twice in Joshua, the Bible says Caleb fully followed the Lord. The prophecy of verse 24 was fulfilled in Joshua 14:13-14.

In verse 25, God warns the people of impending danger and tells them the way of escape if they act immediately.

In chapter 1, 603,550 men are numbered for the purpose of conquering the Promised Land. Only two of those who are called fulfill their calling. Truly, "many are called, but few are chosen" (Matthew 22:14).

Caleb possesses faith in the Lord's promise. On a scale of 1 to 10 in pleasing God, Caleb is a 10! "But without faith it is impossible to please him: for he that cometh to God must believe that he is, and that he is a rewarder of them that diligently seek him" (Hebrews 11:6).

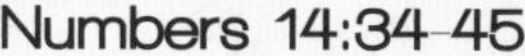

Numbers 14:34-45

What is the writer saying?

How can I apply this to my life?

pray *Spain – Praise – Successful use of music in evangelization. Pray for more musicians and opportunities.*

"Would God that we had died in the land of Egypt! Or would God we had died in this wilderness" (14:2)! God would never let His people return to Satan's domain (Exodus 13:17). So, He gives them their second request. They forfeit the promise and receive one year wasting in the desert for each day of the spies' search. The ten men who cause the congregation to murmur die in a plague (16:49). Of the twelve, only Joshua and Caleb survive the years in the wilderness.

When the people were confronted with the consequences of their sin, they "mourned greatly" and confessed their sin. However, there is no real change of heart. They still "walked in their own counsels" (Psalm 81:12). (To see what the Lord had in mind for them, read also Psalm 81:13-16.)

In willful defiance of the Lord's direct command (14:25), and the warning of Moses (14:42-43), they attempt to possess the Promised Land. The result is a rout by the enemy.

If we are to be successful in the Lord's work on earth, there are some essentials. First, we need a heart to listen and harken to His directives. As we rely upon His promises, He measures to us sufficient faith to accomplish the impossible in His power. Second, we must wait patiently for His timing. We go at His command and stay at His command. Otherwise, His presence will not guide us. We are on our own, and we will fail.

We presume against God when we think we can choose the time to answer His call to salvation. We have no power to come except at His call, and for each there comes a time when He will no longer call. The same principle is true for service. If I don't come at His call, He will choose someone who will. That one will receive the reward He would have bestowed upon me.

Numbers 15:22-36

What is the writer saying?

How can I apply this to my life?

pray *North Korea – Protection and perseverance of nearly 100,000 believers confined in North Korean camps.*

Because they have no heart to possess the land under the Lord's direction, He rejects the service of the first generation of His redeemed people (Psalm 95:10-11). However, He does not abandon His plan to establish the descendants of Abraham, Isaac and Jacob in the land promised to them.

In order to assure Moses of His purpose for the second generation, the Lord at once gives Moses rules of worship and conduct for future use in the land (15:1-2). Verses 3-21 have to do with worship; the remainder of chapter 15 concerns conduct.

Hebrews 5:1-2 tells us that a high priest offers sacrifices for two classes of sins: those committed in ignorance of the law and those committed by people "out of the way." The latter ones know the law but fall into sin when drawn away by temptation. They "have erred, and not observed all these commandments" (v. 22).

Verses 24-26 give the sacrificial procedures for sins of ignorance committed by the congregation. Verses 27-29 concern sins by individuals.

There are no sacrifices for presumptuous sin (v. 30; Hebrews 10:26). Examples are the ten spies and the people who heed them (14:40, 44). Other examples are the man who deliberately violated the Sabbath (15:32-36), and the sons of Eli (1 Samuel 2:12-17). The psalmist cries out to the Lord to keep him from presumptuous sin which he called the great transgression (Psalm 19:13).

We tend to measure sin by its degree of atrocity and repulsiveness. God measures sin by the condition of the heart that causes the sin. The willful heart is unrepentant because it despises the Word of the Lord (v. 31). The vilest of sins can be forgiven when there is true repentance (2 Samuel 12:13).

39 Friday

Numbers 17:1-11

What is the writer saying?

How can I apply this to my life?

pray *Korea – For youth ministries working among South Koreans, as they disciple believers to maturity.*

Chapter 16 tells of a rebellion against Moses and Aaron led by Korah, a fellow Kohathite. He convinces a large following, mostly Levites, that Moses and Aaron are usurping authority that belongs to everyone (16:3). He also blames them for the failure to enter the Promised Land (16:13-14). The Lord opens up the earth, and it swallows Korah and his leaders 16:32-33). Then fire from the Lord comes down and consumes the 250 men Korah has appointed as priests (16:35). The congregation accuses Moses and Aaron of killing Korah and his followers (16:41). The Lord sends a plague against the complainers, which kills 14,700 before the plague stops through the ministry of Aaron (16:48).

Chapter 17 tells how the Lord leads Moses to authenticate Aaron's priesthood. The leader of each tribe brings a rod from an almond tree. Moses lays the twelve rods before the presence of the Lord. Aaron's rod miraculously buds, blossoms and bears fruit. Then the twelve rods are shown to the congregation. Aaron's rod is placed in the Ark of the Covenant (Hebrews 9:4), where the golden pot of manna (Exodus 16.33) and the Ten Commandments (Deuteronomy 10:5) have been placed.

Aaron's rod that buds points to Jesus Christ, the "root out of a dry ground" (Isaiah 53:2), who bears much fruit in His resurrection. He grows up in a spiritual desert and is "cut off" for the transgression of His people (Isaiah 53:8), after His soul is an offering for sin, and in the pleasure of the Lord, He prospers (Isaiah 53:10).

Every aspect of the Ark of the Covenant speaks of Christ. The wooden chest overlaid with gold presents His humanity enveloped in eternal deity. The cover (mercy seat) depicts His judgment combined with mercy. The cherubim show forth His holiness. The combined picture is Immanuel, God with us!

Numbers 20:1-12

What is the writer saying?

How can I apply this to my life?

pray *Dominican Republic – For God to send workers to the 4,000 villages that have no Gospel witness.*

Chapter 18 presents details concerning the position and duties of the priests and Levites and provision for their sustenance. Chapter 19 describes procedures for the purification of defiled persons by means of the ordinance of the red heifer.

Based upon the dating information in Numbers 33:38 and Deuteronomy 2:14, we conclude that 20:1 is speaking of the first month of the fortieth year since departing Egypt. We are now following the journeying of the second generation. Notice they begin at Kadesh where their fathers stopped thirty-seven years previously. Not one step of forward progress has been experienced towards the Promised Land.

They begin with the same problem, no water. Their solution is the same, revile the leadership and look to Egypt. They must learn that the only source for the water of life in a desert is the smitten rock (Exodus 17:6; 1 Corinthians 10:4). Moses and Aaron are completely dismayed that they face the same problem again. Moses becomes so exasperated that he fails to listen and heed the instructions that are not the same as before. The rock has already been smitten. Access to the water of life from the smitten rock is by faith, not by force.

The Lord graciously supplies the need from the smitten rock, but Moses teaches the wrong lesson to the people. He loses privilege and blessing because of unbelief, anger and disobedience. The people lose the lesson that their need is met because of the Lord's graciousness, not by Moses' authority over the rock.

According to 1 Corinthians 10:11, this very episode is recorded for our admonishment. We tend to deal harshly with the faults of others when their conduct causes a problem for us. How can we be of most help to contrary people?

QT

Numbers 20:23-21:9

What is the writer saying?

How can I apply this to my life?

pray *Italy – Pray for the more than 30,000 communities without an established gospel witness.*

Aaron is identified with the generation who forfeits entry into the Promised Land. At age 123 (33:39), his work on earth is done. His son, Eleazar, is made spiritual leader of the new generation.

Though they are at the border of the land, they must be tested in battle and then cross over by a miracle of God in order to observe His might on their behalf. Their route passes through the kingdoms of Edom and Moab on the east side of the Dead Sea. Edom refused to allow passage (20:14-22). So they take a circuitous route that brings confrontation with King Arad, the Canaanite. The Lord gives them a great victory, and they continue around the land of Edom.

The arduous journey discourages the people and they rebel against Moses. Manna is God's provision for the wilderness. His plan is for them to eat it for thirteen months and then feast upon the bounty of the Promised Land. Because of their repeated rebellion, they ate it for forty years and came to loathe it!

When poisonous snakes appear among the people, they recognize it as judgment from the Lord and confess their sin. Moses intercedes, and the Lord provides a way for them to live.

Brass (bronze) signifies divine judgment. The serpent represents sin and Satan. Lifted up, the brazen serpent points to the judgment of sin and Satan on the cross of Christ (John 3:14; 12:31-33). One look by faith upon the Lord's provision for sin brings the believing one life out of death.

Each of us has been bitten and poisoned by sin (Romans 3:23). We shall surely die in our sin (Romans 6:23) unless by faith we look upon God's provision for sin. Eternal life does not come through a process over a period of time. It is a gift to be received in a moment. We must lift the cross high so all can see.

Numbers 22:1-15

What is the writer saying?

How can I apply this to my life?

pray *For summer teen and children's camp staff needs to be met; lifeguards, nurses, wait staff, housekeeping,, groundskeepers, office staff, etc.*

After swift and complete victories over King Arad, the Canaanite (21:1-3), King Sihon, the Amorite (21:21-32) and King Og of Bashan (21:33-35), Israel encamps in the plains of Moab, across the Jordan River from the Promised Land. Balak, king of Moab, observes with fear and allies himself with Midian. Their wise men advise him to hire Balaam, a prophet from idolatrous Mesopotamia.

The story of Balaam's attempts to get God to curse Israel covers three chapters (22-24). Each time he tries to curse Israel, God puts words in his mouth that reveal wondrous future events for Israel.

Before we reach a conclusion about Balaam and his ministry, we should consider what the rest of the Bible says about him. He is soon slain in a battle between Israel and Midian because his counsel brought about trespasses against the Lord by the men of Israel (31:8, 16). Moab is barred from the congregation of the Lord forever because they hire Balaam to curse Israel (Nehemiah 13:1-2). Joshua calls him a soothsayer, and makes comments about him (Joshua 13:22; 24:9-10). Micah warns about Balaam's doctrine concerning the righteousness of the Lord (Micah 6:5).

The New Testament says his way is wrong because he loved the wages of unrighteousness (2 Peter 2:15), he errs because he is greedy for reward (Jude 11), and he teaches a doctrine of idolatry and fornication to God's people (Revelation 2:14).

Balaam believes in the power of the true God. He prays to Him and hears from Him. When he speaks words from the Lord, they are true words. However, he serves self instead of God. Through familiarity with God's written word, false prophets do the same today. The indwelling Holy Spirit is able to teach you from the Word of God who is true and who is false (John 16:13; 1 John 2:27).

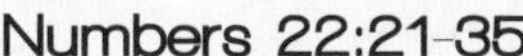

Numbers 22:21-35

What is the writer saying?

How can I apply this to my life?

pray *Mexico – For discipleship programs that effectively teach how the Bible impacts family life.*

Why is God angry with Balaam for going with the princes of Moab after giving him permission to go (v. 20)? Previously God has plainly said, "Thou shalt not go with them" (v. 12). Balaam knows God's will, but he has his heart set on personal gain and hopes to hear something from God more pleasing to him (v. 19). So God gives him his desire even though He foreknew that Balaam would soon die for his folly (31:8). God is just in using Balaam's mouth to bless Israel in the presence of their enemies (23:5; 24:10).

Are we to believe that a dumb donkey actually carries on an intelligent conversation with a man? Writing under the inspiration of the Holy Spirit, concerning Balaam, the Apostle Peter says, "but was rebuked for his iniquity: the dumb ass speaking with man's voice forbad the madness of the prophet" (2 Peter 2:16). Remember, God empowers Satan to converse with Eve using the mouth of a serpent.

Miraculously, God permits the ass to see what the *seer* could not see until God lets the *seer* see. When the angel of the Lord calls Balaam perverse, and lets him know that the "perverse" ass has saved his life, Balaam confesses his sin and agrees to turn back. However, God has plans to use Balaam's perverseness to accomplish His purposes. He uses the submissive Balaam to bless the Lord's people in the presence of their enemies. That story is the subject of chapters 23 and 24.

If we see our own salvation as a miracle of God's grace, we have no problem believing any of the miracles recorded in the Bible. If we see our salvation resulting from the observance of procedures we follow, we have difficulty with miracles that defy natural laws. The natural mind *explains away* such actions by God.

Numbers 27:12-23

What is the writer saying?

How can I apply this to my life?

pray *Austria – For missionaries not to be discouraged with all the obstacles they encounter.*

Chapters 23 and 24 consist of prophecies concerning Israel that the Lord puts in the mouth of Balaam. He is hired to curse Israel, but only words of blessing issue from his mouth. Chapter 25 tells of the seduction of the Israelite men by the women of Moab and Midian, deriving from Balaam's counsel to Barak (31:16). 24,000 Israelites die in the ensuing plague. The numbering of the second generation is the subject of chapter 26. The first eleven verses of chapter 27 provide the rules of inheritance when there are no sons in the family.

Mt. Abarim (also called Pisgah) is a range of mountains rising 4,000 feet from the eastern shore of the Dead Sea. The highest peak is Nebo. From that vantage point, the Lord shows Moses the land he is not permitted to enter because of his disobedience.

When Moses learns of his imminent death, he expresses concern for his people. He envisions them "as sheep having no shepherd" (Matthew 9:36).

The successor to Moses must be chosen by the Lord, controlled by the Spirit and publicly charged with the responsibility of leadership by the laying on of hands. The charge to Joshua by Moses is recorded in Deuteronomy 31:7, 8. The laying on of hands is the outward symbol showing the transfer of authority and honor to the new leader (Deuteronomy 34:9).

Joshua is to receive counsel from the Lord's ordained high priest through the means provided by the Lord (Exodus 28:30).

"I have gone astray like a lost sheep" (Psalm. 119:176). God's people still need shepherds (1 Peter 5:1-4). Their entrance into office is very similar to Joshua's. Through the Holy Spirit's enlightenment of the Word, we are adequately equipped to discern those chosen by the Lord to be pastors (John 7:17; 1 Thess. 5:12; 1 John 2:27).

Numbers 32:1-15

What is the writer saying?

How can I apply this to my life?

pray *Romania – For the lifting of government restrictions, which are hindering effective ministry growth.*

Chapters 28 and 29 provide detailed instructions concerning the sacrifices offered throughout each year. Chapter 30 gives instructions concerning vows. Chapter 31 is the account of the conquering of Midian and the dividing of the spoils of that campaign.

Now the assignment the Lord gave to Moses 40 years previously is being transferred to Joshua. It is to bring the tribes of Israel into possession of a particular land currently possessed by seven strong heathen tribes (Deuteronomy 7:1). It is bounded on the north by the mountains of Lebanon, on the east by the Jordan River and the Dead Sea, on the south by the Sinai Desert, and on the west by the Mediterranean Sea. These boundaries form natural defenses. God's plan is to establish them in this small area and then enlarge their borders (Exodus 23:30; 34:24) to include all the area promised to Abraham (Genesis 15:18). Thirty-eight years earlier, the Lord was ready to bring them in from the south. However, that generation rebelled and died in the wilderness. Now, the Lord is ready to bring a new generation under a new leader into the land from a new direction.

However, two tribes don't want to possess the land across the Jordan. They have their own idea of a good place to live and have no heart to wholly follow the Lord. Like Lot, they *saw*, then *chose* and now want to *dwell* (Genesis 13:10-12). Like Samson, what they *saw* pleased them well (Judges 14:1-3). A dismayed Moses preaches to them.

This history pictures the past, present and future ministries of Christ. He is called out of Egypt (Hosea 11:1; Matthew 2:15) as deliverer to enter the land from the south. But "his own received him not" (John 1:11). Like Moses, He then becomes our Intercessor (Romans 8:34). He will enter the land from the east as conquering King (Zechariah 14:4).

Numbers 32:16-31

What is the writer saying?

How can I apply this to my life?

pray *Taiwan – Greater sense of responsibility among believers who tend to let leadership do everything.*

"We will..." "We will not...". The Reubenites and Gadites are willing to be a part of the Lord's program as long as they choose how to serve. Crossing Jordan to help fight the battles is a necessary means to the desired end. They did "that which hath proceeded out" of *their* mouths.

More than twenty times in the books of Deuteronomy and Joshua, the land the Lord gives to possess is said to be over the River Jordan (the west side). (See Deuteronomy 3:20; 4:21; 12:10 and Joshua 1:2, 11.) In contrast, the possessions of Reuben and Gad are described as that which "Moses gave" (Numbers 32:33, 40; Deut. 3:12-20). When speaking to Reuben and Gad, Joshua made the same distinction (Joshua 1:12-15).

There are some detrimental aspects to possession on the east side of the Jordan. The Promised Land is good for fruits and grain. The possessions of Reuben and Gad, who are joined by half the tribe of Manasseh is pastoral. The times of the three annual feasts are so planned that they do not interfere with necessary attendance to crops. The men are required to go to Jerusalem while many family members could also attend. Distance and occupational requirements make it difficult for Reubenites and Gadites to observe the worship laws. Their boundaries are not clearly defined, and there are incursions by surrounding heathen tribes. They are the first to fall into idolatry and the first to be taken into captivity (1 Chronicles 5:25-26).

Many of the Lord's people today are possessed by their possessions. Boats, summer cottages, avocations, supplies and various recreational vehicles take time, money and effort. Our time for the Bible, prayer and public worship is consumed, and we drift backwards spiritually to our eternal detriment.

Numbers 35:9-25

What is the writer saying?

How can I apply this to my life?

pray *Paraguay – For the maturity of new believers among the Lengua, Angaite, Chorote, and Toba Indians.*

Chapter 33 lists in order all of the encampments of Israel in the journey from Egypt to the Jordan River (33:1-49), and then gives instructions for possession of the Promised Land (33:50-56). Chapter 34 tells the boundaries of the Land and names the leaders for each tribe. Chapter 35:1-8 sets apart forty-two cities for assignment to the Levites.

"Behold therefore the goodness and severity of God" (Romans 11:22). In His governmental instructions to Noah, God decrees that a murderer forfeits his life at the hands of man (Genesis 9:6). This edict is incorporated into the Law of Moses (Exodus 21:12). The Law also provides a way of escape for those who kill unintentionally (Numbers 35:11).

Cities of refuge are provided to save the life of the slayer until he has an opportunity to prove that he did not kill maliciously. The Bible devotes most of three chapters to the subject – Numbers 35, Deuteronomy 19 and Joshua 20. Each passage contributes details. Numbers 35:19-21 lets us know who is designated to carry out the death sentence upon the murderer. The avenger of blood is the nearest kinsman of the victim. The illustration in Deuteronomy 19:5 is particularly helpful in understanding who qualifies for the protection afforded by the cities of refuge. Joshua 20:6 tells of the ultimate restoration of the slayer.

The passage from Numbers 35:26-34 continues the subject of the cities of refuge, and chapter 36 further instructs concerning inheritance of ancestral land.

"...who have fled for refuge to lay hold upon the hope set before us" (Hebrews 6:18). Jesus Christ is our city of refuge. Our sins slew Him upon the cross, but when we sinned, we didn't know that. So He has provided a way of escape! "Which hope we have as an anchor of the soul, both sure and stedfast..." (Hebrews 6:19).

The book of Galatians is generally recognized as Paul's earliest epistle. It is written to the group of churches that Paul founded on his first missionary journey. These would include Iconium, Lystra, Derbe and Antioch. Paul's visit to these cities is recounted in Acts 13 and 14. He revisits them briefly on his second journey (Acts 16:6) and some of the northern cities on his third missionary journey (Acts 18:23). Because the Epistle to the Galatians references a number of historical events, we are able to place the date of writing with some certainty. Paul mentions his trip to Jerusalem to meet with Peter (1:18). This probably corresponds to Acts 9:26. In Galatians 2:1 Paul speaks of a visit fourteen years later. This is most likely the *famine visit* of Acts 11:27-30 as opposed to the Jerusalem Counsel visit referenced in Acts 15. While there are some plausible arguments for this being the latter, the fact that Paul does not invoke the conclusions of that counsel to bolster his argument would seem to exclude it. Therefore, the letter is most likely written in 49 A.D. just prior to the Jerusalem Council.

The purpose for this letter is very clear. A theological battle has been brewing in Galatia ever since Paul's first visit to those cities. Certain Jewish religious leaders claiming the support of both the apostles and the church leaders in Jerusalem have begun to teach a *hybrid* Gospel. This Gospel tries to maintain a *by grace* salvation coupled with a *by-law* sanctification. This way they are able to enslave church-age believers to the Mosaic Law. They teach that circumcision is absolutely necessary for keeping oneself saved.

This short epistle may have ignited the flames of controversy that ultimately lead to the counsel in Jerusalem the following year. These false teachers, generally called Judaizers, would follow and plague the ministry of Paul throughout his whole life. The following is a brief outline for the book:

1. Introduction (1:1-9)
2. Paul Defends His Authority – Autobiographical (1:10-2:21)
3. Paul Explains His Theology – Doctrinal (3:1-4:31)
4. Paul Exhorts Proper Christian Living (5:1-6:10)
5. Conclusion (6:11-18)

41 Sunday

QT

Galatians 1:1-9

What is the writer saying?

How can I apply this to my life?

pray *Honduras – For a compassionate outreach by churches to the more than 8,000 exploited street children.*

The normal opening found in Paul's other letters would be to: (a) introduce himself with a salutation, (b) pray for those being addressed, (c) offer thanksgiving to God for the spiritual progress of his readers, and, finally, (d) move on to the main subject of his letter. Here, there is no thanksgiving to God; they are not progressing! Rather there is an indictment given that charges the Galatians with moving away from their faith in the *grace of Christ* (1:6).

Paul selects a form of the Greek word for *removed* (v. 6) to express two charges against the Galatians: (1) The present tense ("I am making a cake," not past tense, "I made a cake") is used to indicate that the Galatians are in the process of defecting from the truth although they have not yet completed the process. Paul is writing with the intent of turning around this process (5:1). (2) The word, *removed*, is also in the middle voice (active voice: "John *hit* Tom"; passive voice: "John *was hit* by Tom"; middle voice: "John *hit himself*"). Paul is saying that, while there are others present who are teaching a false gospel (vv. 7-9), the Galatians are responsible for *removing themselves* from the true Gospel. This word is used in the Greek world of someone who has *deserted* one army for another. An example would be Benedict Arnold who, during the American Revolutionary War, *removed* himself from the American army to join himself to the opposing army of the British.

Loyal follower or deserter? What influences from "this present evil world" (v. 4) will you face today that will encourage you to *remove yourself* from your walk of faith with the Lord? How must you prepare yourself to respond to those influences so that you may "stand fast" (5:1) in your walk of faith? What are three or four things that you can be doing today to keep yourself *loyal* to the Lord?

Galatians 1:10-17

What is the writer saying?

How can I apply this to my life?

pray *Poland – Young people are skeptical of traditional religion but are open to the good news of Jesus - pray that many would give their lives to Him.*

Paul opens this section with a series of questions. These questions reflect the accusations being used to discredit Paul and his Gospel message (i.e., salvation is only by faith in Christ's death on the Cross, "Who gave himself for our sins," v. 4). The word "now" (v. 10) is key to understanding the accusations. "*Now*" implies an antecedent of *back then*. The false teachers are saying that *back then*, Paul sought to "persuade" (to win over) Jews by observing the Law and by presenting a message that would please the Jews. But "*now*" Paul is seeking to "please" Gentiles by saying they do not need to keep the Law, and by altering his message to conform to the current situation.

In response, Paul contends that his Gospel is not obtained from other men (vv. 10-11) or other apostles (vv. 16-17). Nor is it obtained through the labors of studying in school (the intent of "neither was I taught it," v. 12). Rather, Paul received his message by the "revelation of Jesus Christ." "Revelation" literally means, *to remove a cover*. It gives us a picture of Christ giving a gift box to Paul that contains the true Gospel message, which Paul then *unwraps* for us in his letters.

To further establish his claim that his Gospel is from Christ, Paul reminds them that they know of his life before he was saved (v. 13, "ye have heard"). They knew he had been "zealous" in pursuing the "traditions of my fathers" (v. 14, i.e., trusting in the rites and ceremonies of Judaism). They know he had "persecuted" Christians (v. 13). Yet they also know he had been "called" of God (v. 15) to a new life based upon God's "grace" and not Paul's former zealous works to earn righteousness.

Notice how Paul points to his own life history as an endorsement of his gospel message. How can you live today so that your life *endorses* the truth of the Gospel of Christ that is the basis of your salvation?

Galatians 1:18-24

What is the writer saying?

How can I apply this to my life?

pray *For the unblocking of Christian radio broadcasts that reach into North Korea with the Gospel.*

Paul continues his defense against those who claim that he has changed his message. They charge Paul with being an unscrupulous preacher. To defend his former activities, Paul uses the forceful courtroom terminology, "before God, I lie not" (v. 20, equivalent to our *Do you solemnly swear to tell the truth?*). The Galatians would have understood that Paul is willing to go to court to defend the truthfulness of his past actions.

Apparently, the false teachers are implying that Peter held their position, at least in practice, yet they conveniently overlook the fact that Paul corrected Peter's lack of consistency and that the matter has been resolved. In Galatians 2, Peter is the one who changes his teachings! Paul's purpose in today's passage is to support his claim that his Gospel message is by "revelation of Jesus Christ" (v. 12). This is best seen by Paul's choice of words "to see Peter." The Greek word translated, "to see," is used only here in the New Testament. It means, *to come to know by personal enquiry,* thus, *visiting someone to get acquainted.* It is used of one who visits a famous place; thus, it is the basis for the English word *history.* The Galatians would have understood that this word *did not* permit a suggestion of Paul being taught by Peter during Paul's short visit to Jerusalem. Rather, Paul has been directly taught by Christ Jesus. Thus Paul's Gospel message is genuine; a man is justified by faith in Jesus Christ alone (2:16).

Notice the implied warning for us today: Our beliefs must be based upon the *revelation of Jesus Christ*! Take a minute and list the different ways you are regularly taught about God. Do these avenues of teaching use the Bible as their only foundation for instruction? Are they, like Paul, directing your focus back to the *revelation of Jesus Christ*? Similarly, are you able to trace your foundational beliefs back to the Word of God?

Galatians 2:1-6

What is the writer saying?

How can I apply this to my life?

pray *Italy – For people to turn from the occult to Christ and for the city of Turin, a global center for Satanism, to be invaded by the power of the Gospel.*

Today's passage continues to support the claims of the first chapter, namely, that Paul, from the beginning, has declared the same message and has had the same mission. Both come directly from God.

First, notice that Paul is directed "by revelation" (by God's leading, not by Peter's command) to go to Jerusalem. Paul desires to "communicate" to the apostles at Jerusalem (*to lay before* for the apostles' consideration) what he preached. He does not want his efforts to be *rendered useless* ("in vain," v. 2) because of a misunderstanding between the ministry of Paul and Barnabas to Gentiles, and the ministry of Peter and James to Jews.

Next, notice that the apostles, who are men of importance to the church at Jerusalem (v. 2), "added nothing" (v. 6) to Paul's message. This means they (1) agree with the gospel message that Paul *lay before them,* and they (2) have nothing new to add to Paul's teachings.

Third, notice Paul says, "That gospel which I preach" (v. 2). The Greek form of the verb, "I preach," asserts the fact of continuous action from the past to the present. Today he would have to say, *This is the gospel that I have, in the past, always preached and, now, continue to preach!* Again, Paul declares he has consistently preached the same gospel message; a person is saved by faith in Jesus alone.

Finally, notice that Titus, a Greek, "also" comes to Jerusalem (vv. 1, 3). Titus is Paul's proof that his message has been consistently the same: salvation for Jews and Gentiles is by faith alone and does not require the keeping of the additional religious rituals of the Jews.).

Consistency in life and ministry is the trademark of Paul's defense. How about you and your life and ministry? While it may not be a *flashy* lifestyle, what elements of your life will be noticed by others so that they will say, "There is a person who seeks 'God's leading' in his life!" Also, consider if there is an area of your life that needs more consistency!

41 Thursday

QT

Galatians 2:7-14

What is the writer saying?

How can I apply this to my life?

pray *Netherlands Antilles – For the Papiamento Bible that was published in 1997 to be an impact on those who use it.*

Paul now turns his defense to those who "seemed" (three times in vv. 6, 9) to be "pillars" (v. 9) in the church (i.e., those who were the *supports* of the church). The idea here is that Peter, James and John are men who are recognized by all as leaders of the church at Jerusalem and, thus, those to whom the "gospel of the circumcision" (v. 7, to the Jews) is committed. Paul says these three "saw" (v. 7) that the "gospel of the uncircumcision" (to the Greeks and other Gentiles) has been committed by God to Paul.

There are different Greek words for "see" in the Bible. Here the word for "see" (eido) means, *to take a long look with the mind,* which is to say, *to observe something so that the mind becomes aware of the significance of it.* Here we must ask, what happens to cause them to see something of significance in the ministry of Paul and Barnabas (likewise with "perceived," v. 9)? The answer centers on an understanding of the words: "wrought effectually," and "mighty" (v. 8).

"Wrought effectually" and "mighty" are different forms of the Greek verb, "energeo." It means, *to be instrumental in a work* or as we might say, *the power source that produces a work*. Our word, *energy,* comes from this Greek word. It is used throughout the Greek Old Testament to describe God's mighty works. Peter, James, and John "saw" that the same "mighty power" that *energized* God's great works in the Old Testament, and that *energized* their own ministries was now *energizing* the ministry of Paul and Barnabas. For this reason they have extended to Paul and Barnabas the "right hands of fellowship" (v. 9), as they recognize Paul as a co-equal apostle to themselves.

God has been and wants to continue being the energy source behind your life and spiritual ministry! What is an area of your life that needs to hook up to God's "mighty" battery charger?

Galatians 2:15-21

What is the writer saying?

How can I apply this to my life?

pray *Uganda – For God to call witnesses to the Sudanese, Congolese, and Rwandan refugees.*

The Judaizers claim that the ways of the Jews are "by nature" (v. 15) superior. Paul says, no, your only advantage is the revelation given to you in scripture. The word "knowing" (v. 16) picks up on this idea. Here the Greek form of "knowing" is saying, *We Jews, above all people, came to know in the past and continue to know now that the observance of religious rituals will not justify us.* Paul then answers the question, how do we Jews come to know that we were not justified "by the works of the law"? He quotes David from Psalms 143:2, "And enter not into judgment with thy servant: for in thy sight shall no man living be justified." David is saying *do not judge me by Thy Law* since "no man" has kept the whole Law and thus "no man" could be "justified" by the Law. So Paul is reminding us that David was relying upon his faith, not his works, to be justified before God.

Notice that "justify" is used four times (vv. 16-17) and "righteousness" is used in v. 21. "Justify" is the verb form and "righteousness" is the noun form of the same Greek word, *dikaios*. It is a common legal term meaning, *to declare a person to be righteous who had been found guilty*. In the secular courts of that day, a person guilty of an offense could be declared righteous by a judge after the person *worked off* the debt of his offense. Paul makes it clear that the Old Testament teaches that no man, Jew or Gentile, is able *work off* his spiritual debt to God for his sin. Rather, Paul declares that we are declared right before God only by "faith" in Christ who paid for our violations by His crucifixion and resurrection (v. 20).

Are you seeking "justification" by your own works or by the work of Christ? Are you trying to work off the debt of your own sin ("works of the law," v. 16)? Or have you "believed in Jesus Christ" (v. 16) as the One who *worked off* your debt?

Galatians 3:1-9

What is the writer saying?

How can I apply this to my life?

pray *India – For godly officials who will bring an end to the widespread practice of aborting females.*

Paul has finished his defense and is now moving on to teach the Galatians the true basis of being justified (v. 8, also "righteousness," v. 6) before God. Paul begins by rebuking them since they were "foolish" (v. 1, 3) in not perceiving the significance of the evidence that has been set before their eyes (v. 1, "evidently set forth").

"Foolish" literally means, *not applying the mind*. Also, he says they have been "bewitched," a word that draws from the superstitions of the day. It was a commonly held fear that staring into the eyes of an evil person could result in the evil person gaining control over them so that he might draw them into great harm (like a modern magician saying, "look into my eyes"). It is used figuratively here to express that the false teachers are drawing them into evil doctrines. Paul is telling the Galatians to use their minds and *see* the truth before their "eyes."

Now notice that "faith" (a noun), "believed" (a verb) and "faithful" (an adjective) are used seven times in verses 2-9. All three words come from the same Greek root word, *pistis*, which means, *to have a firm persuasion or conviction*. What is Paul's doctrine of justification by faith?

1. verse 6, Abraham "believed" was the basis of his righteousness.
2. verse 7, All who are of "faith" are in Abraham's spiritual family.
3. verse 8, The Old Testament Scriptures (Genesis 12:3) foretold of the Gentiles coming to God by the same "faith" as exercised by Abraham.
4. verse 9, All those of "faith" will be "blessed" (to cause to prosper) by God just like "faithful" Abraham was blessed.

Think back to that time period just before you were saved. How did God cause your mind to *see* the truth about Christ so that you were *firmly persuaded* of your need to trust in Christ as your means of justification before God? How has God "blessed" your life since you believed?

QT

Sunday 42

Galatians 3:10-16

What is the writer saying?

How can I apply this to my life?

pray *Ecuador – Pray for God to call more laborers to reach the impoverished of Quito and Guayaquil.*

Yesterday, we looked at the blessings (v. 9) that come upon the Galatians when they, by faith, are *justified* before God. Today, Paul argues from the opposite view: if one seeks to be *justified* by "the works of the law," he is under the "curse" of the Law (v. 10). The word "cursed," *to call down wrath upon,* is an Old Testament term found especially in Deuteronomy when Moses is given the Law. The "blessings" and "cursings" are included to warn the people concerning their response to the Law (Deuteronomy 30:19, "I have set before you … blessing and cursing").

The curse of the Law signifies being handed over to the judgment and wrath of God. From our judicial system, we have a similar picture of a convicted criminal being delivered to the electric chair for justice to be carried out. This is a serious thing made worse by being linked here with the word "under." Rather than merely facing the possibility of a future punishment, "under" emphasizes that the follower of the Law is already subject to the wrath of God upon sin.

Paul closes with the declaration that Christ "redeemed" us from this hopelessly bleak situation of being "under the curse" of God. In the New Testament world, a person could be redeemed from slavery when someone paid the slave's debt, thus buying the slave's deliverance. This image is applied here to Christ's death on the cross (v. 13, "hangeth on a tree"). His death is the price paid to deliver "us" (v. 13), who have placed our faith in Him, from our slavery to the curse of the Law.

Think of it! Redeemed from slavery to the curse of the Law and receiving the blessings that "come on the Gentiles through Jesus Christ" (v. 14). Take a minute and write a note to Jesus, thanking Him for paying the price that freed you from your hopeless situation.

Galatians 3:17-22

What is the writer saying?

How can I apply this to my life?

pray *Nigeria – For the staggering growth of the church to continue and for the body to become mature.*

Again, we have a key word that is central to Paul's next point in his on-going line of argument, which is: a person is saved by faith in the death of Christ. "Promise" is used eight times in this chapter, which is the greatest concentration in the New Testament. In the Greek world, "promises" (with the definition of *notification of an agreement*) are made between parties after pledges are negotiated in a contract.

A second definition is also used for "promise": *to announce an intention.* This definition is used when Greeks pledged to give a *free-will* offering (no two-way contract implied) to one of the Greek gods. It is significant that Greek gods are never said to give *free-will* promises to men. In contrast, the very character of the Old Testament is built around the free-will promises of God! The first promise of God is to Eve, found early in Genesis (3:15). Late in Old Testament history, when Israel's sins against God are at their worst, God gives His most revealing promises concerning the coming Messiah (e.g., Isaiah, Daniel).

Foremost in Paul's thinking is God's promise to Abraham, Genesis. 12:3, "in thee shall all families of the earth be blessed," which Paul quotes in Galatians 3:8. In 3:17 and 18, Paul points out that God's covenant and promises to Abraham are separate from the Law. The two are separated by both a great time period and by purpose. The Law is "added" (3:19) later because of sin. The Law does not "disannul" (*to render cancelled,* v. 17) the promises. Rather, the Law is "added … till the seed should come" (v.19), since the "seed" ("which is Christ," v. 16) is the thing promised to "them that believe" (v. 22).

Since God is faithful to His promises concerning both our initial salvation and our on-going Christian walk, which promises will you claim today?

Galatians 3:23-29

What is the writer saying?

How can I apply this to my life?

pray *Ukraine – For the failure of any doctrine that is contrary to biblical truth.*

Paul now gives an illustration of how the Law is to assist the Old Testament believers. The illustration centers on the words "schoolmaster" (vv. 24, 25) and "children" (v. 26) and refers to a Roman household of a wealthy person. The lord of the household would acquire a slave trained as a "schoolmaster," literally a *child-leader*. This *child* (Greek, *pais*) refers to a seven to fourteen year old boy. A pais has no privileges and is considered just a member of the household, the same as any other slave. The schoolmaster's primary responsibility is to guard the children under his care against temptations and danger. He is responsible for their moral and physical well-being, which includes disciplining the children. While he teaches the children informally, he is not their teacher; rather he is responsible to take his charges to school. It is important to note that Jesus is commonly recognized in this role as the *teacher* (same as *master*). Thus, the role of the Law, in the household of God, is to bring those under the Law to the true Teacher, Jesus Christ.

The word "children" in 3:26 is a different Greek word, *huios,* which is used of a man over twenty-five who is a legal heir. A *huios* could be either the natural offspring or an adopted son. An adult-son is released from the schoolmaster (v. 25) and is granted the legal privileges as the recognized heir of the lord of the household. Paul says that "by faith" (v. 26) we have become the *acknowledged sons* in the household of God. This is a new concept for believers since the Jews only viewed themselves as the *pais* of God; little children in God's great household. Thus, Christians now have a better relationship to God!

You have been adopted into God's family and have been recognized as an adult-son in the household of God! What are some of the privileges granted to you? What are some of the responsibilities extended to you?

Galatians 4:1-7

What is the writer saying?

How can I apply this to my life?

pray *Dominican Republic – To escape occultism's bondage by responding to the call of the Holy Spirit.*

Today's key word, "heir" (4:1), picks up where yesterday's "heirs" left off (3:29). The word "heir" comes from a family of Greek words that deal with inheritances. The Bible's idea of inheritance is a very rich study. First, an inheritance is a reminder that man is neither an independent, self-sufficient being, nor is he an isolated being. It is a reminder that a person receives what has been passed on to him from God's workings in past history. Second, it is a reminder and a comfort that a person of faith receives even greater blessings as he looks forward to the future.

Paul reminds us that an heir, while he is still a minor, is treated as a household slave. He would one day be "lord of all" (v. 1) the property, yet as a minor he is required to obey the "tutors" (*guardians who sanctioned and limited a child's activities,* v. 2) and the "governors" (*one who serves as trustee of all the inheritance*) until the child becomes an adult. The illustration teaches that mankind is like a minor in God's household-world. Mankind is under the control of external laws and demands of the world (v. 3). But, when Christ came, He redeemed (*paid the slave's debt and set him free,* v. 5a) those under the Law and He caused us to "receive the adoption of sons" (*we who were homeless outsiders become heirs to the household-heaven of God,* v. 5b).

Just like the father orders that a signet ring be given to the prodigal son upon his return (Luke 15:22), we are given the Spirit. The ring is a token that shows the father has recognized the prodigal as his son and has granted the son full identity, privilege and authority as his son. The presence of the Spirit in our hearts (v. 6) is our signet ring from God.

As an "heir of God through Christ" (v. 7), how has your identity changed? What privileges has He given you? How will men see the Spirit in you?

Galatians 4:8-18

What is the writer saying?

How can I apply this to my life?

pray *Canada – For more missionaries to be called to this vast country (second largest country in the world).*

Previously Paul has been arguing against the Jews who are seeking to add the Jewish religious rituals to the predominantly Gentile churches of Galatia. Now Paul appeals to these Gentiles with the following four points:

(1) verse 8, Pre-salvation *bondage*: Because the Gentiles are ignorant of the true God, they "did service unto them," all the "no-gods" (idols, demons, and other men who exalted themselves).

(2) verse 9a, Post-salvation *liberty*: *Knowing God* is a summary phrase for all that happens when a person is saved: freedom from their bondage to sin to become partakers in the blessings of the new life in Christ. Being "known of God" includes an acknowledgement that God has sought them out to save them. It also gives the idea of being welcomed into God's family as a son and heir.

(3) verse 9b, Interim-"turning again" to *bondage*: "Weak" means *without-strength*, thus one who is feeble or sick. "Beggarly" literally means, *poor and unable to work*, like a crippled beggar. Thus, the Galatians have become sick and crippled as they turn to the false belief of Jewish ritualism. This new "bondage" is powerless to justify them before God. It could not work to enrich their walk with God.

(4) verses 12-13, Final-return to their first *liberty*: Paul's words, "be as I am," are saying, *When you heard the graciousness of my Gospel you begged to hear more. Now I beg you to return to that attitude of admiring the graciousness of God's plan of salvation.*

Which will it be: Liberty in Christ or bondage by the works required of religious rituals? What influences from the world "zealously affect you" (v. 17a)? How can you avoid those things that seek after you, desiring to "exclude" (*lock out*) the blessing of God from your life (v. 17b)?

Galatians 4:19-26

What is the writer saying?

How can I apply this to my life?

pray *China – Special need for study Bibles and children's Bibles and safety for those transporting them.*

Paul desires "to change my voice" (v. 20) towards the Galatians for he has been speaking with a harsh voice of rebuke. Since he loves the wayward Galatians, he prefers to speak with the voice of a loving mother to her newborn (v. 19). Yet his harsh words are necessary because the false teachers are placing them in bondage "under" the Law (v. 21). Since the Judaizers claim to understand the Law of Moses, but they actually pervert the Law by claiming that salvation is faith plus law-observance, Paul chooses to draw an analogy from the Books of Moses.

The analogy is from the life of Abraham (Gen. 16, 17, 21) and it looks at an event where Abraham seeks to *work* at fulfilling the promises of God rather than by merely *trusting* God to fulfill His own promises. Abraham feels he needs to *add something* to his simple trust in God's promise (Gen 12:2-3; 15:4) lest he *miss out* on the fulfillment of God's promise. Likewise, the pagan Galatians have become Christians through simple faith in the promise that they could trust in the death of Christ. Now they were *seeking after* the false teachers who are saying the Galatians need to *add something* to their simple trust in God's promise or they too would *miss out* on God's promise to them.

It is important to note that this story of Abraham ends with God demonstrating that Abraham's additional work to fulfill God's promise failed to *help out* God. In fact, Abraham's works were ultimately harmful to his children (v. 29).

Learn from Abraham's mistakes! When faced with uncertainties, do you patiently wait on God? When you question whether faith in Christ's death is enough for your salvation, do you remind yourself that God, who is always faithful, has declared you to be a "child of promise" (v. 28)? Take a minute and write out a "Declaration of Faith" in God's promises.

Galatians 4:27-5:1

What is the writer saying?

How can I apply this to my life?

pray *Korea – Protection and perseverance of nearly 100,000 believers confined in North Korean camps.*

Paul is building on his contrast between *freedom* and *bondage.* Paul's argument is that just as Isaac was the *child of promise* to Abraham and Sarah, so those who trust in Christ by faith are also the *children of promise.* As such "all" (4:26) people of faith are (a) *free* from bondage to paganism (4:8), (b) *free* from bondage to Jewish legalism (4:5) and (c) *free* from any other teaching that seeks to draw those of faith back into the "yoke" of works (5:1) to earn salvation.

Today's passage rolls over into chapter 5 to complete the word-contrast between *freedom* and *bondage.* First, note that the Greek word for "liberty" (5:1) is the noun form of the word, *free,* which is used later in this verse and is used several times in Chapter 4. Verse 5:1 extends the word-contrast with two Greek imperatives (*a word form that gives a strong command*), "stand fast" and "entangled."

"Stand fast" gives the positive command, *be standing up straight with feet fixed,* and suggests the negatives, *don't be pushed over* and *don't be driven away.* The word is illustrated by a line of soldiers standing with weapons ready and with feet fixed as they are prepared to meet an on-rushing enemy. The opposite form of the word is used in 5:12, "trouble," where it means *to cause one to flee his station.*

"Entangle" literally commands *don't be held in* and is illustrated by a bird caught in a net with its wings being held in. It is coupled here with the picture of a slave who is forced to bend over because of the straps that bind him into a yoke.

Which of these illustrations better fits your spiritual life?
(1) A soldier courageously standing, facing his enemies!
(2) An eagle soaring "free" with outstretched wings.
(3) A soldier fleeing his post when enemies "trouble" him.
(4) Or perhaps, a bird snagged in a net unable to fly.

43 Sunday

Galatians 5:2-6

What is the writer saying?

How can I apply this to my life?

pray *Kenya – For church leaders to have wisdom and boldness when speaking out against sin.*

Paul here uses a form of the verb, "circumcised" (v. 2) to express a *continuous idea* beyond the normal physical circumcision. Thus, continuing circumcision refers to an ongoing keeping of all the Jewish religious ceremonies and practices, circumcision being just the first step. The Galatians are being taught that these are needed to maintain an additional layer of acceptance before God. Paul emphatically states that there can be no *double foundation* upon which a person's salvation rests. Righteousness must either be obtained by faith in Christ or the keeping of "all" (3:10) the practices of the Law. By adding the Jewish rituals to their faith, the Gentiles of Galatia are in danger of making their walk (not their salvation) with Christ "of no effect" (v. 4). "Of no effect" means, *cut off from*, thus, ceasing to be connected with the grace of Christ needed for daily living ("fallen from grace," v. 4b).

In contrast with v. 4, Paul presents the true basis for salvation (v. 5): (a) "we through the Spirit" and (b) "wait for the hope of righteousness" (c) "by faith"

a) "*Through the Spirit*" acknowledges that it is the Spirit who works in us, drawing us to Christ and then imputes the righteousness of Christ to us.

b) "*Waiting for the hope of righteousness*" refers to the fact that, at salvation, a believer is declared righteous but some of the benefits promised to a believer are not received until he gets to Heaven.

c) "*By faith*" in Christ, without any mixing with personal works, is the means by which people receive acceptance before God.

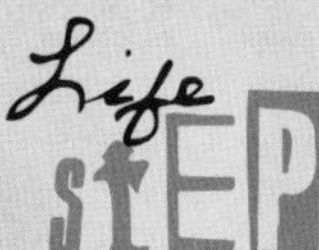

Are you seeking acceptance by God through a mixture of trusting in Christ and trusting in the religious deeds you may have done to *earn* salvation? If you are trusting in Christ alone for your salvation, then think back through the *work* the Holy Spirit did to bring you to Christ!

Galatians 5:7-15

What is the writer saying?

How can I apply this to my life?

pray *Argentina – Pray that Argentina's church leaders would be committed to pursuing unity, personal holiness and discipleship.*

Today's passage could be entitled, "Running or Hindered?" The phrase, "Ye did run well" (v. 7a) refers to the Greek stadiums where foot races were conducted. "Well" means *with excellence* and here refers to the character of the runner and his *excellent* conduct in the race.

The next phrase, "who did hinder you...," continues the metaphor of running a race. The Greek word, "hinder," literally means *to cut into* referring to a retreating army that would cut into (*break up*) a road to make it temporarily impassable, thus delaying their enemy. Later, it is used with the idea of *to cut short, to check,* as in checking the course of a ship (*turning to stop forward motion*). It is also used of a runner who comes across the course to jostle an opposing runner, causing him to stumble and fall out of the race. Paul uses it here to picture the false teachers who are building up spiritual obstacles in front of the Galatians and deliberately *pushing* the beliefs of the Galatians. They are seeking to hinder the Galatians' faith in God and to *check* their walk with the Lord.

Next, Paul says, "I have confidence in you through the Lord" (v. 10). In what is Paul confident? Paul expects the Galatians to again "run well" as they had before. Paul then goes on to define what he has in mind for their renewed *run*. The Galatians are (a) to "serve one another" (v. 13), (b) to "love thy neighbor" (v. 14), (c) to "take heed" of their conduct (v. 15), (d) to walk (v. 16) and live (v. 25) in the Spirit (tomorrow's study) and (e) to desire humility (v. 26).

Are you *running well*? Which of the above areas of spiritual *running* do you need to practice so that your game can become *excellent*? Which area needs you to ask for some help from God?

43 Tuesday

Galatians 5:16-21

What is the writer saying?

How can I apply this to my life?

pray *Nigeria – For churches and youth ministries to reach the nearly 1,400,000 children orphaned by AIDS.*

"Walk in the Spirit" (v. 16) is in focus today. First notice the little word "in." Let us picture the subjects of today's passage in relation to the boundary of a marathon race course. The Holy Spirit has provided the markers that define the boundaries *within* which we can "run" free (v. 7) and "live" free (v. 25). Also notice that failing to "walk" (v. 16) *in*side the Holy Spirit's boundaries results in our always failing to "do the things" we want to do (v. 17)! Now notice that Paul gives two lists. One list of seventeen items, "the works of the flesh" (vv. 19-21), is the out-of-bounds area. The other list of nine items, "the fruit of the Spirit" (vv. 22-23), is *in*-bounds and is tomorrow's passage. So let's look at the first list:

- *Adultery, fornication, uncleanness,* and *lasciviousness* all involve sexual impurity that abandons godly morals.
- *Idolatry,* worshipping idols, also anything taking God's rightful place.
- *Witchcraft* is the use of drugs (potions) in sorcery, enchantments.
- *Hatred,* a personal quarrel with others leading to a desire to murder.
- *Variance* means arguments and strife resulting from selfishness.
- *Emulations* are jealousies that make war on the good in another.
- *Wrath,* an outburst of uncontrolled anger due to a lack of self-control.
- *Strife & seditions,* taking sides by selfishness that destroys harmony.
- *Heresies,* divisive and destructive views on doctrinal beliefs.
- *Envyings* are active and often treacherous desires to get even.
- *Murders,* intentional killing, the destroying of another's character.
- *Drunkenness* & revellings are unrestrained carousing and partying.

Does your life, at times, run *out-of-bounds*? For example, do you find yourself wanting to get even for some wrong done to you? Well, that is out-of-bounds! How can you keep from going out-of-bounds? How can you work together with the Holy Spirit, your *race referee,* to stay inside the Spirit's boundaries for your life's race for God?

QT Wednesday 43

Galatians 5:22-26

What is the writer saying?

How can I apply this to my life?

pray *Poland – For God to protect missionaries and ministry equipment from criminal activity.*

Today we get the good list, the *in-bounds areas* that allow us to "run well" (v. 7). Let's begin by noting that there are no laws (v. 23) like our speed limits or construction zone restrictions that require us to drive slowly when using today's list. Remember, Paul has been arguing against those who wanted to install the Old Testament Law into the churches of Galatia. Here, Paul is also pointing out that neither the Old Testament Law, nor any other set of religious rules, can give a person love, joy, peace, etc. These are only obtained when a person places himself under the Holy Spirit and thereby removes himself from being under religious rules and rites.

The nine "fruit of the Spirit" (v. 22) are the crops that the Spirit *grows* in our lives. These are the expected *harvest* of the Spirit's working in the *soil* of your life as a Christian. Let's look at His crops:

- *Love,* (Greek: *agape*), a self-giving devotion that does what is best for the other person regardless of what that person does in return.
- *Joy,* a cheerful attitude, delighting in God, regardless of situation.
- *Peace,* a quiet calmness of heart, knowing my life is in God's hands.
- *Longsuffering,* to suffer long; endurance when wrongly treated.
- *Gentleness,* showing kindness, conveying consideration, patience.
- *Goodness,* good in character, demonstrated by generosity.
- *Faith,* faithfulness in conduct due to a complete confidence in God.
- *Meekness,* an inward submission to God's dealings in one's life, resulting in an outward balance in the expressions of one's strength.
- *Temperance,* having the mastery of self-control over fleshly desires; the right use of the powers given to a man by God.

Since these are *growing* crops or fruit, which of the above do you need to concentrate on producing in your life? How can the Spirit help you? How can you *fertilize* these spiritual crops?

Galatians 6:1-5

What is the writer saying?

How can I apply this to my life?

pray *Portugal – For information technologists to utilize the Internet for evangelization and discipleship.*

Today's passage picks up on the second of two extremes facing Christians in their life of liberty in Christ. The first extreme is the danger of losing one's liberty by coming again "under the law" (5:18) of legalism. Paul already noted that the second extreme is allowing one's liberty to become a license to sin (5:13). Liberty in Christ does not mean lawlessness. Rather, it is every believer's responsibility to "fulfil the law of Christ" (v. 2) which is a law of "love" (5:13) and is accomplished by applying the "fruit of the Spirit" (5:22-23) to the situations of life.

Paul gives an example of this in a brother "being overtaken in a fault" (v. 1). "Overtaken" means *drawn into a trap and taken.* It is coupled with "fault" (*to misplace one's step; to slip and fall*). Thus, Paul gives a picture of a brother who falls into the mud of sin because he was careless, not having considered his steps that led him into the trap. A "spiritual" Christian (*one being led by the Spirit*) cannot say, *Well, it is his own fault, let him suffer! Maybe next time he will be more careful.*

While such a comment may be true, it is not loving. Love demands that the "spiritual" one come to the aid of the one "overtaken" and "restore" him (v. 1, literally, *to set a broken bone, allowing it to heal*). The "spiritual" one must use care ("meekness," v. 1) since broken lives, like broken bones, are very painful. "Meekness" demands the precision, and gentleness of a spiritual doctor who brings health to his patient. Finally, Paul reminds us that people with broken lives, like those with broken bones, often need others to carry ("bear," v. 2) their burdens for a time.

As in the Parable of the Good Samaritan, what spiritually injured person has God placed in your path so that God might teach you how to become "spiritual" through the use of the qualities listed as "the fruit of the Spirit"? Ask God to show you how you might be able to "bear" up that friend of yours who needs you to carry him along for a while.

Galatians 6:6-10

What is the writer saying?

How can I apply this to my life?

pray *South Africa – Protection for believers in a land with a murder rate that is seven times that of the U.S.*

Paul shows the functioning of the "fruit of the Spirit" (5:22-23) in the believer's daily life by giving two applications to the model of "bear ye one another's burdens" (v.2). The first is in yesterday's passage and dealt with serving as a *spiritual doctor* to those who have been "overtaken" by the troubles of life.

Today we look at the second application. Lehman Strauss, in his commentary on Galatians, puts it this way, "The word 'communicate' (v. 6) conveys the idea of sharing, of having things in common. The teacher passes on the great truths of God's word which are the fruit of his labor; the taught acknowledges this by communicating to him 'in all good things' (v.6b)." Paul is implying that the members of the churches of Galatia are neglecting their spiritual leaders ("him that teacheth," v. 6) whose work was the sowing (v. 8) of the word (v. 6). The law of sowing and reaping (vv. 7-8) teaches all men that only a fool thinks he can break God's Law and escape the consequences (v. 7). Paul is urging the ones who are being "taught" (v.6) not to "faint" (v. 9b) or become "weary in well doing" (v. 9a) in their temporal support (salary, housing, food, and other needs) of their spiritual teachers.

Yes, the teacher who ministers in the Spirit, with the "fruit of the Spirit," will reap a great harvest of God's blessing. But, notice here that Paul is emphasizing the reaping of the ones *being* taught: the member in the pew. These also will reap a great harvest of God's blessing by faithfully supporting the work of the ministry with the temporal seeds that they have "opportunity" (v. 10) to sow upon the work of the church.

What "opportunity" seeds has God given you to plant in the garden of your life? Don't become "weary" at working your garden! Take a moment and remind yourself of the great harvest you are going to "reap."

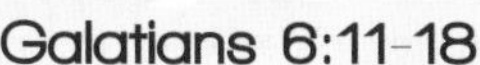

Galatians 6:11-18

What is the writer saying?

How can I apply this to my life?

pray *Netherlands – For those crossing social and cultural barriers trying to spread the Gospel to the lesser reached people.*

To stress its importance, Paul takes the pen from his scribe and writes with bold letters this last paragraph. The three sections of the conclusion correspond, in reverse order, to the three sections of the letter.

First, he warns that the false teachers, who "constrain" (v. 12b) the Galatians to be "circumcised," are not interested in the spiritual welfare of the Galatians. Rather, they, being self-serving by seeking (a) to obtain a "fair shew" (v. 12a, *win favor with their religious superiors*), (b) to avoid "persecution" (v. 12c) by staying in good standing with the Jews and (c) to "glory in your flesh" (v. 13) by making a display of the number of Gentiles they had won to the Jewish ritual).

Second, Paul makes a final defense of his own credentials. Notice the contrast given by the repeating of the word, "glory" (vv. 13-14, *basis for boasting*). Paul rightly boasts in the "cross of our Lord Jesus Christ" (v. 14). Paul has in mind more than just the cross upon which Christ died. He is emphasizing all that was accomplished by the complete work of Christ. Paul points out two aspects: (a) Paul is now *dead* to the world (v. 14, "crucified") and (b) he is now *alive* to Christ (v. 15, "a new creature").

Third, Paul says he has "marks" (v. 17b) on his body to prove that his arguments in this letter are true. The word, "marks," refers to the scars on his body. The "marks" declare that Christ owns Paul. There are three classes of people in the ancient world who were branded: soldiers, slaves and devotees. The religious devotees would voluntarily accept branding to announce that they belonged to a certain God.

What *proof of ownership* can be found from your conduct during the past week? In what will you seek "glory"; self-serving things that give you a "fair shew" or self-sacrificing things that *show Christ* in you?

In Biblical usage, the word "proverb" refers to a brief, pithy statement of practical wisdom usually providing moral direction. "Knowledge" is the accumulation of facts. "Understanding" is the appreciation or the correlation of these facts. "Wisdom" is the practical application of knowledge and understanding of real-life situations. In the Bible, and especially here in Proverbs, wisdom is seeing life from God's point of view. We know from Deuteronomy 17:18 that God expected every king to hand-copy his own copy of the Law. Some have suggested that the book of Proverbs is Solomon's distillations of practical applications to the Law of Moses.

Ancient proverbs are designed principally for oral transmission. They are structured to impact the hearer and also for ease of memory. A frequent device is the contrasting couplet: "A fool uttereth all his mind; but a wise man keepeth it in till afterwards" (29:11). "Commit thy works unto the Lord, and thy thoughts shall be established" (16:3) is an example of a completive couplet; whereas "Better is a little with righteousness than great revenues without right" (16:8) is a comparative couplet.

The book of Proverbs includes not only proverbs, but also other types of literature such as parables, poems and oracles. Proverbs 1:1, 10:1 and 25:1 tell us that King Solomon authored Proverbs with the exception of the last two chapters, where Agur and Lemuel are named as authors. According to 1 Kings 4:32, Solomon spoke three thousand proverbs.

1 Kings 4:31 says, "he was wiser than all men." That statement, of course, was no longer true when Christ became a man, for in Him "are hid all the treasures of wisdom and knowledge" (Colossians 2:3). The story of how Solomon acquires such wisdom is found in 1 Kings 3:5-12.

Some of the virtues commended in Proverbs are the pursuit of wisdom, respect for parents, liberality, marital fidelity, honesty, humility and piety. Vices condemned include lust, drunkenness, lying, cheating, laziness, strife, greed, pride, folly, gluttony and vengeance.

The principle theme of the book is wisdom. The words "wise" and "wisdom" occur more than one hundred times in the text.

Proverbs 11:1-11

What is the writer saying?

How can I apply this to my life?

pray *Bulgaria – Freedom from legal restrictions aimed at believers caused by the slanderous Orthodox media.*

The book of Proverbs is somewhat disjointed because most of the proverbs cover one topic in just one or at most a few verses before the subject is changed. Therefore, we can only provide a general outline for the book. In chapters 1-9, Solomon covers the topics of wisdom and foolishness. In chapters 10-15 he contrasts the lifestyles of the righteous with the wicked. Here in 11:1-11, each verse is a contrast usually noted by the word "but" in the middle. Verses 1, 2, 4, 7 and 9 start with the wicked and end with the righteous, while the others start with the righteous and end with the wicked. There does not seem to be a standard pattern. Notice the depth of God's resentment against cheating in business ("abomination" is used elsewhere of gross immorality; compare with Deuteronomy 24:4). Sometimes it is not spelled out why a particular attitude or action is bad, but we can tell by the context. The "pride" of verse two obviously leads to some sort of foolish public mishap that brings shame to the proud person, whereas, the humble person is able to wisely avoid looking stupid. Solomon has everything a man could desire and therefore, could authoritatively argue that riches are fleeting. We can only be happy if we live with eternity's values in view. Like the villain who drowns because of the gold bars in his pocket, the evil that men do drags them down to a Christ-less eternity. This section concludes with a generalization to a whole social unit (in this case, a city). It could just as easily have been applied to a whole nation.

As go the parents, go the children. As go the children, goes the family. As goes the family, goes the city. As goes the city, goes the nation. As goes the nation, goes the next generation. Humanly speaking, there seems to be no hope, but fortunately God can break the downward cycle.

Proverbs 11:12-21

What is the writer saying?

How can I apply this to my life?

pray *Costa Rica – Pray for the Holy Spirit to break the bonds of materialism, apathy, and ritualism.*

God's plan is for men to love and be at peace with each other. The foolish person antagonizes those around him for selfish reasons. The Hebrew word for "despiseth" is an onomatopoeia (sounds like what it represents). It is the angry sounding word *buzz*. Like the angry buzzing of a bee, gossip and slander goes forth. Holding peace means not gossiping about and tearing down the reputation of others. Being quiet about other people's failures acknowledges that we wouldn't want our shortcomings advertised. Verse 14 provides the universal truth that humans function better in coordination than in solo attempts at success. Rugged individualism may have a place, but no man is an island, and for the sake of the community we should stand together lest we hang separately (consider the U.S. in 1776). "Surety" and "suretiship" refer to those responsible for covering a loan that is in default. Money can come between friends and certainly is a problem with untested strangers who can abuse your trust. In this passage are several key theological terms that we should know and honor. "Gracious" (v. 16) is the Hebrew word for grace, pronounced *chen*. Many know the New Testament Greek equivalent, *charis*. "Merciful" (v. 17) is covenant loyalty (*chesed*). It speaks of loving kindness, goodness and mercy. It is the Old Testament equivalent of agape love. The "froward" heart (v. 20) is the one twisted from God's way of righteousness. Even though the wicked stand together, they *will* hang together (v. 21).

Much of today's passage announces the rewards of godly living. The godly woman is honored (consider Ruth). The godly man enjoys his material blessings (consider Job). The merciful man finds mercy and internal peace (consider Abraham). Not only does godliness bring a reward, it *is* a reward.

Proverbs 11:22-31

What is the writer saying?

How can I apply this to my life?

pray *Kosovo – For healing from past wars, for missionaries working there, and for new believers threatened due to converting from Islam.*

Parables are powerful because they take something ordinary and concrete from daily life that we all can identify with, and they use it to explain an abstract and/or unfamiliar concept. What a comical mental picture verse 22 conjures up! Our old world is wracked with pain and suffering because of the evil acts of wicked men. Ironically, in their grasping attempt to get more, they actually wind up with less. This seems to be the lesson of communism in the 20th Century. It is almost as though God has created a law of economics and social interaction, that those who voluntarily contribute to any process are themselves blessed by that process (true for both capitalism and random acts of kindness). There is a story of a farmer who relied on irrigation for his produce. Every night his neighbor would break the retaining wall so his field would get all the farmer's water. Finally, the farmer stopped fixing the wall and just watered his neighbor's field as well as his own. It resulted in apologies and a lasting friendship that improved the production of both fields. Verse 26 speaks of price manipulation that for a luxury item might be acceptable, but when people are starving it is an atrocity. Notice how these proverbs bring to mind some of our modern sayings, such as, *What goes around comes around* (v. 27). In verses 28 and 29 notice that the physical is unsure and fleeting while the abstract is enduring (righteousness, godliness, wisdom). Verse 30 is a classic, very similar to Daniel 12:3, "And they that be wise shall shine as the brightness of the firmament; and they that turn many to righteousness as the stars for ever and ever."

Notice that the tree of life is not the reward given to the righteous person (we are saved by faith not works), but rather it is the fruit of the righteous life – other people getting saved eternally.

Proverbs 12:1-10

What is the writer saying?

How can I apply this to my life?

pray *Ukraine – For God to give youth a passion to live for Him and reach their land.*

He who can, does. He who can't, teaches. This mean-spirited evaluation has some basis in real life, but is not the final word on the value of instruction. Ideally, a teacher should both *do* and *teach*, in both word and by example. The receptive student, even when his pride is wounded by the critique, will flourish. The headstrong will be retarded in moral, social and intellectual advancement. Firm foundations are important to buildings and to lives. Wickedness is quicksand. Liars must remember to whom they said which lie. The honest person does not have that burden to bear. It is important that your spouse and children are assets and not detriments to your testimony and ministry. Therefore, there is the need to choose your spouse prayerfully and carefully. We can imagine Hitler or Saddam Hussein planning to kill someone, but the Bible implies that even the somewhat *peaceful* person can cause murderous activity as their philosophies are molded by atheistic principles. Note all the lives lost due to communism or women's reproductive rights in the 20th Century. Verse 6 is not saying that the wicked are having discussions about whom to kill, but rather that they use their words publicly (such as by lying under oath) to destroy others. The righteous, on the other hand, speak the truth that frees the innocent. "Perverse heart" (v. 8) refers to a morally crooked way of thinking. Verse 9 is difficult. Apparently it means the proud person has spent all his money on appearances and therefore, lacks daily bread. Finally, in verse 10 a person's character is demonstrated even in the way he treats animals.

It is interesting that our word *wrong* comes from the Old English word *wrung* (to twist), as in *He wrung the chicken's neck.* Sin is destructive by nature.

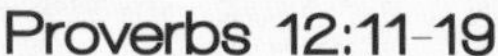

Proverbs 12:11-19

What is the writer saying?

How can I apply this to my life?

pray *Ecuador – For those in authority to deal honestly, to resist social bribery, and to receive Christ.*

Verse 11 teaches that hard work puts food on the table while wasting time with questionable characters leads to hunger. Tragically, most people on welfare could work if they willed to do so. The "net" (v. 12) refers to what evil men steal. Other evil men envy the thief's possessions, but the righteous man pays his own way in life. He leaves behind more than he takes. Verses 13-19 all relate to talking or listening. Sinful talk traps the wicked. Good words encourage the heart of the speaker. His hard work with mind, lip, and hands are rewarded in this life and in the life to come. The fool rejects guidance, but the wise man accepts the good advice of others. The wise man is positive and doesn't accentuate the negatives of life. The foolish man is quick to vent his criticisms. "Truth" is an eternal absolute. It is not based on a command of God (such as the temporary command not to eat of a particular fruit tree in the Garden of Eden), but rather on the very character of God. Therefore, truth is part of righteousness. It is also "righteous" in that the context is again a court of law in which a false witness is not only deceitful, but also deadly. Even in non-legal contexts, poorly chosen words can be very hurtful. This is especially important in husband/wife and parent/children relations. *Verbal abuse* is real and has life-long consequences. Conversely, even a few kind words are incredibly powerful in the lives of those around us. A kind word is *good medicine.*

Our good words become part of an eternal record. Lying words are immediately useless ("for a moment" is literally *the blinking of an eye*).

QT

Friday 44

Proverbs 12:20-28

What is the writer saying?

How can I apply this to my life?

pray *Canada – Effective ministry among the Innu People (First Nations) in Northern Quebec.*

So much of what an evil man plots leads to violence and destruction. Therefore, the opposite activity of the righteous man is described as "peace." This well-known Hebrew word, *Shalom* is the root of Solomon's name (*Shlomo*). It is the word for wholeness or completion. Theologically, we are at war with God, other men and ourselves. God's salvation brings peace to all of these hostilities. The wicked are not promised this peace and in fact will sow to the wind and reap the whirlwind. The promise of protection to the just must be qualified by God's larger plan. Certainly saints will suffer troubles. Normally God protects His own and when He doesn't, the troubles are purposeful, temporary, and not eternal, as will be the punishment of the wicked. "Lying" occurs eight times in Proverbs, "lips" or "tongue" sixty-one times and "truth," "true," "truly" eleven times. This is obviously an important issue with God. The wise man stores up ("concealeth") knowledge for future use but does not parade his information, while the fool ignores instruction and spouts his own opinions. *Better to keep your mouth shut and be thought a fool, than to open it and remove all doubt.* A man's gifts make room for him while a lazy person will eventually be forced into undesirable tasks. As a man thinketh in his heart, so is he. The attitude of the heart will affect the man's personality (v. 25). Verse 26 means that the righteous will be a helpful guide to his neighbor while the wicked only use other people. The lazy man doesn't even prepare himself a good meal (or can't because he has no game), while the diligent man enjoys the work of his hand. Righteousness leads to temporal joy and eternal life.

God says "joy," not happiness, because happiness depends on what is happening to you (circumstances), while joy transcends circumstances.

Proverbs 13:1-13

What is the writer saying?

How can I apply this to my life?

pray *Angola – For the Holy Spirit to ignite a passion for youth evangelism among believers.*

The wise son listens to his father, while the bad son ignores his father. The unwise son is a mocker, someone who does not show proper respect. Good communication leads to good provisions. Evil communication leads to physical destruction. The tongue is a small member but can get us into big trouble. Those who know the least seem to talk the most and the loudest. In the multitude of their words, there is a multiplication of opportunity to hurt, offend, and destroy. The profit motive is alive and well in the Book of Proverbs. "Loathsome" (v. 5) means, *to cause a stink*. It is interesting that wicked men arrogantly abuse the righteous in life, but at their funerals, the wicked want nice words said about them, indicating they understand "shame" but refuse to change their lifestyle to avoid it. Not only are we commanded to be righteous, but also as we practice righteousness it helps us stay righteous. Likewise, the wicked are further trapped by their wickedness. Evil men might achieve riches, but they are poor while the righteous are "rich," no matter what their bank account says. The other thing a righteous poor person never has to worry about is being kidnapped for his wealth (v. 8). Verse 9 indicates that on the average, the righteous person lives longer that the unrighteous person and that period of life is much merrier for the righteous (compare life "more abundantly" in John 10:10). Contention is based on the sin of "pride." Pride brought sin into the universe through Satan (Isaiah 14:12-14) and was the cause of Eve's sin (Genesis 3:5, 6). Money attained through wickedness is lost, while honest money is multiplied. Failed expectations depress, but the patient is eventually rewarded and that reward is sweeter for the wait. God's Word is our life.

Why would anyone even consider going Satan's way instead of God's way?

Proverbs 13:14-25

What is the writer saying?

How can I apply this to my life?

pray *Canada – Effective ministry among the Innu People (First Nations) in Northern Quebec.*

The *Fountain of Youth* does not exist, but the superior "Fountain of life" does. It is the Word of God and wise men derive wisdom from it. Not only is it refreshing in the heat of the battle, but it also prolongs life helping the observant person to avoid a premature death. It is hard to understand why sinners find years of a sinful lifestyle attractive. Certainly there is momentary pleasure, but what a price is paid by years of smoking, drinking, immorality, brawling, etc. Sinners get old before their time. The word "hard" in verse 15 implies a calloused life that blinds the individual to the stupidity of his way. The righteous follower of God's way is a truth merchant. The fool has nothing to offer but his folly. The fool is an enemy, not only to himself, but also to anyone who trusts him with an important task (v. 17). One of the marks of a wise and righteous individual is his willingness to accept correction and to improve himself. Not only does this impress others, but also it increases the likelihood of success, which brings further honor. The righteous get to rejoice at their successes and rewards while the fool can't bring himself to leave his evil ways to give success a chance in his life. Poor company corrupts manners (compare v. 20). The sinner is his own worst enemy. Generally, the righteous are blessed in this life and certainly in the life to come. The righteous have food to spare, leave an inheritance for the next generation and even wind up with the fool's money as *a fool and his money are soon parted*.

Many of the *promises* in Proverbs are principles that on occasion are violated by a larger purpose of God or conflicting principles. For instance, some righteous die young, are murdered, martyred, etc., as part of God's plan. Or, "train up a child ... he will not depart" can be violated by the child's God-ordained freewill.

45 Monday

QT

Proverbs 14:1-12

What is the writer saying?

How can I apply this to my life?

pray *Nigeria – For the Lord's guidance and direction in the training and follow-up of new converts that are won to Christ through evangelism.*

Not only the wise man but also the wise woman benefits others. The bottom line is this: Do you love and respect the Lord or not? Arrogant men speak boldly against the Lord, His servants and His ways. These words lead to their own destruction while the wise will be saved by the Lord they love. The fool hates to clean up messes such as those made by oxen. Of course, they then have no help to plow their fields and feed themselves. There is no such thing as a free lunch. If you want profit you have to expend time and energy. Habits of life mold the future. The liar continues to lie by nature and habit. The scorner is blinded by his mental attitude so he never perceives wisdom while it is second nature to the righteous wise man. Note that the problem is not that the scorner doesn't want wisdom but that he can't recognize it when he stumbles across it. Since bad company corrupts good morals, the wise man limits his time interfacing with fools. Verse 7 is the first command in this section of Proverbs contrasting evil and righteous living (10:1-15:33), underscoring the importance of that bit of advice. Being *self-aware* is a characteristic of the wise man and a weakness of the fool. He is self-deceived, a hero in his own mind, convinced by his own press releases (v. 8). It is hard to argue with a snicker. Fools make the righteous feel foolish for being so *straight* but in the end, it is the righteous who come out on top. "Intermeddle" (v. 10) means *to share.* Both bitterness and joy are usually private experiences that cannot be shared. The wicked may build a substantial dwelling ("the house"), but it will nevertheless fall (due to the poor foundation), while the flimsy dwelling of the righteous ("the tabernacle" *tent*) will survive and even thrive.

If blind and walking in an area where one misstep spells death, you better rely on someone who sees perfectly.

Proverbs 14:13-23

What is the writer saying?

How can I apply this to my life?

pray *Korea – For the message of the gospel to penetrate North Korea's isolation from the modern world.*

As long as there is sin in this life, we will never experience untainted joy. How often a minister goes from performing a wedding to presiding over a funeral. Only once safely on the shore of heaven will we know ceaseless joy. The morally retarded ("backslider") receives the evil fruit of his evil ways while the righteous will be pleased with the fruit of his righteousness. Perhaps less odious than the fool, the simple also are to be pitied. Mindlessness is dangerous no matter why the person is careless. The wise person thinks before he leaps. The fool is led by his emotions rather than his mind and heart (v. 16). His emotions blind his judgment and cause his behavior to be publicly offensive. The naïve ("simple") receive the same inheritance as the fool while the careful thinkers wear their well-deserved knowledge as a crown upon their brow. Sometimes in this life, and certainly in the life to come, wicked people will be forced to honestly acknowledge the superiority of good people. Money is an issue in this life. It shouldn't be that way as verse 21 concludes. There is coming a day when a man's relationship to Christ will be demonstrated by his relationship to the despised and persecuted of this world (the *sheep and goats judgment* of Matthew 25). "Happy is he" (v. 21) is the definition of *beatitude,* perhaps the most famous of Christ's teachings. "Blessed are the poor in spirit: for theirs is the kingdom of heaven" (Matthew 5:3). Since there are more poor people than rich people, we have the opportunity to make more friends and receive more appreciation by befriending the poor. Besides, many times the rich don't seem to want or need our *help.* Good dealings with fellow men bring truth and loving kindness to the perpetrators. Talk is cheap. You have to follow through with actions to reap a reward.

Satan has gone through the department store of this world and has changed all the price tags. Check God's list for the right prices!

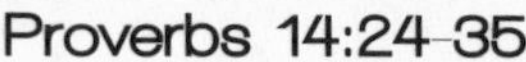

Proverbs 14:24-35

What is the writer saying?

How can I apply this to my life?

pray *Guatemala – For more willing hearts to join the 100 missionaries sent from Guatemala in the last 15 years.*

The wise man lives in such a way that he is financially secure. He doesn't waste his money on sinful pursuits (gambling, drinking, drugs, smoking, etc.). He is successful in his business because of his diligence. "Fear" refers to reverential awe. It is the beginning of wisdom as the Lord is the only true source of wisdom. The wise man finds protection for himself and his offspring. It is also a fountain of life because it protects the individual from behavior that hastens death. Leading with no one following ruins the resumé. The rush of emotion that comes with anger fogs the brain and produces foolish thoughts, words, and behavior. "Sound heart" (v. 30) refers to a peaceful mental state that lowers the blood pressure and enhances the health of the physical body. "Envy" refers to a jealous longing for that which belongs to another. *Green* is associated with both envy and jealousy—because it is the color of sickliness. God has created both the poor and the rich. He loves them both. He does not respect the one more than the other. Neither should we. If we oppress the poor, it is as though we actually despise the Lord. We might envy the wicked rich person, but two seconds into eternity he will care nothing for all his wealth. The fool may attempt to hide his evil thought patterns, but they will eventually be revealed, even if occasionally he produces a *wise* thought (v. 33). "Wisdom" here is personified in Hebrew by a feminine pronoun as in chapter 1. "Exalteth" means *to lift up either in prestige or morals.* Here it probably means morally. Sin is a disgrace to the whole nation. The Lord, as the King of the universe, is angry at the nations that behave shamefully.

The Canaanites are an ancient example of a disgraced nation. Nazi Germany is a modern example. Where will immorality leave us?

Proverbs 15:1-11

What is the writer saying?

How can I apply this to my life?

pray *Dominican Republic – Pray for the more than 3,500 villages that have no evangelical witness.*

Many of the Proverbs deal with interpersonal problems, since interfacing with other people is one of our biggest challenges each day. Verse 1 warns against pouring fuel on the fire. The tongue can do great and irreparable damage. Nothing we think, say, or do is hidden from the Lord. Therefore, we should be conscious of His watchful eyes at all times. Godly speech gives life. Evil speech tears the speaker's soul and the souls of others. Parents are to be respected both for their position and their wisdom. They have lived longer and therefore should know more than the child. The child that learns from parental correction will be farther ahead of those who go it on their own in life. The righteous has much to offer society. The fool is all take and no give. Out of the heart of the wise flows forth helpful information. Out of the fool comes only useless comments. Verse 2 says that folly *bubbles up* out of the fool. God rejects even the *good works* of the fool, while the Lord delights in the words spoken to Him by the righteous (v. 8). For the second time in two verses something is said to be an abomination to the Lord. The particular Hebrew word for "abomination" here (there are four used in the Old Testament) is used elsewhere of the sins of homosexuality and idolatry. By way of contrast, the Lord delights in the righteous. Correction and reproof may wound the pride, but ignoring them destroys body and soul. God is omnipotent (all powerful), omniscient (all knowing) and omnipresent (everything is before His person). His omnipresence includes even the grave (*sheol*) and death (*abbadon*). Therefore, it is a small matter for Him to also know what is in our hearts.

It is a fearful thing to fall into the hands of Almighty God. The hands that threaten are the same hands that heal. Receive healing not destruction.

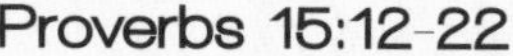

Proverbs 15:12-22

What is the writer saying?

How can I apply this to my life?

pray *Ghana – Pray for the nearly 5,000,000 people who are followers of Islam and other African religions.*

Pride motivates the fool to reject correction and the wisdom of the righteous man. Here the word for "reproveth" is a stronger Hebrew word than used earlier. It refers to a stern warning or *rebuke*. The fool is not quiet in his pride but actually scorns the righteous wise man. Therefore, we can also conclude that someone who mocks others is probably a fool. (Please remember that in the Bible, a "fool" is not intellectually inferior, he is not stupid, but rather it refers to moral and theological error.) Happiness, like beauty, can be only skin-deep, but sorrow goes all the way into the deepest recesses of our being. Our mental and emotional health is drastically affected by our heart attitude which can be controlled by God and His word. The success of the righteous life lies in the fact that it is self-reinforcing. Once a little knowledge is gained, there is hunger for more (v. 14). Unfortunately, the same is true with foolishness. How else can we account for the amazing degeneration of the Hollywood industry? Despite the confusion around us, the joyful righteous person can live life to the fullest (v. 15). And that joyful life does not have to include lots of *things* (v. 16). Most righteous husbands and wives would never qualify as Hollywood's idea of a romantic couple, but the sweet irony is that most righteous couples enjoy greater romance than those on the silver screen (v. 17). Control of passions (v. 18) and control of laziness (v. 19) brings success to the wise man. He is a joy to his father while the fool disgraces even the woman who bore him (v. 20). Walking successfully through the mountainous terrain of life requires wisdom and advice from trustworthy counselors (vv. 21-22).

Tolerance is the cry of the Hollywood industry. Actually they are tolerant of everything except God's Word and His people.

QT Saturday 45

Proverbs 15:23-33

What is the writer saying?

How can I apply this to my life?

pray *For the United States and its leaders on this Independence Day to see their need for the freedom that only Christ can provide.*

The pen is mightier than the sword. Historians argue that the real influencers and shapers of the world have not been politicians and soldiers, but rather thinkers. The right word at the right time changes the destiny of whole nations. Avoiding "hell" in verse 24 is not a reference to eternal damnation (although that is the ultimate destiny of the fool), but rather is referring to physical death (*sheol*). Wisdom prolongs physical life on this earth. The proud, rich fool becomes poor while the Lord protects the defenseless, righteous widow. Even the thought life of the wicked man disgusts the Lord, while He delights in the words of the pure. Greed leads to compromise, which leads to trouble. Refuse a bribe and you will not be indebted to another sinner (v. 27). Look before you leap and make sure your brain is engaged before putting your mouth into gear (v. 28). While God knows all, He only "heareth" (*pays attention to*) the prayers of the righteous. He delights in His child and wants to hear his voice. In verse 30, it is the light in the righteous man's eyes (*friendly appearance*) that encourages others. It is the righteous man's kind words (*good news*) that bring health to others ("maketh the bones fat"). Listening to the words of the righteous man, both encouraging and rebuking, eventually turns one into a wise/righteous person. Rejecting discipline is self-defeating (v. 32). What attitudes are mandatory if a person wants to be an honored wise man among his fellow countrymen? He must fear the Lord and humble himself (v. 33).

The composite picture of the wise/righteous man is that he reverences God, not himself. He submits to God's way, not his own way. He allows other wise men to guide him, not going it alone. He seeks to give more to society than he takes.

Thessalonica is located one hundred miles from Philippi and is a key city in northern Greece (Macedonia). The Egnatian Way (a major East/West road) goes though her walls. She also has a splendid harbor, making her the chief port of Macedonia. She is the largest city in Macedonia with 200,000 inhabitants. There are some Jews, but it is basically a pagan city.

History:
315 B.C. City is named after Alexander the Great's sister.
168 B.C. Romans divide Macedonia into four districts and make it capital of its district.
146 B.C. Named capital of all Macedonia.
42 B.C. Declared a *Free City* (allowed to control its own affairs) as a reward for helping Octavian (the future Caesar Augustus) against the murderers of Julius Caesar.
Today It is called *Salonika* with a population of 300,000+

Paul visits Thessalonica on his second missionary journey (Acts 16:8-17:10). Paul is forced out of Philippi. Silas and perhaps Timothy are with him. Paul's practice is to hit the major centers of Roman administration, Greek culture, Jewish colonies, and trade/transportation hubs. He goes to the Jew first (the synagogue), where more Gentile proselytes to Judaism respond than those born Jews.

Acts 17:1-2 mentions "three Sabbath Days" (twenty one days) in Thessalonica, but it would seem that he stays there longer than three weeks. Philippians 4:16 tells us he receives not one but two offerings from Philippi during his stay at Thessalonica. We know from 1 Thessalonians that the converts are won from paganism. To disciple them would seem to require a greater length of time. Therefore, he might have been there up to six months.

Eventually jealous Jewish leaders run him out of town. He is charged with "turning the world upside down" and "treason." A bond is taken from Jason to ensure Paul would not return. Paul does visit again on the third missionary journey (Acts 20:4) and later takes Aristarchus with him to Rome (Acts 27).

Acts 17 and 18 tell us Paul travels quickly from Thessalonica to Berea, Athens, and then to Corinth. He is worried about the young converts. He sends Timothy to check on them. Upon receiving a good report from Timothy, he writes 1 Thessalonians. In the letter, he praises their endurance though persecution, refutes slander against him, exhorts them to greater Christian living and answers eschatological (doctrines about death and its aftermath) questions (vv. 1:10; 2:19; 3:13; 4:15; 5:23).

The first epistle is dated 51 A.D.; the second, within the next twelve months. According to Acts 18, Paul is at Corinth for eighteen months. Gallio is Proconsul at Corinth. We know that proconsuls only hold office for one to two years, therefore, from Roman history we can rather accurately date Paul's stay in Corinth. This makes Thessalonians one of Paul's earliest epistles (This is about twenty years after Christ died and rose again. Paul has been saved for about eighteen years. Paul has been a missionary for about eight years).

2 Thessalonians is written in response to the reaction of 1 Thessalonians. Apparently, word comes back to Paul that some have quit their jobs, expecting the immediate return of Christ and have become a financial burden to the church. There is also confusion about the Day of the Lord, some thinking that they were already experiencing it. Each chapter addresses an area of confusion: Chapter 1, Persecution; Chapter 2, Prophecy; and Chapter 3, Practice.

1 Thessalonians 1:1-5

What is the writer saying?

How can I apply this to my life?

pray *Pray for the salvation and protection of those serving in the United States military around the world.*

Paul went by his Hebrew name, Saul, before he was saved. Living in the Roman city of Tarsus, "Paul" would have been his Roman (Gentile) name. The Hebrew name is a proud name, both because it is the name of the first king of Israel and also for what it means: *Asked for.* Paul, on the other hand, is a humble name meaning *Little.* It is also appropriate for someone whose main ministry is to Gentiles. "Silvanus" means *of the forest.* He was also called "Silas" which is a Greek variation of "Saul." He replaces Barnabas as Paul's traveling companion and is instrumental in determining how Gentile converts would be treated at the Council of Jerusalem in Acts 15. He is jailed with Paul at Philippi and ministers at Corinth. He apparently also ministers with Peter (1 Peter 5:12). We know more about "Timothy" (*He who honors God*). The little word "in" speaks of our sphere of blessing. Jesus is given three names. "Lord" is the Greek word for *Jehovah,* which describes His essence as deity. "Jesus" is His human name, the Greek form of "Joshua" which means *Jehovah is Salvation.* This speaks of His mission to the planet. "Christ" is a title. It is the Greek equivalent of "Messiah" (*Anointed One*) referring to His kingship. Notice the key theological terms: "Grace ... peace," which are also the Greek and Hebrew greetings of the day. What a prayer life Paul has! Paul says they were patient in their persecutions, which can be graphically defined as *optimistic fortitude in spite of indignities suffered.* "Beloved" (v. 4) is in the Greek perfect tense, indicating a past event with presently continuing results.

Election is God setting His love on us in His past councils so that in the present we respond to the Word as convicted by the Holy Spirit.

1 Thessalonians 1:6-10

What is the writer saying?

How can I apply this to my life?

pray *Portugal – For a Bible believing church in each of the more than 300 counties that currently have none.*

The believers at Thessalonica are primarily Gentiles (1:9 says they "turned to God from idols"). They apparently are undergoing social ostracism because of their newfound faith. In verse 6, this "affliction" (*tribulation*) is a word that refers to the pressing of grapes to get the juice. Despite the pressure, they become followers (*mimics*) of Paul and "received" (*to welcome as a guest*) the Word he preached to them. They are so noble under their persecution that they became "ensamples" (examples from *tupos,* the Greek word from which we get the English word type.). "Macedonia" is northern Greece, "Achaia" is southern Greece. Their good testimony *echoes* ("sounded out") like a trumpet blast or thunder bouncing off of distant mountains. Verses 9 and 10 amplify the three phrases of 1:3. Their "work of faith" is their past salvation. Their "labour of love" is their present service. Their "patience of hope" is their longing for the future reunion with Christ. In the midst of struggles, Paul encourages them with the blessed hope of the return of Christ. Statistically, one out of every thirteen verses in the New Testament refers to the return of Christ. When He returns, He will deliver us from the wrath to come (a future wrath). Since fire is already a punishment for the unsaved dead and Colossians 1:13 says that we are already delivered from hell, we conclude that this wrath must refer to the judgments of the tribulation period. This deliverance is "from" (*out of*) the wrath to come. This small Greek word (*ek*) implies complete exemption from, not just protection within (see Revelation 3:10). Theologically, this wrath is described as something determined for the unsaved (earthdwellers Revelation 3:10) and Israel (Jeremiah 30:7; Daniel 9:24).

Keep looking up, your redemption draweth nigh.

1 Thessalonians 2:1-8

What is the writer saying?

How can I apply this to my life?

pray *Ukraine – For believers willing to begin a work within each of the 20,000 villages without one.*

In chapter 2, Paul turns to the issue of his own credibility as an apostle. They know that his message has supernatural power. The phrase "not in vain" means *not devoid of power,* Holy Spirit power. He could not have had ulterior motives because of the personal price that he is paying. He suffered (physically) and was mistreated (emotionally) at Philippi (Acts 16). There is opposition at Thessalonica as well (Acts 17). Opposition is the word *agony* which is also used for the sport of wrestling. In his preaching, Paul exhorts (*parakaleo*) them. It means, *called alongside to help*. It is not deceitful (compare the "cunningly devised fables" of 2 Peter 1:16). It is not delivered with unclean motives (seeking personal benefit by way of manipulation). It is not preached with "guile" (from the word for *catching a fish by baiting a hook*). In fact, God continually "trieth" his heart. This word for *approved* ("allowed") is in the Greek perfect tense, meaning that God approved him in the past, and that approval continues right up to the present. Some of the details of that approval process are mentioned in other books. Paul is personally taught by Christ for three years in the wilderness near Damascus. He worked for seven years in Tarsus and at the church in Antioch. On the first missionary journey, he experiences disappointment with John Mark's defection, danger at Lystra, and a dispute with Peter (leading to the Council of Jerusalem in Acts 15). He concludes in verses 5-7 that his motives and behavior are pure. He is no smooth-talking religious huckster. He does not use a mask of deceit ("cloke of covetousness"). He is motivated neither by greed nor glory. He is like a professional nanny taking care of her own children (v. 7).

Approved. What a blessed word to hear from the Lord!

1 Thessalonians 2:9-13

What is the writer saying?

How can I apply this to my life?

pray *Pray for those serving in your local government.*

Paul is motivated not for personal gain, but rather the spiritual benefit of his converts. Even though as an apostle he has the right to financial support, he often would not ask for it; working as a tent-maker to pay his own way. As a result he labors "night and day." In that, part of the time is devoted to preaching, teaching, and discipling, while the other time is devoted to working to earn money. According to the Talmud (an encyclopedic collection of the beliefs and practices of Judaism), every Jewish father is obligated to do three things for his son: 1) Circumcise him (bringing him under the covenant of Judaism); 2) Teach him the Torah (Law of Moses); and 3) Teach him a trade (lest he become a thief). Paul's father apparently taught Paul how to take the skins and wool of animals and sew them into tents. This is interesting because working with the skins of dead animals borders on the Levitically *unclean.* When God is getting Peter ready to take the Gospel to the Gentiles, he places Peter at the home of Simon the tanner. The words "labour" and "travail" in verse 9 both refer to agonizing activity. "Labour" comes from a word that means, *to strike* and would be comparable to our English saying, *I'm whipped!* In verse 10, Paul creates a courtroom atmosphere as he calls the Thessalonians and God to testify that indeed he is above reproach in his financial dealings with them. "Unblameably" means *not able to find fault* as in a court of law. "Exhorted" comes from *parakaleo,* meaning called alongside to help. "Comforted" is even tenderer (*alongside to console*). In verse 13 Paul concludes with a strong statement about the self-authenticating nature of the Word of God (compare Hebrews 4:12, "quick, and powerful, and sharper than any twoedged sword").

We are children of the King. Let's live up to that position.

1 Thessalonians 2:14-20

What is the writer saying?

How can I apply this to my life?

pray *Korea – For opportunities to be given to godly Chinese businessmen so they may use their easy access to North Korea to share the Gospel.*

Gentile converts in the first century might have felt like *Johnny-come-latelies.* The Judaizing tendency (Hebrew Christians promoting Gentile observance of the Law of Moses, as rejected at the Council of Jerusalem in Acts 15) doesn't help their feelings of second-class citizenship. Paul argues in verse 14 that they were "followers" (mimics from the Greek word *mimeo*) of the Judean Hebrew Christians in that they also are persecuted by their fellow countrymen for the faith. The New Testament in general, and Paul in particular, are accused of being *anti-Semitic.* Since most of the authors of the New Testament are Jews themselves, this is rather strange. If you look at the Gospel of John, his condemnation of the Jews does not refer to Jewish people but rather to the Jewish religious leaders of the day. Likewise, Paul's reference to Jewish persecutors can be accurate without also being anti-Semitic. Actually, even in Thessalonica, it is some in the Jewish community who run Paul out of town (Acts 17:5). Paul feels abandoned ("taken" means *orphaned*) and he lusted ("with great desire") to see them again. Satan "hindered" them. This is a military word that means, *to break up the road.* Paul concludes with the happy thought that even if in this life they can't get back together, at the rapture there will be a joyous reunion. "Coming" (v. 19) is *parousia,* meaning to be alongside of, refers to the Lord's Coming/Arrival. Since it is the word also used for the arrival of kings in the ancient world, it is also called, *The Royal Visit.* This is the first time in the New Testament it occurs. It is only used of Christ's return to the planet, never of His first coming.

Every generation of the church has anticipated the return of Christ. One generation will get to experience it!

1 Thessalonians 3:1-5

What is the writer saying?

How can I apply this to my life?

pray *For the many summer children's camp leadership and staff, as they share the Gospel with hundreds of children.*

In 2:19 Paul uses one term for Christ's second coming. There are two others to consider. Apocalypse (*apokalupsis*) means revealing or revelation. Epiphany (*epiphaneia*) means seeing, especially His glory. These terms are used for both the Rapture and the return at the end of the tribulation period. This does not require that they are one and the same event. They are *qualifying terms* (descriptive of an action) not *quantifying terms* (identifying one and only one event). Having reflected on that great reunion with the saints when Christ is revealed in all His glory in His coming, Paul continues with the account of his attempts to be encouraged by them. His heart pain is so strong, that even though it means being left alone in hostile territory there in Athens (Acts 17), he nevertheless sends Timothy to see how they are doing. "Left" (v. 1) is used elsewhere of being abandoned by the death of a spouse (Mark 12:19). In verse 2, Paul identifies Timothy (*He who honors God*) as a "fellowlabourer." Fellowship has been defined as *two fellows in one ship*. What would "fellowlabourer" be? Actually, in the Greek text it says *God's fellowlabourer*, which implies that both Paul and Timothy are in the harness with God. The word "establish" is a construction term; the *buttress* used to support heavy stone walls. "Comfort" is our old friend *parakaleo*, (called alongside to help). The English word actually means *with* (com) *strength* (fort). It means that God wants to strengthen us before the task, not just make us feel better when hurt in the task. The word "appointed" in verse 3 refers to careful planning and is used of the building of a city (*set*) on a specific location.

Satan is alive and well on planet earth. We should encourage one another in the struggle to make sure our fellowlabourers don't slip away.

46 Saturday

1 Thessalonians 3:6-13

What is the writer saying?

How can I apply this to my life?

pray *Taiwan – For teachers and counselors who will provide a vibrant witness within the educational system.*

Timothy's great report is a *gospel* to Paul's ears; *good news*. Even though this doesn't alter Paul's physical living conditions, the emotional support greatly improves his frame of mind. The "affliction" of verse 7 is defined as *choking care* while "distress" is *crushing trouble*. "Affliction" refers to an internal stress such as that brought on by lack of finances. "Distress" is external and, in fact, elsewhere is translated *persecution* and *tribulation*. In all this, he is *parakaleo-ed* by their love. Some English versions flip the words "distress" and "affliction." This is not a change of word order but the translators' idea of the best English word for the underlying Greek word. Since the words are so close in meaning in both languages, it is hard to say which is the superior translation. When you see the word "distress," it is not necessarily translating the word that means, *crushing trouble*. You need to check the Greek. In verse 8, Paul's happy exclamation could be phrased, *Now we really live!* The "if" doesn't mean that Paul has any doubts and could also be rendered *since*. If Paul could spend more quality time with them, he would be able to give them more instruction about the Christian faith and life. He launches into a doxology ("Now"). There is a plural subject (God the Father and our Lord Jesus Christ), but a singular verb indicating that in Paul's mind they are of equal essence (deity), authority, and purpose. As with all the chapters in 1 and 2 Thessalonians, Paul refers to the coming of Christ as a motivating hope. The "saints" (*holy ones*) of verse 13 can refer to angels or saved humans. In this case, probably both are in mind as both will be involved in the Second Coming of Christ.

Love of the brethren is a chief marker of a true follower of Christ.

1 Thessalonians 4:1-8

What is the writer saying?

How can I apply this to my life?

pray *Honduras – Continued economic success for the Christian bookstores that provide resource materials.*

Paul first addresses a problem and then makes practical applications. Having handled the problem of his separation from them and his desire to be assured of their spiritual well being, he now exhorts them in the area of personal holiness. In verse 1, "beseech" is a term of request that would be made between socially equal parties. In verse 2, superiors give "commandments" to subordinates. The topic is sexual purity. Paul requests it, the Lord Jesus commands it, and in verse 3, God wills it. In verse 1, "walk" refers to our whole manner of life. Paul is confident that they are already living careful lives, but he wants to reaffirm the importance of personal holiness. Jesus's command is particularly convicting because He already lived a holy life in the flesh. "Sanctification" means *to be set apart.* It is the root word for sanctify, holy, and saint. The specific issue is "fornication" (*pornea*). It refers to any type of sexual misconduct. The "vessel" (body) of verse 4 can refer to a person's own body or the body of the spouse as the appropriate object of sexual expression. Both usages occur in Scripture (1 Cor. 9:24-27, 1 Peter 3:7). "Concupiscence" refers to greedy, self-centered satisfaction of fleshly desires. Even in marriage, romantic expression is to be for the benefit of the partner. The Gentile pagan world not only uses sex for recreation, but also religion. Therefore, this warning is especially appropriate to the culture of Thessalonica. Sexual sin defrauds or *steals from* another person. This would include both the other person and the present spouse if married, or the future spouse if currently single. In verse 8 Paul warns that to treat sexual impurity lightly is to treat God lightly. He empowers us for purity with the indwelling Holy Spirit.

There is hope. What our flesh can't do the Holy Spirit can!

47 Monday

1 Thessalonians 4:9-12

What is the writer saying?

How can I apply this to my life?

pray *Portugal – For biblically sound Christian musicians who will surrender their talent to God's use.*

Beyond personal purity, Paul also urges a continuation of their noteworthy love for the brethren. "Brotherly love" is *philadelphias*. This is not *agape*, the highest expression of love, but rather the love that binds the children of one set of parents together (*blood is thicker than water*). Paul tells them about this, but also reminds them that God Himself has included this in His written instruction manual (Leviticus 19:18). Thessalonica is a city in northern Greece, which at one time is called Macedonia. In fact, the *classical* Greeks such as Homer, Socrates, Plato and Aristotle all come from Achaia (Southern Greece). Those in Achaia consider the Macedonians to be backward. It is Philip of Macedonia (the father of Alexander the Great) who unifies Macedonia and Achaia. He hires Aristotle to tutor Alexander. It is Alexander who not only creates the *Greek Empire*, traveling all the way to India in his conquests, but also spreads his adopted Greek culture everywhere he goes. This is three hundred years before the birth of Christ, but clearly sets the stage for the language of the New Testament and Christian missionary expansion ("But when the fullness of the time was come, God sent forth his Son" Galatians 4:4). In verse 11, Paul asks that they be distinguished in being quiet. Taking everything that Paul says about work in 1 & 2 Thessalonians, apparently a number of the believers have lost their jobs due to persecution, or quit workng because they think they are in the end times. As a result, when they run out of money, they begin to bother others, and therefore become a poor testimony.

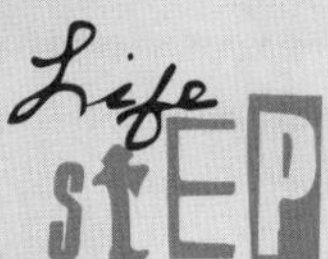

Notice how working and minding your own business go hand in hand. The donkey doing all the braying is not the one out pulling the plow!

1 Thessalonians 4:13-18

What is the writer saying?

How can I apply this to my life?

pray *Don Lough Jr., wisdom as he directs the Word of Life Inc.*

This is the earliest written account of the Rapture. The Rapture is not mentioned in Matthew 24 because there has to be a church before you can have the Rapture. The doctrine of the church isn't introduced until the Book of Ephesians. Contrast Matthew 24 and 1 Thessalonians 4 to see all the differences between the Rapture and the Second Coming of Christ. Paul doesn't want the Thessalonians to think that their dead, believing loved ones would miss out on anything. "Sleep" is a kind way of referring to death. Certainly believers are *awake* in heaven after death (see 5:10; Philippians 1:23; Luke 23:43). God lovingly *put them to sleep* (passive voice). Christ will lead them back as in a triumphal military parade. In verse 13 in the Greek text, Paul uses a double negative for emphasis: "by no means no way." Christ Himself (emphatic) will lead the way. The "shout" is a military cry of command (see John 5:28). The only archangel we know by name is Michael. He is always seen protecting Moses (Jude 9) or Israel (Daniel10; Rev.12). Trumpets are used for the monthly new moon, the annual New Year, and as commands on a battlefield. Therefore, it signifies *assemble and go forward*. If this is the "last trump" (1 Cor. 15:52), then the first trump is the one associated with the giving of the Law (Exodus 19:13; also Hebrews 12:26) which launches Israel. It is a qualitative not a quantitative term, just like the *First Resurrection* which includes several resurrections under the concept of *believer's resurrection*. The phrase, "dead in Christ" occurs forty times in the Bible, always referring to church saints. The word *rapture* ("caught up") is used elsewhere of Philip (Acts 8:39); Paul (2 Corinthians 12:2); and Jesus (Revelation 12:5).

Encourage one another with these words. It is no encouragement if we have to go through the Tribulation before being rescued!

1 Thessalonians 5:1-8

What is the writer saying?

How can I apply this to my life?

pray *Costa Rica – For God to keep the doors open for the Gospel to be preached in Schools.*

It is clear from 5:1 that Paul is changing subjects. The Greek phrase, *peri de* (here translated "but") is used by Paul eight times. Each time it indicates a change of subject (see 4:9). Having covered the Rapture of the church in chapter 4, Paul now turns his attention to that which follows the Rapture, namely the tribulation period (Daniel 9:24) also called, "the day of the Lord." There is no need to discuss *timing*, because it is unknowable. Just as a thief (cat burglar) does not announce his coming, likewise the start of the day of the Lord is sign-less. The day of the Lord is an Old Testament doctrine (see Isaiah 2; Joel 2; Zephaniah 1). Thirty Old Testament passages are similar to the events in Revelation 6:12-17. Not only is a thief unexpected, but also the homeowners are unprepared. The unsaved are lulled into complacency by the peace and safety of the era. Peace is the platform that brings the Antichrist to power. Peace certainly is not a characteristic of the end of the tribulation period where some want to start the day of the Lord and a rapture of believers. Labor pains are an Old Testament illustration (Isaiah 13). They have three characteristics that apply to this event. They are sudden, intense, and inevitable (both in the eventual coming and the outcome). The day of the Lord events are the *birth pangs of the new age*. Paul argues that these events will not "overtake" or *seize* believers. Our moral alertness allows us to be taken from the earth. As we wait for this deliverance, we are to continue the attitude of alertness by putting on the whole armor of God. We do this by "putting on" Jesus Christ according to Romans 13:14.

Live like children of the King in anticipation of the great position that awaits us when He returns.

1 Thessalonians 5:9-15

What is the writer saying?

How can I apply this to my life?

pray *China – For the 44,000,000 members of unregistered house churches, persecuted by officials.*

Those who teach a *Post-Tribulational Rapture* (the church will go through the Tribulation and be raptured at the end) argue that 1 Thessalonians 5 presents Christians persevering on earth in the midst of moral darkness. If we only had verses 5-8, we might grant their argument. However, verse 3 says "they" are saying, "Peace and safety," and the day of the Lord will come upon "them" and "they" shall not escape. Verse 4 says, that day shall not overtake "you" (believers). Finally, verse 9 explains that "God hath not appointed us to wrath." We deduce, therefore, that the day of the Lord is a period of God's wrath upon earth-dwelling sinners. The only way to avoid a Pre-Tribulational Rapture is to argue that either, a) the church goes through the day of the Lord/tribulation period, but none of the judgments touch believers; or b) the day of the Lord is not the tribulation period, but only refers to the judgments following the return of Christ at the Battle of Armageddon. Both of these explanations seem forced, so the easiest understanding is to say that we miss the wrath of the day of the Lord/tribulation period because we leave earth before it begins. Notice the Christ centered nature of the discussion in verses 10 and 11 (not centered on the Antichrist!). In verses 12 and 13, Paul gives a *Pastoral Job Description* using three participles. Pastors "labour," "are over you," and "admonish you." "Admonish" means to put in mind, coming from the Greek word *noutheo*, which is the name given to a popular theory of confrontational Biblical counseling. Notice that Paul expects them to follow a chain of command even though they are all the same age in the Lord. In verse 14, the "unruly" are *soldiers not in proper rank*. "Patient" means *to go a long way before overheating.*

It may be simplistic, but *be good to everyone* covers it all!

47 Friday

QT

1 Thessalonians 5:16-22

What is the writer saying?

How can I apply this to my life?

pray *Thailand – For believers to be wise stewards of the new prosperity that their society is experiencing.*

Verse 16 has the distinction of being the shortest verse in the Greek New Testament. (It takes fewer letters in Greek to say, "rejoice evermore" than "Jesus wept.") People say, *Praise the Lord anyway*. This is not accurate. Verse 16 is asking us to *Praise the Lord because of it*! This may be humanly hard to do, but as we learn to rest in the absolute plan and power of God, we eventually learn that "all things work together for good" (Romans 8:28). The verb used in "pray without ceasing" is used elsewhere of a repetitive, uncontrollable cough. It doesn't mean constant coughing/praying, but rather periodic, spontaneous prayer. Verse 18 indicates that the only way we can be thankful for all things is to live "in Christ Jesus." "Quench" means *to put out a fire*. The Holy Spirit is the fire of God leading us to do certain things (such as witness to a friend). We should not resist the Holy Spirit's leading and throw cold water on His plan. Elsewhere it says that our sin "grieves" the Holy Spirit. This refers to His emotional distress. We grieve the Spirit when we do what we shouldn't do, and we quench the Spirit when we don't do what we should do. Apparently, the Thessalonian church is so careful about false prophetic utterances that they completely ignore anyone with the gift of prophecy. This is the opposite problem of the Corinthian church that shows no restraint or discernment in that area. Verse 21 strikes the proper balance, namely, don't be gullible. Check the message and messenger against the standard of the Word of God. Finally, verse 22 is not saying that we should avoid appearing as though we are doing evil. It is saying that we should avoid every type of evil.

Our morning devotions with the Lord should set the stage for a whole day's worth of quick communications to heaven for help and guidance.

1 Thessalonians 5:23-28

What is the writer saying?

How can I apply this to my life?

pray *Pray for safety for those in your church who will be traveling this summer.*

"Sanctify" means *set apart*. It does not immediately mean *morally pure*, but because we are set apart unto God, and since He is morally pure, we should then be morally pure as well (the Greek word is also the root for "saint" – not perfect one but *set-apart one*). Paul then asks that their entire person be "preserved blameless" (*no accusations*) until Christ comes (His *Parousia*). It is certainly possible that we are tripartite beings, however, verse 23 does not prove that we are. Elsewhere, the Bible talks about our heart, mind, strength, will, and conscience. Therefore we might have more than three parts or some of these terms are synonymous. We know that in Scripture the words soul and spirit are used interchangeably, so all we can say for sure is that we have a physical part ("body") and a non-physical part ("spirit and soul"). We particularly need to avoid developing other teachings based on an assumption that indeed we have three parts. Some argue that in salvation, our dead spirit becomes alive. Actually, salvation affects our whole being, not just our spirit. Others argue that Christians can be demon possessed in the soul since the Holy Spirit is only related to the spirit. This is also invalid. A few argue that the unsaved go out of existence at death because only a human with a spirit lives for eternity. God is faithful and will see us safely to the end of our journey (v. 24). The "holy kiss" is fulfilled in today's culture with a holy handshake or other socially acceptable forms of warm greeting. "Charge" (v. 27) means, *bind with an oath*.

Of all the adjectives he could use to describe God it is interesting that he chooses "peace." Sin brings discord into every area of life, but God and His plan of salvation brings harmony – between God and us, within ourselves and between each other.

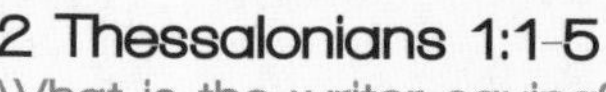

2 Thessalonians 1:1-5

What is the writer saying?

How can I apply this to my life?

pray *Chile – Outreach among the middle and upper classes who have proven to be resistant to the gospel.*

Chapter one deals primarily with the problem of the persecution which the Thessalonians are experiencing. Paul's typical salutation occurs in the first two verses. "Paul" is a Greek name meaning *little*. Perhaps he felt it more appropriate than his old Hebrew name "Saul" which means *asked for* (such as a child who becomes the pride and joy of his family). "Silvanus" means *of the forest*. Paul sends him back to Antioch with the decision of the Jerusalem Council in Acts 15. He joins Paul on the second missionary journey after Paul's falling out with Barnabas. Later, he is Peter's secretary. "Timothy" means *he who honors God*. He is the favorite *son* of the Apostle Paul, as well as recipient of his last will and testament in 2 Timothy. This is the last time that these three appear ministering together (at this time, in Corinth). Notice both the typical Greek ("grace") and Hebrew ("peace") greetings. Notice also the way in which God the Father and God the Son are mentioned together on equal footing. In 1:3-12 we have the first major section of the outline: *Paul's Thanksgiving for the Thessalonians*. Paul is proud of his spiritual children. "Are bound" means *ought*, indicating his moral obligation to say this. The Greek word translated "groweth" (v. 3) only occurs here in the Bible. It speaks of the rapid expansion of a vigorous plant. "Abounding" speaks of their love spreading with the aggressiveness of a flooding river. In verse 4 Paul claims *bragging rights*! Verse 5 is difficult. Paul seems to be saying that their patient endurance under the persecution is proof that God is working in their lives and in the situation. Since God is working, then He will eventually rescue them and punish their tormentors.

Witnessing is bragging on Jesus. Paul brags on the Thessalonians for bragging on Jesus despite great opposition.

2 Thessalonians 1:6-12

What is the writer saying?

How can I apply this to my life?

pray *Canada – For outreach into the Asian Indian, Chinese, and Arabic-speaking immigrant communities.*

"Tribulation" refers to the persecution of believers in many passages (see also v. 4). It also refers to God's judgment on sinners, as in verse 6. Therefore, believers of all ages can expect "tribulation" from the world, the flesh, and the devil. However, there is coming a special tribulation period, when God will pour out His wrath on sinful mankind. Verse 7 speaks of Christ's Second Coming at the Battle of Armageddon to finalize this judgment. This verse does not mean that church saints, Paul or these particular saints, are on the earth when Christ returns, but that the punishment is finally executed on all sinners. Their punishment is termed *everlasting destruction*. This is not annihilation, for other passages speak of eternal conscious punishment in Hell. It does speak of the horrors of eternal separation from the only one that can make life worthwhile – the Lord God. Verse 10 says that Christ will be glorified "in" (not by) His saints. In our glorified state, we will reflect His glory at His return. Paul prays that the Thessalonians would remain faithful and not crack under the immediate pressure of the persecution (vv. 11-12). This prayer is designed to empower them for further service. God desires to be glorified through our lives and accomplishments. The *secret* then is to think of and pray for things that would bring Him glory. For a third time in chapter one, God the Father and God the Son are mentioned on equal terms. Notice it is the name of God that is to be glorified. This does not refer to the letters that make up His title. It speaks of character – everything that makes God, God. Therefore, to glorify His name we repeat and meditate on all of His attributes.

Paul's prayer life must have been incredible when you consider the number of times he tells people that he is praying for them!

48 Tuesday

2 Thessalonians 2:1-5

What is the writer saying?

How can I apply this to my life?

pray *Angola – Pray for churches to develop a unity in Christ that transcends tribal loyalty and politics.*

Paul now shifts to a doctrinal discussion: The return of Christ and the day of the Lord (2:1-12). In verses 1 and 2 we have the reason for Paul's instruction. Apparently someone has spread a rumor that Paul is publicly teaching that the day of the Lord has already begun. Since this upset them, they must have expected to be raptured before the day of the Lord. The "coming" of verse 1 (*parousia*) can be used of both the Rapture and the Second Coming. Context has to decide which coming is in view. In the second half of the verse, it is the coming in which we are "gathering" to Him. For the Church Age saint, this is clearly the Rapture as described in 1 Thessalonians 4, and located time-wise as Pre-Tribulational (1 Thessalonians 1:10; 5:9; and Revelation 3:10.) They are "shaken" (such as a sudden shock to a ship in a storm) and "troubled" (as in the ripple effect of the initial shock). This rumor comes in three avenues: a prophecy, a report, and a letter claiming that the day of the Lord has begun. Verses 3 and 4 teach that before the day of the Lord can come, the *apostasy* must come first. This is a reference to the colossal departure from the faith by organized Christianity in accepting the Man of Lawlessness (the Antichrist, Beast, Little Horn, Prince that Shall Come, Willful King). Verse 4 contains the only reference to a tribulational temple in the church epistles. Once is enough and clearly demands a restored Israel and temple worship in order to be fulfilled. Paul is a tad frustrated in verse 5. He feels that he has been perfectly clear on the scenario in his previous teachings and is disappointed that they don't realize this rumor was false.

We sometimes feel that it is *childish* to long for the return of Christ, but it was a daily consideration for Paul and the early church.

2 Thessalonians 3:1-5

What is the writer saying?

How can I apply this to my life?

pray *Nicaragua – For godly politicians with the credibility and wisdom to end divisive disputes.*

The rest of the book (chapter 3) deals with the practical application of *abstract* doctrine. In the first three verses, Paul requests prayer. Notice that with one-third of the book left, Paul (as with many preachers) has the audacity to say "finally." Actually "finally" doesn't mean in conclusion, but rather, *my final topic.* The "us" would be the men mentioned in 1:1, Paul, Timothy and Silvanus. "Free course" means, *spread rapidly or run.* Paul envisions the Gospel catching on like wildfire or growing profusely like a healthy vine. "The word" is the *logos.* It is the background to our English word logo (as a saying, or the insignia for an organization). It can mean the written or spoken word. It refers to Christ as the living Word (communication) from God. It also is the ancient Greeks' concept of ultimate thought, philosophical thought – the logic that controls the material and immaterial universe. Christians, therefore, possess ultimate logic, "the way, the truth and the life" (John 14:6). Paul prays that this precious gift of knowledge is recognized and prized by others. Verse 2 expresses concern about the (in Greek) "unreasonable and wicked men." Paul has a particular conflict in mind, perhaps the one he is enduring as he writes from Corinth (Acts 18). While the average man is faithless, God is faithful and will protect the child of God from (Greek) "evil" (namely Satan). Paul encourages the Thessalonians in 3:4, 5. He is a master motivator. He uses the technique of positive reinforcement to ensure that the Thessalonians do what he requests. By stating his confidence in them, his exhortation becomes a self-fulfilling prophecy.

Patience is a virtue. It is also a command as we wait for the Lord to intervene in the affairs of men and set things straight on planet earth.

2 Thessalonians 3:6-18

What is the writer saying?

How can I apply this to my life?

pray *New Zealand – For continued transformation of lives through effective prison ministry.*

Apparently, some believers are begging instead of working. The Thessalonians are to "withdraw" from such people in order to shame them into repentance. Paul says that they "ought" (moral obligation) to follow Paul's example. "Follow" is the Greek word *mimic.* Paul does not beg (3:8). *No work, no eat* is a familiar concept to students of American history. In the early settlement at Jamestown, the governor, John Smith, had to insist on this principle to ensure that every person carried his own load in the difficult task of building a successful community in the new world. Eventually this became known as the Protestant Work Ethic. Verse 11 is a play on words. Instead of being busy (i.e., working), they were "busybodies" (using the time they had on their hands to mind other people's business). The "quietness" of verse 12 means *settle down,* probably over the agitations of the rumor about the day of the Lord. "Note that man" literally means to *brand* him. He is to be shunned by other believers giving him the message that they do not approve of his behavior and will have nothing to do with him as long as he behaves that way. The goal is not punishment, but to shame him to a point of repentance and return to fellowship. In a pagan society, it would get lonely real fast. Paul says that he is to be admonished with love (3:15). "Admonish" means *to put in mind of the truth*. Sometimes it is not a matter of not knowing, but not remembering what the truth requires of us. Paul uses a secretary to dictate his letters, perhaps because of poor eyesight. He says he signs all of his epistles so that they would be able to recognize forgeries.

In the past, we were not able not to sin. In the present (in Christ) we are able not to sin. In the future (glorified) we will be not able to sin!

QT

Monday 49

Colossians 1:9-14

What is the writer saying?

How can I apply this to my life?

pray *For the perseverance of fellow believers and unashamed boldness for those who preach the Gospel (Ephesians 6:18 – 19).*

When Paul hears Epaphras' good report about the Colossians, he is further encouraged to pray that the Colossians would be filled with a knowledge of God's will. The present participles "pray" and "desire" reflect the intensity of Paul's prayer for them. Why is Paul fervent in his prayer for them? Because he fears false teachers might lead them astray. To avert this, Paul prays that they would have a full knowledge of God's will, that is God's Word. God reveals His will through His Word and averts our lapsing into error. A proper knowledge of God's Word also results in wisdom – knowing how to apply God's Word to life's experiences. When a believer conducts himself in a way that is pleasing to the Lord (Philippians 1:27; 1 Thessalonians 2:12), four things will result:

1) He is constantly *bearing fruit* in every good work (John 15:5) while revealing the life of Christ through himself (Galatians 2:20) as he learns to glorify God in *every* realm of life.

2) He is constantly *growing in the knowledge of God* and fellowship with Him (2 Peter 3:18).

3) He is constantly being *strengthened by God's power*. Note that the verb is passive, meaning we do not do this, but God empowers us (Ephesians 3:16; 6:10) with a supernatural result: steadfastness amid difficulties, and patience in forgiving and tolerating others.

4) He has a characteristically *thankful spirit* because God has, through His grace, qualified him to share in the glorious, heavenly inheritance in Christ. The reason we rejoice is because of His provision of redemption, Christ has delivered us from the realm of Satan's power (Ephesians 2:2) and translated us into the kingdom of Christ!

The best security against deception by false teachers is feeding daily on God's Word. How much time have you spent in His Word this week?

Colossians 1:15-19

What is the writer saying?

How can I apply this to my life?

pray *South Korea – Complete renewing of the mind for South Koreans saved out of Buddhism and Confucianism.*

The crux [or crucial point] of Christianity is Christ. The true, unblemished Deity of Jesus Christ is the doctrine that separates Christianity from cults and religions. Jesus is God! In battling the false philosophy in Colosse, Paul instructs the believers concerning the supremacy of Christ. He is supreme in the universe and in the church. Just as the image of George Washington reveals what the first president looked like, so Jesus is the exact image and likeness of God – He reveals what God is like (v. 15; Hebrews 1:3). As the second person in the Godhead, Jesus is equal with the Father.

Jesus is also the "firstborn," which does not mean He was created, but rather emphasizes His uniqueness in having authority over all creation. Firstborn stresses the preeminence, lofty position, dignity, and authority of Christ. He is sovereign over all creation (Psalm 89:27).

Moreover, in countering the false teachers who taught that intermediary angels created the world, Paul informs us that Christ, in His preeminence, has created *all* things (v. 16; John 1:3; Hebrews 1:2). Clearly, if Christ created all things, He is un-created and eternal. Christ created the visible and the invisible – destroying the argument of the heretics who teach that matter is evil, but spirit is good. Christ created all things for the purpose of glorifying God; all creation is to adorn the majesty of God. Christ has no beginning. He is eternal (v. 17; John 1:1; 8:58) and He is also the cohesive force of the universe (v. 17; Hebrews 1:3). The ultimate purpose of the fullness of Deity dwelling in Him, is that He might have first place in the church and in believers' lives (vv. 18-19).

Take some time and reflect on one of the many facets of the doctrine of the Deity of Christ. Also, ask yourself this: *Since I am in union with Christ, and Christ is God, what difference should that make in how I conduct my life today, this week, and throughout my life?*

Colossians 2:1-7

What is the writer saying?

How can I apply this to my life?

pray *Pray for the many summer Christian camp counselors, supervisors, and teen staff to serve Christ wholeheartedly.*

Paul's strenuous struggle reveals his love and concern for the believers in Colosse and Laodicea. Paul fights like an athlete against the false teachers for the purity of the Gospel (see Ephesians 6:10-20). His purpose is that they would be encouraged and united in love. Legalism discourages; grace encourages and unifies. Love is the cohesive force among Christians, knitting them together through the Gospel of grace. Through love, believers attain to all the wealth that comes from a full understanding of Christ – He is the believer's riches! This is experiential knowledge – being guided by the Spirit in applying the truths of Scripture to the issues of life. It means knowing Christ in fellowship and recognizing He is the true source of wisdom and knowledge. Christ supplies a rich storehouse, a wealth of knowledge that we can apply to all the circumstances of life.

True knowledge is essential to prevent being led astray by persuasive but false arguments. Paul sees the believers' good discipline in spiritual matters. Like military soldiers, they don't break rank; they are not moved away from the Gospel of grace. Individually, they are spiritually disciplined and, corporately, they are stable. What a commendation!

The Gospel of grace begins and ends our spiritual journey. We receive Christ by grace through faith and we walk with Christ by grace through faith (v. 6). In this way, we are firmly rooted in our faith. Jesus Christ is the rich soil that causes the believer to grow. Like a building under construction, in Christ we grow to maturity; faith being the cement of our spiritual building.

Since Jesus Christ is the epitome of wisdom and knowledge, do you seek constant fellowship with Him through His Word? How can you become mature and be firmly rooted in this spiritual life supplied by Christ?

Colossians 2:8-15

What is the writer saying?

How can I apply this to my life?

pray *Germany – For government leaders to tackle the unresolved issues that face them.*

Zealous for the *Gospel of Grace,* Paul continues to warn the believers against worldly false philosophy and deceptive traditions that would lead them astray. Truth is found in Christ – He is the complete and final revelation of God. The fullness of Deity dwells in Him. This is invariably the doctrine that divides true Christianity from the cults. Jesus is God! And the benefits that accrue to the believer are numerous:

1) *Complete in Christ* (v. 10). Through Christ's redemptive work, we stand spiritually complete in God's presence.

2) *Circumcised in Christ* (v. 11). We have been united to Christ in a spiritual circumcision. This spiritual circumcision occurs at the time of one's salvation. It removes sin's power over the new believer by "putting off" (v. 11) sin's control over him (3:9).

3) *Buried with Christ* (v. 12a). At salvation, we are baptized into (or plunged into) union with Christ and one another (1 Corinthians 12:13). This is not water baptism, but water symbolizes the union.

4) *Raised with Christ* (v. 12b). As Christ was raised from the dead, sin having no power over Him, so the believer has been raised in union with Christ. Thus, sin no longer has authority over him (Romans 6:11).

5) *Alive in Christ* (v. 13). While we were dead in sin, Christ gave us spiritual life, making us *alive,* "quickened together with Him."

6) *Forgiven in Christ* (vv. 13-14). Out of His abundant grace, God forgave us all our sins – past, present, and future.

7) *Triumphant in Christ* (v. 15). As the Romans held a victory parade after battle, so we spiritually triumph in Christ. Sin is defeated!

To help you remember all you have gained by your salvation through Christ, take a colored pencil and number or highlight in your Bible all these *in Christ* benefits. Then pick one that causes you to especially rejoice in Christ and return a prayer of thanksgiving to God for this blessing!

Colossians 3:8-17

What is the writer saying?

How can I apply this to my life?

pray *Fiji – Reconciliation of the body of Christ still suffering from division caused by racial prejudice.*

The new life in Christ is likened to *taking off* old, dirty clothes and *putting on* new clothes (vv. 8-10). The old life of sin is to be removed like dirty clothing. Not only are acts of sin to be set aside (v.5), but also attitudes reflected in deep-seated and blazing anger, hatred, slander, filthy talk and lying (vv. 8-9). Why? Because believers have laid aside the old self. *Positionally*, at salvation, the old nature was crucified with Christ; *practically*, we daily lay aside the old self, which is the old way of life as we used to live it, before coming to Jesus in salvation.

At salvation we put on a *new nature*, like a *new set of clothes*, that is constantly being renewed in progressive sanctification (Romans 12:2; 2 Corinthians 4:16) into the image of Jesus Christ (v. 10; Ephesians 4:23-24). In this new life, cultural and social distinctions are erased; we are one in Christ (v. 11; Galatians 3:28). Because believers are the chosen and beloved of God, we are called to put on new spiritual attributes: compassion, kindness, humility, a gentle spirit, patience, bearing with others, and especially forgiveness, these are to mark the new life.

We are to be "forgiving one another" out of grace. Even if we have a legitimate complaint, we are to forgive. The reason? Because Christ has forgiven us. "Even as" we have been forgiven, "so also" (v. 13) we must forgive. This is a critical issue for all of us. *We must forgive others, no matter what the complaint.*

The final piece of clothing to wrap around us is *love*. This is the attribute that ties us together in unity (Galatians 5:22).

Finally, the peace of Christ must direct our decisions through the Word of Christ (v. 16), guiding us to honor Christ in everything we do.

Ask yourself: Am I harboring a grudge or bitterness against someone? Do I need to go to someone today and ask forgiveness? Take a minute and ask God to help you "put on" this difficult set of clothing!

Colossians 3:18-4:1

What is the writer saying?

How can I apply this to my life?

pray *Pray for those in your church who have lost a loved one this year.*

Perhaps there is no passage in Scripture like this one that emphasizes Christians do not follow culture for their beliefs. For the home to survive, it is imperative that we follow the Bible's teachings. The command for wives to be subject to their husbands comes from a military term meaning, *to rank under*. While spiritually a husband and wife are equal before the Lord, in function they are different (1 Corinthians 11:3).

Man's headship is based on the order of creation, and judgment because of deception (1 Timothy 2:13-14). The woman is enjoined to be subject to her husband because it is a duty "in the Lord." Husbands are instructed to love their wives. Love (*agapao*) is more than an emotion. It is a selfless, reasoned-out love that loves the other person regardless of the response one receives. The present tense of love emphasizes the love is continuously expressed. Husbands are warned not to be harsh and bitter toward their wives – they are not to be dictators. Rather, husbands are to honor their wives (1 Peter 3:7).

Children are instructed to be under their parents' authority by obeying (*listening to*) them because it is honoring to the Lord. Children should not be discouraged through a father's provocation. They must be nurtured through discipline and instruction (Ephesians 6:4).

Finally, for an orderly, biblically directed society, there must be proper relations between slaves and masters. Employees are subject to their employers and must obey them – not superficially pleasing them when they are watching, but with undivided loyalty, out of honor to the Lord. Masters, meanwhile, must treat their servants justly and fairly, recognizing the Lord is in authority over them.

How can you be applying the biblical instructions given above? What are some practical ways that you can be a biblical husband or wife, son or daughter, employer or employee? Be specific.

Colossians 4:12-18

What is the writer saying?

How can I apply this to my life?

pray *Cuba – For the persecuted Christians to be encouraged and continue their service for the Lord.*

Concluding words in a letter are frequently significant summary statements, and so it is in this letter. Paul, a Jew, mentions *Epaphras*, a Gentile, in considerable detail. His concern for the Colossian believers is so intense, that Epaphras is "labouring fervently" for them in prayer. The picture is graphic: the word is *agonize*, as a wrestler would struggle physically. Epaphras prays intensely for their spiritual welfare. His concern is that they would develop spiritual maturity, with a conviction that they understand the will of God. Epaphras's concern is pictured as strenuous labor, exerted to the depth of his soul for them (v. 13).

Luke, the traveling companion of Paul and the beloved physician also greets them, as does *Demas*. But Demas does not remain with Paul. Later, Paul writes that Demas has forsaken him because of his love for the world (2 Timothy 4:10). Not all who start well, finish well.

Paul sends greetings to the believers in Laodicea, located across a valley ten miles northeast of Colosse. He also sends greetings to *Nymphas* (a female name), since the church meets in her home (like Lydia in Philippi from Acts 16:15,40). Paul's love and concern for the believers is reflected in these words.

Paul's final charge is for *Archippus* to be vigilant and persistent in the ministry: *don't quit, Archippus, your ministry is a lifetime commitment!* As a solemn reminder, Paul points to his own imprisonment – he has been faithful in the ministry to the point of suffering imprisonment. We are called to that kind of commitment.

What kind of an example of spiritual commitment is your life? Are you an Epaphras, wrestling with great zeal at your spiritual task? Are you a Demas, who gives up because he loved the things of the world? Or perhaps you are like Archippus, having a difficult time in your spiritual work. Ask God to help you live for His glory.

The Apostle Peter writes to Christians in Asia Minor (modern Turkey) towards the end of his earthly life (A.D. 67) from a Roman prison (the "Babylon" of 1 Peter 5:13). It is Peter's *Last Will and Testament.*

Impetuous Peter is a beloved character because we can identify with his shortcomings and admire his zeal for the Lord. After his dismal denial of the Lord at His initial interrogations by the high priest, Peter is given three opportunities to publicly proclaim his love for his Lord (John 21). Peter is the key leader in the early chapters of Acts, but as the Jews continue to reject the preaching of the kingdom, the Book of Acts transitions to the ministry of Paul among the receptive Gentiles. Peter and Paul agree that Peter should concentrate on the Jews and Paul the Gentiles (Galatians 2:7-9). The last time Peter is mentioned by name in the Book of Acts is in his miraculous release from prison (chapter 12). Paul rebukes him in an undated encounter at Antioch (Galatians 2) that must have transpired before the issue (Mosaic Law observance) is settled by the Council of Jerusalem in Acts 15 (about A.D. 50).

The believers Peter writes to are a mixture of Jewish and Gentile converts. Peter draws heavily on Old Testament Scripture and analogies. Asia Minor is Paul's territory, so it very well could be that Peter is writing to people influenced by Paul. Peter also demonstrates knowledge of Paul's writings, including Ephesians (compare 1 Peter 1:1-3 and 3:1-6 with Ephesians 1:1-3 and 5:22-24). The "Babylon" of 1 Peter 5:13 could refer to the actual city in Mesopotamia where a large Jewish population would benefit from Peter's ministry. It could also be a cryptic reference to "Rome" as the current enemy of God. Trustworthy tradition places Peter's death in Rome during the persecutions of Nero (reigned A.D. 54-68). Peter supposedly was crucified (as a non-Roman) but requested to be hung upside down, feeling unworthy to die in the exact manner as his Lord.

In 1 Peter, Peter reminds the believers of the grace of God, developing the concepts of the believer's salvation (1:1-22); sanctification (1:23-2:12); submission (2:13-3:12); servitude (3:13-4:11) and suffering (4:12-5:14). The Greek grammar of 1 Peter is much better than that in 2 Peter, indicating that his associate, Silvanus, edited the letter for him as he wrote it (cf. 5:12). 1 Peter concerns itself with the *External Pressures of Suffering,* whereas 2 Peter is concerned with the *Internal Pressures of False Teachers,* a theme also echoed by Jude. Peter calls upon his readers to remember correct doctrine ("know" occurs 16 times in the 3 chapters). Chapter 1 discusses the *Development of the Faith.* Chapter 2 contains the *Denouncement of False Teachers.* And chapter 3 presents the *Design for the Future.* Key features of 2 Peter include: the impact of the Transfiguration (1:16); the inspiration

2 Peter 1:5-9

What is the writer saying?

How can I apply this to my life?

pray *New Zealand – The need for focused Youth Pastors and leaders.*

In verses 1-4 Peter challenges us to conform ourselves to God's image (see Romans 12:1-2). He now rattles off a list of eight items that detail the lifestyle of one made in the image of God. We are to do this with "diligence" which involves an expenditure of effort and is done with haste. "Faith" apparently sums up verses 1-4 as a synonym for salvation (saving faith). It would also refer to our daily walk as we are not only saved by faith (past tense), but we are being saved by faith (present tense). The entire Christian life is a *faith walk.* To our constant trusting in God's care for us, we are challenged to add "virtue." Virtue is a word that describes intrinsic excellence. Not only do we do good works but we look and act like someone who would be expected to do good works. To this we are to add "knowledge." It is the word for *intimate, experiential knowledge,* such as in marriage. We can't just know God theoretically or superficially. We must know Him deeply and intimately in order to be conduits of His blessings. "Temperance" refers to the ability to respond to situations as though we really are convinced that God is in control. It literally means *in strength,* referring to self-discipline. "Patience" means *to abide under,* similar to our concept of someone *holding up well under pressure.* "Godliness" does not have the word "God" in it in the Greek language. However, the concept is the same as the Greek is: *good + to be devout.* It speaks of the character of one devoted to a holy God. Such a one loves the brethren (those of his own family – *Philadelphia*). That is not the highest love. *Agape* love is. It is self-sacrificing – not demanding anything in return. "Abound," not just meeting the minimum standards, is stipulated.

The *what* of the Christian life is easy. The *how* is the challenge.

51 Tuesday

QT

2 Peter 1:10-14

What is the writer saying?

How can I apply this to my life?

pray *Korea – For the unblocking of Christian radio broadcasts that reach into North Korea with the gospel.*

One of the puzzles of the Christian life is that many verses indicate we can do nothing to merit or keep our salvation. It is a work of God from the start to the finish. We certainly condemn as heretical those branches of Christianity that teach we earn the right to go to heaven by our good works. On the other hand, there are many challenges for us to put forth effort in our walk with the Lord. The balance is that we cannot do this on our own any more than we can merit our salvation on our own. Therefore, both the initial salvation event and the ongoing Christian life (*sanctification*) require our faith, asking God to supply the power to obey His commands. The *effort* then is directed, not at being a good person, but in studying what God defines as a good person, what promises He offers to help us be a good person, and then asking Him to give us the wisdom, insight, and power to practice what we have learned. In verse 10, Peter says that since we are sons of the King then we ought to act like it. Our entrance into heaven is not in doubt. We can, however, have a glorious entry by harnessing all the power and accomplishing all the tasks that God has offered us. Fully aware of the weakness of the human nature, Peter says he wants to constantly remind his readers of these things. He knows they know these things, but it is his duty to make sure they are always thinking this way. He is also mindful of his soon departure and wants the most important things to be emphasized and remembered. "Established" comes from the word for *prop* and therefore, means *to fix firmly in place.* Back in Luke 22:32, Peter is commanded by our Lord to establish his brethren. Peter is faithfully doing what the Lord commanded right to the very end.

If the Lord told us when we would die, how would that change our lives?

QT

Friday 51

2 Peter 2:10-16

What is the writer saying?

How can I apply this to my life?

pray *Pray for the President of the United States to submit to the wisdom and guidance of the Holy Spirit.*

False teachers are motivated by fleshly desires. They resent authority. They are a law unto themselves. They are stubborn. They arrogantly condemn other leaders (human and angelic). They are not like the holy angels who demonstrate true meekness, which is power under control. They are true to their unsaved sin nature and behave like animals. Their end is beastly. This is not annihilation, but rather the loss of contact with God for all eternity, the only thing that makes existence worthwhile. Their sin is particularly heinous because it is done under the guise of religion, preys on the weak and gullible, and draws people away from a satisfying life with God. Peter likens them to Balaam, who, in Numbers 22-24, pretends to be a *prophet of Jehovah*, but clearly is really a *prophet for hire*. He is willing to try to influence any of the gods for his human clients. Balak, King of Moab, hires him to curse the Israelites as they are attempting to cross from Egypt through Moab to the Promised Land. At first, God tells Balaam he is not allowed to go. Then God agrees to allow him to go, but only if he would say whatever God tellls him to say. Balaam agrees, but God wants to make sure. Along the way God challenges him. Initially only his donkey sees the angel, and that amazing conversation takes place between Balaam and his donkey. When Balaam arrives he gladly takes Balak's money. Every time he opens his mouth to curse the Israelites, out came a blessing. Since Balak is getting mad and Balaam is in danger of losing his paycheck, Balaam says, *I can't curse them but here's what you should do. Send your women to them to entice them to intermarry and worship your gods. Then God Himself will curse them.*

Money is the root of every kind of evil. Use it but don't be used by it.

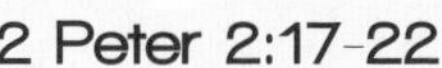

2 Peter 2:17-22

What is the writer saying?

How can I apply this to my life?

pray *Japan – For an end to cult growth, which far exceeds the growth of Christianity.*

The Middle East is a dry area of the world and water is a vital issue. Whole armies were lost in antiquity by dry wells in the wilderness. After the long, hot summer, puffy clouds would blow up from the Mediterranean, but they would drop their water before they arrived at Jerusalem. Useless mist they have offered, and useless mist will be their abode for eternity. "Wantonness" refers to sexual immorality. Apparently they are teaching the Gnostic heresy that a believer could indulge the flesh and still consider his spirit to be pure and acceptable to God. This is doubly tragic because the ones they are enticing have just recently escaped from that polluted lifestyle (v. 18). The false teachers consider this open-minded approach to be liberating, but it really is bondage. Free love is neither *free* nor is it *love.* Those who follow after righteousness are looking forward to the day when sinners are exposed as fools, as in the fable, *The Emperor's New Clothes.* Verses 20-22 could be used to argue that salvation can be lost, as it appears that these false teachers at one-time knew the truth and then willfully left the truth and now are under God's damnation. Other clear passages in Scripture will not permit that conclusion. Since salvation is neither won nor kept by works, then a person cannot *lose salvation* by bad works. These individuals tasted salvation, and were attracted to the teachings of Christ ("the Lord" not *their Lord*); but before they made a true commitment, they were led away by their sinful flesh. Their current behavior proves that they never possessed saving faith. Their condition is now worse because they will be less likely to consider the claims of Christ a second time.

The price of freedom is constant vigilance.

2 Peter 3:13-18

What is the writer saying?

How can I apply this to my life?

pray *Uruguay – For God to save and call witnesses among the upper middle-class, which is estimated to be the largest group not evangelized.*

The righteous look forward to and long for a return to the Garden of Eden. Initially, this will be on the millennial earth. Righteousness will be exalted in the beginning because every person entering the messianic kingdom will be saved, and Christ will rule with a rod of iron. In these one thousand years (Revelation 20) babies will be born. They will have the choice to accept or reject Christ as their Savior. Outward rebellion will not be tolerated, but unfortunately, some will be *Secret Service Unbelievers*. At the end of this period, Satan will be released to attempt one final revolt (Revelation 20), but it will fail. At that point, the current heavens and earth will be destroyed and new heavens and earth will be created. Never again will sin spoil the Garden of Eden (read Milton's *Paradise Regained*). Peter does not doubt God's promise, even as he faces his own imminent death. How should we then live? Not stained by sin, but at peace with God, ourselves and others. "Longsuffering" means *to go a long time before boiling over*. God's patience is not a delay but an opportunity for more people to come to Christ. Peter's reference to Paul shows his respect and demonstrates the cooperation among the apostles in the early church. The fisherman agrees that the rabbi is learned but does not excuse people for misunderstanding him. Study is hard work. Notice how often Peter refers to his audience as "beloved." The word for "steadfastness" (v. 17) is the opposite of the word "unstable" in verse 16. The root idea is that of both a strong and a wide base upon which one can safely stand without toppling over or breaking through. Growth must continue. The opposite is not stagnation but death. Our growth is found by getting to know a person better.

We can fellowship with the greatest personality in the universe.

Jude is identified as the half-brother of the Lord Jesus Christ and the full brother of James, the leader of the church in Jerusalem and the author of the Book of James (Matthew 13:55). His name means, *Praised*. It is an abbreviation of "Judas" which comes from "Judah."

Like Peter in the Book of 2 Peter, Jude is concerned about the inroads false teachers are making in the early church. In his short epistle, the size of one piece of ancient papyrus paper, Jude gives his urgent warning. Verses 1-16 proclaim the ever-present danger of false teachers. In verses 17-23 Jude exhorts the believers to due diligence. It appears that the type of false teaching Jude is attacking is a form of Gnosticism that allowed for immoral living.

Gnosticism comes from the word *to know*. Adherents claim to have secret knowledge (see Colossians 2:18). They deny the Deity of Jesus, postulating that He is just one of many *emanations* from the one true God. They teach that God did not create the world, since He is too holy to be involved with the carnality of physical existence. The job was done by one of the emanations (analogous to angels). Gnostics do not respect physical existence, and as a result either have no morals (you can't help yourself – eat, drink and be merry for tomorrow you die) or go to the other extreme of severe asceticism (which Paul confronts in Colossians).

In Revelation 2:6 Christ condemns the "deeds of the Nicolaitans," who apparently excused immorality and compromise with pagans. The "deeds of the Nicolaitans" becomes "the doctrine of the Nicolaitans" by Revelation 2:15. In Revelation 2:24, the Gnostic thought can be paraphrased as: *In order to defeat Satan you have to experience evil deeply*. This is Satan's approach with Eve in the Garden of Eden.

Gnosticism is also reminiscent of the so-called *New Age* movement (actually *Old Age* paganism and 1960's-style flower-child philosophy). Notice the frequency with which New Age practitioners make contact with *highly evolved extraterrestrials* and the demonic teachings that are *channeled* from these spirit beings (demons), such as *you are gods*, and *there is no damnation to fear*.

Jude 1-7

What is the writer saying?

How can I apply this to my life?

pray *United Kingdom – Alcholism is higher in the UK than in any other Western European country. Pray that young people will avoid this vice.*

Jude, like Peter and Paul, refers to himself as a "servant." He is the brother of James and half-brother of Jesus. He writes to believers. The Greek text behind the King James calls them "sanctified" while the text behind the New American Standard has the word *beloved*. The difference in spelling between these two words is slight, hence the potential for scribal change. Theologically, both concepts are accurate. They are *preserved*. This Greek word is in the perfect tense which refers to a past activity with ongoing consequences into the present. While it is true that Christ is our sphere of blessing and preservation, the grammar of the sentence probably means that believers are being preserved until the coming of Jesus Christ for them (*kept for Jesus Christ*). Saints are "called" which is the root of the word for *church*. Instead of grace, Jude uses "mercy" (God withholding the punishment we deserve). "Multiplied" comes from the same root as that vivid word, *plethora*. Jude says he had started to write about salvation, but switches to a warning about false teachers. "Earnestly contend" means *wrestle intensively*. It comes from the Greek word *agonize*. "Once" means that it is a finished product. We are not to expect more and certainly not different information. Evil men try to change the revealed Word of God. They are "ordained" (*written before*), probably refers to the fact that believers are warned that evil men would come and their punishment is certain; not that the specific individuals are predestined to this sinful behavior. Peter and Jude use similar illustrations of the fact that God's judgment cannot be avoided.

What a privilege to catch the heartbeat of someone barely known and yet who had the opportunity to grow up with Jesus Christ.

52 Thursday

Jude 8-11

What is the writer saying?

How can I apply this to my life?

pray *South Africa – Fruitful ministry of the nearly 2,000 South African missionaries serving abroad.*

Jude says that false teachers are antinomian (against the law) and anti-lordship (v. 4). They are immoral, anarchists and profane (v. 8). The "dignities" of verse 8 would be spirit beings (angels, demons and Satan). In contrast, even the highest angel in heaven – Michael the archangel – is respectful when he talks to Satan. The particular episode Jude alludes to occurs in Deuteronomy 34 but without these details. *The Assumption of Moses* is an ancient religious writing that Jude may have read. That he relates information from non-Biblical sources does not imply that they are inspired. It only means that God led the author to use information from that source. These false teachers are promoting an early form of Gnosticism, which teaches that physical matter is intrinsically evil and therefore, allows for immorality. It is not clear why they would speak evil of angels. Over in Colossians 2:18 a group is condemned for worshiping angels. At any rate, a very important principle is developed here. One of the marks of a false teacher is that he proudly brags about being able to boss Satan and demons around. If anyone criticizes his excesses, he wishes he had a Holy Ghost machine gun to blow them away (in the words of one current heretic). Ironically, the Gnostics claim to have superior, hidden knowledge of the spirit world. Both Peter and Jude say that they don't have a clue (v. 10, see also 2 Peter 2:12). They are condemned along with: Cain, the first murderer who refused God's required method of worship (Genesis 4); Balaam, the prophet for hire (Numbers 22-24); and Korah ("Core"), the Levitical priest who challenged Moses's authority and wound up seeing some of his followers burnt by God, and others swallowed up by the earth (Numbers 16).

It is an awesome thing to fall into the hands of the living God.

Jude 12-19

What is the writer saying?

How can I apply this to my life?

pray *Pray for the single parents in your church to be consistent and to persevere in patience and love.*

Jude uses six illustrations of the false teachers' uselessness. They are a stain at the church's communion table. They are pigs feeding themselves and not others. They promise spiritual drink, but can't satisfy anyone's thirst. They are fruit trees that not only have no fruit, but they are up-rooted. They are violent waves pouring forth pollution. They are shooting stars – all sound and fury, but vanish as soon as they appear. Their destiny is eternal blackout. Jude quotes godly Enoch (who walked with God and God took him, Genesis 5). The quote does not come from the Bible. It comes from the so-called Book of Enoch that is part of the Apocrypha. It almost certainly is not written by Enoch, for it does not appear in human history until the first century B.C. God's inspiration overcomes any weakness in the source. In fact, God could have told Jude that this is what Enoch said, without any other written source. The information communicated, however, is all known from other biblical passages such as Daniel 7:9-14. "Ungodly" occurs four times in verse 15. It refers to an aggressive antagonism to the person of God. Antinomian means *against the law* while "ungodly" means *against God Himself.* It is gratifying to think that not only sinful behavior, but also the arrogant words men speak against God, will be publicly judged and in the process, corrected. These false teachers manipulate others with flattery (v. 16). Other apostles have already warned that this is how sinful men behave apart from the Spirit of God.

To be forewarned is to be forearmed. We should brace ourselves for the disdain of sinners and have a gentle response to continue to interest them in the claims of Christ.

Jude 20-25

What is the writer saying?

How can I apply this to my life?

pray *Nicaragua – For gifted Bible teachers committed to the development of future church leaders.*

Jude is rushing to get this urgent communication to his beloved brothers in Christ. The amount of words might have been limited to the paper Jude has at hand. Since time and space is limited, the communication is terse and pointed. These are the items foremost on Jude's mind. The recipients are "beloved" (v. 20). The root of the word is *agape,* the word for "self-sacrificing love." "Building up" (v. 20) comes from three Greek words: *to build* plus *house* plus *upon.* The key is the foundation which is specified as "your most holy faith." We are saved by faith, and we continue to grow by faith. Our faith is bolstered by our prayer life in which the Holy Spirit guides our thoughts and prayers, and interprets our weak words to God the Father. Notice that in verses 20 and 21 all three members of the Trinity are mentioned. The Greek word *tereo* refers to believers twice in Jude. In verse 1 we are "preserved" in Jesus Christ. In verse 21 we are to keep ourselves in the faith. This is the only sphere in which God's love and mercy can be given. This does not mean that we *lose* salvation if we *lose* our faith. It does mean that someone who is truly saved would never *lose* his or her faith. Perseverance to the end is a mark of a truly born-again individual. As we seek to influence others for Christ, in some cases we take a low-key approach (v. 22) while in others we must be firmer in our admonitions (v. 23). Verse 22 is probably referring to weak believers who are being swayed by the heretics. Verse 23 is referring to the unsaved heretics who are still savable if they repent, but the rescuers need to be very careful because their error is toxic.

After many warnings Jude closes with a magnificent benediction. God is great, God is good, and we thank Him for everything He does.

"Ruth" means *Friendship*, and "Boaz" means *Lord of Strength*. In this little gem of a book, we have an idyllic love story that unexpectedly places a Moabite woman into the line of Christ! By tradition, it is written by the great prophet Samuel, who also wrote most of 1 Samuel, the book that describes his anointing of the first two kings of Israel: Saul first, followed by Ruth's great-grandson, David. David is anointed king about 1010 B.C., which would put the story of Ruth around 1120 B.C. This is the period of the Judges in which, unfortunately, every man did that which was right in his own eyes (Judges 21:25). Samuel is the transitional figure from the time of the Judges (he being the last judge, as well as a prophet) to the monarchy.

Chapter One is *Ruth in Moab*; Chapter Two, *Ruth in Bethlehem*; Chapter 3; *Ruth in Boaz's Barn*; and Chapter 4, *Ruth in Boaz's House*. Boaz's relatives are moved, either by gross spiritual dullness or financial desperation, to leave Bethlehem-Judah (*The House of Bread and Praise*) to seek better farming in the neighboring enemy country of Moab. The boys of the family marry Moabite women, including Ruth. Despite the poor spiritual example of her in-laws, Ruth is drawn to true Jehovah worship. Despite the immense obstacles that face her as an unwanted foreigner, she goes to Bethlehem. It is harvest time as the love story unfolds. Therefore, in Jewish tradition, the Book of Ruth is read every year for the holiday of Pentecost, since Pentecost is the *Wheat Harvest Holiday*. It is also considered to be the anniversary of the giving of the Law on Mt. Sinai (the real *Bread of Life*). It is appropriate to remember Ruth at this time as a convert to the Law. Also, by Jewish tradition, King David is born at Pentecost and dies on Pentecost. More significantly, the Holy Spirit is given to start the Church Age on Pentecost, a great reminder of the transition from the Age of Law to the Age of Grace and the fact that the Holy Spirit is the *Staff of Life* for the Church Age saint. In the Jewish celebration of Pentecost, two loaves are waved before the Lord in thanksgiving for the wheat harvest. Perhaps they can symbolize for us the Jews and the Gentiles that now comprise the Church.

From this little book we receive a view of the lifestyle during the period of the Judges. We see that Gentiles could believe and participate in the blessings of the Jews. We see that there is Gentile blood in the line of Christ (not only Ruth, but also Rahab and Tamar). Later on we can understand why David would flee to Moab from King Saul – he is visiting relatives! The book illustrates international relationships, the Law of Gleaning (Leviticus 19:9), Levirate Marriage (Deuteronomy 25:5), and the Jewish Court meeting in the gate of the city. Ultimately, Boaz, as the *Kinsman-Redeemer*, becomes a picture of Christ as our great *Redeemer*. According to the Law, the *Kinsman-Redeemer* has to be: 1) a blood relative (2:20); 2) have the money to purchase the land (4:10); 3) be willing to pay (4:9); and 4) be willing to marry the widow (4:10). Christ fulfills all four in relationship to His Bride, the Church.

53 Sunday

Ruth 1:1-14

What is the writer saying?

How can I apply this to my life?

pray *India – Effective ministry to nearly 400 million youth, many of who are in crisis.*

The period of the Judges lasts about 350 years, from the entrance into the land to King Saul (1440-1050 B.C.). It has some noble moments, but the general evaluation of the period in Judges 21:25, is that every man does that which is right in his own eyes. God uses famine in Abraham and Isaac's lives to test their resolve to stay in the Promised Land (by the time of Jacob's famine, it is God's will for them to go to Egypt). Elimelech (*My God is King*) and Naomi (*Pleasant*) apparently are unaware of the history or felt the challenge doesn't apply to them. The region is known as "Ephratah," *Fruitful.* They live in the *House of Bread and Praise*, but their sons bear names speaking of their frustration: Mahlon (*Sickly*) and Chilion (*Pining*). The Moabites are related to the Israelites through Abraham's nephew, Lot, but they have long since become antagonistic to the Jews (see Numbers 20-36). Orpah means *Fawn* and Ruth means *Friend.* God allows the three men to die. This puts all three women in financial straits and causes Naomi to head home, since she has no living relatives in Moab. The girls apparently love Naomi. She strangely tries to discourage them from returning with her. Perhaps out of embarrassment? She certainly is spiritually insensitive, for by this time in history the Moabites worshiped Chemosh, offering human sacrifices to him. Verse 11 refers to *Levirate Marriage.* The widow is to marry a family member to raise a child to the memory of the dead husband. Again, either out of ignorance or embarrassment, Naomi does not mention that there might be eligible relatives in Bethlehem.

Too often believers who should know better overlook opportunities to be a witness for the true God. Whose salvation can you pray for today?

Ruth 1:15-22

What is the writer saying?

How can I apply this to my life?

pray *Canada – For translation of their English Bible material for French-speaking countries.*

Naomi rather forcefully tells Ruth to return with her sister-in-law back to her native land. She even reports that Orpah went "unto her gods." The implication is that she doesn't care whether the girls worshiped Chemosh or Jehovah. The Moabites made a hollow bronze idol of Chemosh with outstretched arms. They would light a fire inside of the idol and when the arms and belly were red-hot, they would lay babies in the outstretched arms and *worship* to the screams of their burning babies. It is never stated why Ruth longed to be with Naomi. Is it an indicator of the great love she had for Naomi's son, Mahlon? Is there something about Naomi that Ruth found attractive? Despite the poor testimony of the family, did Ruth already come to love and worship Jehovah? Whatever her motivation, it is clearly a sacrifice to leave the land of her birth, her family, and her heritage to go to a place she does not know, has no assurance that she would be welcome, and has no guarantee of financial success. Verses 16 and 17 are often used in weddings due to the tender sentiments they express. However, remember this is said between women, not a husband and wife! Over ten years have passed (1:4), but everyone recognizes Naomi. The village is small, even hundreds of years later (Micah 5:2), probably only a few hundred people live here. Without any media to distract them, social events (including births, weddings, and funerals) are the main attractions. "Mara" (1:20) means *bitter*. It is more fitting to her circumstances than her given name *Pleasant*. It is the spring of the year (April). The barley harvest is celebrated during Passover in the First Fruits Festival.

Never in her wildest imaginations could Ruth have ever guessed what God is planning for her! Can you trust God for what He has planned for you?

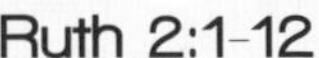

Ruth 2:1-12

What is the writer saying?

How can I apply this to my life?

pray *For the missionaries from your church to find favor with the governments of the foreign countries in which they serve.*

Naomi's character is further illustrated, in that she never tells Ruth about the potential for family help by way of gifts, gleaning or Levirate marriage. Either she is numb from grief or too proud to ask for help. She doesn't even volunteer to go looking for food. It is up to Ruth to take the initiative to provide for their household. "Ears of corn" is Old English for *heads of grain*. Ruth expects that she will have to ask permission ("find grace" v. 2, also compare to v. 7), not knowing that the Law of Moses demands that landowners allow gleaning by the poor (Leviticus 19:9-10). "Her hap was to light..." (v. 3). What a beautiful Old English turn of a phrase to capture the incredible sovereignty of God in our affairs. Notice the cultural and social items in the story. Ruth asks permission to go and the older Naomi grants it. Ruth asks for permission to glean and the servant grants it. Ruth feels free to take a break in the cool of an enclosure (v. 7). Eventually, she is encouraged to work closer to the reapers (she was humbly hanging back), to drink from the water jars (she was drawing her own water), and not to fear the young men (despite general protection given women in the Law of Moses, there is still a crudeness in the society that put women at risk in the open field; see Judges 21). In this passage we are introduced to Boaz, *Fleetness*. He is wealthy and godly. His typical greeting indicated his concern for the spiritual welfare of his associates. In Hebrew it is pronounced: *Adonai immachem*. Their response: *y'barekka Adonai*. To this day in Israel, it is common to hear the Biblical words *peace, praise the Lord*, and *blessed be the Lord* in everyday conversation. Boaz speaks kindly to Ruth calling her "my daughter," which indicates their relative ages. Ruth's reputation has preceded her.

Every day is another opportunity to alter the course of human history!

Ruth 2:13-23

What is the writer saying?

How can I apply this to my life?

pray *Bermuda – Pray that Christians in Bermuda would get more involved financially and spiritually to support missions.*

Ruth politely thanks and praises Boaz for his kindness. He invites her for lunch, giving her bread and sour wine for flavoring. Bread is the *staff of life* and is the featured commodity at every meal. In addition, there might be olives, olive oil as a dip, cheese, yogurt, figs, grapes and dates. Meat is only for special occasions. He also roasts some of the fresh grain to share with her. While perhaps not *romantic*, it certainly would have thrilled the heart of this outsider to be so graciously received into her new village. To further help her without embarrassing her or demeaning her work ethic, Boaz arranges for abundant grain to be available for her to pick up. At the end of the day, she has about a half a bushel of grain – enough to make meals for several days. She shares her bounty with her mother-in-law, and Naomi immediately realizes that something special has taken place. In 2:12 Boaz pronounces a blessing on Ruth. Here in 2:20 Naomi pronounces a blessing on whomever it was that had been gracious to Ruth. These pronouncements foreshadow their marital blessing and the happy end of the story. Once Naomi learns the man's identity, she blesses him again, not only telling Ruth that he is a relative, but also indicating that Boaz is giving signals that he would stand ready to be their kinsman-redeemer. "That they meet thee not in any other field" (v. 22) probably refers to the danger of abuse by evil workers if Ruth went to another man's field. Ruth spends over two months with Boaz, as the wheat harvest (Pentecost) comes seven weeks after the barley harvest (Feast of First Fruits). You can imagine the conversations around the table every night at Naomi's house!

One second you are down for the count and just about out. The next thing you know, God has intervened and life has taken a dramatic turn.

Ruth 3:1-18

What is the writer saying?

How can I apply this to my life?

pray *Bahrain – Pray that Christians would be able to have the courage to share the love of Christ with others despite rules against evangelism.*

Naomi finally gets around to explaining the Levirate marriage custom to Ruth (see Deuteronomy 25). This is not unique to Jewish culture, but the details would have been different enough that Ruth would need guidance. "Rest" (v. 1) refers to marriage. How does Naomi know that Boaz would be threshing barley that night? Either the farming schedule is very specific or Naomi has been out gathering intelligence (she has her sources). What follows sounds strange and some have turned it into a risqué episode. However, both parties are known for their integrity and a sexual interpretation is demeaning. Boaz has given every indication of his willingness to be the kinsman-redeemer. Due to his age, perhaps he feels it awkward to make a direct offer. In Deuteronomy 25, the woman is pictured as taking the initiative. Ruth does make herself presentable for this special occasion. Up until this moment, Boaz has only seen her in her work clothes. Even though Boaz has addressed her in public, it would not be appropriate for a poor woman to initiate a social conversation or ask for a private audience. Naomi's planned meeting is designed as a formal request for marriage in a private setting. Boaz is asleep. No one else could see Ruth approach and uncover his feet to gradually awaken him. The startling realization of her presence and the simultaneous realization of what she would ask adds to the preciousness of the moment. "Spread therefore thy skirt" is a request for protection (see Ezekiel 16:8). Boaz praises her for not desiring a younger man, calls her virtuous, and protects her virtue by having her leave early in the morning before anyone could see that she had been there. "Kindness" (v. 10) is the word for *covenant loyalty* or *loving kindness.*

In all thy ways acknowledge him and he shall direct thy paths.

QT

Friday 53

Ruth 4:1-12

What is the writer saying?

How can I apply this to my life?

pray *Pray for those who are persecuting believers around the world (Matthew 5:44).*

As Naomi predicts, that very day Boaz goes to the Jewish Court which met in the city gate. The gate would supply shade from the sun and also is a centralized meeting place as a main thoroughfare. By contrast, in a pagan town the court meets in the temple in the center of town. "Ten men" is called a *minyan* in Hebrew. To this day, a minyan is required for a worship service. Boaz brings the closer relative before the ten elders. Why wasn't anyone interested in Elimelech's land until now? In ancient Israel, land is never permanently sold. When Elimelech left Bethlehem, he would have leased his farmland to another farmer who would have use of it until the next Jubilee, at which time it would revert to Elimelech's family. To "redeem" the land means to buy the lease out ahead of time. Since there are no heirs to inherit the land, it is added to the land of the closest relative. This individual is able and willing to buy the lease until he finds out that there is a living widow. In that case, he is also obligated to impregnate her to raise a child who could inherit the land. Since he already has an heir, he doesn't want to have to share his current holdings with another child. Boaz is then authorized to buy Elimelech's land and marry Ruth. Why isn't Boaz already married? Why doesn't he have an heir? We can only guess that his wife must have been barren and/or dead. Possibly he has other sons, but his wealth is so great that he could afford to take on another heir. (His godliness does not preclude polygamy since godly men both before and after Boaz had multiple wives.) The elders graciously bless the decision and pray that God will richly bless this marriage in Israel. The mention of Tamar is particularly significant since she is a Gentile like Ruth.

"... exceedingly abundantly above all that we ask or think." (Ephesians 3:20).

Ruth 4:13-22

What is the writer saying?

How can I apply this to my life?

pray *Pray for unity among the staff and the membership of your local church.*

We don't know how long Ruth had been married to Mahlon but obviously God had prevented them from having children. Now God, the author and giver of life, gives Ruth and Boaz a son. The people of Bethlehem are very kind to Naomi. They see in her life a tremendous reversal of fortune. Instead of *Bitter*, she could now really enjoy her name, *Pleasant*. She has financial protection, she has a grandson to enjoy, she has the psychological satisfaction of knowing that her husband and son live on in her grandson, and most importantly, she knows true love – Ruth's love. Seven is the number of perfection. To have seven sons (a quiver full) would have been the ultimate mark of God's blessing on the family. But the women of Bethlehem state that this Moabite woman is even better. Throughout the story "kinsman" and "redeemer" have occurred. The Hebrew term for this specialized function is *Goel*. It comes from the Hebrew word *redemption*. Jesus Christ is the ultimate Goel. Normally the father names the child but in this case, public opinion named the boy. He was "Obed" – *Servant*. He would serve Naomi well in her declining years. This has been a precious story, but it also has a theological and historical purpose. For you see, this is the story of the grandfather of David, the great King of Israel and the progenitor of Jesus Christ the Messiah. Verses 18-22 give the whole genealogy from Judah (the kingly tribe according to Genesis 49:10 & 11) to David. The only detail to remember is that in Hebrew "father" and "begat" does not necessarily mean *immediately*. There can be gaps in the genealogies as demonstrated in Matthew 1.

The Goel has to be able to redeem, want to redeem, and be a close relative to redeem. Jesus Christ fulfills all three qualifications!

The following chart is provided to enable everyone using Word of Life Quiet Times to stay on the same passages. This list also aligns with the daily radio broadcasts.

week 1	Aug 24 – Aug 30	Psalms 51:1-56:13
week 2	Aug 31 – Sep 6	Psalms 57:1-63:11
week 3	Sep 7 – Sep 13	Psalms 64:1-68:35
week 4	Sep 14 – Sep 20	Psalms 69:1-72:11
week 5	Sep 21 – Sep 27	Psalms 72:12-76:12
week 6	Sep 28 – Oct 4	1 Timothy 1:1-4:8
week 7	Oct 5 – Oct 11	1 Timothy 4:9-6:21
week 8	Oct 12 – Oct 18	Leviticus 1:1-23:14
week 9	Oct 19 – Oct 25	Leviticus 23:15-26:46
week 10	Oct 26 – Nov 1	Mark 1:1-3:12
week 11	Nov 2 – Nov 8	Mark 3:13-5:20
week 12	Nov 9 – Nov 15	Mark 5:21-7:13
week 13	Nov 16 – Nov 22	Mark 7:14-9:29
week 14	Nov 23 – Nov 29	Mark 9:30-11:11
week 15	Nov 30 – Dec 6	Mark 11:12-13:23
week 16	Dec 7 – Dec 13	Mark 13:24-14:65
week 17	Dec 14 – Dec 20	Mark 14:66-16:20
week 18	Dec 21 – Dec 27	1 John 1:1-2:27
week 19	Dec 28 – Jan 3	1 John 2:28-4:21
week 20	Jan 4 – Jan 10	1 John 5:1 - 3 John 14
week 21	Jan 11 – Jan 17	Ezra 1:1-5:5
week 22	Jan 18 – Jan 24	Ezra 5:6-8:36
week 23	Jan 25 – Jan 31	Ezra 9:1 - Haggai 2:23
week 24	Feb 1 – Feb 7	Nehemiah 1:1-4:23
week 25	Feb 8 – Feb 14	Nehemiah 5:1-13:14
week 26	Feb 15 – Feb 21	Acts 1:1-3:11

week 27	Feb 22 – Feb 28	Acts 3:12-5:32
week 28	Mar 1 – Mar 7	Acts 5:33-8:13
week 29	Mar 8 – Mar 14	Acts 8:14-10:8
week 30	Mar 15 – Mar 21	Acts 10:9-12:25
week 31	Mar 22 – Mar 28	Acts 13:1-15:12
week 32	Mar 29 – Apr 4	Acts 15:13-17:21
week 33	Apr 5 – Apr 11	Acts 17:22-20:12
week 34	Apr 12 – Apr 18	Acts 20:13-22:30
week 35	Apr 19 – Apr 25	Acts 23:1-25:27
week 36	Apr 26 – May 2	Acts 26:1-28:31
week 37	May 3 – May 9	Numbers 1:1-8:18
week 38	May 10 – May 16	Numbers 8:19-13:25
week 39	May 17 – May 23	Numbers 13:26-20:12
week 40	May 24 – May 30	Numbers 20:23-35:25
week 41	May 31 – Jun 6	Galatians 1:1-3:9
week 42	Jun 7 – Jun 13	Galatians 3:10-5:1
week 43	Jun 14 – Jun 20	Galatians 5:2-6:18
week 44	Jun 21 – Jun 27	Proverbs 11:1-13:13
week 45	Jun 28 – Jul 4	Proverbs 13:14-15:33
week 46	Jul 5 – Jul 11	1 Thessalonians 1:1-3:13
week 47	Jul 12 – Jul 18	1 Thessalonians 4:1-5:28
week 48	Jul 19 – Jul 25	2 Thessalonians 1:1-3:18
week 49	Jul 26 – Aug 1	Colossians 1:1-2:15
week 50	Aug 2 – Aug 8	Colossians 2:16-4:18
week 51	Aug 9 – Aug 15	2 Peter 1:1-2:22
week 52	Aug 16 – Aug 22	2 Peter 3:1 - Jude 25
week 53	Aug 23 – Aug 29	Ruth 1:1-4:22